PAYING THE PIPER
Music in Pre-1642 Cheshire

PAYING THE PIPER
Music in Pre-1642 Cheshire

By Elizabeth Baldwin

With a Contribution on Music in the City by David Mills

Early Drama, Art, and Music
Monograph Series 29

MEDIEVAL INSTITUTE PUBLICATIONS

WESTERN MICHIGAN UNIVERSITY

Kalamazoo, Michigan
2002

Baldwin, Elizabeth.
  Paying the piper : music in pre-1642 Cheshire / by Elizabeth Baldwin ;
with a chapter on music in the city by David Mills.
      p. cm. -- (Early drama, art, and music monograph series ; 29)
Includes bibliographical references (p.   ) and index.
  ISBN 1-58044-040-1 (alk. paper) -- ISBN 1-58044-041-X (paper : alk.
paper)
  1. Music--England--Cheshire--History and criticism. 2.
Music--England--Chester--History and criticism. I. Mills, David, 1938-
II. Title. III. Series.
  ML286.7.C48 B35 2002
  780'.9427'1--dc21
                                                        2002003901

ISBN 1-58044-040-1 (casebound)
ISBN 1-58044-041-X (paperbound)

CONTENTS

Acknowledgments vii

Introduction 1

I. Music in Context 14

II, Part 1. Music in the City 54
    By David Mills

II, Part 2. Music in the County 79

III. Music and the Gentry 119

IV. The Musical Instruments 143

Appendix I. Inventories of Cheshire Musicians 187

Appendix II. Named Musicians 195

Notes 211

Bibliography 248

Index 265

ACKNOWLEDGMENTS

My particular thanks are due to David Mills, who has provided a chapter on music in the city of Chester for this book, and who has also encouraged me in my writing. The basis of the present book is material collected for the Records of Early English Drama project on Cheshire, a project in which David has been involved for many years and which I joined in 1992. I am also grateful to Richard Rastall for reading the manuscript and offering expert advice on musical questions, and to Clifford Davidson for overseeing the production of the book. Ephraim Segerman has generously answered my questions about musical instruments and their construction, and Veronica O'Mara has very kindly checked references for me at the Brotherton Library in Leeds. Anthony Leiman listened to much of the book before it was written, and was unfailing in his encouragement.

I acknowledge with thanks the help provided by staff at the Cheshire and Chester Archives, the Bodleian Library, the British Library, the Borthwick Institute for Historical Research, the Denbighshire Record Office, the John Rylands University Library, the Public Record Office, and the mayor and borough of Congleton.

Finally, this book could truly never have been written without the support, moral and financial, of my mother, Daphne Baldwin, and it is to her, and to the memory of my father, that the book is lovingly dedicated.

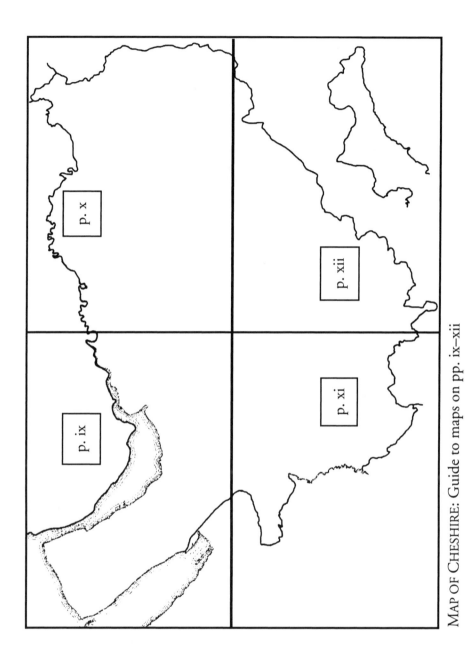

MAP OF CHESHIRE: Guide to maps on pp. ix–xii

p. x

p. xii

p. ix

p. xi

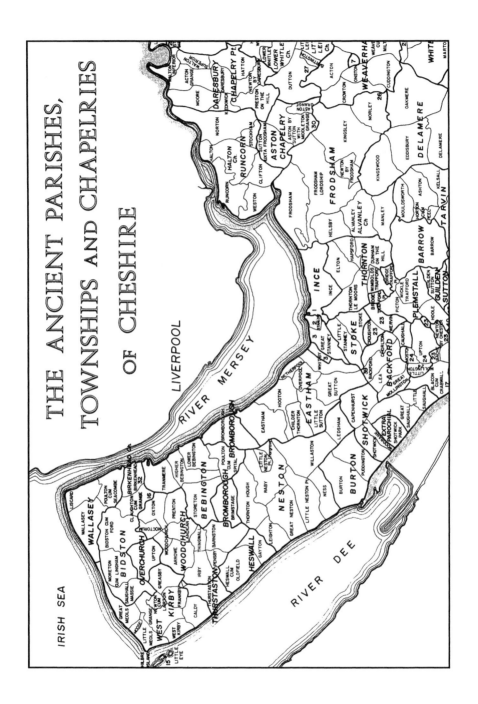

THE ANCIENT PARISHES, TOWNSHIPS AND CHAPELRIES OF CHESHIRE

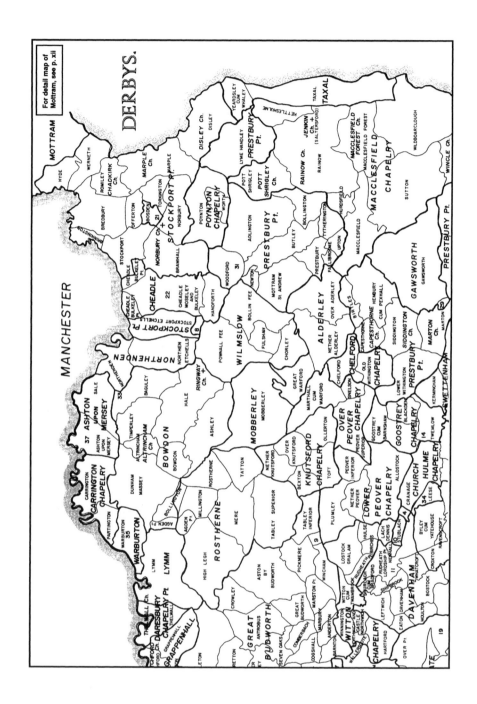

For detail map of Mottram, see p. xii

MOTTRAM

DERBYS.

MANCHESTER

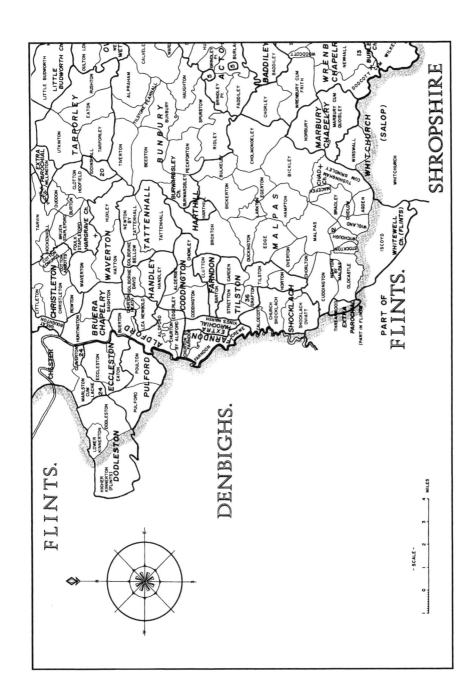

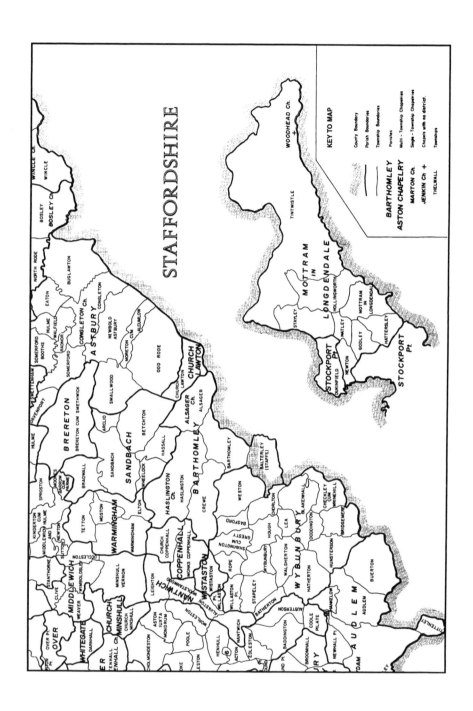

xii

INTRODUCTION

General Aims

Much of the work that has been done on early music has con-
centrated on surviving manuscripts of music or on known composers
and musicians. By far the greater part of this type of evidence relates
to sacred music. Even those studies that have been done on minstrels
as a group have focused on the royal minstrels of the high Middle
Ages. The present work proposes instead to look at the situation in a
single county, Cheshire, from the late Middle Ages to the beginning
of the English Civil War. The documentary evidence for this study has
been collected as part of the ongoing Records of Early English Drama
(REED) project, whose aim is to "find, transcribe, and publish ex-
ternal evidence of dramatic, ceremonial and minstrel activity in Great
Britain before 1642."[1] The material drawn upon here forms part of the
collection for the forthcoming volume on Cheshire. Because of the
nature of the project on which this book is based and because so much
has been done on sacred music already, the focus is on music outside
the regular control of the Church, although the division between
sacred and secular is not always clear-cut. Church musicians performed
in secular situations, and the Church sometimes made use of secular
musicians. Most Church music was centered on large foundations such
as St. Werburgh's Abbey, later Chester Cathedral (see chapter II, part
1). Also, a secular performer or performance may have religious implications in an era when politics and religion were as closely interwoven
as they were in the late sixteenth and early seventeenth centuries. The
temporal and geographical limits are also set by the surviving evidence
and the nature of the Cheshire project, which provides the data for this
study, but some mention will be made of neighboring counties and
post-Civil War practices for purposes of contrast.

The focus of this study is not only on the musician in the sense of
musically literate, trained professional, but also on the music-maker,
the performer, trained or untrained, depending on music as a means
of livelihood or not, who provided entertainment at guild feasts, in
alehouses, and in gentry households. The true amateur, the lady or
gentleman who performed for pleasure rather than necessity, must also

1

be considered. From the gentleman who takes music lessons, to the saddler who plays a cittern, or the alehousekeeper who plays the pipes, the music-makers refuse to be strictly categorized.

Social attitudes towards performers of music changed over the course of the sixteenth and seventeenth centuries, and we owe much of the evidence of their existence to the desire of the Puritans to see the Statute of Vagabonds enforced against minstrels. This study attempts, impossible though the task may be, to set the performer of music in a social, economic, legal, and possibly political context in the county of Cheshire. Who was performing music, where, when, and why? What instruments were played, and by whom? What attitudes were there towards music, and how did they vary according to circumstances and religious affiliation? Did Cheshire's special status with respect to the Statute of Vagabonds really make any difference to the performers in the county?

Geographical and Administrative Boundaries

As the research for this book is based on that done for the Cheshire volume of Records of Early English Drama, the basic focus is Cheshire and the *musicians* of Cheshire. The term is used loosely in this instance since it includes a wide range of music-makers from the member of the gentry who plays as an amateur, to the piper who is classified as a 'rogue and vagabond.' Chapter I provides a discussion of the terms 'musician' and 'minstrel,' and I have tried to use the terms as precisely as possible. Precision is not always available in the records themselves, and complete consistency has not been possible.

The intention is not to provide a biographical discussion of individual musicians but to look at the role of music and music-making in the society of Cheshire, with particular attention to the changes over time, particularly in the wake of the Reformation. Musicians from other counties, whether 'wandering minstrels' or visiting court composers, are discussed when they enter the boundaries of Cheshire, and evidence for Cheshire musicians, such as the Chester waits, traveling outside the county, is also discussed.

However, as much of the evidence comes from ecclesiastical and judicial records, it is important to remember that the geographical boundaries are not as important as the administrative ones, and that there are several different administrative boundaries to consider, some of which overlap with other counties, some of which are subdivisions of the larger county unit. For example, the ecclesiastical structure of Cheshire poses certain difficulties. Up until 1541, Cheshire was part of the large diocese of Coventry and Lichfield; relatively little ecclesiastical evidence survives for this period which may reflect the remoteness of Cheshire from the see cities. By the fourteenth century the archdeacon of Chester had some autonomy within the diocese, but it was only after the Reformation that Chester became a separate diocese and St. Werburgh's was elevated to the status of a cathedral. However, this diocese was still very large and distinctly unwieldy, including as it did the county of Lancashire, the deanery of Richmond in Yorkshire, and parts of Westmorland, Cumberland, and Wales.[2]

The diocese was divided into seven deaneries,[3] but the basic administrative unit was the parish, as it was nationally. Several of the older parishes in the county are very large, perhaps reflecting the outlines of ancient estates that once existed. Malpas, for instance, contains twenty-five townships, two of which are over the Welsh border in Flintshire. The Malpas townships are at least geographically contingent. Prestbury, with nineteen townships, is scattered in four sections, and several other parishes are split into two or more sections. Prestbury itself formerly contained as many as thirty-one townships, which help to fill up the gaps between the sections.[4] This has implications for the concept of the "wandering minstrel" since an individual could travel from township to township without technically leaving the parish, the unit on which his residency status was based under the Elizabethan Poor Laws.

As far as the judicial administrative boundaries are concerned, the two main divisions are the hundred and the township. By the sixteenth century, there were seven hundreds (see General Description of the County, below). The boundaries of the townships did not always correspond with those of the parishes, nor the boundaries of the hundreds with those of the deaneries. It is not unusual to find a township falling in two parishes, and even in one case two deaneries.[5]

Evidential Limitations

Despite the large number of documents relating to music and musicians in Cheshire collected for the Records of Early English Drama volume on Cheshire,[6] it is important to remember that the evidence is still very sparse. Although approximately seven hundred documents have been found which relate to music or musicians in

Cheshire, the evidence is limited in a number of ways. Most documents relate to the sixteenth or early seventeenth centuries, although there are several items from the fourteenth and fifteenth centuries and important references to earlier traditions. It is thus necessary to consider a span of six or more centuries, with evidence that is very heavily weighted toward the end of that period. The number of documents concerning music relative to the total number of documents examined is small—and becomes smaller still when one takes into account the loss of documentary evidence over the years, and the fact that the search for material has been directed towards the most likely sources. A recent visit to the Public Record Office only produced a rate of eight documents concerning entertainments (not only music) in Cheshire per thousand documents examined.

Music and musicians were only of interest to the writers of documents in certain circumstances. Indeed, the most significant feature of most documents concerning music or musicians is that their primary interest is not in music for its own sake. A piper is mentioned in a parish register because he marries, has a child christened or buried, or is buried himself. He appears in a set of accounts because he is paid, but the accounts make no comment on the performance. He appears at the assizes on in the ecclesiastical court because he has become involved in an infringement of the law. This may involve his musicianship, as in the case of the numerous citations for "piping on the sabbath," but the documents are not interested in anything beyond the barest facts of performance. The role of music-makers in society and society's attitudes towards them are rarely stated, and when they are stated it is usually in the form of opposition from the more extreme reformers, whose opinions may or may not coincide with those of the majority of the population at any given time.

More than two-thirds of the documents used in this study can be divided into the broad categories of *judicial* and *financial*. The term 'judicial' is used to cover documents from both the secular and the ecclesiastical courts since performers might come under the jurisdiction of either. The ecclesiastical material ranges from cases in the consistory court to episcopal and metropolitan visitations of the diocese. The attitude towards music and music-makers is more consistently negative in the latter documents, as sabbath-breaking is one of the items specifically inquired for by the officials. In the secular court, documents vary more widely, from simple recognizances to long depositions in Quarter Sessions or even Star Chamber cases. In some of the longer cases, music and music-makers are mentioned only in passing. These mentions are often of considerable interest since they tend to be more detailed and less negative than the responses to inquiries initiated by the authorities such as those regarding the "harboring" of minstrels. Although by far the largest group of documents can be described as "judicial," this is to a considerable extent owing to the more careful preservation of such records. It also reflects the fact that an activity or an individual is more likely to be recorded for breaking the law than for keeping it.

An open mind is required toward the documents that survive. Documents relating to legal processes have an inherent bias since the law courts are concerned with the infractions of the laws, and an activity may be legal in one century and illegal in another. The predominance of cases against performers for "piping on the Sabbath" in the late sixteenth and early seventeenth centuries reflects the fact that this became a legal issue with the rise of sabbatarianism in the Church of England, particularly among those who considered that the Church had not gone far enough in reformation. It does not necessarily indicate an increase in the number of instances of pipers playing on Sunday, but neither does it prove that pipers were traditionally accustomed to playing on Sundays in previous centuries and were restricted by laws introduced by the reformers. Furthermore, it must be remembered that a legal document does not necessarily contain the "true facts" of a case. Parties in a dispute, even without the added problem of perjury, present a case in such a way as to be most favorable to themselves. When only one side of the pleadings remains, it is all the more difficult to determine "what really happened" in a given dispute. The purpose for which a document was written, the attitude of the writer, the amount of actual knowledge possessed by the writer, and the scribal accuracy of the document are all relevant to the determination of the facts. Unfortunately, in most cases such information is simply not given, and sometimes cannot even be deduced. Some documents, such as parish registers and accounts, can be taken more or less at face value since the purpose of the document is transparent, the attitude of the author known or irrelevant, and the actual knowledge and scribal accuracy generally indeterminable but less problematic than in other documents. For legal pleadings, Puritan polemic, and other documents where the purpose is less obvious or less neutral, one must use caution. The attitude of the author or informant, if not stated, must be deduced as far as possible, and the possibility of there being another side to the story must always be borne in mind. At the same time, one has to work with the evidence that is available, and at some point it is necessary to say "If these allegations are true, what do they tell us about music and music-makers? If these allegations are not true, what do they tell us about the attitude towards music and music-makers?"

The financial records, on the other hand, treat the performers as entertainers to be rewarded for their performance. The majority of the surviving records of payment come from the guild accounts of Chester and relate to the Chester waits, who had an established position and respectability not available to all performers. This reflects the continuity of guild accounting and the better survival of guild records as well as the relative status of the Chester waits. The Chester waits are discussed in Professor David Mills's section on "Music in the City" in chapter II, part 1.

Other financial records, such as the accounts of an individual member of the gentry, show that payments to musical performers were not limited to important occasions or to established groups such as the waits. Although these records are limited in the detail that they give— often not even indicating the name of the performer—they do provide a valuable counterweight to the judicial evidence and the Puritan polemic. Despite all the disapproval expressed by the Puritans and implicit in many of the judicial documents, musical performance was an accepted—and even expected—part of the social life of the time.

The other records, which cannot be classified as either judicial or financial, are varied in both their nature and their attitudes. Parish registers are perhaps the most neutral in tone, and their information, although limited, is valuable because it provides biographical details. The problems offered by parish registers tend to be in the field of scribal accuracy and identity of individuals. For instance, it is impossible to be sure if the scribe has accurately recorded the musician's preferred instrument, or whether "piper" is a generic term. Variant spellings of names make it more difficult to trace the activities of a single musician. It is even possible for scribal attitude to enter into the parish registers, and in these cases more information is usually provided, as when suspect deaths or illegitimacy are noted. Wills and inventories are slightly more positive in their attitude since they demonstrate an interest in music on the part of the gentry and, in some instances, evidence of the wealth or otherwise of musicians. Letters, whether personal or official, vary in tone, but generally reveal their bias clearly. Personal letters tend to reveal a more positive attitude on the part of the gentry, who are evidently performers as well as patrons of music. Official letters are often written with the intention of enlightening the authorities about the perceived danger to the public order from activities associated with music and music-makers. Some printed works, such as William Hinde's *Life of John Bruen*, were written by those with a reforming interest and therefore are strongly negative towards activities such as music on Sunday. However, even the works of the reformers have to be read in context, and it is important to remember that much of the objection to music was associated with the time or place of performance rather than with music itself.

One other fact that emerges from these documents is that the same individual who sat as magistrate was also likely to be present at a guild feast or a civic function—or to be a patron, and indeed a performer of music, in a private capacity. The personal attitude of individuals to music and musicians must be taken into account as well as the official attitude, and it is evident that there can be some variance between personal and official attitudes even in one individual. Personal attitudes can become politicized, either by the individuals concerned or by others; a lenient magistrate who allows a traditional wakes entertainment, with music and dancing, to proceed, may be accused of recusancy by a magistrate of a more reforming turn of mind who had forbidden the same activity. Parishioners might seek to antagonize a reforming preacher by playing on his objections to piping on the sabbath.[7]

The evidence provided by the documents is limited by its subjectivity, by the fact that musical performance was often not the principal interest of the writer, and by the lack of detail provided. Very often we learn nothing more about a musician than his name, occupation, and (sometimes) place of habitation. All three of these vary: names can be spelled in a number of ways, as with "Tompson," "Thomson," and "Tomson," or the Cally/Kelly family of waits of Chester, where the identity of the individuals is sufficiently clear that the two can be treated as equal alternatives (see chapter II, part 1, for a discussion of the Cally/Kelly family). General terms such as 'minstrel' or 'musician' vary with a more exact description such as 'piper' or 'fiddler' (see chapter I for a discussion of nomenclature), although even these are at times frustratingly vague. Change in place of habitation may reflect the movements of a single musician rather than different individuals, or they may reflect scribal inexactitude; both factors probably apply in the case of Richard Metier, variously described as "of Withington," "of Lower Withington," "of Sidding-ton," and "of Swettenham" (see chapter II, part 2).

The limitation of detail is further imbalanced by the fact that documents opposed to music-makers, such as Puritan writings or court cases, provide more detail than neutral or positive documents such as parish registers or financial accounts. The picture that emerges of what actually happened at a musical occasion is therefore much more negative than it might be if we had similarly detailed accounts of, for instance, the program of music at a guild feast. Doubtless there were occasions on which performers were involved in breaches of the peace or when the music itself became a public nuisance; the same can be said in modern times. Doubtless, also, there were many occasions on which music was performed without incident, without opposition, and without being recorded in any surviving document.

Social and Economic Context

It is perhaps misleading to speak of a social and economic context for musical performance as if there were only one. Music occurred at all levels of society, and was performed both by those who relied on it for subsistence and by those who considered it a necessary accomp-lishment of a gentleman or a lady. There are therefore a number of social contexts, some of which overlap, between the various levels of musical performers. The role of the gentry, both as patrons and per-formers, is discussed in chapter III. Musicians who were themselves gentry or able to mix with the gentry as something a little more than servants are also discussed in chapter III. The musical instruments themselves, including the expense involved in purchasing them, are discussed in chapter IV.

Economically, it must be remembered that Cheshire was a rela-tively poor county, although not to the same extent, for instance, as Cumberland or Westmorland—or even Lancashire. Although there was a strong, and highly interconnected, web of gentry families, there were no powerful magnates resident in the county.

The deterioration of the term 'minstrel,' which is discussed in chapter I, reflects the fact that the social and economic position of the performer who relied on music for his livelihood was often precarious. Even the Chester waits, who had a certain degree of monopoly over music-making in Chester, were dependent on the good will of the mayor and assembly, who could dismiss them (see chapter II, part 1). Music-makers who did not have the protection of a specific patron, whether an individual or a corporation, were in a more vulnerable situation. Nevertheless, it must be remembered that those who were arrested for performing in illegal alehouses were likely to be those lower down the socio-economic scale, and also that they might not have been much poorer than their audience. On the other hand, there is evidence that some musical performers did manage to make a sufficient living. The economic situation of professional or semi-professional musicians is discussed in chapter II, part 2.

The social context of Cheshire after the Reformation must also be considered in terms of religion and politics, matters which were so interconnected at the time that they can hardly be considered separately. Cheshire was a county that was considered, like the rest of the Northwest, to be potentially recusant, and the national Church accordingly took the step of appointing clergy of reforming tendencies to Cheshire parishes. There was also a strong reforming interest among some of the gentry. This led to tensions between those of a reformist and those of a traditionalist tendency, and one of the areas which became a focus for this debate involved traditional entertainments, many of which involved music-making. The conflict between the pipers and the preachers is discussed in chapter I.

Legal Context

The minstrels of Cheshire were ostensibly in a unique position nationally. In the 1572 Statute of Vagabonds an exception is made in favor of Cheshire which recognizes the hereditary right of the Heir of Dutton to license minstrels in that county (see chapter III).[8] On the surface, this would appear to give Cheshire a special status and Cheshire minstrels special protection from the potentially harsh punishments of the Statute of Vagabonds—punishments which included forced labor, branding, and ultimately hanging, all legislated at one time or another. The questions that must be asked are to what degree this section of the statute actually protected those performing music in Cheshire and how much it was seen to be beneficial to them. It certainly does not amount to *carte blanche* for minstrels in the county of Cheshire, nor does it necessarily result in a more positive attitude towards minstrels in that county. It is, furthermore, difficult to determine whether or not a minstrel is licensed, and it may be that some performers, who were resident in one area or had another means of livelihood as well as music, did not or could not pay the four pence annual fee for the licence. The Dutton minstrels' licences operated as a form of taxation. The particular role of the Dutton Minstrels' Court is discussed in chapter III and also, as it relates to the city of Chester, in chapter II, part 1.

In addition, the authorities were concerned in the late sixteenth and early seventeenth century with the proliferation of illegal ale-houses. The alehouse was frequently a venue for musical performance, and much of the surviving evidence about musical performance is concerned with time and place. The role of the alehouse is discussed in chapter I, as are some of the difficulties encountered by the authorities in attempting to enforce legislation that sought to control entertainment such as piping in these establishments.

General Description of the County

Cheshire's status as a county palatine gave it some measure of independence from central control, although in the Tudor period government became more centralized and more aspects of life came under governmental control. Geographically, also, Cheshire was outside the orbit of London. Strategically, Cheshire—and particularly Chester —remained important because of its proximity to Wales and the sea-route to Dublin and, via the Irish Sea, to ports on the Continent. This resulted in a regular flow of traffic from outside the county: soldiers and courtiers bound for Ireland, traders to Wales, Ireland, and the North, and, with them or in their wake, the minstrels, singingmen, and other performers in whom we are interested. Cheshire's proximity to Lancashire, a strongly recusant area, meant that there was considerable official focus on traditional activities such as wakes and ales at which music was performed—and that official concern with illegal alehouses could take on a political and religious significance as well as an administrative one.

Cheshire lies in the northwest Midlands, separated from Lancashire in the north by the river Mersey. The river Dee in the west forms the border with Wales (Flintshire) for much of its length, although several Cheshire parishes and townships near Chester lie to the west of the Dee. In the south, Cheshire is separated from Staffordshire by the Ellesmere moraine, and in the east the foothills of the Pennines divide it from Yorkshire and Derbyshire. Cheshire has no substantial coast-line, although the Wirral peninsula does extend to the Irish Sea. The Dee was navigable as far as Chester in former times but even by the sixteenth century was silting up.[9]

Southeast Cheshire forms part of the Midland Gap, and there is a major divide along Congleton Edge and Mow Cop. The Midland Gap is "an important routeway from north-west England to the Midlands and the south-east."[10] The county is also divided north-south by a sandstone ridge "which, as it approaches the Mersey Valley, turns east to Alderley Edge, where it abuts upon the Pennine foothills."[11] Cheshire is divided between a series of escarpments in the east and shallow valleys in the west by the Mid-Cheshire Ridge, which is broken by a series of gaps from east to west that give access to the eastern lowland.[12] Primarily, Cheshire is country best suited for pastoral agriculture, with an important salt industry going back to Roman times in the area of the three wiches (salt places) of Middlewich, Nantwich, and Northwich. The county was more heavily populated in the south, while some parts, such as the Wirral, were very sparsely populated in our period—a fact which is reflected in the geographic distribution of music-makers (see Appendix II). Chester was the county seat and principal town and dominated the western part of the county. As noted above, its city waits had a recognized status as professional musicians despite their occasional quarrels with the city (see chapter II, part 1). Smaller towns in eastern Cheshire had resident performers but on special occasions might rely on the expertise of the Chester waits, as at Congleton in 1621, when "Cales the musitian of Chester" was paid for playing for the Scholars' play on 14 February (twenty shillings) and later for the Townsmen's play on 5 April (3*s* 4*d*).[13] Nantwich, which has the fullest parish registers, had a number of resident musicians, but as no borough accounts survive it cannot be determined if they were maintained by the town or not.

Cheshire has both navigable waterways and Roman roads, making travel within the county possible if not always easy. The principal lines of communication run north-south and northwest-southeast, and there are also east-west routes through Wales and the Pennines.[14] If the music-makers of Cheshire were "wandering minstrels," then they must have wandered along these routes, though in spite of the county's special status with regard to the Statute of Vagabonds they were not exempt from judicial control—or from being regarded as "rogues and vagabonds." In examining the travel patterns of music-makers, it will be relevant to look at the organization of the shire.

As noted above, the principal secular administrative divisions were the township and the hundred. Originally, Anglo-Saxon Cheshire was divided into twelve hundreds, consistent with 1200 hides of the ancient shire. This division was probably made sometime in the tenth century for military purposes and as a response to Norse raids, but it may reflect earlier administrative divisions.[15] By the sixteenth century, seven hundreds remained: Broxton, Bucklow, Eddisbury, Macclesfield, Nantwich, Northwich, and Wirral. Of these seven, only Bucklow corresponds to one of the Anglo-Saxon hundreds (Bochelau),[16] although probably its boundaries had changed over the centuries. The City of Chester, while geographically located in Broxton hundred, was administratively separate.

The basic ecclesiastical unit, the parish, was also important as a unit of secular administration. It was the parish which was ultimately responsible for the care of the destitute, and it was to the individual's home parish that vagabonds were returned. If after the Reformation many of the Cheshire parishes were large—including several townships, not always connected geographically—some of the pre-Reformation parishes had been even larger. Prestbury, which after the Reformation eventually reached thirty-one townships, was even larger in the early Middle Ages, when it included Gawsworth, Taxal, and Nether Alderley and hence formed over half of the ancient district of Hamestan.[17] Large parishes which include a number of townships probably represent the remains of ancient estates.[18] Movement from township to township within the parish was likely to be viewed differently than movement from parish to parish. The fact that Chester was not a separate diocese until 1541 is also of significance. When Cheshire was part of the large diocese of Coventry and Lichfield (and earlier of Lichfield only), visitations were fewer, and consequently evidence regarding musical performers and their relationship to the Church and canon law is sparse. Even after Chester was made a separate diocese (which included Lancashire and part of Yorkshire), it was still "a poorly endowed, monstrously large and administratively unmanageable ecclesiastical unit."[19]

A Note on Transcriptions

In keeping with the practice of the Early Drama, Art, and Music Monograph Series, dates are given according to the New Style whenever possible. However, some documents, particularly guild and civic records, work on an accounting year that does not begin on 1 January. Frequently the year begins at Michaelmas (29 September) or some other feast day, and there is not always consistency from one year to another. It has therefore been necessary to adopt the system used by the Records of Early English Drama of indicating both years (e.g., 1573–74). Where certainty is possible, an exact date has been given.

Abbreviations are expanded in the transcriptions as italics, but superscripts are generally lowered. Interlineations are indicated by the use of a caret (^) before and after, with an extra caret when one is in the text. Interpolations in a different hand and scribal errors are only indicated when it is necessary to avoid confusion or when they may provide added information. Deletions in the text are indicated by square brackets ([ ]), and material which is lost because of damage to the manuscript is indicated by angle brackets and ellipses (< . . . >).

I
MUSIC IN CONTEXT

Nomenclature

Minstrel *and* Musician

In c.1576, Thomas Whythorne wrote:

> þen for such az served for pryvat rekreasion in howzes, which wer
> for þe nobilite & wurshipfull, þes wer no les esteemed þen þe
> oþerz, till tym þat þe Raskall and of skumm of þat profession, who
> be, or owht to bee kalled minstrels (alþoh now A daiz many do
> nam þem miuszisions) þez I say did and do mak it kommen by
> offring of it to evry ʒak, going abowt evry plas and kuntrey for þe
> sam purpoz, as partly it iz towcht affor.[1]

One source of confusion in the records has always been the exact
significance of terms such as 'minstrel' or 'musician,' both of which are
used as both generic and specific terms for makers of music. The
question is made more difficult by the probability that the scribes
using the terms may not have been using them in as exact a sense as
we—or even their contemporaries such as Thomas Whythorne—
would wish, and the certainty that the exact meanings changed over
time. This can be particularly observed in the deterioration of the term
'minstrel,' which after the fifteenth century became increasingly
pejorative and was apparently replaced by 'musician' or 'musicioner,'
as the quotation from Whythorne at the head of this chapter indicates.
There is also a question as to the range of meaning of the two terms.
As Timothy McGee notes, originally the term 'minstrel' "takes in a
broad category of people who shared a common function of entertaining in some way,"[2] with musical performance as only one of a
number of performance skills. During the course of the sixteenth
century, the picture changed. Specialization took place and with it a
lowering of status of the term 'minstrel.' At the same time, 'minstrel'
became more specifically associated with music-making, originally a
sub-category under this term, while other activities, which had pre-

viously been part of minstrelsy, were taken over by specialist jugglers, tumblers, bearwards, and so on. Certain specialist instrumentalists such as trumpeters or waits also rise above the level of the common minstrel and tend not to be referred to as minstrels.

The term 'musician' does not appear in the Cheshire records until 1567–68 (in the form "musicioner"). Whythorne's comments would appear to suggest that it was being used more loosely—and possibly further down the social scale—than had previously been the case. His distinction between the musically literate and those who played by ear is a valid one in identifying "professional" status for musicians.[3] But how clear was the distinction in the popular—or indeed the official— mind? Early uses of 'musician' or 'musicioner' in the Cheshire records include waits such as Edmund Cally or Kelly, who might reasonably be expected to have had some musical training, and an otherwise unknown woman, Agnes Rowley, wife of a tinker, who in 1573–74 was ordered to depart the city within two days.[4] Whythorne's comment suggests that performers without any claim to musical knowledge were passing themselves off or being carelessly referred to as musicians when they should by rights be termed minstrels (and, by implication, be subject to the penalties of the Statute of Vagabonds). The case of Agnes Rowley agrees with Whythorne's complaint. It is therefore important to consider the context in which terms such as 'musician,' 'musicioner,' and 'minstrel' are used. The description of an individual as a player of a specific instrument may be more neutral than either minstrel or musician, but certain instrumental terms, such as 'piper,' do seem also to acquire a pejorative sense in official documents. The term 'musicioner' was also used specifically in the context of the Statute of Vagabonds as early as 1572 in a recognizance for Edward Jonson, described as "Music*ion*er," who is charged with playing "vpon his Instrument of musick" and "vsing the same contrary to the tenor of An Acte of p*ar*lyament against such vagarant and idell p*er*sons this p*re*sent yere made and p*ro*vided."[5]

Confusion of the terms 'minstrel' and 'musician' in the case of a single individual is not usual, but it is possible. In 1589, John Tompson of Nantwich is described in the parish register, a fairly neutral source, as "mvscition" on the occasion of his daughter's baptism. In 1597, at the burial of his wife, he is described as "pyper," but when he appears in the Crown Books in 1613 for making "a lewd marriage," he is described as "minstrell." Both the term and the context would appear to be censorious. At his own burial in 1624 he is again described as "pyper."[6]

There are a number of possible explanations for this variation in terminology. The first, albeit unlikely, is that more than one individual is involved, a musician/piper in the late sixteenth century, and a minstrel, possibly a piper, in the early seventeenth. It is unlikely that the John Tompson, musician, of the earliest mention is not the piper who buried his wife eight years after the baptism of his child. If he is not the John Tompson, piper, who is later buried in 1624, then what happened to the earlier John Tompson? Did the earlier John Tompson leave the parish (not an easy thing to do) and another John Tompson, piper, move into the parish? It is possible, although there is no record of baptism, that he was even the son of the first John Tompson. There are indications elsewhere in the parish registers that not all children were baptized. It seems more likely, however, that we are dealing with one individual who may have gone down in the world or perhaps suffered because of the hardening of attitudes towards performers of music. The three descriptions of him as "minstrel" are all in official court documents, all relating to the same case, and therefore probably copied one from another. The mention of him as "musician" in the 1589 parish register may indicate that he called himself a musician in response to the parish clerk's questioning of his occupation. Whether his use of the term was opportunistic, as Whythorne suggests was the practice, or indicates that he had some official status in the town, is not clear. Several Nantwich instrumentalists are described as "musician" or "musicioner," and, while it is possible that the town had a wait or a small band of waits, there is no way of determining this in the absence of borough records.[7] It may be that the musical performers of Nantwich were simply successful in appropriating the term 'musician.'

The difficulties of ambiguity in the terms 'minstrel' and 'musician' also affect the present work. I have attempted, where it can be done without undue awkwardness, to substitute terms such as 'performer,' 'musical performer,' and 'music-maker.' I have, however, on occasion had to use 'musician' and 'minstrel.' The latter I have used particularly to apply to music-makers whose circumstances would cause them to be subject to the provisions of the Statute of Vagabonds, in which case 'minstrel' is a legal classification, not dependent on skill or professionalism. 'Musician' has been used when an individual is so designated or when he is clearly musically literate and professional. It has, however, been necessary to use 'musician' sometimes as a blanket term for all makers of music, professional and amateur. It is hoped that the context in which the terms are used will make clear the distinctions between them.

The earliest mention of a named individual minstrel—or indeed of any type of musician—in the accounts is William le Synger in 1342–43.[8] Synger was clearly a minstrel in the wider medieval sense, not purely an instrumentalist. Although he may have played a musical instrument, he seems to have been principally known for his singing. It is interesting to note that he is the only minstrel mentioned in the Cheshire records for the fourteenth century. Synger was one of only six performers mentioned in the fourteenth century altogether, and of the remaining five, four are designated harpers and one a piper. One of the earliest mentions of a harper is in 1354 when Hugh de Walay was given a pardon by the Black Prince for a land transaction.[9] In the fifteenth century, however, the situation began to change: twelve minstrels, seven harpers, five pipers, two fiddlers (to which must be added one of the minstrels whose surname is given as Fiddler, indicating his choice of instrument), one horner, one trumpeter, one organmaker, and one luter. These numbers probably reflect a variety of factors at work. The increase in the survival rate of documents, and the requirement, introduced in the fifteenth century, to specify the occupation of an individual, enhance the chances of named musicians being recorded. Harpers, however, are no longer the dominant group. John Southworth mentions that there was a decline in the popularity of harpers as court entertainers from the beginning of the fourteenth century, although this trend would probably be more gradual outside of court circles.[10] Harping may have remained popular longer in Cheshire because of influence from Wales. The increased use of 'minstrel' may, in the fifteenth century, be due to the same factors that led to the use of 'musician' in the sixteenth. There were complaints in the fifteenth century about false claims to livery by minstrels—serious enough that a commission to inquire was set up in 1449. This commission, however, specifically excluded Cheshire, which had a separate licensing system (see below, and also chapters II, part 1, and III for discussion of the Duttons' Minstrels' Court).[11]

In all, thirty-eight named individuals are designated as "minstrel" in the Cheshire records: one in the fourteenth century, thirteen in the fifteenth, eleven in the sixteenth, and fourteen in the seventeenth. Although this would appear at first to be a stable number, it actually is relatively a much smaller proportion of the overall numbers of named performers in the sixteenth and seventeenth centuries than in the fifteenth.[12] The number of performers recorded in the documents rises steeply over the centuries: a mere six in the fourteenth century, thirty-one in the fifteenth, rising to fifty-three in the sixteenth century, mainly in the latter part of the century, and jumping to 122 in the first half of the seventeenth century. There is, of course, some overlapping of names between the late sixteenth and the early seventeenth centuries, as performers appear in more than one document. The number of named minstrels in the seventeenth century is therefore proportionally the lowest: 11.5%, as opposed to 21% in the sixteenth and 41% in the fifteenth century. The use of 'minstrel' or 'minstrels' as a general term also shows change over time. In the fifteenth century, it occurs only seven times, always in connection with the Duttons' hereditary right to license minstrels for the county, a usage which may be considered static since legal terminology changes more slowly than other forms of language. The sixteenth century shows a greater variety of usage of the term 'minstrel.' As well as a greater variety of licensing references, there are also other legal documents, such as alehouse recognizances, which use 'minstrels' because that is the term found in the relevant statute. More revealing is the use of the term by guilds in their records of music provided at guild dinners. Between 1559 and 1582, 'minstrels' is used eight times to describe performers at various guild dinners.[13] After that, there is only one such usage, in 1606. 'Musician' and 'musicioner' begin to be used in the 1590s, but by far the most common usage is simply "the Musick." Increasingly after 1590, minstrels are mentioned generically and negatively in official orders, warrants for arrest, alehouse recognizances, and puritan complaints.

The increased number of minstrels in the fifteenth century may be connected to the licensing of minstrels in Cheshire under the Duttons, but it may also reflect the rising number of entertainers who described themselves as minstrels in hopes of attracting a greater reward because of a perceived connection with royalty or nobility. Traditionally, the origin of the licensing of minstrels is traced to the twelfth century, when Ranulph III, Earl of Chester, was besieged in Rhuddlan Castle by the Welsh:

> He sent to Roger Hell (alias Lacy) Constable of Chester, to Come
> to his ayde. Which Roger, calling his ffrendes together: desyred
> them to make as many men as they could, & to go with hym. At

whose Request Ralf Dutton, his Sonne in Law, being a Lusty
youth: Assembled all ye players & Musicians in the Cittie (for this
chaunced at ye ffayre tyme) And went forth, with ye said Constable
against ye walshmen, who fledd vppon the sight of such a nomber
of people. |

. . .

The Erle being delyuered out of Danger: granted to his said
Constable, dyvers freedomes & priveleges, within the Cittie, and
in other places. And granted to ye sayd Ralf Dutton: The Rule &
ordering of all the Musicians, within the Countie, which his heires
enioy, even at this day.[14]

By 1433, the right to license minstrels was a recognized part of the
Duttons' hereditary rights.[15]

A large number of the performers who appear in the records are
not designated as either 'musician' or 'minstrel' but by terms that suggest the particular instrument they played, such as 'harper,' 'fiddler,'
'drummer,' or 'piper.' It would appear that, as far as can be determined, these terms were of lower status than the terms 'musician' or
'musicioner,' which seem to be associated mainly with waits and other
more established performers.[16] By far the largest group comprises the
pipers to the extent that 'piper' seems to have become almost a generic
term, like 'minstrel,' and implying similarly low status. The term may
have been found objectionable by some performers such as Richard
Preston of Warrington, who in a Quarter Sessions Examination in
1594 describes himself as a "musicioner."[17] The document has "pip"
crossed out immediately before "musicioner," and it is clear that the
scribe began to write "piper" but corrected himself or was corrected.
Had the document been something other than a statement taken from
Preston, the scribe may have let the term stand. "Musicioner" is more
likely to be Preston's description of himself. "Piper" replaces "mynstre"
in a jury's presentment of Henry Clutton of Malpas in 1618;[18] in this
case, there is an earlier document which describes Henry Clutton as a
piper, and the alteration was probably made by the scribe in order to
be consistent in the identification of Clutton. But the scribe thought
"minstrel" first, and "minstrel" rather than "musician."

Another important factor in the decline of the status of minstrels
is change in musical taste in the sixteenth century. According to
McGee, the Statute of Vagabonds did not establish the low status of
the minstrel but simply reflected a lowering of status resulting from a
change in musical taste.[19] Both McGee and Southworth associate the

change with the loss of the minstrel's role as storyteller, the dif-
ferentiation between court musicians and chamber minstrels, and the
emergence of the players as a separate group.[20]

The association of the term 'minstrel' with untrained performers
meant that it came to refer increasingly to those who were relegated to
playing on informal, low-status occasions, the alehouse gatherings and
sabbath dances, rather than entertaining the gentry and the guilds,
although this division is not absolute.[21] The combination of change of
taste and legislation gave the medieval minstrel—and by extension the
performer of traditional monophonic music—a lower social status.
McGee remarks:

> The demand in the late sixteenth-century was for specialists whose
> performance skills included reading music and the most up-to-date
> instruments and repertory on the one hand, and for trained actors
> on the other. The respected repertory was that transmitted in
> writing, and the minstrel/storyteller, with a repertory of traditional
> monophonic ballads and tales transmitted orally over the centuries,
> had the wrong repertory and lacked all the contemporary skills.
> The medieval English tradition of minstrelsy was overshadowed
> and replaced by the latest trends from the continent: in part it was
> an early casualty to the rising popularity of the skill of reading.[22]

The increased use of the term 'musician' from the later sixteenth
century thus reflects the specialization of the former minstrels, the
lowering of status of minstrels as a group from royal servants to vagabonds, and the division between the musically literate and illiterate.
The term 'minstrel' in the earlier records may mean, but is not limited
to, instrumentalists, as minstrel names such as William le Synger
(1342–43), Robert Gyster (1407–09), and Thomas Fiddler (1488)
indicate.[23] Whythorne's distinction, based on musical literacy and
social and economic status, probably meant less to the average listener,
who have might regarded the same individual as either minstrel or
musician depending on context, prejudice, or mood.

Professionalism

What characteristics are necessary for an individual to be identified as a musician? And where is the line to be drawn between
professional and amateur? Whythorne's comments (see below) indicate

an attitude towards professional and amateur musicians that reverses modern assumptions.[24] It was the amateur—the gentleman or gentlewoman who played and sang, who read music, and who could critically appreciate music—who was respected, not the performer who made music a means of earning a livelihood. Difficulties can therefore arise in applying the terms 'professional' and 'professionalism' to performers in the early modern period. Both 'minstrel' and 'musician,' as used in the records, imply some degree of professionalism, in the sense of identity and status. But what was required for an individual to be identified as 'minstrel' or 'musician,' and what is to be understood by professionalism in this context? Modern critics are not agreed on a definition of musical professionalism in the medieval and early modern periods, and different definitions can be equally valid. Richard Rastall discusses it in terms of musical training and specifically the ability to read music.[25] John Southworth argues that professional minstrels must depend primarily or exclusively on their performing skills for their livelihood.[26] Rastall's definition is more appropriate for distinguishing between trained church musicians, able to read music and sing complicated polyphony, and secular musicians outside the court circle: "Secular musicians performed entirely in an aural tradition, unless in an intellectually high-powered courtly context, until well into the sixteenth century, and the methods by which they turned a tune into an acceptable instrumental piece or song belonged to the same tradition."[27] As Rastall points out, the sixteenth century marked a change in musical training and musical literacy which had implications for the professional minstrels. Rastall sees the introduction of a simpler form of music notation and the printing of music as contributing factors bringing about "the virtual end of medieval minstrelsy in this country."[28] Even in the medieval period distinctions were not so clear-cut:

> The question of a minstrel's professional status must often have been difficult to determine, for instance. An independent minstrel could hardly claim to be a professional unless he had served a seven-year apprenticeship: yet many villages must have relied for their music on men who also plied other trades. Disputes over a minstrel's right to perform were no doubt common.[29]

Southworth's definition of professional would seem to exclude those men from the category of 'minstrel' "who also plied other trades," unless music was their primary vocation. Part of the difficulty here is

determining an individual's primary trade, especially as not all trades
are listed in a particular instance, so that one must first identify that
"John Smith, piper" and "John Smith, alehousekeeper" are the same
individual—a difficult task in itself—and then decide which occupation is the primary one. Nor does the use of more than one identifying
description for one individual mean that that individual is necessarily
relying on several trades to support himself. Wealthy guildsmen might
belong to more than one craft and might describe themselves as "husbandmen," having property outside the city, in order to avoid the
expenses of civic office.

Simple distinctions between professional and amateur, between
minstrel and musician, remain elusive. It is probably more useful to
think of a range of professionalism, of a variety of factors making up
the individual's identity as a musician or minstrel. One must also be
constantly aware that the status of a single individual can vary according to the point of view of those around him. Thomas Whythorne,
himself a musician in the sixteenth century, is precise and particular in
his definitions of who is and is not to be considered a musician, but it
is doubtful if his distinctions were widely followed. Even he speaks of
the varying degrees as all being musicians, descending from the doctor
and bachelor of music, through "miuzisians vnkomenced," organists,
teachers of music (including pricksong) (usually schoolmasters),
singers in churches (including children), those who teach music
privately (in their own or, more often, in others' houses), down to
those who go about the country with their instruments to cities, towns,
villages, and private houses. These last he does not consider truly to be
musicians, and for them he prefers the term 'minstrel,' which to him
is wholly pejorative:

> lastly þer bee þ<oz> do ywz to go with þeir instruments abowt the
> kuntreiz to sytiez, tow(nz) and villaȝes, wher also þei do go to
> pryvat howses to such as will hear þem eiþer publikly o<r>
> pryvatly, or els to markats, fairz, marriaȝes, assembliez, taverns,
> Alhowzes, and such lyk plases. and þar to þoz þat will hear þem þei
> will sell þe sowndz of þeir voises and instrriments. also to
> banketterz, revellerz, mummerz, maskerz, daunserz, tumblerz,
> plaierz and such lyk, þei sell also þe sowndz of þeir voises and
> instrriments. Đez in awnsient tym were named Minstrels. and az
> þe forsaid *Marcus Aurelius* did banish þis sort of peopull for þeir
> misywzed lyf, so hav þei bin of lat in þis owr realm restrained
> sumwhat from þeir vakabond lyf, which sum of þem ywzed. Đoz

maʒestrats and ʒiustizes be not well adyzed (with reverens I do speak it) who do gyv lisenses vnto minstrels vnder þe nam of miuzisians to go abowt þe kuntrey with þeir miuzik in such sort az iz befor rehersed, and if þei do remember þem selvz, þe statiut nameth þem minstrels, and so owht þei to do in þeir lisenses geven to þem.[30]

Whythorne is here invoking the statute as a reason for using what has become a pejorative term, and has a clear idea of "musicianship" as linked to musical literacy and formal training in polyphony, whereas "minstrelsy" probably reflects an older, popular, aural style of music-making. The division is one that is still seen today in the distinction between "classical" or "classically-trained" musicians and "popular" musicians, although there are instances of classically-trained musicians becoming popular musicians—and certainly of classical musicians performing popular music.[31] Even in modern times the term 'musician' itself is ambiguous and can cover a wide range of musical ability, training, and reliance on music as a means of earning a living; nor are the three factors always interconnected. It is possible for a trained musician to be unable to earn a living from music alone, and it is also possible for a musician, at least in certain types of music, to be successful without being able even to read music.

Virtually all of Whythorne's categories are represented in the Cheshire records, although by far the largest group is the one which Whythorne would designate *minstrels*. There are a few trained musicians making appearances in the records: Mr. Evans, singer in the choir at Chester in 1608–09, whose name implies some status; Thomas Jones, bachelor of music, at Chester in 1625; Henry Lawes, the court composer, visiting the Legh family of Lyme Hall in 1635; Richard Nuball, organist of Chester cathedral, in 1641; and Mr. Woodson, an organist—and possibly a composer—at Cholmondeley, in 1643.[32] These men all may be presumed to have been musically literate, and there are other singingmen, usually associated with Chester Cathedral, who would have had to be able to read music. In 1642, the parson of St. Bridget's, Chester, was informed against at the Quarter Sessions because Henry Hughes, the sub-sub-sexton, was ignorant "in the science of Musicke."[33] The late date makes it likely that there was disagreement in the parish between traditionalists and reformers about the role of music in church services. The Chester waits and some of the "musicioners" in places such as Nantwich were also musically literate, at least by the seventeenth century. Whythorne does not actually include waits in his catalogue of musicians. His interest is in discriminating between the low-class minstrel and the university-trained teacher or performer; in short, he is interested in establishing his own status and thus draws a sharper line between the trained and untrained than may have been visible to the casual observer of the time. His list includes musicians who satisfy both Rastall's and South-worth's definitions of professionalism, musical training and music as a source of livelihood. He gives a higher status to musical training, and regrets the use of 'musician' for untrained performers but does not deny them a degree of professional status. He raises, by protest, a third important factor in the identification of professionalism: common fame. A musician is a musician when he is seen as such by his neighbors; if a tailor plays the pipes at village festivities, it is immaterial which is his principal source of income. He is seen by his neighbors as fulfilling two functions, the value of which depends on the perspective of the observer. A saddler who plays the cittern for his own amusement may nonetheless attract an audience. To that audience, the distinction between musician and minstrel would have been largely subjective.

Contexts of Performance

The possible venues for musical performance are more varied than for other forms of entertainment such as bearbaiting or plays. In addition to private performances in houses, Whythorne lists "markats, fairz, marriaȝes, assembliez, taverns, Alhowzes, and such lyk plases" as potential venues or occasions for music, and associates music with "banketterz, revellerz, mummerz, maskerz, daunserz, tumblerz, plaierz and such lyk."[34] A single piper or fiddler can potentially perform any-where, and music can be either a source of entertainment in itself or part of the background to a banquet, or it can be an integral accom-paniment to other forms of entertainment, as Whythorne's list shows. Dancing is of particular importance since it is in most cases a par-ticipatory activity which requires music. In most contexts, the mention of dancing may be taken to imply the presence of music, and music is undoubtedly associated with dancing on many occasions where there is no explicit reference to it.

The where and when of musical performance are not always of interest to those keeping the records and tend to be specified when there is a perceived inappropriateness, such as in the numerous citations for piping on the sabbath, or in the churchyard, or after dark in the alehouse. Nevertheless, there is still a wide range of venues listed, and most of those on Whythorne's list are represented. Musical performances took place in the homes of the gentry, at guild dinners, in churchyards, and even on occasion in the church. Musicians performed at church ales, in alehouses, on the village green, at wakes, rushbearings and bearbaitings, and even before the stocks. They are frequently presented for playing at night, but they also played on the sabbath at the time of the service, in the afternoon, after evening prayer and in the evening. In short, virtually any leisure time was potentially an opportunity for music, and virtually any place was a potential venue.

Despite the seemingly negative attitude of the Statute of Vagabonds, there are many musical performances that are recorded in a positive context. They are more likely to occur in association with entertainment for the upper levels of society, whether in the homes of the gentry or at guild feasts. The Chester waits, individually or collectively, were paid for performing at a variety of guild feasts: special occasions such as Midsummer and the Account Day, and associated "drinkings" at the houses of the aldermen and stewards (see chapter II, part 1). Guild drinkings with musical accompaniment continued to be held during the Civil War and Commonwealth periods on occasions such as Shrovetide and Midsummer. Professor Mills has found instances of musical performance at guild feasts in the late 1670s.[35] The accounts do not indicate whether the musicians' performance was provided as background music to the feast or as an entertainment in its own right. On one occasion at least dancing was certainly involved since in 1658–59 the Painters, Glaziers, Embroiderers, and Stationers Company paid one shilling to "the maydes at Alderman Holmes house, for Rubbing the Chamber after their danceing in it." James Robinson "the musitioner" was paid three shillings on the same occasion.[36] The entry is ambiguous, as it could have been either the maids or the members of the company who danced. The term 'minstrel' or 'minstrels' is used in the accounts of the Cordwainers and Shoemakers Company, the Painters, Glaziers, Embroiderers, and Stationers Company, and the Joiners, Carvers, and Turners Company at various drinkings, feasts, weddings, and other social occasions, particularly from the late 1560s to the mid-1580s.[37] The specific terms 'wait' and 'waitmen' are used more regularly after 1585, but in some accounts both minstrels and waits are paid.[38]

Members of the gentry continued the medieval custom of having musicians among their liveried retainers (see chapter III). A piper apparently in the livery of the Legh family of Lyme ("which had Sir Peeter Leighes Cloath") was involved in an affray at Wilmslow in 1610,[39] and two brothers of the Cally dynasty of Chester waits, George and Robert, served respectively the Earl of Derby and Sir John Savage. Edward Clarke, who testified in 1607 that he was born in the Isle of Ely and that he was "by profession a Musicioner," claimed to have been a servant in the house of Mr. Legh of Baguley for one year. He was interrogated as being suspect for the theft of jewels from Mr. Legh and his daughter at the end of his service.[40] He was presumably employed by Mr. Legh as a musician, probably to teach his daughter. His employment lasted one year and, according to Clarke, seems to have terminated naturally. The outcome of the case against Clarke does not survive; as a servant who had recently left the household, he would be an obvious suspect when items were missing. It is clear, despite Whythorne's claim that those who taught privately in houses had a higher status than the common minstrels, that Clarke was not regarded as being of any higher status than any other former servant, and that once he had left Mr. Legh's employment he became liable to suspicion as a wandering minstrel.

There are, as indicated above, musicians who enjoyed quite high status and could mix on equal or near-equal terms with gentlemen. Sir Peter Legh of Lyme was on friendly terms with Henry Lawes (1595– 1662), the court composer who created the music for Milton's *Comus*, as can be seen from Lawes's letter to Sir Peter in 1635, discussed in chapter III. Francis Pilkington, lutenist and composer, who was also a minor canon and singingman of Chester Cathedral, dedicated his *First Booke of Songs or Ayres of 4 Parts* to the Earl of Derby in 1605, his *First Set of Madrigals and Pastorals of 3, 4, and 5 Parts* to Sir Thomas Smith of Hough, Cheshire, in 1612, and his *Second Set of Madrigals, and Pastorals of 3, 4, 5, and 6 Parts* to Sir Peter Legh of Lyme in 1624.[41]

In any case, musicians were an important part of civic entertainment. The presence of a musician could even be in itself the occasion of a celebration. The mayor and aldermen of Congleton spent 3s 4d on entertaining gentlemen such as Sir John Brereton, Sir Randall Mainwaring, and Mr. Henry Mainwaring "when the pyper was in Towne."[42] Musicians in the service of gentlemen or nobles would also visit smaller towns or country houses. Congleton hosted the Chester waits in 1618, and the Earl of Derby's trumpeter was paid six pence as he passed through the town on his way from the Low Countries in 1623.[43] Baroness Newton, writing the history of the house of Lyme in 1917, cites payments to visiting musicians listed in a Household Account Book which now appears to be lost: "Given | in reward to 4 Trumpetters of my Lo: of Pembrookes — iii s iv d," "Given in reward to a piper of Sr Thomas Smith, i s."[44] The Sir Thomas Smith here is probably Sir Thomas Smith of Hough, dedicatee of Pilkington's first book of madrigals. Evidence from Lancashire reveals that Sir Peter Legh had musicians who traveled since the Household Accounts of Sir Richard Shuttleworth show a payment of one shilling in 1584 to "the musicions of sir piter lyghe."[45]

The examples quoted above demonstrate a generally more positive attitude towards musical performance than might be found in, for instance, the diocesan visitations. Music was happening at all levels of society, but, like drinking, it was more acceptable at some levels than at others. The guildsmen who gathered at an alderman's house for their drinking, listening, or dancing to the music of George or Robert Cally and their waits would draw a definite line between their behavior and that of the piper arrested for playing in an alehouse at night or on the sabbath. And, as noted above, the gentry were often music-makers themselves, as can be seen by the number of references in wills to musical instruments in the sixteenth and seventeenth centuries as well as notations in account books such as Thomas Wilbraham's that reveal the borrowing and lending of musical instruments to friends or relations and other musical activities (see chapter III).[46]

The attitude of the local gentry towards music could also have an effect on what happened further down the social scale. A justice of the peace of Puritan tendencies was far more likely to treat minstrels as rogues and vagabonds and to attempt to suppress activities such as maypoles, wakes, and dancing, all of which would involve music. Where local landowners were of differing sympathies, popular entertainment could become a focus for their dispute. In 1594, John Egerton of Oulton forbade the constables of Little Budworth to hold their traditional wakes, which he considered had been "ouermuche superstycyously vsed" and likely to attract "great store of the worsest sorte," resulting in disorder, misdemeanors, and breaches of the peace. The constables promptly went to John Starkey, esquire, of Darley, and his wife and son, whom the constables knew to be "greatly affected & supersticiously <..>clyned to the observinge & kepinge of the same wakes & such other lyke vayne & abolished Trashe" for permission for the wakes to be held.[47] The resulting dispute went as far as the Star Chamber. Music was not mentioned to any great extent but was an understood part of the festivities, which included maygames and dancing.

The only form of music that is actually mentioned is drumming, and that only because it was associated with an assault on Mr. Egerton's servants:

> One Bennet Hardinge William Carter Elizabeth Salte otherwise called Bounsing Besse and iij or iiijor persons more with them whose names he this deponent nowe remembreth not, towardes the evening of the sayde sayde[48] wake daye being weaponed somme of them with staves and somme with Swordes came verye merelie by the hedgsyde next adioyning to a Cowpasture of the Complainantes In which pasture the servantes of the said Complainant were mylking or Redye to mylke ther kyne, And when they came against ther kyne stryking on a dromme, This deponent being at the hedg syde nere to the said pasture wylled them that they would forbeare that noyse vntyll they were past the kyne for fearing of them And on of the same Companye badd hime that Caryed the dromme strike on And this deponent aunswered that yf they would not giue ouer the noyse he would strike out the bottome of his dromme. And thervpon, and vpon some other speeches passing emongest them One Laurence Yewoode and other of the servantes of Mr Iohn Starkey Came vnto this deponent and somme of them did hold this Deponent by the armes, and ^the^ sayd Yewoode with a Cudgell did breake the head of this said deponent, being there about his Mr his busines in peaceable manner.[49]

The drum may have been a tabor, frequently used to accompany dancing. Egerton alleges that it was used solely to frighten the cattle and that the incident was intentional, "procured" by the Starkeys and carried out by their servants, who were on their way from the wake at Little Budworth to John Starkey's house at Darley. Egerton's own servant allegedly did no more than "quietly reprehende" the rioters, for which he was "daungerously & cruelly" beaten.[50] The interrogatories in the case suggest that the company with the drum were traveling to John Starkey's house in order to dance and that this might have been a usual practice at the Starkeys:

whether dyd yow and your Company that eveninge with your
drumme goe to the hall of Darley, and there daunce and make
mery in the presenc, and by the allowance & request of the said mr
Starkies weyf, and was she accostomed to haue such druminge
daunsinge and sport at other tymes and how often.[51]

The answers to the interrogatories reveal that the drum was carried by
"one Chester a drummer"[52] but deny that there was any malice afore-
thought in the actions of Mr. Starkey's servants. It seems most likely
that the drumming incident was simply an expression of a deeper
divide between the two gentlemen, carried out by their servants. Their
different attitudes towards music and dancing suggest that Mr. Egerton was more puritan in his sympathies, and he implies that the
Starkeys were recusant in theirs. The religious divisions of the
sixteenth and seventeenth centuries do affect every aspect of life, but
they are particularly relevant in relation to the popular attitude
towards music and music-making because of the rise of the puritans
—and as a result of Sabbatarianism—in the latter part of Elizabeth I's
reign. This further deterioration in the attitude toward music and
musicians is an important part of the context in which music was performed.

Puritans and Sabbatarianism

I thinke that all good minstrelles, sober and chast musicions
(speking of suche drunken sockets, and bawdye parasits as range
the Cuntreyes, ryming and singing of vncleane, corrupt, and filthie
songs in Tauernes, Ale-houses, Innes, and other publique
assemblies) may daunce the wild Moris thorow a needles eye. For
how should thei bere chaste minds, seeing that their exercyse is the
pathway to all vncleanes. Their is no ship so balanced with massie
matter, as their heads are fraught with all kind of bawdie songs,
filthie ballads, and scuruie rymes, seruing for euery purpose, and
for euery Cumpanie.[53]

Although reforming preachers and puritans were associated
particularly with opposition to popular musical entertainment, the
above quotation represents an attitude that had as much to do with
social class as with religious persuasion. Even the more extreme reformers were not opposed to music completely, and their anxieties
about what they saw as related activities to music were shared by many

of the ruling class. Puritan writers were able to make use of official concerns about social problems in their arguments against musicians, wakes, and other forms of popular entertainment.

The term 'puritan,' although unsatisfactory in many ways, is still perhaps the most convenient to designate that branch of the Church of England which favored more extreme Protestant reform than the main body of the Church. They were characterized by a more definite rejection of ceremonies and ritual and an advocacy of stricter observance of the sabbath and biblical teaching. They might also be distinguished by a soberness of dress and a rigidness of moral standards. These, along with their self-identification as "the godly," set them apart to some extent, and made them more visible targets for the "ungodly," who were apt to take exception to having their traditional entertainments curtailed.

The terms 'precisian' and 'puritan' began as terms of abuse. As with recusancy, much depended on the attitude of the person using the terms, and there is a range of attitudes subsumed under them. 'Puritanism,' or extreme Protestantism, was regarded with some suspicion by the national authorities since it could become non-conformism, and clerics were punished for going too far in reformation. Nevertheless, Cheshire had a relatively large proportion of clergymen who would qualify as puritans and who were tolerated—and at times encouraged —because of the threat of recusancy in the Northwest.[54] It is hence important to stress that the 'puritan' opposition to music was coming from within the established Church and frequently had the full approval of ecclesiastical and secular authority.

The recusancy of Cheshire has been linked to passive conservatism rather than active proselytizing from abroad. According to Christopher Haigh, only Bunbury and Malpas developed "substantial recusant groups, and in both cases this seems to have been due to the work of parish clergy who became recusant priests and led some of the people out of the Church of England."[55] The response of the authorities was to appoint preaching clergy of puritan tendencies to these parishes. William Hinde, vicar of Bunbury, was evidently chosen to counteract recusancy. He was also connected with the local reformist gentry and wrote the life of his brother-in-law, John Bruen of Bruen Stapleford, as an example of "godly living." Both Hinde and Bruen apparently considered music to be dangerous in particular because of its association with dancing. Although in his youth Bruen "was drawn by desire and delight into the Dancing-schoole,"[56] Hinde's text inveighs on his behalf against the opportunities for sin which mixed dancing afforded:

> Sober and single dancing of men apart, and women apart, hath had his use, and praise also, not | not only among the Heathen, but amongst the people of God, when by the nimble motions and gestures of the body, they have expressed the great joyes of their hearts, for some good of their owne, or to set forth Gods glory. But mixt dancing of men and women, with light and lascivious gestures and actions, framed in number and measure to please a wanton eye, and provoke one anothers lust, or to serve the humour of some wicked *Herod*, hath ever beene held, both of the ancient Fathers within the Church, and of the best Authors that ever wrote amongst the Heathen without, to bee utterly unlawfull, sinfull, shamefull, carnall, sensuall, and divellish, as hatefull unto God, as hurtfull unto men.[57]

Music and dancing, while not sinful in themselves, could so easily provide the occasion for sin as to be dangerous and better avoided. Although writers such as Stubbes allow that music and dancing may have benefits if used for the praise of God and healthful recreation, there is a general sense among the puritan writers that the risk of abuse of such activities is so great as to make them virtually irredeemable. Furnivall, in his edition of Stubbes, refers to Bishop Babington's rejection of both dancing and piping: "The scriptures checke it, the fathers mislike it, the councels haue condemned it, & the proofe of Gods iudgements vpon it biddeth vs beware. *Instrumenta luxuriae tympana & tripudia*, sayth one, the inticers to lust are pipings and dancinges."[58]

Musicians were further suspect because of their associations with the Old Religion and the old holy days. Particularly objectionable to a puritan like John Bruen were the wakes, the vigils of the feast-days of the patron saints of the various parish churches, which developed into festivals lasting several days and involving visitors from other communities. These festivities attracted entertainers, including minstrels, from the surrounding area and very likely from further afield. Some of these were probably not above supplementing their takings with some petty crime, and others could have served as messengers between recusants. Bruen was sufficiently concerned about the "popery and profannes" of Tarvin wakes—that is, the celebration of the patron saint (St. Andrew) and the performance of secular entertainment—that he found a means of attacking both problems at once. Over a number of years (Hinde does not specify the exact period, but it must pre-date the death of John Bruen in 1625) Bruen invited several preachers to Tarvin wakes "that spent most part of three dayes in preaching and praying in the Church, so as the Pipers and Fidlers, and Bearewards, and Players, and Gamesters, had no time left them for their vanities, but went away with great fretting."[59] As it was illegal to perform music or hold bearbaits during the time of divine service or sermons—and moreover as the sermons provided an alternative entertainment— Bruen effectively suppressed the wakes at Tarvin. The editor of the 1799 edition of *A Faithfull Remonstrance* notes: "It is remarkable, that there has not been a wake held at Tarvin, from the time here alluded to, to the present period, 1799."[60]

Sabbath Infringements and Sabbath Sports

The question of sabbath observance became to some extent a touchstone of religious sympathy in the late sixteenth century and a decided feature of Cheshire puritanism. It was an issue that concerned secular as well as ecclesiastical authorities[61] as concerns about recusancy were augmented by worries about sedition, plague, and disorder. Opposition to all forms of secular activity on Sunday, whether work or play, was "one of the most prominent features of the clergy's strivings towards reformation and the godly discipline."[62] Music and dancing were only part of the problem. Working, drinking, and gambling on the sabbath as well as not attending church are frequently cited in the Visitation Books. However, activities such as communal eating and drinking, music and dancing, could be part of the older tradition of celebration on festivals such as saints' days. Many of the traditional saints' days, including the wakes held on the patronal festival of a church, had been suppressed or modified at the Reformation. The puritans, quick to assume the connection between sabbath-breaking and recusancy, argued that Roman Catholics encouraged or at least condoned traditional activities that broke the sabbath and that thus people were prevented from attending catechisms and sermons. John Barwick, dean of St. Paul's, in his *A Summarie Account of the Holy Life and Happy Death of the Right Reverend Father in God Thomas Late Lord Bishop of Duresme* (1660) attributes Sunday recreations to Catholic policy:

> It was no small policy in the leaders of the Popish party to keep the people from church by dancing and other recreations, even in the time of divine service, especially on holy days and the Lord's Day in the afternoon. By which means they kept the people in ignorance and lukewarmness, and so made them the more capable to be wrought upon by their emissaries: which gross abuse this bishop endeavoured to redress in his primary visitation.[63]

That every piper who played on a Sunday did so on orders from Rome—or even out of Catholic sympathies—is highly unlikely. Many of those cited for breaking the sabbath were not doing so out of any policy other than that of making money, and they may not even have considered themselves to be doing anything wrong. In many cases, the puritans who were complaining about the music and dancing ironically were likely to be less willing to conform to the religious laws than those about whom they complained.

Nevertheless, there is evidence that some musicians were in fact associated with recusant activities. A fiddler at Rostherne in 1629–30 was identified as a recusant and part of a recusant group: "Con*tra* Isabella*m* Stubbs de Tabley et Ellin*am* servu*m* ib*ide*m, in ead*em* dom*um*[us] Thomam Allin et Katherin*am* vx*or* eius, [Thoma*m* Ashton] et vx*or* ^Thome Ashton^, All these Recusant*es* & the s*ai*d Allen (a fidler by trade) a great seducer" ("Against Isabella Stubbs of Tabley and Ellen her servant, in the same house Thomas Allen and Katherine his wife and the wife of Thomas Ashton . . .").[64] The implication is clearly that Thomas Allen was using his trade as a fiddler to proselytize. Fiddlers were, like peddlers and chapmen, more mobile than most of the population, and may have acted as messengers between recusants. Thomas Allen, if he is the same man as the fiddler Thomas Allen of Lostock Gralam, had been cited as early as 1619 for playing on the sabbath and not attending church. Recusancy is hard to measure in these cases. The information that Allen was a recusant is given (if he was the same individual) when he was away from his home parish. Of course, a performer might participate in an allegedly recusant activity without being actively recusant. A charge was made against Henry Dowse, piper, in 1595 that "he occac*i*oned youth to prophane the sabbothe."[65] This in itself does not mean that either the piper or the youth necessarily had recusant leanings. However, a second citation in the same month makes the recusant connection more definite: "Marye Layton Wyfe of Willi*a*m layton gent*l*e*man* a Recusante Ther was a May pole sett vppe vpon Lawton grene vpon a

Sabbothe or holly day. where a pyper, and dyuers youthe were playinge and dauncinge, the pypers name is henry Dowse."[66]

Musical performances such as Dowse's could occur in the context of traditional Roman Catholic activities such as pilgrimages and wakes. John Harrison, fiddler, was accused of being involved in what looks like a pilgrimage "for drawing people to holliwell [on the] in an assembly on the sabboth" in September 1617.[67] Another, fuller document refers to a trip to "Hallewell" taking place on 27 July in the same year. This excursion involved the constable of Ness and nearly two hundred of the inhabitants of surrounding parishes:

> Richard Holland millar of litle Neston informeth vpon his oath
> that vpon Sunday after St Iames day b<...> the 27 of Iuly last,
> william Barrowe Constable of Nesse did ride vnto <..>llewell
> accompanyed with most of the inhabitantes of Shotwick Rabie
> Puddington & litle Neston to the number [of] neere vnto two
> hundreth, & they had in there Company one Iohn Harrison & his
> boy who are fidlers & dwell as this informert thinketh in Saughton
> vpon the hill or there aboutes, which said Harrisson and his boy
> did ride in like manner vnto Hallewell & spent the whole day in
> fidlinge & danceinge too and fro vntill they Came to litle Neston
> that night, & this informer saith further that one Evans a young
> man who dwelleth in the fflint was in Wirrall the weeke before this
> goinge to Hallewell & there did report that they might Come ouer
> into wales & play & dance & nothinge would bee said to them &
> further saith not.[68]

The authorities are clearly anxious about this activity on a range of levels. In the first place, the number of people involved, nearly two hundred from four separate townships, led by a representative of authority from a fifth township, and representing three different parishes, would have the uncomfortable appearance of an uprising or at least a riot to the authorities. Secondly, there are the recusant associations of traveling in a large group to what is clearly a holy well. Added to this, the first event takes place at the time when wakes were usually held (having been officially moved to St. James day, 25 July, after the Reformation). The second excursion, if it is a different occasion and not simply an entry in the Crown Book of the July excursion, took place on the old Holy Rood day, the feast of the Exaltation of the Cross (14 September), a feast with decidedly recusant associations. Then there is the issue of disruptive behavior and, in particular, behavior inappropriate (and to some extent forbidden) on the sabbath: the fiddling and dancing. This seems to have been at least in part a processional activity, as the fiddler was on horseback and the dancers moved "to and fro" until they reached Little Neston at night. Finally, the words of the Welsh visitor were evidently being construed as seditious in their implication both that the authorities were un-reasonably strict in objecting to activities such as this and that Wales was exempt from such control.

The Pipers and the Puritans

In 1618, the piper William Ashton of Over Knutsford was in-dicted "for saying there had bene a strife for many yeres betwixt pipers & prechers but now (god be thanked) pipers had gotten the victory."[69] The source of this strife was the question of sabbath entertainment, and the "victory" of the pipers was probably seen to be King James I's *Book of Sports*, which specifically identified "puritanes and precise people" as hindering the lawful pastimes of the people:

> Whereas we did justly, in our progresse through Lancashire, rebuke some puritanes and precise people, in prohibiting and unlawfully punishing of our good people for using their lawfull recreations and honest exercises on Sundayes and other holy dayes, after the afternoone sermon or service: It is our will, that after the end of divine service, our good people be not disturbed, letted, or discouraged, from any lawful recreation, such as dauncing, either for men or women; archery for men, leaping, vaulting, or any other such harmless recreation; nor for having of May-games, Whitson-ales, and morris-daunces, and the setting up of May-poles, and other sports therewith used; so as the same be had in due and convenient time, without impediment or neglect of divine service. But withall, we doe here account still as prohibited, all unlawfull games to be used upon Sundayes onely, as beare and bull-baitings, interludes, and, at all times in the meaner sort of people by law prohibited, bowling.[70]

Ashton's view of the situation was clearly not acceptable to the authorities; if nothing else, the "god be thanked" would seem blasphemous and possibly would have made him suspected of recusancy. But by Ashton's time, the puritan leanings of many of the clergy in Cheshire—and even more in Lancashire—had become as much a problem as the recusancy that they had been introduced to combat.

The "strife" between the preachers and the pipers was not entirely metaphorical, nor was it one-sided. Although preachers preached against pipers and other music-makers and had them presented to the ecclesiastical courts for sabbath-breaking, there are cases which show that the pipers had popular support. Piping on the sabbath could even become a means of testing the minister's power and, of course, of annoying him. John Baxter, alias Barne, piper, was evidently being used by some of the Mobberley parishioners to express their dissatisfaction with Mr. Eaton, their vicar. The articles of the charge specify that Thomas Brachgirdle, who is allegedly responsible for hiring the piper, was aware of the Archbishop of York's decree that no piper or minstrel should perform on the sabbath, but that he nevertheless caused the piper

> to plaie vpon his pipes at Moburley & nere vnto the parish Church ther & parsonage house aswell in the great prophanacion of godes holie sabaoth the contempt of the said most godlie order & Iniunction and in despight of mr Eaton Parson of Moburley thy Pastor . . . that the said Mr Eaton thean reproving the said Piper for so prophaning the Lordes sabaoth thou the said Thomas said openly although he the said piper did cease or geve over now to play yet he shuld play [p] againe before night (meaning he shuld playe againe on his pipes that same daie) and letts se who dare take him vpp or wordes to the lyk effect.[71]

Brachgirdle is also alleged to have said that if the rest of the parish would do as he would, "they woold spend fourtie poundes before he shuld geve over playing meaning they wold spend xl li before the piper shuld geve over his playing on his pipes on the sabaoth Daie." Brachgirdle went on to whisper to the piper while Mr. Eaton was trying to catechize him. The court demands that Brachgirdle reveal what he said to Baxter; he may have been giving him the answers to the catechism, or he may have been making comments about Mr. Eaton. The piper played both immediately after evening prayer and also later in the evening, and he was specifically—and it would appear deliberately—stationed near Mr. Eaton's gates as well as near the church. Mr. Eaton certainly saw it as a deliberate attempt to annoy him. Part of the objection is that Brachgirdle was setting a bad example to the rest of the parish and undermining the incumbent's authority. Brachgirdle's father, John Brachgirdle, also becoming involved in the controversy, questioned the vicar's attitude and suggested that he had been more lax in the past:

> the said Mr Eaton [Ea] rep*r*ehending the pip*er* afforenamed for his abuses & being then in the Church at or ready to the exercise of Catechising didst openlie in reproofe of the said Mr Eaton ^^& defense of the said piping vpon the sabaoth daie^ vtt*er* these or the lyk speches and why did you (Mr p*ar*son) suffer the lik piping At grapnall. And y*at* thervpon being required by the said Mr Eaton to hold his peace because neith*er* the place nor tyme did s*er*ve to reason on such Matt*er* thou the said John said openly againe I have spoken to as good a Man as you (or he) and thervpon felle into comparisons saying y*at* his sonne was as good a Man as the said mr Eaton & w*i*th the Lyk disordered behaveo*ur* didst both geve Iust offence to the people ther present & hind*er* that godly exercise of Catechizing so much as in the did lye[72]

The allegations so far would suggest that this was a unique event, organized for the specific purpose of testing the parson's authority and tolerance. But the final item alleges that the piper habitually played on the sabbath, at Mobberley and elsewhere, and mentions a "decre & Iniunction" given by the chancellor of the diocese, David Yale in 1594 or 1595.[73] Mr. Eaton's admonishments did not prevent Baxter from playing later in the evening "at aft*er* Eveninge prayer and in the Eveninge of the same beinge assisted w*i*th a noumb*er* of [his] confederat*es*."[74] Mr. Eaton was a puritan minister and a preacher, whose attitude towards piping on the sabbath would have been known to his parishioners.[75] He had been appointed rector of Mobberley in 1595, but had held the living of Grappenhall since 1582. He continued to hold both livings until his death in 1621.[76] By hiring a piper to pipe specifically on the sabbath—but, it would appear, without actually playing at the time of the services—parishioners might have been testing the law as well as Mr. Eaton's patience. The orders from the archbishop and the chancellor were apparently more severe than the secular law or the *Book of Sports* as they forbade piping at any time on the sabbath. The parishioners may well have regarded these rules with resentment.

Part of the offence in the Mobberley case comes from the location where pipes were played, not just the time. The fact that he played at Mr. Eaton's gates and "nere vnto the parish Church ther & p*ar*sonage

house aswell"[77] is taken to be something unusual. Compared to the
number of documents that specify performance on the sabbath, there
are relatively few which specify or even imply performance in the
churchyard or near the church. Only once is a piper actually cited for
playing in the churchyard as a specific offence.[78] The only other
instance where proximity to the church is mentioned in the document
may not be a specifically musical performance; in 1615 at Shotwick
the preacher, Mr. Burrows, was forcibly kept out of the pulpit on
Christmas Eve, and "there was a horne blowen neare to the Church
. . . with great hallowinge on a Sabbath day not longe before, by one
George Massie" (see also chapter IV).[79] The intention here, as at
Mobberley, seems to have been to disrupt the activities of the preacher.
Massie is unlikely to have been a musician.

    Sabbath infringements thus are seen to be a major element in the
evidence for musical activity in Cheshire. Far more musical performances are cited as taking place on the sabbath than both unspecified performances and performances on other days of the week. This
must in part be attributed to the rise of sabbatarianism and the
increased prosecution of sabbath infringements. But it also reflects the
fact, recognized in the *Book of Sports*, that Sunday was the only day
really available for entertainment: "For when shall the common people
have leave to exercise, if not upon the Sundayes and holy daies, seeing
they must apply their labour, and win their living in all working
daies?"[80] Sunday sports were not simply an issue for the puritan
minority but were of concern to the secular authorities because of the
increasing concern with social control. From the point of view of the
authorities, the sports which James I allowed on a Sunday—dancing,
archery, leaping and vaulting, as well as maygames, maypoles, Whitsun
ales, and morris dances—were harmless, provided that attendance at
church was not neglected. The alternative was seen to be "filthy
tiplings . . . and discontented speeches in their Ale houses."[81] Where
the puritans hoped that the banning Sunday sports would lead to
attendance at sermons and prayers, the secular rulers feared that it
would lead to drunkenness and sedition.

    It is impossible even to guess what proportion of the total sum of
musical entertainment is represented by the surviving evidence of
sabbath infringements. Doubtless there were many occasions on which
people were able to have their "honest recreations" without attracting
the adverse notice of the authorities. Much depended on the attitude
of the local magistrates, churchwardens, and clergy, much also on the

degree to which the entertainment remained within the bounds of acceptable behavior. The definition of what is acceptable of course changes over time and varies with social class and religious persuasion.

The Ale and the Alehouse

But what of the alternative to honest recreation on the sabbath, the "filthy tiplings . . . and discontented speeches in their Ale houses" mentioned in the *Book of Sports*? If the sabbath is the most common time of performance specified in the records, the most common venue is the alehouse. As with the sabbath infringements, this reflects an increased interest in social control, but it also signifies the increasing number of alehouses, many of them illegal and temporary. The alehouse as such only really became common in the sixteenth century; Peter Clark estimates that by 1577 there were 14,000 alehouses in twenty-seven counties and possibly as many as 24,000 nationally. By the 1630s, there were perhaps as many as 32,000 to 35,000 licensed premises and a further 15,000 to 20,000 unlicensed.[82] Clark's table of local returns to the Privy Council on the number of alehouses in 1577 shows Cheshire as having forty-four inns, no taverns, and 390 alehouses, at a ratio of one alehouse for every 51 inhabitants, although he points out that this estimate may be low.[83] The alehouse was the smallest type of victualing establishment, and the lowest in status. Clark comments:

> Essentially it sold ale and beer with the occasional rough spirits (aquavita), cider or perry, which customers either took home or, more commonly, drank on the premises. It also offered food and one or two beds for the foot traveller or lodger. Most alehouses were kept in ordinary houses, in a back room (sometimes behind a curtain) or in a cellar; there are frequent references to them being located in back-alleys.[84]

Accurate counts of alehouses are impossible, as they were frequently temporary expedients to supplement income. The number of alehouses tended to increase in years of poor harvest.[85]

The causes of the increase are various: the introduction of hops changed brewing from a small domestic industry into a viable commercial one. Increased poverty increased both the demand for alehouses and the number of people seeking to supplement their income by selling ale.[86]

The other two establishments in Clark's "victualling hierarchy for the sixteenth and seventeenth centuries,"[87] the inn and the tavern, were also scenes for musical entertainment, but it is the alehouse which caused anxiety for the authorities and as a result produced a higher number of prosecutions. From 1550, there were numerous attempts to control the alehouses by statute, but enforcement was always a major difficulty. Licensing was often lax, and unlicensed alehouses were common. Alehouses catered primarily to the poor, and the alehousekeepers tended to be poor themselves. Keeping an alehouse was often a secondary trade, and many alehousekeepers came from poorer trades such as tailors and shoemakers. In one instance at least a piper was also an alehousekeeper. Richard Metier was described in 1624 as "A pyper, and A Tipler or Alekeeper."[88]

The proliferation of alehouses in the early modern period was not simply a result of economic factors, however. Clark argues that from the sixteenth century "the alehouse, or tippling house, became an ubiquitous, essential feature of the social world of ordinary folk."[89] As such, it tended to replace the parish church as a center of social life, especially since events such as church ales came under pressure from Reformers.

Traditional ales—for example, church ales, help ales, or love ales—differed in that they were single events rather than regular establishments and were principally charitable rather than commercial in function. Church ales had been a traditional way of raising money for the maintenance of the church fabric. Thus in Cheshire in 1492, when Geoffrey Downes left orders in his will that "if the great Bell break yat. then Robert Downes or his Heirs & ye Brethern of our Lady & Ihon make them an Ale for the makeing of yat Bell."[90] Individuals might also hold help ales to raise money for their relief, and Clark also mentions ales held by newlyweds or by pilgrims.[91] But after the Reformation, church ales came to be increasingly associated with recusancy and disorder, although the help ale and the love ale were still found. Usually the authorities dealt more lightly with help ales held by the extremely poor.

The evidence for the performance of music at church ales is less than for alehouses. There appears to be a distinction between "selling ale" and "making an ale," the former referring to an alehouse rather than an ale. A love ale was held at Boughton, probably Great Boughton, on a Sunday in 1618 at which there was drinking, fiddling, dancing, and brawling all afternoon and "the most part of that nyght."[92] An ale on the sabbath at Acton in 1611 may have had drumming; John Spencer is cited "for drum*m*inge on Sabboath daies" immediately after Thomas Hardinge is cited for having an ale on the sabbath.[93] The suggestion that John Spencer drummed on more than one sabbath does not make it less likely that he played at the ale.

With ales, as with everything else, there was variation in what was acceptable and what was not, and the boundaries were not always fixed. Hugh Warde of Astbury was cited at the diocesan visitation of 1601 "for keeping drinkinge harping & dancinge in the sabaoth daie" but pleaded that "beinge a verie poore man hee had an ale and that there was dauncinge & harpinge appon the Saboth daie in the after nowne & not otherwyse & denieth hee selleth anie ale savinge att that tyme."[94] His response argues that there was a perception that an ale, even with music and dancing, was acceptable in certain circumstances and at certain times. He was ordered to confess his fault, but not otherwise punished.

The church ale and the help ale represent the more acceptable side of ale-selling, the idea of drinking as a communal activity and as a form of charity. The alehouse was in itself a necessary institution: it provided affordable food, drink, and lodging for the customers and a source of income for the alekeeper. There were, of course, many who objected to alehouses, particularly as their number proliferated. Christopher Hudson of Preston summed up the puritan opinion of alehouses in 1631 when he spoke of "the multitude of alehouses, which are nests of Satan where the owls of impiety lurk and where all evil is hatched and the bellows of intemperance and incontinence blown up to the provocation of God's wrath in the subversion of a kingdom."[95]

Even so, Hudson and others principally objected to the *excessive number* of alehouses. The authorities were also concerned about the proliferation of alehouses and the potential for disorder. Alehouses were potentially disruptive in a variety of ways. They were places where crimes could be planned; alehousekeepers served as receivers of stolen goods. Alehouses might also serve as small-scale brothels or places of meeting for lovers. Violence was also a potential threat. Clark quotes one case that illustrates how alehouse quarrels could escalate into civil disorder: "At Malpas in 1615 there suddenly erupted a great tumult in the house of an ale-seller which started as a brawl between two drinkers and ended with 'most of the town . . . disquieted'."[96]

All of this forms the wider background against which the performance of music in alehouses must be viewed. The alehouse licenses sought to control not only who could sell ale but when and to whom. The following is a fairly straightforward licence:

> And further that *ye* sayde margarett Stanne, nor any other of her family shall not sell anye Ale, beere, or any kinde of victuall vppon suche daye or dayes as heretofore haith bin vsed or keepte, for wake or wakedayes *wi*thin her sayde p*a*rishe or place where shee nowe dwelleth, nor *wi*thin the space of three dayes before, or Seaven dayes nexte after suche seue*ra*ll wakedayes, vnlesse hit be for necessarye victuallinge of souldiers, passengers, or travaylars, not beinge com*m*on sturdye beggers, mynstrelles, fencers, enterludeplayers, bearewardes, tu*m*blers, Iugglers, and suche lyke. . . .[97]

Other licences add the additional prohibitions that the alehousekeeper is not to permit any unlawful games or to "support any offendo*r* or offendo*rs* herein, knowinge of his or there offence in that behalf, w*i*th meate drinke or lodginge," or to receive stolen goods. He is likewise not to "suffer to be vsed any mysord*er* or like evill rule w*i*thin his said howse or backside" nor sell ale on a Sunday or holy day at service time.[98] To legislate for certain behavior was one thing; to enforce the laws was another. At times those who were responsible for enforcing the laws were also responsible for breaking them. At Harthill in 1617 the High Constable of Broxton Hundred found it necessary to present one of the lesser constables who was also an aleseller: "I Thomas Bressie one of the said high Constables doe present Richard Dod of Harthill Aleselle*r* for keepinge a piper in his house vppon the Saboth day at night being the time of their wakes as himselfe hath confessed being constable and acquinted w*i*th our Iudges Orders notw*i*thstanding."[99]

In reality, the requirements of the licenses were not always observed. The prohibition against selling ale at the time of wakes in particular was likely to be ignored. The wakes attracted crowds from neighboring areas, and the alehouses made a profit. Entertainment in the form of piping, fiddling, dancing, or bearbaiting provided an added attraction, and alehousekeepers both "harbored" wandering performers and also hired them to perform in their alehouses. To the authorities, the entertainers were potentially dangerous carriers of plague, sedition, and moral decay, ready to infect the crowds who gathered at the wakes. Their orders, such as the command given to the constables of Nether Peover in 1631, reflect these anxieties and also the view that the vagrant minstrel, at least, was willfully idle and morally suspect:

> fforasmuch as in theise times of apparent danger wherin the plague is soe much dispersed throughout many parts of this kingdome, and that all resort, and concourse of people in great multitudes may bee a meanes for the further dispersing of it: Theise are therfore to command, and charge you, that now at the accustomed time of your wackes, you doe not permitt nor suffer, any Beare-beatings to bee, nor any Musitians, Pipers, or others to come or to bee entertained within your Townshipp, which may bee occasion to draw a concourse of people togeather, by meanes wherof the infection may bee brought amongst you, by such idle, licentious, and dissolute persons, who take liberty to themselves to wander throughout all parts of the kingdome As alsoe that you see your watch and ward to bee performed with more then ordennary care at the said time And that you give notice to your Alehouses, and all others who are accustomed to lodge, and entertaine all that resort vnto them, that they lodge, and entertaine noe strangers, or persons vnknowne vnto them, for if heerin they offend, wee will suppresse them, and punish them further as wee see cause: ffaile not you heerin, in the execution of the duty of your place at your vttermost perill: Given vnder our hands August 6: .i63i.[100]

But as can be seen from the case of Richard Dod of Harthill, quoted above, the constables might themselves be involved in the very activities they were meant to suppress. An attempt was made in 1616 to make the constables and high constables financially liable for failing to "cause a strong watche to be made, on the saterday night next before every such wakes, and contynue the same both day and night during the same wakes," in order to apprehend "all such idle and disorderly persons, resorting thither." The watch was also required to visit the alehouses and "not suffer any of the said idle or disordered persons to come or resorte to any alehouse within the said Towne or parishe, where such wake shall be."[101] The penalty was £10 for high constables, £5 for petty constables, and any alehousekeeper caught harboring disorderly persons was to be automatically disabled from keeping an alehouse and bound over to appear at the next Great Sessions. There was certainly an increased interest in wakes in 1616. A list of objections to wakes drawn up in that year complained that "as theire is noe one reason to maintayne the vse, soe there is manye that it

sholde not be vsed."[102] Alehousekeepers are alleged to brew "a hundred
Winchester Measures"—an amount entirely consumed in the two days
of the wakes—"w*hi*ch causeth much drunkennesse, Quarrellinge and
much Manslaughter." In order to attract more people, the alehousekeepers hired bearwards, minstrels, and jugglers to provide entertainment. The influx of "Roagues and idle Wandringe beggers" was
not confined to the two days of the wakes but stretched out "a weeke
before and a weeke after." Part of the problem for the authorities was
that the target audience was young, usually financially dependent on
parents or master and liable to be drawn into crime:

> These delight*es* drawe a great recourse of people, especially of the
> yonger sorte, as mens sonnes, daughters and servant*es*, w*i*thout
> regarde of their Maisters occasions (although it be in Harvest tyme,
> as most vsually it is) and if this liberty be denyed them, eyther they
> will refuse their service, or doe it soe repyningly as wilbe noe good
> to the Maisters profitt: Many tymes it is knowne these people
> steale from their Parent*es* & Maisters to spend at this tyme./[103]

The document goes on to make definite suggestions as to how the
justices of the peace may "easily redresse" the abuses of the wakes.
First, the justices should insure that the alehousekeepers did not
provide extra food and ale for the wakes. Second, they should attend
at the wakes to make sure that their orders have been carried out "and
to banish the Berewardes and minstrell*es* from those places, that the
people may haue noe occasion to staye."[104] The justices only need a
little stirring up from the higher authorities to make them attentive to
a duty they have tended to neglect, according to the author of the list,
but the difficulties of enforcement were greater than he allows.
Nevertheless, there do seem to have been greater efforts to suppress
wakes and to search for itinerant entertainers after 1616. Often the
results were negative, showing that the search was undertaken in
response to instructions from above rather than to a local incident.
The following, from the constables of Rowton, is a typical example of
the "nothing happened here" report:

> ffrom the Constables of Rowtoun
> These are to let you vnderstand, that wee did search the 23 and 24
> dayes ^^of august^ at the Alehouses in the nighttyme and found
> not any strangers, likewise vpon the 23 day of the same Mooneth
> wee did Search all the Towne ouer and found not any vagranunt

person in the towne, <.>ee present Thomas ffisher for selling Ale vnbound, and also Iohn Boden for selling Ale vnbound, As for Wakes, piping, or Bearbeating on the Saboth day wee haue not any, and as for Maulters wee haue none in our Towne that buyeth Barley to sell it againe.[105]

Many of the presentments that were made came as responses to disorder rather than the preventative measures envisioned in the idea that the justices could "easily redress" the problems of illegal alehouses.

An illegal alehouse at which an incident occurred was more likely to attract official notice, as at Hatton in 1640 when an affray occurred at Thomas Renshaw's:

& the Constables of the within named Hatton coming to the said Thomas Renshaws house vppon sunday morning aforesaid to see the Kings Ma*jesties* peace kept, did there find fouer fidlers drinking, & some of the *par*ties that had bene in the ffray who were dangerously hurt wherevpon the said Renshawe with many oathes & reviling speeches threatened the said Constables, & in his fury cast a Tobacco pipe at Thom*as* Pickering one of *ye* said Constables.[106]

When the constables arrived the affray had evidently already taken place, and the drinking had been going on all the previous night and most of the day. Of course it is not impossible that they were merely making a routine check of alehouses, but much more likely they were responding to a report of fiddling, prolonged drinking, and an affray. Renshaw sold ale without license, but the presence of four fidlers would have been enough to lose him his license, if he had had one. The advantages of providing music to attract customers must have made it seem worth the risk, particularly to the keepers of illegal alehouses who had no licenses to lose. As well as attracting customers, the dancing which probably accompanied most alehouse music would have increased the customers' thirst.

As shown by the Hatton evidence, not only the day of the week but the time of the day was important in determining the degree of the fault. Many performers who were presented for piping on the sabbath excused themselves by claiming that they played only after evening service had ended. Conversely, constables were frequently presenting performers who played at night in alehouses, or alehousekeepers who offered entertainment at unlawful hours. In the case of Richard Platt of Tattenhall, his breaking of the sabbath in 1620 was also seen as an infringement of his license as a piper: "Richard Platt of Tatnall ./ [ffor] pip*er*, ffor abusing his libe*r*ty of piping by playinge & pipinge at vnlawfull tymes to the great p*r*ophanacion of the sabbath."[107]

This item supports the allegation made by William Hinde in his *Life of John Bruen* that Bruen's cousin, the heir of Dutton, was persuaded to include a prohibition against Sunday performances in the minstrels' licenses:

> *At the same time my cosen* Dutton, *being pressed and charged by some of great place to mainteine his Royalty of Minstrelsey for Piping and Daunsing on the Sabbath day, my Minister, my selfe, and my family were earnest against it, and prevailed so far with my cosen* Dutton, *that he promised that all Piping and Dauncing should cease on the Sabbath day, both forenoone and afternoon, and so his Licences were made, and do continue so untill this day. And so wee had great peace and comfort together; blessed be God.*[108]

This entry is undated but it must be from before 1614, when the last male Dutton heir died. It is indicative of the disputes which led to King James' issuing of the *Declaration for Sports* in 1617.[109]

The constables were occasionally unclear about what exactly was or was not permitted, and alehousekeepers took advantage of the ambiguity of the situation. In 1617, Richard Wilbraham wrote to Sir Thomas Chamberlain on behalf of a constable, James Smithe, who failed to arrest a piper who played on the sabbath. The company told Smithe that they had a "tolleracion from Mr Dutton of Hatton for the said pyper to playe." Wilbraham doubted that this was the case but indicated that credence was given to it by the constable, "beinge a verye silly and ignorant p*er*son, vnfitt to beare any such office w*h*ich makes me the rather to move yo*u*r favor towards*es* him, for otherwise I wolde not sue for any that sholde be vnderstanding and willinge offendors in that kynde."[110] Wilbraham asked that Smithe be spared the fine, or at least that it be deferred until the next Assizes, at which time Chamberlain can see Smithe and judge for himself his "insufficiency." Smithe was evidently a constable in the tradition of Dogberry and Elbow, and certainly many constables were insufficient to the task assigned them but not always because of their personal inadequacy. Even if their allegiance was not divided and their knowledge of the most recent laws and justices' orders sufficient, they were not always equipped to enforce the orders. Alehousekeepers might feel that they were entitled to offer entertainment and resented interference. At Frodsham in 1602 the bailiff presented that on Sunday, 16 July, Richard Williamson "had an Alefeast Pypinge, Bearebaytinge & horsbaytinge, & had companye in his house at 11 or 12 of the clock in the nighte, & said (to the baleff) he might take his advantage at that time, both day & night of seruant*es* & strangers men & women."[111] A list of ten people follows, including three women, one servant, and the bearward, who were found in the alehouse at night. Williamson is also accused of keeping unlawful gaming earlier in July and of playing cards "w*i*th one that sells aqua vite. & sett the said per*s*on in pds in Ale."[112]

Constables could also risk verbal and physical abuse when they attempted to carry out the justices' orders to search the alehouses. Thomas Astle, constable of Siddington, related how he attempted to search the alehouse of Richard Metier in Siddington on a Tuesday evening (11 May) shortly after sunset. Metier was also a piper and had been presented previously for keeping an illegal alehouse. Astle had been informed that there had been company in the house during the day. Metier challenged Astle's right to enter, first on legal grounds, and then defiantly, particularly when the constable was joined by John Fletcher, the minister, between whom and Metier there was a particular animosity:

> And saith that hee soe comminge the said Metyer vsed theise or such lyke speeches to him this Inform*er* before they p*ar*ted (vizt) Askinge this Informer by what warrant hee came to search his house; whervnto this Informer answered that hee thought his office gaue him sufficient warrant soe to doe, or to such effect: And therevppon saith that the said Metyer answered, w*i*thout warrant from a Iustice hee should not come theire; and soe warned him from com*m*inge anie more otherwise to his house, but as aforesaid: Affirminge further that hee had Ale in his house, and would brewe Ale to sell, in spyte of the teeth, of whomsoeuer sayd nay: And further informeth that at the same tyme Mr ffletcher the preacher comminge by him this Inform*er* w*i*th the rest; hee the said Metyer causlesly rayled on and to the *sa*id Mr ffletcher, and then called him, in most base and shamefull manner, a paultrey, beggerie lowsie preist of purpose (as this Informer thinketh) to haue pr*o*voked him, or some of the companie, either to haue quarrelled w*i*th him the said Metyer, or otherwaies to haue rayled and scouled w*i*th him, as hee did.[113]

There was sufficient legality in Metier's claim that the constable did not search the house that day, but returned about a fortnight later with his fellow-constable, Edward Plante, and a justice's warrant to search the house. Their aim was both to serve the warrant and to determine if Metier was brewing and selling ale. Astle's deposition affirms that Metier had been warned both by the constables and by the justices against selling ale. This time also they found access to the house difficult:

> And saith, That at theire said last goinge to the said Metyers house as aforesaid, they found the doore of the said house barred; or locked And soe fyndinge the same; called to knowe who was in the said house; whervppon the said Metyers wyfe came and opennend the said doore, and havinge a pitchforke in her hand therwith kept backe this Informer, and refused peaceably to suffer him to come into the said house; wherby hee was kept out: but saith, That shee was at last contented to suffer his fellow Constable to goe in, but still refused that this Informer, or that Thomas dayne whom the said Constables brought to assist them, should either of them come in to the said house.[114]

A petition from the minister states that Metier beat Thomas Astle (or Ascell) "traveling<.> vppon the highe waye being in the kinges service" and that he had "fearefully and dangerously offered at some tymes in his drunken rage to kill & murther his wief with a knife <...> very deaft & almost blind."[115] If Metier's wife was very deaf and almost blind, the pitchfork may be less a defiance of authority than a protection against an unknown foe. The fact that she eventually allowed one of the constables to enter would support this. Metier was nevertheless a disruptive force in the area and well known for violent behavior. His career will be discussed further in chapter II, part 2.

Not all nighttime musical activity was viewed in the same light. City waits were expected to perform in the city streets at stated times.[116] There seems also to be a difference between regular deliberate flouting of the licensing laws and spontaneous music, nor were the musicians always the ones about whom complaints were being made. Richard Preston of Warrington, musician, was examined in 1594 as to "what abuse was offred vnto him sins his repaire to that Citie." He explained that on the preceding Tuesday he and his company, possibly a group of visiting waits,

> were plaininge vpon there instrumentes vp [thestgate] St warburg lane out of the Eastgate street towardes their hoste foxall his howse

And saith in that Lane Mr Will*ia*m Hicock clerk ^^who came out
of John Stils Tavern^ over toke them and spake to this exa*minate*
and requested this exa*minate* to Lend him this exa*minates* Treble
violen to plaie vpon and this exa*minate* so did ^^whoe plaied very
excelent well theron^ and this exa*minate* did plaie to him vpon the
base vp that lane & vp the north gatestreet vntill they cam*e* very
nere the sad foxall*es* howse ^[^whoe plaied excelent well vpon that
instrument And^] wher the said Mr hicok redeliu*e*red to this this
exa*minate* the said violen w*hi*ch this exa*minate* gaue to his boy.[117]

Up to this point all was well. Mr. Hicock, possibly as a result of
his visit to John Stil's tavern, had amused himself by joining a group
of professional musicians and had impressed them with his skill.
However, when Preston "vpon curtesie" took Mr. Hicock by the cloak
and tried to persuade him to come for a drink in Foxall's house, he not
only refused but "strok vp the exa*minates* heeles with his foote
wherreby this exa*minate* fell and [w*i*th that f] w*i*th that fall this
exa*minates* sword was broken." Mr. Hicock then departed with
Preston's broken sword to his own house, followed by Preston who
was trying to get his sword back. Hicock's behavior at this point seems
odd:

Mr hicok went into his owne howse & caused a Candle to be
Lighted & lockt his owne dore & said Loe now none can make me
cookoulde & thervpon cam*e* forth to this exa*minate* againe & went
vp w*i*th him to the said foxal*es* howse wher this exa*minate* charged
him w*i*th the breking of his sword & Mr hic said that he this
exa*minate* did but iest ther was none suche matt*e*r & in ende Mr
hicok semed to offer violens to this exa*minate* but in ende dep*a*rted
And saith that as yet Mr hicok kepeth from this exa*minate* his
blade hilte & scabard.[118]

Sex, Drunkenness, and Piping

Although passed off as a jest, the incident between Hicock and
Preston shows some of the potential for disorder about which the
authorities were concerned. The concern was not with music in itself
but with music in inappropriate situations or at inappropriate times
such as in an unlicensed tavern in the middle of the night. There were
a number of things that the authorities feared. A list of reasons why
Richard Wright was considered unfit to keep a common inn by the

city of Chester in 1593 includes the fact that he was "A Carnall vicious man," that he had kept other men's servants in his house at night where they danced and feasted, and was a receiver of stolen goods "brought to his house by mens Apprentices & suffers the same to be ther laciviously spent and geven away." He was also accused of "lousgou*e*rment" and keeping "Bawdry" in his house at all hours and receiving all comers without taking responsibility for the government of his house.[119]

That these fears were to some extent justified is shown by the number of prosecutions for music that include other offences. While music and dancing, which are naturally associated, might be innocent in their own right and perfectly acceptable to the authorities in the context of a guild feast,[120] they were nevertheless viewed with suspicion as providing opportunities for sin. The puritans were opposed to mixed dancing on the grounds that it led to immoral behavior, and there is evidence that dancing in alehouses was sometimes linked with illicit sexual relations. A Consistory Court interrogatory in 1571 indicates how a dance might serve as a cover for a clandestine meeting: "Did not yo<.> one wrenburie wake day at night goe as a messenger sundrie tymes for Elizabeth Barker to come to Richard Due before she came, and because the house was full of youths w*h*ich were daunsinge, did not you cause her to goe out of the house one the backsyde, and to come in at a littell dore w*h*ich is made vppo*n* purpose for that baudy place where Due sate."[121] Although music is not specifically mentioned, it may be safely assumed that the dancing was accompanied by instrumental music. At Alvanley in 1638, an adulterous couple sent for a piper, who played at night in the alehouse where they were staying so that they could dance.[122] The case was only prosecuted because the woman, Alice Ash, had disappeared and there was a question of abduction and murder. The evidence of the servants at the alehouse suggested that she was with Thomas Penkett willingly, but exactly what happened is not clear. Keeping a bawdy house was a fairly frequent accusation against illicit alesellers, and small-scale prostitution was probably common.[123] A fondness for dancing could be evidence of a bad character, particularly in a woman. Jane Man, wife of William Man, Master of Arts, was considered in 1578 to have a bad reputation, "w*h*ich infamie she daily confirmeth as I credibly heare by drinkinge, diceing, dauncinge, swearinge and royotinge: so contagious & troublesome a neighbo*u*r that w*it*hin this twoe or three yeares some bloud hath bene shead for her and manslaughter like to have bene, and the quiet have hardly escaped."[124] Dancing was even more suspect in a member of the clergy, as in the case of the curate of Nether Peover who was presented in the same year at Archbishop Sandys's Visitation: "The Curate haunteth alehowses hunteth hawketh and now and then daunceth and plaieth vncomelie for his callinge he doth not instructe the yowth in the Catechisme nor readeth the homilies."[125]

As the preceding cases will have demonstrated, there was a wide variety of activity which the authorities sought to control, especially when practiced inappropriately. Hunting, hawking, and even gambling were acceptable activities for secular upper-class males, but not for lesser clergy or women or for the usual clientele of an alehouse. These of course are not, like dancing, naturally linked to musical entertainment, and only occasionally were connected with it. The number of incidents of violence in alehouses that coincide with the presence of musicians is only a small fraction of the total of disorderly alehouses. At Ince in 1616, Thomas Hale was bound to appear at the Assizes to "answere his beinge an Aleseller his enterteining of pypers and singgers dansinge and fightinge in his howse in the night tyme vppon the Saboth daye at a wake tyme."[126] The timing of this incident is important: at night, on the sabbath, and at the wake time, all times when the official eye was more likely to be turned towards the alehouse. For Thomas Hale, entertaining pipers and singers meant that he would attract more customers, who would buy more ale, particularly if they were dancing as well. That a fight broke out meant that he was more likely to attract official notice, but, as noted above, this must have been a calculated risk for most alesellers. Relatively few documents specifically mention fighting in connection with alehouse music, although there are mentions of "comitting disorder" (Darnhall, 1602), swaggering (Frodsham, 1609), and "revelling" (Tarporley, 1616).[127]

By and large music does not seem to have been associated with violence, although individual musicians might be. The role of the musician as lawbreaker is discussed in the next chapter. Dancing, lewdness, drinking, sabbath infringement, and even recusancy are far more likely to be associated with musical performance than fighting. Anne, the wife of Richard Hughes, was presented to the diocesan visitation in 1628 as "a seduceinge papist and for daunceinge vpon *ye* Saboth daie."[128] Musicians who performed for dances on the sabbath were of course similarly suspect, as were activities such as maygames and maypoles. The greater the numbers involved, the greater the concern of the magistrates. At Bunbury in 1620, there was a series of "disordered assemblies" that involved music and dancing, but the objections to these were also reinforced by linking them with other illicit activities.

> The first disordered Assembly was occasioned by Richard Cod-dingtoun who was putt in womans apparell on the Sabboth day in Iulie last, by Elizabeth Sym*m*e and oth*eres*, at her father*es* house (a disordered Alehouse) w*h*ich Elizabeth Sym*m*e together w*i*th David Wilkinson (two persouns notoriously suspected of Adulterie) were thought to be the cheefe Authors both of attyringe the foresayd Coddingtoun in womans apparell, and vsinge him as a messenger w*i*th a great trayne of rude people tumultuously gaddinge after him from thence to the Church hill to bringe a present of Cheryes to the sayd Elizabeth where shee sate as Ladye of the game readie to receive them.
> . . .
> The second tumultuous Assembly was Iulie 25, occasioned by Thomas Broocke & Thomas Manninge in womens apparell dans-ing like women after one Peacocke a fidler. And by William Arrowsmith and Richard Stubbs both of them in disguised apparell w*i*th naked sword*es* in theire hand*es* daunsing w*i*th those that were in womens apparell, a great multitude of disordered and rude people gadding a longe after them
> . . .
> The third disordered & riotous Assembly was August 5 Thomas Sym*m*e and Margaret Bettely theld*er* cheife Authors of the same gathering together a greater multitude, by carrying about a great & large garland [for th] decked w*i*th flours ribband*es* tinsell & scarfes for the making whereof money was gathered: & Richard Vernon a piper hired, & soe riotinge from on towneshipp to an other, men and women promiscuously & lasiviously daunsed about Thomas Sym*m*e (as about a maypole) bearinge vpp the garland.[129]

The wording of the document is interesting and indicates both the religious concerns of the writer and an attempt to link those concerns with activities that were unambiguously illegal. Bunbury was largely a recusant area but had a succession of puritan clergy, the result of the advowson being in the hands of the London Company of Haber-dashers. This gave the clergy at Bunbury virtual immunity from Church censure but also meant that clashes between the clergy and the parish were likely.[130] The presentation of the material concerning the "disorders" shows that the author was concerned about maygames, rushbearings, mixed dancing, and cross-dressing, but that he may have felt it necessary to emphasize the negative aspects by associating them with disordered alehouses, adultery, riot, promiscuity, and potential violence (the naked swords in the second incident, and the repeated emphasis on the number and disorderliness of the participants).

Performer and Audience

Many of the documents, such as the one relating to Bunbury quoted above, must be considered to be implicitly biased. They represent the official—but not necessarily the communal—view. It is necessary, as well as looking at the complaints made about the performances, to consider the audience or implied audience whose attitude towards the performer was likely to be more positive—or at least less hostile.

Minstrels, in common with other entertainers, occupied a paradoxical place in society. Socially, they were often marginalized.[131] Theologically, secular music was at best trivial and at worst damnable. Economically, only a few minstrels achieved any type of financial security, and even that was precarious, often dependent on the good will of a particular patron or corporation. Simultaneously, the minstrel was a welcome addition to feasts, ales, weddings, and wakes. He was an integral part of the society, yet remained somehow on the margins of it. The audience too was an integral part of the performance, whether it was viewed in a positive or a negative light.

As with all the material discussed in this study, the above statements are subject to fluctuation and variation over time and with regard to social class. The respectability of the performer could be less at issue than the respectability of the audience, although there is often a correlation between the two. If some minstrels were, as Rastall suggests and Whythorne asserts, the dregs of society, so sometimes were their audiences.[132] The official concern was more with the "rude people tumultuously gaddinge" than with the piper who provided the accompaniment to them. The alehousekeepers and villagers who hired pipers and fiddlers to play at the wakes or on the greens were probably on much the same social level as the musicians they hired.

II, PART 1
MUSIC IN THE CITY

By David Mills

When Henry VII granted the town of Chester palatinate status in 1506 in the so-called "Great Charter," he recognized administratively what had in social and political terms long been the case, that the town of Chester was a community separate and distinct from the county in which it was set.[1] It had been founded by the Romans in the first century A.D. on a sandstone ridge that dominated the lowest fording and bridging point of the River Dee but had suffered an extended period of decay after their departure. In the early tenth century, however, it had been substantially rebuilt and the fortress restored, and the Norman conquerors, recognizing its strategic military importance, had established an earldom there and built a castle at the southwest corner of the town. The castle was the administrative seat of the Earl of Chester, a title that from 1237 belonged to the eldest son of the monarch. Around it, within the medieval walls that protected it against invaders—most particularly, the Welsh—the town developed.

By the time of the Great Charter Chester was established in many distinct roles. From Roman times its location had made it the center for the north-south routes from Whitchurch to Lancaster, with roads leading also to Warrington and Manchester. The Dee was navigable to Chester, and the town was the major port of the northwest coast, the embarkation point for Ireland, with trading links across the Irish Sea and into France and Spain. It had always been a garrison town with a transient population of soldiers and their supporting trades *en route* to wars in Wales, Ireland, or Scotland. Around the castle lived the Earl's representatives, his administrative staff, and their families who ran the administration of the area. Chester was a natural trading center through which passed the goods brought through the port and from the surrounding countryside to be sold at the town's markets and fairs. With its own population and that of the county to serve, Chester developed as a manufacturing center. The workmen who maintained the army and repaired the castles of Wales also built the houses of the wealthy.

And Chester was a religious center. Just outside the walls to the southeast the great collegiate church of St. John dominated the riverside. It housed a relic of the true Cross. Briefly it had been the seat of the Bishop of Lichfield (1073–95), and the bishop, a major landowner in the town and county, stayed in its precinct on visits. In 1093, the second Earl, Hugh Lupus, founded a Benedictine Abbey dedicated to St. Werburgh, whose relics it housed, in the northeast corner of the walls and granted the abbot considerable trading rights in the town. The Abbey was evidently conceived as a statement of the Earl's power in opposition to that of the Bishop. Gradually it grew until by the time of the Great Charter it was an impressive building. After its dissolution in 1540, the Abbey church was established as the cathedral of the new diocese of Chester that was created the following year.[2]

The town had a Gild Merchant by c.1200–02 at the latest, and individual companies—craft- or trading-gilds—developed progressively thereafter, each gaining civic or royal charter to confirm its monopolistic privileges and rights. The Great Charter confirmed the status of the mayor, the governing body or Assembly, and the autonomy of the city's courts. The center of civic government was an annex to St. Peter's Church at the head of Bridge Street known as The Pentice, which dominated the road from the south across the Dee Bridge. That road was effectively Chester's ceremonial way, leading to its civic center from whose windows the mayor could look into any of the four Roman streets of the town.[3]

Enclosed by its walls, with its various and conflicting centers of power emblematized in the great buildings among which its citizens moved—castle, church, Abbey, Pentice—the town was perceived as a self-contained community. Only if you were a freeman and a member of a company could you work and trade freely within it. Its government was dominated by a few local families, and offices in its government became almost hereditary. Local gentry families, such as the Savages and the Duttons, had their town-houses there and played leading roles in the political and ceremonial life of the town. As the threat of Welsh attack receded in the sixteenth century, the social and communal life of Chester developed.

This context provided ample opportunities for music-making of all kinds. Though the Latin liturgy of the Catholic Church was, in uneven stages, replaced by the new English forms of worship, the traditions of liturgical music continued from Abbey to Cathedral. The town's servants in their livery, including the town waits, represented the mayor's authority in the town's streets almost daily. The Duttons, who had the privilege of licensing minstrels, used the annual minstrel court as a mark of their family status. Companies, gentry, innkeepers, and others required music for their dinners, dances, and customers. Chester became a meeting point for musicians from a range of different backgrounds and traditions, working together or competing, sometimes physically, for patronage. And the public catalysts for this mixture were the great civic occasions of the Shrovetide Ceremonies, the Whitsun Plays, the Midsummer Show, the Christmas Watch, and, from 1610, the St. George's Day horse-race, all of which only a threat of plague could prevent. Music has to be seen as a component of the wider social, ceremonial, and commercial life of the town. And as a magnet for musicians of all kinds, the town enhanced the musical life of the surrounding area also.

The Music of the Church

When the commissioners of the Crown carried out their inventories of the goods of Chester's churches on 28 May 1553, they listed a pair of organs in each of the major city churches—the Cathedral, St. John's, St. Mary's, and St. Peter's.[4] We know little of the musical life within those churches except for the Cathedral, formerly the abbey church. Even there, specific information begins only with the creation of the Cathedral since most of the early records have been lost, although it may safely be assumed that the usual Benedictine service pattern with its rich musical tradition was maintained. A glimpse of that tradition is provided in the references to the Palm Sunday celebrations in the cathedral accounts for 1544–45, 1555–56, and 1558–59, where gloves and, in 1544–45, a breakfast were provided for "the prophet Apon palme Sunday."[5] The role was taken in 1555–56 by Thomas Barnes, who was master of the choristers—an indication of a soloist singing the traditional music following the first Gospel during the Palm Sunday procession.

An agreement of 22 June 1518 between Abbot John Birchenshaw and a London clerk called John Bircheley sheds more light on the Abbey's music.[6] For an annual sum of £6, all meals, a house free of rent, and other perquisites, John is required:

> to teche all suche bredren of the place as be or shalbe willyng
> heraftre to Lerne to synge thaire playnsonge fafunden prykksong

descant to play on the Organs And to sett songes yf thay be
dysposed to gif theymsellffe therunto And aftre lyke man*ner* to
Instructe six Children for the Chapell and as many other scolars of
the place that haue or shall haue thaire fyndyng within the
monastery aforsaid as the said*es* Abbot and Co*n*uent and theire
Success*ores* for the tyme beyng shall thynke necessarye for mayn-
ten*a*nce of diuine se*r*uyce within the said monastrye / It*e*m to kepe
a ladye masse dayly withe pryksong and organs and an Antemp of
pr*i*ksong foloyng the same It*e*m eu*er*y fryday Iesus masse w*ith*
priksong and thorgans at vj of the Clok in the morowe / And an
Antemp of I*o*hn and of o*ur* Lady withe the pees at aftre Euynsong
as hathe be vsed withe all other masses matyns and Antymps
whiche hathe bene accustomed to be kepte withe pricksonge and
Organs on festyvall dayes at any tyme hertofore or that shalbe
thoght reasonable by the sayd Abbot and Co*n*uent and their
success*ores* at any tyme heraftre.[7]

Pricksong is music in mensural notation, as opposed to the umeasured
notation of plainsong, while descant is defined by the *Oxford English
Dictionary* as "a melodious accompaniment to a simple musical theme
(the plainsong) sung or played and often merely extemporized above
it, and thus forming an alto to its bass."[8] Clearly John's is a standard
contract. It indicates the demanding nature of a post that combines the
roles of organist, choirmaster, and teacher. The final injunction in the
agreement is that John is not to leave without permission, which suggests that such organist/choirmasters could find ready employment
elsewhere.

John Bircheley is the first holder of this post whose name we
know, and he continues to hold it when the Abbey becomes the
Cathedral—a reflection of the continuity of musical tradition. Possibly
the William Pryke "organplayer" who appears in a court case in 1504
was one of his predecessors.[9] As early as 1488 a Richard Paynter
appears in another court case described as "Organmaker"; in 1534–35
Thomas Smyth and in 1536 Thomas Peycock are similarly described,[10]
but we do not know anything specifically about the instruments that
they built.[11]

The musical influence of the Abbey extended beyond the boundaries of the city and county. For example, the abbot of Rushen Abbey
in the Isle of Man, in an indenture of 1504, sent John Dorse to St.
Werburgh's Abbey to study with William Perk—who might be the
William Pryke above—to serve him and "kep his scole" when William
was away.[12] William's duties are set forth:

[He] schal fyrste informe hym of his dayly service anenst God also
to instructe hym in dyscyplyne of good manners & also to tech
hym to synge prykkytsong, Discant of all manner mesurs & to syng
upon a pryksonge fawburdon to cownter of every mesur, & to set
a songe of thre parts iiij or v substancyally, and also to play upon
the organs any manner playsong or prykkytsonge two parts or thre,
and to mak playne & schew hym the secretts & speed of techynge
& instruccyoun of every of the premisses in the best manner &
most speedfull he can.[13]

Evidently John already held a post at Rushen Abbey, possibly as choirmaster, and the abbot's purpose in this case was to have him serve as
an intern who might return and be able to raise the quality of music in
the liturgy of his own abbey.

John Bircheley was not responsible under the Cathedral's
constitution for teaching music to the eight boy choristers, though he
continued as schoolmaster; that duty fell to one of the petty canons.
The statutes of the Cathedral require the appointment of one skilled
in singing and playing the organ who would apply himself diligently
to teaching the boys, playing the organ at such time as he chooses, and
singing the divine office—indicating the amalgamation of the offices
of organist and choirmaster.[14] A succession of organists held the post
during our period, some of national significance such as Robert White,
who came from Ely to Chester in 1567 and held the post until 1570
when he moved to Westminster Abbey; others made their reputation
at Chester—for example, Thomas Bateson (1604–08), who published
his first book of madrigals while at Chester, and Robert Stevenson
(1570–99). And occasionally one such as Robert Jewett (1643–46)
came, having already made a name for himself, in Jewett's case from
Dublin.[15] Francis Pilkington, Bateson's contemporary at Chester, was
also a well known composer of madrigals (see chapter III). In discuss-
ing the tenure of John Allen (1609–13), Shaw comments that "Chester
Cathedral had a good share of musicians who sought the vague status
at this early date of a graduate in music," which surely reflects a policy
of appointment.[16]

The first station of the Whitsun Plays was the Abbey gate, where,
as the antiquarian David Rogers reported, "the monks and Churche
might have the first sight."[17] The playtext survives in eight manuscripts, five containing the full cycle. These cycle manuscripts, dating
from 1591–1607, are all copies made by antiquarians from a lost
original, long after the last performance in 1575.[18] The latest manu-

script (British Library MS. Harley 2124) was the work of James Miller, vicar of St. Michael's Church in Chester and precentor at the Cathedral. Miller's will, which was proven on 28 July 1618, sheds some light on the library of such a man. He had a collection of Latin books, including song books in Latin, and also other music books ("Balladers . . . the sett of ffrench Songes in a Case") as well as books in English ("Historyes, Chronicles and Diuinity," and "Schoole bookes") (see also chapter III).[19]

Miller's manuscript, perhaps significantly given his role as precentor, is the only one to contain a line of music, setting the angel's *Gloria* for the Painters' play of *The Shepherds* (Play 7).[20] Richard Rastall has suggested that the music is a line "from a pre-existent polyphonic piece,"[21] but it may well have been James's own adaptation of a liturgical piece that was of considerable importance to the play.

The Post-Reformation Banns for the cycle command the company to "see that 'Gloria in Excelsis' be songe merelye" (93),[22] and the shepherds respond with admiration and a comically inadequate attempt to piece together the separated syllables of the words. This "church voice" is finally complemented by a popular song (see below).

Interestingly Miller's manuscript contains another musical variant which differs from the other copies. During the Waterleaders' play of *The Flood* (play 3), there is a necessary hiatus in the action when Noah and his family withdraw into the Ark while the Flood rises. The other manuscripts have the direction that Noah and his family go inside the Ark "and for a little space within the bordes hee shalbe scylent" (3.260 s.d.).[23] Miller's manuscript reads: "Tunc Noe claudet fenestram archae et per modicum spatium infra tectum cantent psalmum 'Save mee, O God'" (3.260 s.d.) ("Then shall Noah shut the window of the ark and for a little space within the boards they shall sing the psalm 'Save me O God'").[24] "Save me, O God" is a verse of Psalm 69, unusually in the vernacular, perhaps because the actors were not versed in Latin, which also suggests that they were not chorally trained. Rastall has pointed out that this must be the metrical rendering of the psalm by John Hopkins in 1561 which was "ubiquitous in the second half of the sixteenth century."[25]

The cycle as a whole contains nineteen liturgical pieces in Latin which carry a "church-voice" through the cycle. Most can be traced to standard liturgical texts and seem to require trained singers. But there are exceptions. In the Wrights' play of *The Nativity* (play 6) following line 666, as the Emperor Octavian burns incense before an image of the Virgin and Child in a star, the angel carrying the star sings *Haec est ara Dei caeli*, and the accompanying stage-direction reads: "Let the setting be according to the judgement of the performer" ("fiat notam secundum arbitrium agentis, etc."). The source of the text has not been found, and the freedom given to the performer suggests that there was no fixed setting. The quality of the performance is indicated by the Emperor's response:

> A, Sybbell, heres not thow this songe?
> My members all yt goeth amonge.
> Joy and blys makes my harte stronge
> to heare this melody.
>   (6.667–70)

Company accounts constitute an important form of evidence for cycle plays, although they merely list items of expenditure in a particular year and therefore leave much scope for speculation. There is no reason to believe that the production took the same form at each performance. In Chester, unfortunately, company accounts are late and only a few relate to the period of the plays, all in the later sixteenth century. They include the accounts for the Smiths, who produced the play of *The Purification: Christ Before the Doctors* (play 11) for the years 1554, 1561, 1567, 1568, and 1572. These show that the company turned in those years to the Cathedral for help with the music for their production:

> 1554
> we gaue to barnes & the syngers iijs 4d
> 1561
> Spent in Sr Rand barnes chamber to gett singers iijd
>   . . .
> payd to S*ir* Io Genson for songes xijd. to the 5 boyes for singing ijs vjd
>   . . .
> to Tho ellam xijd
> 1567
> spent on mr chanter in mr pooles Tauerne iijd
>   . . .
> to mr white 4s to mr chanter xijd
>   . . .
> 1568
> to mr Rond barnes 3s 4d to mr wyte for singing 4s[26]

Randle Barnes was a minor canon of the Cathedral who first appeared in the Cathedral accounts in 1551; here it seems he was in charge of the choristers. John Genson, who provided songs, was the Cathedral precentor and is probably the "mr chanter" of the later reference. Mr White was Robert White, the cathedral organist who Rastall postulates may have taken the role of Simeon in 1567 and 1568.[27] The only solo piece, the *Nunc Dimittis*, is sung by Simeon and, as a central liturgical piece, required a good performance.

The Smiths' 1567 accounts also include the item "payd one for Carringe of the Regalls ijd."[28] The regals, a keyboard instrument with reed pipes (see chapter 4), would have been built by an organ-maker. The fact that there is no other similar payment may mean that the regals would have been used on only this occasion, or that someone carried it on other occasions without payment. Possibly it was used to accompany the singing, but the playtext gives no indication of its use.

The Painters, whose play contains the *Gloria*, also sought help from the Cathedral in 1568, 1572, and 1575, the years of their extant accounts:

> 1568
> Item spentt at Thomas Ionsons to speke with mr Chaunter for shepertes boyes ijd
> 1572
> Item spende on the iiij syngarse at rondyll ynces ijd
> 1575
> Item for pouder for the sengers vjd[29]

The three shepherds in the play have a boy called Trowle, and, in an extended version, each of the four has a boy, presumably the "iiij syngarse" here. The reference to "mr. Chanter," probably once again John Genson, indicates that the singers were the boys from the Cathedral choir. The play-text itself makes no provision for a choral piece.

The use of liturgical music and the resources of the Cathedral must have bonded the plays more closely to the Church. At the same time, there were other musical "voices" to be heard in the plays which had very different associations.

Music for the City

The city employed a number of officials who were entitled to wear the city's livery. Among them were the city swordbearer and macebearer. There was also the bellman, whom we might call the town crier, whose bell-ringing was intended to draw attention to his announcements. None of these can be said to be musicians. But there were others, termed "heraldic minstrels," whose role has been described by Suzanne Westfall as "to make loud impressive sound, designed to command quiet and to accentuate the arrival of an influential personage or the presentation of a significant event, analogous to the entering player's cry of 'room' in the interludes."[30] This group would include the city's drummer. His role was certainly one of signaling and summoning, setting the beat for the processions and the step for military drill. So on St. George's Day, "the Warninge by the drum*er* and Cryer shalbe upon Saterday or the day next before St George day not beinge y*e* Saboath."[31] The drum was maintained by the city, as in 1613–14:

> Item paid vnto Peter Ince for two drum head*es* and for dressing it vs vjd
>
>   . . .
>
> Item paid to Gest for mendinge the Corde of the drom vd[32]

The drummer was not infrequently accompanied by a trumpeter. Both accompanied the herald when he read the play-banns on St. George's Day,[33] and a trumpeter accompanied the Dutton's herald to summon to the Minstrels' Court (see below). Companies hired trumpeters on occasion too, as with the Painters who paid 3*s* 4*d* for their trumpeter in 1638.[34] The trumpet was, like the drum, a ceremonial object in itself and could carry the arms of the person or organization heralded. So in 1627 the Painters paid "for taffity Sarcenet & Ruben for ^^it^ to make a trumpet baner iiijs vjd."[35] They also bought new silk for the banner in 1632 at a cost of five shillings[36] and in 1639 paid for "new workinge the Trompett baner."[37] Trumpets were used in the great show of 1610 which inaugurated the St. George's Day race; "a noyse of trumpett*es*" accompanied the shows that bore the King's arms and the Prince's arms.[38] And, of course the trumpets were needed to awaken the dead in the Walkers' play of *The Judgement* (play 24); the angels cry "Take wee our beames and fast blowe" (24.33), and this is confirmed by the stage direction "angeli tubas accipient et flabunt" (24.33 *s.d.*) ("The angels shall take their trumpets and shall blow"). Rastall points out that this is the "the ceremonial buisine, the long straight trumpet that is shown in medieval depictions of the Last Judgment."[39]

The city waits constituted a distinct group within the liveried representatives of the mayor. While from one standpoint they belong to the general pool of city musicians, to which they returned when off official duty, they were, like the other employees of the city, emblems of civic control, carrying the mayor's authority through the streets. They had been in existence for some time before we first encounter them in the second mayoralty of Henry Gee in 1539–40. Gee was a reforming mayor who brought system to the city's legislation and record-keeping. His attention turned to the waits because their duties had not been formally set down, and their observances had become idiosyncratic: "bycause that no certen of ordre Owres nor tymes hath heretofore beyn especially lemytted vnto theym."[40] The order states that the waits had been established "for the worship and pleasure of the Citie" and that they should henceforth observe "suche circuite placys and Owres as hath beyn accustomed in tymes past," though the circuit and places are nowhere stipulated. The order requires them to play "eu*er*y sonday, monday tuysday thursday and saturday" in the evening, and "eu*er*y monday thursday & saturday in the mornyng," weather and sickness permitting. No instructions are given about what they are to play.

The livery of the waits is stipulated in a number of places in the Treasurer's Account Rolls for the city, as in 1588–89: "It*em* to mr. ffletcher drap*er* the xjth of december for xviij yeard*es* of sadd nerve Collored broade Cloth att vij*s* iiij*d* the yeard Viz for three of the eldest waytte men x yeard*es* for iij gownes iij yerd*es* for towe Coate Clothes for towe of the Yonger Wayttmen. . . ."[41] ('Sadd' indicates a dark color; 'nerve' is "striped or banded.") The account demonstrates that the waits had their apprentices, and an account of 1591–92 refers to "the weatement & their Boyes,"[42] while another of 1616–17 budgets £1 16*s* for fourteen and a half yards of cloth "to make the waytemen gownes and the boyes Cloakes."[43] A dispute of 1591 makes it clear that the boys were apprenticed to their fathers in many cases, insuring a family tradition of public office. Reference is made to the sons of the waits who will inherit the instruments "when they shall have served out their yeres as Apprentices to the said exercise."[44] But this was not always the case: in 1625–26 gowns were provided only for the four waitmen, with no reference to boys.[45] In the adverse economic situation of the city after the Civil Wars Chester became lax in its treatment of its waits, who petitioned the Assembly on two occasions for wages and livery.[46]

The dispute of 1591 provides information about the instruments used by the waits—"the how boies the Recorders the Cornet*es* and violens" (see also chapter IV).[47] These had been claimed in part as the property of one of the waits, Thomas Williams, by his widow Alice, but the city took the view that "the said instrum*entes* shall from hensfurth forever remayne Continue and bee the owne proper good*es* of the said Waitesmen and of the s*ur*vivour of them." In a crisis in 1613 when the waits abandoned their duty and apparently took their instruments with them, the relics of the stock passed over to their successors: "one double Curtayle wantinge a staple of brasse for a reede, and one tenor Cornett beinge the Citties instrum*entes*."[48]

In 1604 we have the inventory of William Maddock, one of the waits, which shows that he owned a sackbut valued at 13*s* 4*d*, a double curtal valued at ten shillings, two cornetts valued at ten shillings, and a tenor viol valued at 6*s* 8*d* (see Appendix I).[49] In general, one assumes that the waits would have played wind instruments in their "heraldic" functions in order to make a sufficiently large sound, but they might have also used stringed instruments in their private engagements.

In 1592, we have, apparently for the first time, someone in Chester describing himself as an instrument maker. Thomas Beedle described himself as "A verey poore man brought vp in the occupacyon of a Bowier and in the trade of makinge of Instrument*es* of Musick and Longe staves, for her Ma*ie*stes seruice, w*h*ich said trade he is moste desyerus to set vp, vse and occupie w*i*thin the said Citie."[50] Unlike the organmakers, Thomas does not identify himself solely by his manufacture of instruments, which seems to have been merely one component of a wider range of skills, but also by making bows and "longe staves" or ceremonial wands of a type carried by dignitaries such as aldermen. Nevertheless, he seems to have seen his skill at making instruments as a particular commendation to the Assembly, who granted his request for admission to the city's freedom. Not impossibly musicians in Chester had previously had to look outside the city to purchase their instruments.

The exodus of the waits from the city in 1613 produced a crisis. Waits had official duties in addition to their daily perambulations of the city. They were paid for occasions such as the Shrovetide celebrations ("It*em* geven the weattemen the same day iiijd"[51]), the Midsummer Show, where they were hired by the sheriffs to be part of the procession ("citty wayts xijd"[52]), and the St. George's Day race ("It*em* P*ai*d to the waytmen playinge vpon Sct Georges day

00–01–00"[53]). They were also hired for special occasions, as when in 1632 the Lord Deputy made a ceremonial entry to Chester and was entertained at a banquet: "payd to the wayetmen by mr maiors appoyntment for playeing when the lord deputy Came in and the day after at the bankett ij s vj d."[54]

They also played for company occasions; typical is the Shoemakers' account for their election day in 1581: "Item giuen to the waitmen vpon Martins evine xvjd."[55] Similarly, they might be hired for the dinner which was given on the admission of a new member to the company, as in the Smiths' accounts for 1577: "to the wayte men on the election day xijd to them when Tho Kemp made his dimer xijd."[56]

Payment varies, perhaps indicating the number of times they played or the number of waits involved; in 1582 the waits received twenty pence. On these occasions they were competing for bookings with other musicians in the city and seem to have operated in a semiofficial capacity. In the Smiths' accounts of 1577, we find the waits hired with other musicians: "for pott sack & pott clar at Tho locker dinner xxd to weytes xijd to other minstrells 4d."[57] Further, the waits could take bookings from private individuals. In 1620, John Blymson heard music in the late afternoon and went down the street, evidently Bridge Street, with the waits following him. He knew some of the waits, so he met with them at the bridge, and since their civic duty was over, they went for a drink together in Northgate Street. When the bell at St. Peter's church rang to prayer, the waits left "to plaie att a gentlemans chamber."[58] Their civic duty done, the waits moved on to private business. Doubtless their official position helped them to gain bookings and allowed them to supplement their civic income.

Occasionally, even in the present state of researches into records, we find Chester's waits acknowledged in other Records of Early English Drama volumes in places outside the county, for example when "the waytes of Chester" received five shillings from the city of Coventry in 1584.[59] It is almost certainly the city waits who are described as "the maier of Chesters Mynstrelles" and paid eight pence at Ludlow in 1544–45.[60] Perhaps they are "the musisioners of Chester" who were given twelve pence for playing by Sir Richard Shuttleworth in Lancashire in his accounts for 5 January 1595–96.[61] Presumably they had not made these journeys from their Chester base merely for the small rewards in the accounts.

The value of the office is perhaps indicated by the plight of the former wait Christopher Burton who was, for some unspecified "abuses" self-confessed, removed from his office of wait. He claimed that he had "by the want of the said office fallen into great want & pou*er*tie as also into debt" since he knew no other trade.[62] Christopher's demotion did not prevent his son from being apprenticed as a wait, since the following year, after the death of his wife and continuing problems of penury, Christopher asked the mayor to insure that the money paid to the boy, who was using it recklessly, would be employed for the benefit of the son and the whole Burton family (see also chapter II, part 2).[63]

Sometimes tensions arose between the waits and their employer, the mayor. The departure of the waits in 1613 perhaps reflects such discontent. A case in point is Thomas Williams in 1609, who had been a wait but suddenly after the Shrovetide event refused to continue and was jailed for breaking his contract. He then left jail, went to Brettar in Flint, and played at a nearby town, where he earned five shillings. On returning to Chester, he promised to continue as a wait and was released by the mayor, but then again refused to play a further week with his fellow waits in the streets; he said he would burn his gown—an insult to the city—and uttered words of disrespect about the mayor, William Gamul.[64] Thomas had a supporter in George Cally, who was no less rude: "Mr Gamull had putt him in a paier of boults for Thomas Williams his sake but he shall neuer putt me in boults againe for he hath but a weeke and a twilt to be, and y*a*t he would so end his bloodd with the said williams, and in a scoffinge sorte did putt of his hat and said he would doe him noe more when he should be out of his office."[65] This statement seems to suggest that George too had spent time in the city's Northgate jail.

Williams, unlike Burton, does not seem to have suffered from his disgrace. We find the Coopers in 1618 paying "Thomas williams and his companye for Musicke" 2*s* 6*d*[66] and again hiring him in 1624. Possibly Williams was the son of Alice, widow of the late Thomas, who had unsuccessfully claimed a share of the city's instruments in 1591. At least one of the sons of Thomas Jr. did not follow his father's profession; John Williams became an apprentice tallowchandler in 1624.[67] George Cally or Kelly and the rest of that family of musicians warrant a section to themselves.

The Cally/Kelly Family

George Cally, or Kelly, was one of a family of musicians who were prominent in Chester's music scene from the late sixteenth century and whose names appear regularly in company accounts as well as court records. The first Cally we have found is Peter, up for breach of the peace in 1568. Edmund Cally follows him into court in 1572; he is described as "musici*oner* servant" to John Dutton in 1574.[68] John, Peter's son, was summoned in 1588–89 for "le whistelinge."[69] George Cally enters in 1591 in a breach of peace case with Christopher Burton, the wait who was later dismissed (see above),[70] and John appears at the same hearing on the same charge. And they are followed into court by yet another musician, William Madock. In September of the same year another Chester musician, Thomas Hough, complained against John Cally,[71] and in 1598 the same Thomas Hough was complaining against George Cally,[72] with a counter-claim from George. Robert Cally joined the procession to court in 1599 with a complaint against Christopher Burton.[73]

These "non-musical" sightings of the Callys and other musicians attest both the number of musicians within the city and also the intensity of feeling that could arise. But brothers could also quarrel. On 31 October 1609 George was brought to court, as we have seen, for insulting Mayor Gamul. But the trial illustrates another aspect of the music within the city—patronage and hierarchy.[74] Alice Leevesley deposed that "the said George Cally then said [the] that his brother Rob*er*te Croutched to gett *Sir* John Savage patches which he would neuer doe, and said y*at* he was [the] Lord of darbys man," and Ann Hough deposed that "the said Cally rayled [upon] towardes his brother, and said he would neuer incrouch to s*ir* John Sauage for four patches as his brother did / and then clapped his hands on his owne Colysence and said that S*ir* John Sauages Colycence was not to be Comparde to the Lord of Darbyes." From this we gather that the two brothers were musicians in different households. Robert served Sir John Savage, a member of the local gentry, who lived in a relatively new mansion at Rock Savage, between Chester and Runcorn. George served the Earl of Derby, the Chamberlain of Chester and prominent national figure, whose principal residence was Lathom Hall in Lancashire. George seems to have felt that Robert debased himself in order to gain entry to Sir John's service, and, drawing attention to his livery, he insisted on the superiority of his patron and his own standing. There is probably also a hint that George saw this as confirming his superior professional status.

This fraternal rivalry seems to have led to repeated public disorder, for in 1599 a formal agreement had been drawn up between Robert and George:

> The said parties doe agree and doe promyse either to other. to Contynue be and remayne of one Consorte. and to play vpon their instrum*entes* together still in one Company and be lovinge and frendlie thone to thother ^^& to^ thend of their naturall lyves w*i*thout sep*a*ration or dep*a*rture one from another.[75]

But this does not seem to have been effective, for subsequent payments in company accounts show the two performing separately, as in the Beerbrewers' accounts for 25 November 1610:

> p*ai*d for musicke to George Callie   iijs iiij d
> p*ai*d to Robert Callie   ijs vjd
> p*ai*d to the Waites   xviijd[76]

The two Cally payments are for a consort in each case, not the individual. Similarly, the same year the Shoemakers paid 2*s* 6*d* "to Roberte kelly and his Companye for musicke at the same dynner."[77]

The Callys were therefore musicians resident in Chester with their own consorts taking private engagements, but were also formally the servants of local families whose liveries they wore. The disputes with waits like William Maddock and Christopher Burton may reflect professional rivalry as they competed for private bookings. We see the two brawling Callys when they appeared together at a civic function in 1609:

> in the assize weike last this ex*amina*te and the said George Kelly were in the Sheriffe of the shires Court w*i*th there Instruments with intent to haue plaied there att w*hi*ch tyme the said George kelly gaue vnto one Edward Pemberton (being then in Company with the said Kelly) a boxe vpon the eare and vttred these words in great violence to this / ex*amina*te, sayinge that hee would stabb him the said ex*amina*te and Called him Roague villaine and ^^gaue [e]^ other indecent speeches as Bastard and such like and furth*er* [saith] said that the maior ^^of^ the said Citty of Chester did giue but a meany of raggs and that S*i*r John Savage gaue a meany patches.[78]

Pemberton is probably "pemburton þe waiteman" who played at the Shoemakers' election dinner in 1607 alongside "George kellye and his companye."[79] It seems that both George and the waits were employed by the city to provide music at the entry of the Sheriffs' procession to the Pentice where the court was held. The dispute was again one of status, comparing private patronage to civic patronage as signaled by the livery worn.

Given George's attitude, it may seem surprising that he should have any ambition to become a wait. But in 1613, following that sudden departure of the city waits with most of the instruments, George stepped in: "George Callie Musitian exhibiteth his Peticon Deseringe that he and his felowe Musitians may be admitted waytes of this Cittie in steede of the Waytes now absent fyndinge Instrum*entes* of his owne Charg to p*er*forme the service w*hi*ch is deferred to be graunted vntill it may be vnderstoode what are become of the ould waytes."[80] Despite their cautious approach, the city had little option but to accept George's offer, as they did on 13 May 1613. There is no information on record about the missing waits. Presumably George wished to obtain a monopoly of sorts over the music in Chester and saw this as an opportunity both to regularize his income as well as to keep competitors at bay.

George's ambition and his concern with status manifested themselves in another way. In 1608 he successfully petitioned the Assembly for admission to the freedom of the city. Admitted without fee, he became the first known recorded freeman musician of Chester. In the previous year Thomas Fisher had also petitioned for the freedom since, he claimed, he had been born in Chester and his grandfather "and all his Auncestor<.> before him" had been freemen. He stated that his sole skill lay in music. His petition was turned down by the Assembly.[81] Fisher's claims of his ancestry might, however, indicate that a Fisher-musician could have acquired the freedom previously.

But George still faced competition, which led him to petition the Assembly again in 1615.[82] He says that he is married with ten children and is responsible for the company of five waits; and he "professed musicke and the arte and facultie of teachinge to daunce." His concern with status again breaks through as he claims to be esteemed by "men of the best sort & gen*er*all fashion truelie sensible and respectiue of the like faculties." But he complains of "meere strangers" who have set up in the city to teach and practice dance and music and are winning patronage from certain companies and individuals. George wants the

Assembly to suppress this unworthy competition.

Musicians like the Callys not only performed but also instructed. George took an apprentice called John Bradley from Lancashire whose father had died.[83] Instruction in dance was a necessary adjunct and suggests the demand for instruction in the formal dances which the musicians might play for in the houses of the gentry. In 1613 a truant apprentice absconded from his master's house in Chester to go to a party on the Wirral, and on the way back called on Robert Cally "about 4 of the Clock in the morning and desyred him to teache him daunce & stayed dancing one hower."[84] Presumably the apprentice had encountered a new dance at the party which he wished to learn.

The Chester Minstrels

The waits and "fellow musicioners," normally resident within the city, were the "educated" end of the secular musical spectrum. Beyond them were the "itinerant minstrels" who moved from town to town and played for hire. These minstrels seem to have been largely without formal training and played by ear, usually from memory. The Statute of Vagabonds, passed in 1572, had major implications for all traveling groups of performers—bearwards, actors, musicians, or other entertainers. Its aim was to regulate the growing numbers of vagabonds or idle laborers wandering the country who were proving a potential threat to public order. Henceforth only those in the service and wearing the livery of a nobleman were allowed to travel to perform. One of the first to fall foul of the Act in the city was Edward Jonson, described as "Musicioner," from the Chester suburb of Handbridge south of the river. Jonson came before the court in Chester in 1572 because he had "presumed to play vpon his Instrument of musick within the liberties of the Citie of Chester sithens the said ffeast of St Bartholomew thappostell last past and gone abrode vsing the same contrary to the tenor of An Acte of parlyament against such vagarant and idell persons this present yere made and provided."[85] Jonson was evidently an itinerant musician ("vagarant") who was neither covered by the civic office of wait nor by the special licence available from the Dutton family. His offense was therefore two-fold—playing both within and outside the boundaries of the city.

We have little evidence for minstrels licensed to noble patrons appearing in Chester, but in 1583 the puritan cleric Christopher Goodman decided, in a superscript in a letter to the Earl of Derby, to include minstrels in his complaint against the idle pastimes and displays maintained by the city:

> this Citie hath costom-abley bin geven to maintayne sundrye vayne pastance and vnprofitable spectakles as Bayrbait*es*, Bulbaits, Enterludes, ^^minstrell*es*^ Tumblers & suche like not beseeminge good & christian gover-ment, and thervppon consume and Waste other mens goods and pyke the purses of riche and poore, and Drawe both men & wives, sonnes and daughters, men & maide-servants from theire needfull busines at vnseasonable tymes, late in the night, to heare & behould wanton and vayne playes.[86]

He goes on to say that the city is afraid to displease "such noble personages (to whom the aforesaide Bearward*es*, Players, minstrells, and Tumblers doe appertaine and weare theire lyveries)."[87]

But besides the visits of minstrels in the service of noblemen, there were other minstrels of no affiliation within the city, as Chester, and hence Cheshire, had a special exemption from the Act. The Dutton family's traditional and well-evidenced right to license minstrels at a Minstrels' Court was acknowledged in the 1572 Act. The licences lasted for a year, after which reapplication had to be made to the Court. The recorded history of the Court began in 1477.[88]

Richard Rastall has plausibly suggested that its historical origins may lie in the ownership of Chester's fair by the Earl of Chester who exacted payment to license those trading there. He suggests that the minstrels who wished to perform at fair time would buy licences for the year; this would give them more incentive to march to the earl's aid, under possible threat of losing their licences.[89] But the Court also had a traditional origin (see chapter I), according to which Earl Randle Blundeville (1181–1232) was besieged at Rhuddlan Castle by the Welsh and rescued by the Constable of Chester along with an army of "Fidlers, Players, Coblers, debauched persons both Men and Women" who had been at Chester for the fair.[90] The Earl in his gratitude granted the Constable and his successors the right to license whores and minstrels. The Constable delegated this responsibility to his steward, a Dutton, and the privilege remained within that family thereafter. The Minstrels' Court became a means of publicly establishing the profile of the Dutton family.

The court met on Midsummer Day, the day after the Midsummer Show. No licence survives, and no details of the court proceedings are recorded prior to the description of the ceremony by the Cheshire antiquarian Sir Peter Leycester as occurring in his day "vi*delicet* 1642. Iune the: 24th."[91] The Lord of Dutton or his deputy and supporters rode to the Eastgate, accompanied by trumpeter, drummer, and standard-bearer, and summoned all the minstrels to perform before him. Thereafter they were to go to the courthouse to present their claims and pay homage. Then the company, with minstrels playing, processed to St. John's Church where "A sett of the Lowd Musique vpon their Knees playeth A solemne Lesson or Two; which ended they arise vpp with this congratulation, God blesse the Kinge, And the heire of Dutton."[92] The company processed to the courthouse, one of the inns, where a jury was empanelled, and each minstrel was interrogated: did they know of any treason towards the King? Had they exercised minstrelsy without the Court's licence? Had they profaned the sabbath by unlicensed playing? Had they heard slander about the house of Dutton? The licences cost 2*s* 2*d* in 1642, 2*s* 6*d* in 1666.

The ceremony seems to have been somewhat elaborated; Sir Peter Leycester believed that it was originally only a court. The purpose was clearly to glorify the Dutton family, but the emphasis upon loyalty to the King, in both the call at the end of the "concert" and the questioning, suggests something of the troubles at the approach of the Civil Wars. Chester was a Royalist city, and the reference to the cost of the licence in 1666 perhaps suggests a politicized revival of the ceremony much as the Midsummer Show was revived by express command of the Earl of Derby. Otherwise, minstrels could find ready employment in the city by playing in inns, at company dinners, and on civic occasions. Probably each had a specialty. The Joiners in 1602 record payment of 3*s* 6*d* "to three sort*es* of Mynstrels at our dynner at Alderma*n* Kenderickes house."[93]

While it is not always possible to establish the status of a "musicioner" from the records, those designated "fidler"—John Butler (1488), Robert Chalner (1488), James Reynold (1525–26), John Seton (1589–90), and the "2: fidleres" who "were syngyng of the last Triumphe of england against the spaniards" in 1588[94]—may reasonably be thought to belong in the category of *minstrel*. In 1597 Thomas Yemouth from a village five miles outside Derby came before the Chester courts and "saythe he ys a mynstrell & dothe vse to playe vpon the bagpipes / w*hi*ch instrument he left at home"; his insistence that he was not traveling as a minstrel reflects his concern that he might be classed as a vagrant.[95] Harpers, too, may have moved around the county, though there are relatively few examples in the Chester records—John le Wrugh (1397) and Henry Frenway (1424).[96] In 1436 Thomas Bradford sought compensation for, among other items, "harpstrynges."[97]

Pipers, too, such as Richard Jackson (1574), Henry Shurlock (1588–89), Richard Chatterton, who is clearly defined as "ministleo & piper,"[98] and John Peacock who "Came vnto this exa*mina*t*es* house . . . a piper by profession" in 1612[99] seem also to have been licensed travelers. Peacock's case provides an insight into the activity of the piper. He played in the house of the vintner William Moores "vntill Eleven of the Clocke in the night or therabout*es*," and Elizabeth Craddock "danced after him for a while w*i*th an ould man. whose name she knoweth not." Some idea of the bonding and links between the various minstrels may be suggested by the collection of people who came to the Sheriffs' Court in 1488–89 when the fiddler Robert Chalner and the "horner" Richard Hey complained against the minstrel William Marshall, the hooper John Harper, the pardoner David Johnson, and the minstrel Thomas Roper.[100]

Most company accounts include payments to minstrels for performing at dinners, sometimes alongside payments to other groups such as the Callys' consorts or the waits; for example, the Shoemakers' accounts of 1603 report 9*s* 4*d* "spent and geven to the wetmen and henrye Shorlock the viij daye of novembar being our meyting daye."[101] Henry Shurlock, as we have seen, was a piper. The Shoemakers were particular patrons of minstrels: one notes the reference to the cobblers in Leycester's account of the Minstrels' Court. Thus in their accounts for 1578–79 there are twelve payments to minstrels[102] ranging from sixpence "at the shirreffes," presumably part of a collective contribution, to three shillings "at Roger chantres drincking." A solitary minstrel earned twenty-two pence for playing on the evening of Election Day. These payments gain some perspective from the fact that while "at petr bockosos dynner" the minstrels earned sixteen pence, a tumbler on that occasion was paid two shillings.

Minstrels were also hired for weddings; the Coopers' accounts for 1578–79 record 4*d* "payed at Raffe conpares at a wedynge to the mynstrel*es*."[103] And when the two daughters of Sir Piers Dutton married jointly on St. John's Day, 24 June 1540, the day of the Minstrels' Court, the wedding party was met on its return from the church by the steward, the standard bearer, and all the licensed musicians, whose playing escorted the two couples through the city (see chapter III).[104]

The Midsummer Show, held on St. John's Eve, provided further employment for all the musicians of Chester, both at the Show and at the dinners that followed (e.g., "to 2 Pypers on Midsom*er* Eve before the Gyants 00–02–00"[105]). In 1610 a fracas erupted between the city waits and the Duttons' servants, who took the musical instruments from the waits. While the cause is not known, it seems possible that it related to some professional rivalry between the city musicians and the Dutton minstrels (see chapter III).[106]

Minstrels were also required for the Whitsun Plays. The Post-Reformation Banns enjoin the Smiths that for their play of *Christ Before the Doctors* (play 11) they should "gett mynstralles to that shewe; pype, tabrett, and flute" (118), and the accounts of the Smiths indicate that they usually complied:

> 1554
> to the mynstrells in mane   ij s
> 1561
> to the minstrells 3s 6d payd for drinke for ther breckfast before they play & after they had done when the were vnbowninge them iijs
> 1567
> to mynstrells   ij s
> 1568
> at the hyerynge of the Menstrells & Consell of Simion   iij d
> 1572
> to the waytes & our musysyens xij d to mynstrells vj d
>   . . .
> to the minstrells for our pagent 3s 4d
> 1575
> to the menstreleles at our generall rehers and midsamar and w*i*th our pagan v s[107]

The Banns seem to suggest three kinds of minstrel instrumentalists. They were to be available for rehearsals and the performance, presumably to accompany the singing. The 1575 reference seems to distinguish the rehearsal, the performance ("midsamar"), and the carriage ("pagan"), perhaps indicating that the minstrels also provided music either along the way or at each station while the carriage was being set up. They also received a subsistence allowance in 1561. The Smiths also hired choristers and singingmen from the Cathedral as well as minstrels, though the two groups probably performed at different points in the production rather than together. The payment of only two shillings to the minstrels in 1567 is in the year that payment was also made for carrying the regals, the portable organ, perhaps indicating that different music was used with the play in that year. Possibly the pairing of the hiring of the minstrels and the "consell" of Simeon in 1568 relates to that. The 1572 entry also distinguishes three groups of musicians: the minstrels; the city waits; and "our musysens," whoever they might be.[108]

The extant play manuscripts include cues for minstrels to play at various points in the performance. These directions are typically in English in the margins of the manuscripts, as opposed to the Latin stage directions in the body of the texts, and may be production notes which copyists had included in the "Reginall" or master copy. The moments when minstrels play may cover entries or movements from one location to another within the play. In the Drapers' play of *The Creation and Fall of Man: Cain and Abel* (play 2), minstrels are to play as God leads Adam to Paradise before the Tree of Knowledge (112 *s.d.*); as the naked Adam and Eve cover themselves with leaves (289 *s.d.*); as they leave Eden (304 *s.d.*); to bridge the gap from the expulsion to Adam's speech which introduces the Cain and Abel section (424 *s.d.*); and during God's entry to rebuke Cain (616 *s.d.*). One manuscript also directs minstrels to play at the beginning of the play. At line 144 of the Merchants' play of *The Magi* (play 8), minstrels are to play as Herod's messenger returns to his master to announce the arrival of the kings. This music evidently signals Herod's entrance.

Impromptu and Popular Music

There is, understandably, little evidence for amateur performances and popular levels of music in the city. Some indication may be found in the Painters' play of *The Shepherds* (play 7) where the Welsh shepherds, as national stereotypes, praise the angel's singing and respond to the Latin "church voice" with their own. Debating what the syllables meant, the Third Shepherd says, "nayther singes 'sar' nor soe well 'cis', / ney 'pax merye Mawd when shee had mett him." (7.410–11). This appears to be a reference to a popular song—and evidently a somewhat bawdy one in view of the allusion to the kiss of peace. The shepherds eventually head for Bethlehem and seem to invite the audience to join them in a song, with Trowle leading:

Singe we nowe; lett see,
some songe will I assaye.
All men nowe singes after mee,
for musicke of mee learne yee maye. (7.444–47)

The following stage direction reads "Tunc cantabunt et postea dicat Tertius Pastor" ("Then they shall sing and afterwards the Third Shepherd shall speak"), and in the margin the direction appears: "Here singe 'troly, loly, loly, loo'" (447*s.d.*). James Miller alone is unspecific, requiring only "hilare carmen" ("a comic song"). The marginal note is clearly a cue for a particular song, which may have been used only for a particular performance. Richard Rastall suggests that, if this is a title, the only song that would so begin is one by William Cornish dating from c.1515.[109] Christopher Goodman, writing to the Archbishop of York in 1572 to complain of the absurdities of the plays, noted:

> The foolish descanting of the Shepherds upon Gloria in excelsis
> The angels suspected of the Shepherds to be sheep-stealers. with a lewd merry song.[110]

The Shepherds also carried instruments. The First Shepherd has a horn, but as a signaling instrument only to summon his fellows (7.48 *s.d.*, 151, 155, 160, 161–64). Trowle, their boy, however, was provided with whistles, according to the Painters' accounts:

> 1572
> It*em* payde for iiij wyestlles ij d
> . . .
> Item for ij wystyles for trowe ij d
> 1575
> It*em* for wystelles ij d[111]

Rastall suggests that the whistles were dog whistles in view of their price.[112] But there are four whistles specified separately from Trowle's whistles in 1572, and there are four shepherds' boys. Moreover, the Third Boy presents the Christ Child with a pipe in terms that suggest that he can play tunes on it:

> alas, what have I for to give thee?
> Save only my pype that soundeth so royallye
> elles truely have I nothinge at all.

> Were I in the rocke or in the valey alowe,
> I would make this pipe sound, I trowe,
> that all the world should ringe,
> and quaver as yt would fall.
>   (7.626–32)

Moreover, Trowle himself announces his intention to "pippe at this pott like a pope" (189), which also seems to suggest music. One recalls "le whistelinge" at night for which John Cally was brought to court in 1588–89.

In the Waterleaders' play of *The Flood* (play 3), one manuscript prefaces the speech of Mrs. Noah at 225–36 with the words "The Good Gossippes Songe." What follows to 232 is in a different rhyme-scheme from the rest of the play. If this is what is intended, it refers specifically to the rising flood and could not be a song in popular use. But possibly the copyist misunderstood a marginal note, omitted by the other copyists, which was intended to indicate that the Gossips entered singing. As with the Shepherds and the Angel's song, the "popular" voice of the drinking gossips would provide a contrast with the vernacular psalm which Miller's manuscript requires from Noah in the Ark (above).

Popular ballads on contemporary events, like the two fiddlers singing of the defeat of the Armada in 1588, could be heard in the taverns of the city. And there could be spontaneous gaiety in the streets. In 1585 William Helen observed four women "dalyinge amonge theym selues, and disburtheninge theym, two beinge manske borne (as it seemed) vsed such straunge kynde of daunce, singinge, and wanton toyes."[113] Singers also are sometimes recorded as performing at dinners, as in 1608–09 when "Richard Barlow man pickeringe" was given six pence "for singinge."[114] But the company from Whitchurch who burst into the dinner of the Grand Jury in Castle Lane, Chester, on 2 April 1642 had other aims:

> beinge fidlers and Rouges by the Stattute; did singe scandelous songs; to this purpose; viz: that whereas the parliament hath Cleer<.>d diverse persons from theire banishment as Doctor Bast-wicke and <.>r Prinn, said the must bee cannanized saints and Ieered att the parli<.>ment for that pious deede
>   Secondly the abused his Maiestie and the parliment for theire settlinge of peace betwixt England and Scottland and said that when his Maiestie was in Scottland he yeilded to all their demands

and that they had noe crosse in baptizme nor prayers in the
Congregacion and scoffed ffurther att the parliment and said
reformacion would bee perfected with vs when the divell is blind
which speeches the often related over which was the keepinge of
the songe.[115]

Meantime, the gentry were acquiring musical instruments, and
presumably skills to play them (see also chapter III). Virginals occur
with increasing frequency in the inventories of gentry such as John
Cooper, whose inventory of 1579 shows that he had owned a pair of
virginals valued at twenty shillings, while in 1589 William Glaseor left
"a paire of virginalls with the frame" valued at thirty shillings in his
house at St. John's in Chester.[116] The instrument, as Suzanne Westfall
has demonstrated, was the favorite for aristocratic musicians.[117]
Surprisingly, given the numerous instances in the county and across
the kingdom, we have so far found only one reference to the ownership
of a lute in the records of the city of Chester; in 1586 John Coppock,
described as "gentleman," bequeathed "my ^^lute^ and Lutinge
booke."[118] Most unusually, an Irish harp was left in pledge in 1575–
76.[119] A social difference is instrumentally signaled by the inventory of
the innkeeper Thomas Jones in 1637 who owned "2 Instrvmentes
Called a bandore & a Kitte" valued at £1 (see also chapter IV).[120] The
episode in 1594, when William Hicock, clerk, "plaied excellent well"
on the treble violin accompanied by Richard Preston (see chapter I)
shows that a Cestrian who was evidently an amateur musician was
sufficiently skilled to win the praise of a professional, and the two
could play together.[121]

Chester was the meeting point of a variety of musical traditions
and their exponents, sometimes working together and sometimes in
competition so fierce that it threatened public order. How far these
traditions cross-fertilized to produce new musical forms cannot be
determined, for we know something of the musicians but little about
their music aside from the known compositions of Francis Pilkington
and Thomas Bateson.[122] But it may safely be surmised that the city
attracted all kinds of musicians to the county through the opportunities it offered and the licences available through the Minstrels'
Court. Chester, in music as in commerce, was the hub of the county.

II, PART 2
MUSIC IN THE COUNTY

It is axiomatic to the point of cliché that minstrels wandered, just as players strolled. The Statute of Vagabonds, by specifically classifying minstrels as vagabonds, supports the view that they wandered from place to place, from fair to market to wake, and thus changed their audience in order, it has been suggested, to compensate for a limited repertoire.[1] However powerful this image may have become, it needs to be questioned. The terms 'wandering' and 'vagabond' suggest a purposelessness that is belied by the evidence. The terms are to some extent derivative from the Statute of Vagabonds, which was concerned with social control and the perceived problem of a breakdown in society caused by "masterless men." To what extent were minstrels truly vagabond, and how far from home must a minstrel be in order to be considered "wandering"? Was it really necessary for him to vary his audience to the same extent, for instance, as players? Did the Statute of Vagabonds make a noticeable difference to the habits of minstrels?

Many of the music-makers in the Cheshire records seem to have wandered on a fairly local basis and appear also to have had regular engagements in one place. This would suggest that varying the audience was not as necessary as might have been thought. A limited repertoire would not be a serious obstacle if the music were used as an accompaniment to dancing.

The following is a case in point: "Rondull Moreton late of Hart-hill in the Countie of Chester taylo*r* found pipeinge in Bickerton in the said Countie vppon Whitsunday being the xxviijth of May last at the time of divine service, contrarie to a statute in that case provided."[2] Moreton clearly has another occupation, but is able to provide entertainment on special occasions, and indeed on a regular basis, as he is mentioned in a 1617 order to the constables of Egerton:

> Whereas it hath pleased the Right Reverend Iudges of his *Ma*jesties great generall Sessions out of their Godly and Religious care to endevoure the suppressinge of many vile abuses and shamefull disorders too much practised and maintained in theise *partes* amongst w*hi*ch the prophanation of the Saboth by pipeing and

minstrelsie is not one of the least. And being given to vnderstand
that some of thinhabitant*es* of *you*r towneship have hyred on
Rondull Moorton to pipe every Saboth day vppon *you*r greene
contrarie to the intent of the Iudges said ord*ers* whereby God is
both highly dishonoured and his Saboths greatly prophaned.[3]

Though one document suggests that Moreton was regarded as a vagabond, a minstrel who wanders from fair to fair, yet he had a definite
place of habitation as well as another occupation. Furthermore, Harthill and Bickerton are adjacent townships, and Egerton lies just on the
other side of Bickerton. The fact that he was hired to pipe "every
Saboth day vppon *you*r greene" in Egerton indicates a regular event,
probably piping as an accompaniment to dancing, serving to supplement his income as tailor. He would only have had to travel a few
miles. His audience would probably have remained largely the same,
and certainly had some consistent elements, since "some of thinhabitant*es* of *you*r towneship" who have hired him would undoubtedly
have done so for their own benefit, whether as dancers or as alesellers
hoping to profit from the attraction of a dance on the green.

     That minstrels did not perform in only one place is undeniable.
In one instance at least, a piper appeared playing in two different
townships on the same day. Randle Walker of Little Budworth, piper,
was cited for playing on the sabbath, 20 August 1609, at both Tarvin
and Tarporley.[4] The Tarporley jury's presentment includes a number
of pipers and bearwards and is probably connected with the wakes.
The Tarvin entry, from the Crown Books, only specifies Randle
Walker piping at Tarvin. In each case the name of the location is
spelled out, and there does not seem to be any possibility of scribal
error other than a case of mistaken identity by the jury. Nor does it
seem likely that there would be two Randle Walkers of Little Budworth who were pipers at the same time. Although a father/son combination is possible, elsewhere the records distinguish between "Sr."
and "Jr." even when both individuals are not present. Since Tarvin and
Tarporley are only about five miles apart, it was quite feasible for
Walker to walk from one to another and to perform in both on the
same day. His home parish of Little Budworth is about three miles
from Tarporley, in the opposite direction from Tarvin. He would
therefore, if he began and ended in Little Budworth, have about
sixteen miles to walk. It is, of course, possible that he had been traveling and took in Tarvin and Tarporley on his homeward route, or that

he stopped overnight in whichever place he performed in last. This is more likely to have been Tarporley, as the entertainments there continued on 21 August with a bearbaiting. This case shows that a minstrel could have a definite local habitation and still travel in order to perform without being necessarily considered a vagrant. A. L. Beier estimates that wandering within about twenty miles of one's home village was probably tolerated to a certain extent.[5] Walker's offence is sabbath infringement, not vagrancy, and a sixteen-mile round trip is not impossible given sufficient incentive, although an overnight stay in Tarporley possibly provided a break in the journey.

Vagrancy was an increasing problem in the Tudor and early Stuart periods, and the various statutes enacted against vagabonds show that it was perceived as a threat to the social order. Minstrels, who included a wide range of performers, not all of them musical, were classed as rogues and vagabonds by definition, as were other entertainers such as bearwards and players. Their position was at best ambiguous, and they might expect to receive both welcomes and whippings as they traveled about the country. A. L. Beier defines vagrancy as "perhaps the classic crime of status, the social crime *par excellence*. Offenders were arrested not because of their actions, but because of their position in society. Their status was a criminal one because it was at odds with the established order."[6] Minstrels were vagrants not because they wandered but because they were classified as such whether they wandered or not. It must also be borne in mind that minstrels are a sub-set of the list of entertainers classed as rogues, and that entertainers are in turn a small sub-set of the much larger number of the vagrant and migrant poor. Truly vagrant minstrels must have formed only a fraction of the overall total, whether of vagrants or even of minstrels, but they would have been noticeable because they would necessarily have called attention to themselves by performance.

It is sometimes difficult to determine whether a performer is local or a wanderer. Frequently when a place of habitation is given, it is found to be a neighboring or not-too-distant village, as in the case of David Jones of Chester and his fellow, both of them fiddlers, who were in an alehouse in Dodleston, about two miles from Chester, and were "soe drunke that they slept in the feilds and could not get home."[7] Similarly, John Vaughan of Nantwich, piper, was cited for playing pipe and tabor at Wistaston, a neighboring parish to Nantwich, at service time in 1605.[8] But if no place of habitation is given for a performer, is it because he is local, and therefore known, or because he is

a wanderer and unable to supply any definite place of abode? Both
situations probably occurred, and in many cases we cannot get beyond
supposition and guesswork. Henry Boone, who piped in the adjacent
townships of Chelford cum Astle and Marthall in 1619, may have
lived in either of them or may have come from outside. The fact that
his name is provided would tend to support the former supposition,
just as there is a stronger likelihood that an unnamed performer,
particularly in an alehouse connection, was a wanderer, such as the
fiddler at Frodsham in 1609. In this presentment, two other men were
charged with being in the alehouse at midnight on Sunday, accompanied by many people "with theim swagrine with fidler with theim."[9]
The two men, Ralph Middleton and Ralph Huntsman, were described
as dwelling in Overton, which at first glance would seem to make them
wanderers, as Overton is a township in Malpas parish, in the extreme
south of the county, whereas Frodsham is in the extreme north. However, an unrelated document from Frodsham refers to a pair of bagpipes seized at "Evensonges howse by the Bridgend in Overton within
the parishe of ffrodsham," which would indicate that these were
known local men.[10] The fiddler, however, may have been a stranger,
and he may have managed to avoid arrest.

Vagrants might also have attempted to evade punishment by
obtaining false licences. At Congleton in 1587–88, a man had to be
sent to Sutton to speak with a "badger there that had lost his lycence
which was found here vppon a stranger beyng a trompeter."[11] A badger
was a pauper who was licensed by his community to beg and who wore
an identifying badge. The licence may have been genuinely lost, or it
may have been stolen, or sold. In any case, it was not adequate for the
trumpeter, who may have first attracted the attention of the authorities
because he was a stranger.

Definite unnamed wanderers can be found lodging in alehouses,
as at Sutton in 1582 where, in response to a question whether he had
taken in any vagabonds, the keeper of an illegal alehouse admitted that
he had "about the x[j] daie of this Ianuarij lodged one piper whom
greatly in his house abused the curate of the Churche and was let goe
without any further staye."[12] This was the type of wandering minstrel
at which the legislation was aimed—and the type of alehouse that the
authorities sought to suppress. True itinerants were probably rare, as
Southworth notes, at least in places where their presence is recorded.
However, the notion of "vagrancy" may have been largely one of perception. On Southworth's definition, any minstrel owing allegiance to

a Minstrel Court, such as that presided over by the Duttons in Cheshire, could not be considered itinerant: "their guild membership or court licence gave them identity and status, however lowly."[13] Nevertheless, the magistrates and constables may not have seen an absolute divide between the vagrant and the locally itinerant minstrel. A great deal depended on the attitude of the authorities at any given time and on the individual behavior of the performer.

Traveling may have been seen as exacerbating offences such as sabbath infringement or at least as potentially putting the minstrel in the category of vagabond. Two minstrels from Malpas, Hugh Byrsley and Henry Clutton, were censured for "Travelinge Dyvers Sabboth Dayes att the tyme of Dyvine Service to play on a Greene" in 1625.[14] The location of the green is not specified. Byrsley and Clutton evidently did not perform their penance, which led to their names being presented to the Consistory Court. The term 'minstrel' is used for both of them, an unusually late usage which may have been intended to enforce their status under the Statute of Vagabonds in a case in which they in fact do not seem to have been true vagabonds. Whether they were licensed or not is not specified, and indeed this would only rarely have been mentioned in the documents. Only in cases of egregious abuse of privileges did the licensing of the Minstrel Court become an issue, as in the allegations against Richard Metier, discussed below.

Nevertheless, a number of musicians did come from further afield, and these could probably be considered vagabonds in the proper sense of the word. They might have come to official attention as objects of charity, as in the case of "one potinge*r yat* came bare out of Ireland a schol*ar* a musitian" who was given 2*s* 6*d* by the Cathedral Treasurers in Chester in 1607–08.[15] The Cathedral Treasurers also paid five shillings to "a poore singinge man w*hich* came from Ireland" in 1611–12.[16] More frequently, vagabond musicians attracted the attention of the law either because they were illegally lodged or performing in illegal alehouses, or because they were suspected of more serious crimes.

Illegal inmates were not necessarily vagrant, although they were poor. Richard Minshull was a resident of Nantwich, as his son was baptized there in 1606.[17] He is described in the parish register as a musician and is evidently a fiddler since he was presented at the 1622 diocesan visitation for fiddling all afternoon on Palm Sunday. The correction book describes him as being "de Pillory Streete," and specifies that he had received communion before performing.[18] He makes a final appearance in 1623 in a list of illegal inmates as "Richard minshull ^^fidler^ rec*eive*d — margery mynshull."[19] Since this part of the list is for those born in the town, he was not a wanderer. It is not quite clear whether he is receiving or giving shelter, but there is very probably a familial relationship between Richard and Margery, possibly parent and child. One of them at least must have been a native of Nantwich, and Richard Minshull's previous connection with the town suggests that he is the one who was born locally. Local paupers were of course the responsibility of their own parish, and musicians occasionally were eligible for poor relief. A list of paupers in the Chester Cathedral Treasurers' Accounts includes a singing man who was given 2*s* 6*d* in 1617–18. Presumably he had been a member of the Cathedral choir.[20]

Individuals might be temporarily out of their principal place of abode and illegally lodged somewhere else without being more than technically vagrant. The John Peacock, piper, who was lodged at the house of William Moores, vintner, in Chester in 1612 (see chapter II, part 1) and provided music there, may very well be the same individual as John Peacock of Beeston, piper, who, with his sister Jane, was accused of threats and assaults against John Rowland of Peckforton in 1615.[21] Beeston would appear to be his home. A trip to Chester would not be excessive, and providing entertainment at his lodging may only have been a secondary activity. His host points out that none of the watch came to the house to tell them to stop the music, which went on until about eleven at night.[22] Peacock was only a short-term visitor, but musicians from areas outside Chester might lodge there for some time. Thomas Stokes of Stretton, minstrel, was sued by his landlord, William Clowghe, described as "yoman," "for fyve or six weekes meate drinke and lodging." The sum payable was 6*s* 2*d*.[23] As the debt was an old one, it is not possible to determine when Stokes was staying in Chester. We do not know if he was in the city during the festive season when musicians might be more in demand or whether his presence had in fact nothing to do with his occupation.

Thomas Yemouth, who described himself as being from "vn'thorborse within the co*un*ty of derbye / fyve myles fro*m* derbye," claimed to be "a mynstrell & dothe vse to playe vpon the bagpipes / *whi*ch instrument he left at home."[24] He was apprehended and examined in 1597 because of boots, spurs, saddles, and girths which he claimed to have bought in Chester to sell in Derbyshire. The authorities were suspicious that he was involved in stealing horses. Yemouth claimed that he came to Chester in hopes of meeting his kinsman, Jehan Yerton, described as "a husbandman / being a sodier," but failed to find him. He claimed to have brought twenty-five shillings from Derbyshire with him, and had about twenty-three shillings left by the time he arrived. He was interrogated about his acquaintance with "Jenions wyff at Lyttelton," although the document does not say why, as well as about his knowledge of horse thieves and whether he had been in jail.[25] Yemouth claimed never to have met Jenion's wife—nor to have been in jail, nor to know any horse thieves. Whether or not he was telling the truth, he is a good example of a minstrel who traveled across county boundaries and engaged in activities other than music—whether commerce or theft—in order to supplement his income, while at the same time he also shows the suspicion which could attach automatically to a stranger of an already dubious occupation. If he was telling the truth about the amount of money he brought with him and the five shillings he left with his wife, who lived thirty miles away from his house "at fargery / being greved in hir legges of a dropsye," then he was not destitute.[26]

Edward Clarke of the Isle of Ely may have been putting himself higher on the social scale than Yemouth in 1608 when he claimed the profession of musician,[27] but that did not prevent him from being suspected of theft by his employer (see chapter I). Unfortunately, neither the Yemouth nor the Clarke case is complete, and it is impossible to determine whether the musician in each is an opportunistic thief or a victim of circumstances.

Crossing the county boundary was seen as suspect, an indication in itself of vagrancy. William Plymley, piper, allegedly "Contrary to the Statute wandreth from Contrey to Contrey."[28] His roaming across county boundaries was offered as corroborative evidence in a petition to have him bound to keep the peace for making threats against Thomas Chester. Plymley's son, James, was also implicated, and was described as "a Notorious Lewd person, a Night walker and hath been suspected for diuers Criminall yll Accidentes & alsoe hath seuerall tymes robbed the Peticioners orchard."[29] Criminality and vagrancy are clearly associated here. It may also be that by crossing the county boundaries Plymley jeopardized the protection which allegiance to the Cheshire Minstrels' Court would otherwise afford him; the plaintiff may have intended to suggest that Plymley was to be considered vagabond in the fuller sense of the 1572 statute. Despite the benefits of the

Cheshire Minstrels' Court licences, not all Cheshire minstrels remained in the county. John Tomson of Stockport was charged with piping on the sabbath at Manchester in 1601.[30] Stockport is so close to Manchester that there is nothing remarkable in a performer from Stockport appearing at Manchester.

Minstrels might on occasion cross county boundaries for specific purposes in spite of official disapproval and potentially in controversial ways. This appears to have been the case in 1642 when Thomas Cowper and his company from Whitchurch in Shropshire disrupted the Grand Jury dinner in Chester with anti-puritan songs (see chapter II, part 1). Cowper and his company are specifically referred to as "Rouges by the Stattute";[31] would they have been regarded as such if they had come from within Cheshire and had licences from the Minstrel Court? The Statute of Vagabonds, as we have seen, defines minstrels as rogues and vagabonds not because of their actions but because of the nature of their profession. It therefore becomes difficult to determine how much true roguery and vagabondage were present among musical performers. This is made more problematical by the fact that so many documents that mention them are concerned with infringements of the law.

Performers from outside the county who came to Chester could be made to leave again, as in the case of Henry Tailer of Standish, Lancashire, in 1589. An entry in the Mayor's Book records that he was to leave the city the same night ("hac nocte") and not to return under pain of having to pay forty shillings. A Chester musician, Henry Concord, was ordered not to wander about the city after nine at night under pain of paying £40.[32] The difference in the penalties is less likely to be concerned with a perceived difference in the offences than with the greater necessity of controlling the musician who remains in the city. Once Henry Tailer had left Chester, he was no longer their problem, and only needed to be penalized if he returned.

Certain occupations linked with music, however, can suggest vagrancy. In 1573–74 John Rowley, tinker, who is described as being of the city of Chester, and his wife Agnes, described in parentheses as "(she being a muscon)," were put under recognizance to leave the city within two days and not to return for more than two days at a time. They were also required to behave themselves "as becometh honeste Civill persons" when they were in the city.[33] Tinkering was a traditionally vagrant occupation, and Agnes may have supplemented her husband's income with what she could make from her music. The city, however, was anxious not to have them as residents.

Migration as well as vagrancy is a factor in the movement of musicians, although it can be difficult to determine whether an individual with a name indicating a different place of origin is vagrant or migrant. The movement from one place to another can be gradual, and great caution must be exercised when comparing names that occur in different locations. John Challyner of Oswestry, musician, whose name appears in the Chester Mayors' Book for 1572–73 with a memorandum that he is to appear at the next sessions or pay a penalty of £10, was probably at least attempting to settle in the city.[34] Hugh de Walay, who was granted land in Foulk Stapleford by the Black Prince, sounds like an immigrant from Wales.[35] Sometimes an early surname carries a double place name, such as Robert de Overwhitley of Northwich, which suggests migration from the first place to the second.[36]

Where the same name occurs in more than one place, there are several possible explanations. The individual may be a vagrant, either genuine or by status, a migrant over a short or long distance, someone who is traveling for genuine reasons not connected with music, or a musician resident in the general area traveling to perform. An individual might occupy more than one of these categories at once, depending on who was defining his status. Thomas Yemouth was suspected by the authorities as a possible vagrant but presented himself as one who was traveling for valid reasons and, although a minstrel, was not practicing his minstrelsy on his journey. Richard Preston, who was performing in Chester with his company of musicians, deposed that his residence was in Warrington, but he and his company were lodging in Chester at "their hoste foxall his howse."[37] Were he and his company attempting to migrate to Chester, or were they only there for a short time? The authorities do not seem to have considered them vagrants even by the statute definition, so were they a recognized band of waits, licensed to travel under the protection of their patron? Alternatively, were they a group of musicians who were trying to take over the territory of the Chester waits in a situation similar to that which caused George Cally to petition the Assembly in 1615 (see chapter II, part 1)?[38] Although it is necessary to be cautious about assuming that two instances of the same name represent the same individual, it is likely that "Thomas towres yoman," presented in 1610 for playing on his pipes for dancing at Upton-by-Chester, is the same as "Thome Towers de Barrowe," as he was described in 1603.[39] He might also by 1638 have become "a Piper. Vizt old Towres" playing for dancing in an alehouse in Alvanley.[40] Given the length of time involved, he could have moved from one place to another, but he need not have been a migrant and is unlikely to have been a vagrant in the true sense. Barrow is virtually equidistant between Upton-by-Chester and Alvanley, and not far from either. To get to Upton from Barrow, Towers would have had to cross two parish boundaries, but would have traveled less than five miles. To get to Alvanley, he needed only to go into the next parish, and again would have traveled less than five miles. He may, therefore, have been a resident musician in Barrow who played in neighboring parishes.

The position of parish boundaries, some of which have outlying townships, can make it difficult to tell whether an individual was moving from place to place or not. In 1617, the parish registers of Malpas parish recorded the baptism of the daughter of "ffrances Seaer of the lower wiche in Iscoyd pyper."[41] At first glance, this might appear to be an immigrant from Wales, but Iscoyd in Flintshire was nevertheless part of Whitewell chapelry, which in turn was part of Malpas parish.[42] A similar, but less clear, case occurs in the parish of Rostherne, which includes the township of Over Tabley. Nicholas Ashworth, alias Piper, described as "late of ouer taybley," was accused at Archbishop Piers's visitation in 1590–91 of bigamy.[43] Had he moved from Over Tabley to another part of the parish in order to be with the second wife?

A definite case of gradual although possibly not entirely voluntary migration can be seen in the case of Richard Metier, although this also is complicated by the question of parish boundaries. We have for Metier a series of documents that relate to a single individual in more than one place. The surname is not a common one, the places involved are all close together, and the behavior pattern consistent. In addition, there are instances of repetition in the names of other individuals in the cases. There is therefore little doubt that a single individual was involved. Metier is described as being "of" a series of places: from 1609 to 1612 and again from 31 March 1617 to 13 May 1617 he was described as "of Withington."[44] He appeared on 31 August 1617 as both "of Withington" and as "of Lower Withington," and on 15 September 1617 and 13 April 1618 he was "of Lower Withington."[45] It is clear from this that at this time Metier was a resident of Lower Withington, not the adjacent township of Old Withington, which in any case was in a chapelry of Prestbury parish, the same parish in which Lower Withington was situated. All the documents for the

Withington locations are connected with disorderly behavior: fighting, slander, and keeping a disorderly alehouse. In 1623 Metier was connected with both Siddington and Withington when he was cited for intimidating witnesses in a paternity case.[46] In 1624 and 1625 there is a case against him as a resident of Siddington (which is also adjacent to Lower Withington, and in yet another chapelry of Prestbury parish) for offences including keeping an illegal alehouse, abusing the constable and the curate, slander, and disrupting church services. The petition of the curate, Mr. Fletcher, gives a long list of complaints against him and alleges:

> That this Metyer hath formerlie abused other Preachers, And that hee was A longe tyme ymprisoned in the Castle of Chester for abusinge one mr Coller then Parson of Swettenham, And ever since this Metyer was proferrd to be A pyper, hee hath bene an Arrogant Contencyous quarrelor wherby hee hath bene maymed and beatton, And hath bene many tymes Compleyned ^^of^ to the Iustices, And dyvers tymes the good behaviour graunted against him ffor abusinge many gentlemen and honestmen of this Cuntrye, And also hee standeth Indicted ffor a Comon Baretter by mr Baskervyle.[47]

Metier makes his final appearances at Swettenham, from 1 March 1631 to 3 July 1632, again disturbing the peace, slandering his neighbours, and making trouble.[48] Swettenham is adjacent to Lower Withington on the other side from Siddington but, being a separate parish and formerly part of the larger parish of Astbury, is in a different parish. Metier would therefore seem to have been mobile on a limited scale but not necessarily wandering very far outside his own parish. He may have been living in Swettenham when he abused the parson, but he could equally have traveled from Withington or Siddington to do so. The period of imprisonment in Chester Castle may have come between 1617 and 1622, or it may have been earlier, in the period between 1612 and 1617, for which there are no other records. He appears in the records as early as 1597, when he is mentioned at Chelford (adjacent and to the north of Old Withington, and in the same chapelry) as someone likely to be willing to do murder for hire, although his place of abode is not specified there.[49] Between at least 1609 and 1632, therefore, and probably from 1597 to 1632, not counting periods of imprisonment, Richard Metier was associated only with three different townships. Indeed, until he moved to

Swettenham he remained within one parish, albeit he did move from one chapelry to another.

Initially, however, Metier seems not to have been properly resident in Withington. One of the documents is a constable's presentment from 1617 which cites "william ffoden of withinton for takeynge Receaueynge & harberinge Richarde Me^^a^tyre pyper a lewde disordered person to the great disturbaunce of his neighboures synce the first of Aprill i6i6 vntill the fyrst day of may last past as an Inmake contrarye to the forme of the Statute in that case provided."[50] It would appear from this that he lived with William Foden for over a year as an "illegal inmate" and technically a vagrant. After that time he must have acquired some lodgings of his own since he is cited in 1618 for running an illegal alehouse in his house. William Foden was again involved: "for selling ale vnbound & for keepinge great disorder in his house Richardus meteerley de lower withington for setting his house to the said meteerley to mayntayne disorders Williamus ffoden de lower withington. . . ."[51] By the time he came to live in Siddington, Metier seems to have owned some property since Fletcher's petition mentions "Metiers nagge," which he has impounded. There is evidence that he traveled from one parish to another. In the articles objected against him in the consistory court it is charged that "the said Richard Metyer within the said parishe of Prestburie and othere parishes and places neere adioyninge hast most irreuerently and inhumanely blasphemed the most sacred and blessed name of God by swearinge most blasphemously, by his woundes, by his bloode, by his fleshe, by his heart, and by othere partes of his most sacred and blessed bodie to the greate dishonor of Allmightie God, vtter ruine of thy owne soule and evill example of others. . . ."[52]

There is one other document connected with Richard Metier that relates to the mobility of pipers. In 1611, John Metier, brother to Richard and also himself a piper, was described as being of Biddulph, Staffordshire.[53] He was bound over to keep the peace for having threatened Thomas Dale, whom he alleged had slandered his brother Richard as a thief.[54] Richard Metier of Withington and Galfridus Bentley of Knutsford are the sureties for John Metier in January 1612, but a subsequent recognizance, dated 28 April 1612, has John Bentley of Knutsford and John Bradshaw of Allostock.[55] It may be that the earlier sureties were not found to be sufficient.

The fact that John Metier was of Biddulph is significant in that he had his dwelling in a different county and therefore was subject to the

Statute of Vagabonds in a different way than his brother. But Biddulph is only just over the border and a few miles from Withington, Siddington, and Swettenham. It is not, therefore, surprising that he was able to hear of Thomas Dale's remarks about Richard. Unfortunately, the records do not show where the house in which he made his threats was located, but it must have been within the boundaries of Cheshire since the case was tried in this county. The fact that John Metier is "of" Biddulph, while his brother is variously "of" several places not far from Biddulph but in Cheshire, raises the question as to where the two brothers originated. Were they Staffordshire men, one of whom had moved to Cheshire and managed to get a licence from the Duttons? Or were they Cheshire men, one of whom had moved to Staffordshire and managed to find a patron there? Could John Metier possibly have had to leave the county after the commission of a crime?

Another question is whether the size and sometimes scattered formation of the parishes allowed minstrels a means of circumventing the vagrancy laws. Poor relief was the responsibility of the parish, and vagrants were to be whipped and returned to their home parishes. But what is the situation if a minstrel can claim to be traveling from one part of the parish to another? If he moves from one township to another, but remains within the same parish, is he wandering? The authorities do cite it as one of Metier's offences that he blasphemed both in Prestbury parish and other adjacent parishes. They were more concerned about the blasphemy than the crossing of parish boundaries, however.

At first glance, then, it might appear that traveling automatically made a musician suspect. This was not universally the case, although, as noted above, traveling could make a musician accused of a misdemeanor *more* suspect, and it would certainly have increased suspicion if the musician were obviously poor. There are, however, examples of travel in a more positive context, and it is likely that in a law-abiding musician travel was considered tolerable, provided he did not become a burden on the parish. The status of the musicians was often a decisive factor in determining the acceptability of his traveling. On 14 February 1621, "Calis the musitian" was paid twenty shillings "for his paynes in comminge from Chester & playinge, for the Schollers in their play on Shrouetuesday" at Congleton. This was undoubtedly a member of the Cally family of Chester waits who would have provided music and possibly advice on the selection of the music for the scholars' play. He evidently gave satisfaction since he was given a further 3*s* 4*d* on 5 April "when the Townesmen played their play in Mr Greenes court."[56] Musicians such as the Chester waits were expected to travel, to a certain extent, providing it did not interfere with their duties at home. Their visits to Ludlow, Coventry, and Lancashire are discussed in chapter II, part 1. The Shuttleworth family also paid the musicians of Sir Peter Legh twelve pence in 1584. The Shrewsbury waits visited Chester in 1549–50, and Congleton spent money entertaining various members of the local gentry "when the pyper was in Towne."[57]

Chester naturally attracted visiting musicians in spite of the protectionist rules governing the performance of music in the city. The Preston family of Warrington seem to have been frequent visitors to Chester, and the son of one of them was apprenticed to a Chester painter.[58] Three Prestons of Warrington were musicians between 1594 and 1639–40: Richard (1594), who is described as playing with his company, John (1600), and James (1639–40). The first two at least may have been part of a group of waits, like the Cally/Kelly family of Chester. A Preston was a trumpeter, seemingly in an official capacity, at Chester in 1635–36.[59]

Making a Living

The pattern of mobility is to some degree linked with the social status of the performer. It is impossible to determine how many of the rising number of unemployed in the late sixteenth and early seventeenth centuries were—or pretended to be—minstrels. At the lowest level, minstrelsy was probably only one of a variety of methods of making an extremely precarious living. It is not the intention of this book to argue that all minstrels were misunderstood, persecuted individuals, marginalized by their society. Many of them no doubt were "the dregs of medieval society, charlatans with little skill, often using minstrelsy as a cover for vice and petty crime,"[60] and would have been whether they were legislated against or not. The interrelationship between poverty, social marginalization, and crime is no doubt a factor in this image of the minstrel, but we should be very careful of assuming either that all the performers cited for playing on the sabbath were necessarily incompetent musically or that they were involved in petty crime. There was a recognized place for the locally resident musician or musically inclined tailor or saddler. Minstrelsy of course had its attractions for the potential miscreant, for which musical talent was irrelevant, particularly in Cheshire where a piper might obtain a licence giving him some measure of protection and legal status. Richard Metier, surely the dregs of any society, is alleged to have been arrogant and contentious ever since he "was p*r*oferrd to be A pyper."[61]

We have very little evidence of how much a piper or fiddler might expect to earn. Unlike players and bearwards, they do not appear as recipients of payments in civic accounts. Those who, like Richard Metier, combined alehousekeeping with musicianship, probably gained by being able to attract greater numbers to their alehouses, especially if music were provided for dancing. Alehousekeepers or others might hire musicians on a regular basis, as in the case of Rondull Moreton in 1615–17, but we are not told how much they paid. Moreton also had another source of income, and the regular weekly musical performance may have been simply a supplement—or it may have been a substantial portion of his income.

For a minstrel who relied on music only, the important thing was to find a paying audience. The amount paid would probably vary according to both the means of the audience and the skill or reputation of the performer. One of the allegations against alehousekeepers who hired minstrels and other entertainers was that their audience was made up of young people "as mens sonnes, daughters and servant*es*," who "steale from their Parent*es* & Maisters to spend at this tyme."[62] Minstrels were thought to be not only potential criminals themselves but also the cause of crime in others. We need always to remember that alehousekeeping was itself an occupation of the poor, and the alehouse's customers were generally poor; hence minstrels who played in alehouses were also unlikely to have received large sums from their listeners.[63]

The only payment detail we have, other than guild payments from the city of Chester (see chapter II, part 1), is in the account book of Henry Bradshaw of Marple, who records that he gave one shilling to the "Musitioner att Stock*port*" in January 1638 and six pence to the fiddlers at Stockport in March of the following year. In 1640, he only paid the fiddlers four pence.[64] We are not given any context for these entries, nor are we told why the single musician in 1638 received twice or three times as much as the fiddlers of 1639 and 1640. The payment may be simply a gratuity, the amount varying with Bradshaw's mood and spare cash, or the different terms used for the performers may indicate a difference in status. But fiddlers seem to have been proverbi-

ally paid very little. A note in J. B. Leishman's edition of *The First Part
of the Return from Parnassus* (1598) for the line "he drew mee out twoo
leane faces, gaue mee fidlers wages" points out that in 1699 "'fidler's
pay' meant 'thanks and wine'," according to *A New Dictionary of the
Canting Crew*, and fiddler's money was small change.[65]

One document does speak of the annual income of a piper, although its value is doubtful. Thomas Chester's petition against James
Plymley in 1630 complains "that William Plymley father of the said
Iames Plymley beinge a piper and Contrary to the Statute wandreth
from Contrey to Contrey, hath given forth in speech That he Careth
not for any of xx li landes ayeare for he Can spend more then xx li
ayeare by his pipinge as alsoe hath threatned the peticioner that yt had
ben better for him that he had neuer medled with his sonne & wold be
even with him & that his sonne was a better man than he or any of his
kynne, with further reprochfull termes as your peticioner Can Informe
your lordships & the rest."[66] The implication is that Plymley is to be
blamed for making this statement, particularly as he crosses county
boundaries and puts himself in danger of being considered a vagrant.
His claim to earn more than £20 yearly was seen as a presumptuous
attempt to put himself on a level with the gentry with the implication
that he is not subject to their censure. Whether there was any sub-
stance to his claim is not clear. It may be that it was a ridiculous piece
of bombast from a vagrant piper; on the other hand, Plymley may at
least have believed it himself. Would it be possible for a piper to earn
£20 in a year, assuming for the sake of argument that Plymley spent as
much as he earned? In order to earn £20 in a year, Plymley would have
had to earn about 7s 9d a week. This seems unlikely unless he was paid
more than the few pennies that Bradshaw records as his payments to
fiddlers. Even a payment of one shilling would not be enough unless
he played every day and even twice a day occasionally. A payment of
more than one shilling is not impossible but is unlikely to have been
a regular occurrence. Even the Chester guilds tended to pay only four
pence, six pence, or one shilling to single musicians.[67] It also seems
unlikely that Plymley would be able to find a paying audience every
day, especially if he was wandering from county to county, or that he
would be able to perform every day.

These calculations are, of course, highly speculative since we have
so little information about the sums involved or the number of times
in a week a piper might perform. They also do not take into account
payments in kind. A piper or fiddler performing in an alehouse might

well expect to receive his board and lodging—and probably the occasional pint of ale to keep him going when he got thirsty. Minstrels might also receive gifts from the gentry whose houses they visited or whose servants they were. In 1566, Thomas Wewll of Middlewich, piper, was presented at the Quarter Sessions "*pro caliges contra formam Stat*'" ("for shoes contrary to the statute"),[68] in this case presumably sumptuary legislation. Wewll could have received the shoes as a gift from a patron. More useful was the patronage which obtained for Thomas Foster, alias Huntsman, a "great paire of droane bagpipes" which had fallen to the Savage family as a deodand on the suicide of Robert Laithwood (see chapter IV). Huntsman was "a sutor vnto Cap*ten* W*illia*m Saunders for the havinge of those Pipes" who requested them of Sir Thomas Savage and eventually obtained them.[69] But even allowing for payments in kind, making a living by one's musical performances alone at the lower levels of the profession, as Plymley had done, was difficult. The lives of such performers, without a patron or the relative security of a position as a city wait, must have been quite precarious.

Whythorne complained that minstrels went about touting for business and making music "kommen by offring of it to evry 3ak, going abowt evry plas and kuntrey."[70] Alehouses, taverns, and greens were popular venues as minstrels were likely there to find paying audiences who wanted to dance—or alehousekeepers who wanted to encourage dancing. A runaway adulterous couple in 1638 had music and dancing in the alehouse at Alvanley where they stayed: "& further saith, y*at* on y*e* foresaid Saturday & Sunday at night they had a Piper . Vizt old Towres & y*e* said Ales & Penkett did dance together, & y*e* said Alice paaid for y*e* Musick, & the said Alice called her selfe on Mr Ionsons daughtor, & shee called her selfe by the name of [a gentleman] a gentlewoman but this examinat hath credibly heard shee hath beene laide of y*e* ffrench pox & y*e* said Alice & Penkett left vppon y*e* score at Colliers howse i9s 9d."[71] Unfortunately, we are not told how much Alice spent on the music. They were four nights at the alehouse; even if they left without paying their bill at all, they must have been spending heavily at a rate of almost five shillings a day, if the alehouse's bills are not padded. In such a situation, a piper might receive more than one shilling, but it should be noted that this was extraordinary, and he only performed on the Saturday night, not on every night of their visit.

There are surviving inventories for three known Cheshire musi-

cians, two in Nantwich and one in Chester (see Appendix I). The two
Nantwich inventories are discussed below, but it is worth noting the
relative value of their goods. William Worrall of Nantwich left goods
worth £19 8s 2d in 1637; Roger Vaughan of Nantwich, goods worth
£28 4s 8d in 1648.[72] William Madock, the Chester wait, was wealthier
than either of them, with goods worth £44 18s 5d, even though he
died much earlier in the seventeenth century, in 1604.[73] It is, however,
the poorest of the three who seems to have been most reliant on music
as his means of livelihood. Worrall's music books and musical
instruments account for almost ten percent of the total value of his
estate. Roger Vaughan, by contrast, owned "a house and ground in
lease vpon the racke for one liffe"[74] which was his principal asset,
worth over a third of his estate. Musical instruments only account for
about five percent of his goods.

William Madock also seems to have had other sources of income
than music. The number and nature of the goods listed raise the
possibility that he was also running an alehouse or a tavern. He had
several rooms to his house, including a hall, two parlours, one of
which is designated as being "in the Row," a gallery over the hall,
another chamber over the parlour, a "streete chamber," and a kitchen
and buttery. He also had a cellar, a brewing house, and a stable. All
these suggest that he was brewing ale to sell and that he was lodging
travelers. Musical instruments, although he had several, formed under
five percent of the total, and the largest single item in the inventory
was £4 for "one fishing boate and one neat & apece of a nett & nett
cord*es*."[75] It would appear that Madock was further supplementing his
income as a city wait by fishing.

Groups and Families of Musicians

Many of the records reveal musicians playing in groups, both
informally and formally. The relationships between musicians are
interesting and sometimes complex. On one level, they are in
competition with each other—a competition which could become
fierce and vituperative, as in the quarrels among the Chester waits (see
chapter II, part 1). Combinations between musicians could lead to
greater rewards, however, as a group would have a greater range of
music and possibly a greater variety of instruments. Although they did
not necessarily command a higher price than individual performers,
groups might have greater opportunities for performance. A group

with a patron would also have a measure of respectability, and for a group without a patron there might be a certain safety in numbers. It is of course difficult to determine who received more, a group or an individual performer, and the number of performers was probably only one of a number of factors determining pay. The Smiths who record in their accounts for 1557–58 that "the Company neuer mett at Tauarne or any howse *with*out musick" paid varying sums for their musical entertainment in that year. They gave twelve pence to "barne a kyndertons mynstrells," eight pence to "the waytmen," and ten pence to two named minstrels, William Luter and Randle Crane.[76] The last named is elsewhere specified as being the company's own minstrel.[77] The waits were therefore receiving less than the two individuals, even if there were only two waits involved. Distinctions in pay evidently could also be connected with the status of the performers, as in 1571–72, when the Smiths paid twelve pence to "the waytes & our musysyens" but only six pence to "mynstrells."[78]

We know most about groups such as the Chester waits and very little about any groups that might have existed outside Chester. There are places, however, which had a concentration of musicians that might well have necessitated cooperation, and there are instances of several musicians of a single surname and location which suggest a family link. This can be seen, for instance, with the Preston family of Warrington that has been mentioned above. Some groupings are clearly fortuitous: the presence of William Hesketh of Aston, Boswicke, a harper, and Morgan Hopton, a stranger, all of whom were presented for piping on the sabbath at Tarporley in 1609, does not suggest that they were an organized group.[79] The fact that Morgan Hopton is specifically described as a stranger suggests that the others were at least known locally even if not locally resident. The occasion was evidently Tarporley Wakes, and the performers were opportunistic. One would expect to find more than one musician at wakes because of the crowds and the increased chances of profit. Combined performances would have been practical in these circumstances.

There are instances in which musicians were accompanied by a "boy" or a "fellow," as at Dodleston in 1620 when David Jones, fiddler, and his companion (by implication fellow-fiddler) were overtaken with drink and unable to return to Chester that evening.[80] "Iohn Harrison & his boy who are fidlers" of "Saughton vpon the hill" (probably Great or Little Sutton on the Wirral) has been mentioned in connection with a procession to Holywell and a day of fiddling and dancing in 1617 (see chapter I).[81] These are the only two mentions of pairs of musicians with an established hierarchy. It is interesting that both instances involve fiddlers. What exactly was the role of the "boy" in these cases? Was he an apprentice, and if so, why do we have no evidence of apprentices for other instruments? Was a second performer desirable because of the relatively soft dynamics of the instrument, or were they playing different types of fiddle—or in combinations such as fiddle and rebec? Two fiddlers also had performed together in 1588. We are actually told something about their performance in this case because of the subject-matter of their song (fiddling is only implied in their occupation), which was about the defeat of the Spanish Armada —a topic only relevant, as far as the court was concerned, because Francis Barlow, "saying let vs not reioice before the victory," objected to the song.[82] Fiddlers did seem to perform in pairs more often than pipers, as far as can be determined.

More established companies of musicians were also in evidence. Thomas Cowper and his company of fiddlers from Shropshire, mentioned above, was one such.[83] The diocesan visitation of 1605 reports another possible company at Rostherne:

> con*tra* Joh*ann*em Cooke
>> for pypinge vpon the sabaoth daie but hee & his companie
>> goinge vsuallie to morninge & eveninge praier[84]

The company here could, of course, refer to the dancers rather than other musicians, but there is possible corroboration in an unlocated jury presentment from 1618 which lists Peter Cook, John Cook, George Ashton, and John Heywood for piping on the sabbath.[85] Peter Cook appears elsewhere in the records in combination with Richard Cross at Over in 1619.[86] John Heywood is described as being of Lostock Gralam, but does not otherwise appear in the records. George Ashton, piper, features in a Quarter Sessions case in 1630 for lodging a stranger who was pregnant. He was apparently resident in Agden at that time.[87] Part of Agden lies in Rostherne parish, and both parts are not far from Rostherne township. Lostock Gralam is further away, and Over further still. It is possible that the group listed in 1618 was not a formal company, and certainly it does not seem to have been a stable arrangement. The appearance of two Cooks raises the possibility of a family relationship, although the surname is not sufficiently rare to be certain.

Some of the smaller towns of Cheshire have a sufficient number of documents associated with them that it is possible to attempt to consider the musical life of the town. Others are surprisingly lacking in information about music. The borough accounts of Congleton are rich in payments to players and bearwards but say very little about musical performances. There are indications that Congleton did not have a strong local music base since on two occasions they had "Calis the musitian" performing at local plays.[88] They had regular drumming at the rushbearing, and there is a John Waringes, minstrel, described as being of Congleton in 1575. Otherwise musicians seem to be visitors to Congleton rather than residents. The visit of a piper in 1624 was sufficiently important to be used as an identifying event for money spent in entertaining the gentry:

> Bestowed by Consente vpon [the said] ^^S*ir* Iohn Brereton and the reste of the gentlemen then in Towne, when the pyper was heare ij s x d^
>
> . . .
>
> paide at mr Robert Buckleys howse for beere bestowed vpon S*ir* Randull manweringe and mr henrie manweringe by consente Two Aldermen beinge theire when the pyper was in Towne   vj d[89]

Musicians at Malpas

The parish registers of Malpas cover a wide area, as the parish comprised twenty-five townships, one of which was over the border in Flintshire. There is also very little information from other sources about minstrels from the parish of Malpas, and no overlap between the parish registers and other sources. This fact serves as a useful reminder of the limitations of the evidence. In spite of the legislation, the licensing system, and the hostility of puritan clergy and magistrates, an individual such as "Iohn Kersleye al*ias* clubfoote Pyper"[90] of Malpas could go through life with no other record of his existence than the registry of his burial. The note "nihil" at the end of the entry indicates that he was a pauper, and his nickname informs us that he was disabled, possibly to an extent which precluded other forms of labor.

Malpas is one of the places that records musicians from earlier than 1500. In 1417, David le Pyper of Malpas, who in addition to his surname is described as a piper, took part in one of a series of riots connected with the collection of a subsidy. The other rioters consisted principally of yeomen, husbandmen, "knaves" (presumably servants), and a few with occupations such as miller or ironmonger. A substantial number are either specified as Welsh or have Welsh names.[91] The piper in this instance seems to have been part of the community, not a marginal figure, but at the lower end of the social scale.

The Malpas parish registers usefully mention musicians from various townships within the parish such as Francis Seaer of Iscoyd, piper, whose daughter was baptized in 1617, and Mr. Woodson of Cholmondeley, organist, who was buried in 1642.[92] Mr. Woodson naturally would appear to have been higher on the social scale, and may in fact have been a known musician. There are two known musicians named Woodson at the time, although the exact date and place of death is not known for either of them. Leonard Woodson, who was an organist and who is presumed to have died c.1641, is perhaps the more likely. He was born c.1565 and became organist at Eton College in 1615. He is mentioned regularly in the Eton accounts until 1641, and appears to have been replaced by 1645. A mention of him in 1647 is probably an error. His death in 1641 is presumed because he is represented in John Barnard's *First Book of Selected Church Musick*, published in that year and purporting to contain no music by a living composer.[93] Another candidate could be Thomas Woodson, who was also a composer, though nothing is known of him after 1605. He became a member of the Chapel Royal in 1581 and in 1605 sold his place to William West of Canterbury.[94] The presence of an organist at Cholmondeley is probably connected with the private chapel of the Cholmondeley family.[95] Although Mr. Woodson may simply have been visiting the family when he died, the wording suggests that he was a resident of Cholmondeley.

The connection of Malpas parish with Wales is found in names such as John Lloyd of Malpas, organ drawer, and Humphrey Lloyd, singer, who had children baptized in 1626 and 1631, respectively. There is no indication whether Lloyd the organ drawer and Lloyd the singer were related, and it is not even clear from which township the latter came. There also seem to have been two musicians named Peacock in Malpas parish: Peacock the fiddler, whose daughter Sisley was baptized in 1637, and Peacock the piper, whose son Humphrey was baptized in 1640.[96] As there was a "humfrey Peacocke ^^thelder^" piping at Tarporley in 1616, this might seem to reveal another family, like the Callys of Chester, who produced more than one generation of musicians, whether the two Peacocks in the records were related or not.

Musicians at Nantwich

Nantwich is a small town in the southeast of Cheshire which in the seventeenth century had a number of resident musicians. The evidence from the parish registers is particularly useful because Nantwich was a small parish, made up for four townships and part of a fifth, all of which are contiguous. A musician whose name appears in the Nantwich parish registers would have been resident within easy reach of the town. The parish registers use the term 'musician' more freely than do the court records, but by no means indiscriminately. Drummers are not described as musicians, although pipers and fiddlers may be, and some of those who are described as musicians seem to have had a genuine claim to the title. There are in all nine individuals who between 1581 and 1648 were resident in Nantwich and who were classified as musical performers of one type or another. The registers provide only very bare details of baptisms, marriages, and burials, and the amount that we know about any one individual varies. Thomas Weedall, musician, was buried in 1607.[97] We do not know if he was young or old, married or single, a long-time resident or an itinerant who happened to die in the parish, or what type of instrument he played. We know only slightly more about Thomas Baker, harper, who was married in 1581 and buried in 1592.[98] In some cases, sparse information in the parish registers is supplemented with information from other sources. Roger Lether, drummer, had a son baptized in 1602.[99] He is not otherwise mentioned in the parish registers, at least prior to 1642, but his petition to the justices of the peace in 1639 informs us that he had served in Queen Elizabeth's wars in Ireland and that he was, in 1639, 87 years old and unable to work. He petitioned for a pension as a maimed soldier (see chapter IV).[100] He would therefore have been born in 1551 or 1552, making him about fifty when his son was baptized. He was still performing in 1619, at age 67, when he was presented at the diocesan visitation "for druminge in the streetes vpon the Saboth daie haueinge not beene at morning nor eveninge prayer the same daie."[101]

Sometimes the bare facts of the parish registers invite speculation. Zachary Gill, musician, had at least five children, but only two sons had their baptisms recorded. One daughter is mentioned as being buried in 1629, and twin daughters, Margaret and Marie, were buried on 9 May 1640. Six days later, on 15 May, Zachary Gill was found drowned in the Weaver. Another son, not otherwise mentioned in the

registers, was buried in 1649.[102] Why were so few of his children
baptized? Was Gill's drowning accident or suicide, and in either case
was it related to the death of his daughters? Gill was not the only
musician to fail to baptize some of his children. William Worrall,
musician, had a son, John, baptized in October 1629 and another,
Thomas, in March 1631.[103] Then in February 1633 he had three
children baptized together: "Dudley, Iane, & Ellen, Children of
william Woorrall musition baptized, besydes .2. not baptized."[104]
Dudley Worrall was buried in 1634, and another son, William, in
January 1635.[105] In May 1636, William Worrall had a son, William,
baptized, who must have been a replacement for the son who died the
previous year. Worrall himself was buried in June 1637.[106] The first
son named William was presumably one of the two who are listed as
"not baptized" in 1633. One would expect him to be older than the
other children, as he has his father's name. There is no indication how
old the children were when they were baptized, but it is unlikely that
Dudley, Jane, and Ellen were triplets, although they could have been
close in age. Worrall therefore had six children who are known from
baptisms, one who is known only from his burial, and two who are
alluded to as not being baptized. Even if the first William was one of
the unbaptized ones, Worrall had at least eight children.

Worrall is particularly interesting because an inventory of his
goods survives which gives us information about his wealth and the
instruments he played. The parish register describes him as a musician,
and that seems to be the most appropriate term, even by Whythorne's
standards. The total worth of his goods as noted above, was £19 8*s*
2*d*—not, perhaps, great wealth, but not absolute poverty either. He
owned several instruments valued at £1 18*s* 0*d*: "One Bandore One
Alferiall one base vyall 3 treble vyall*es* with Instrument books."[107]
These suggest not only that he was a versatile player himself but that
he may not always have played alone. The instruments include at least
half of those required for a "broken consort," which consisted of treble
viol or violin, flute (recorder or transverse flute), bass viol, lute, cittern
and bandora.[108] In addition, the orpharion would have been able to
play the lute part in a consort,[109] though by 1637 the quality of wire
that was available would have required it to be tuned at a lower
pitch.[110] The necessity of playing at different pitches may supply the
reason for Worrall's possession of more than one treble viol.[111]

Worrall had sufficient instruments for a group of six to play at
once, and it may be that this grouping represents an alternative consort

group. The question then becomes whether there were any other known musicians in Nantwich at that time who might have performed with him. Of the ones who were listed at some point as *musician* and whose dates overlap with his, there are Roger Vaughan (who died in 1648), Richard Minshull (possibly, but not necessarily, the same as Richard Minshull, fiddler), and Zachary Gill. John Tompson, musician/piper, who died in 1624, and John Axon, fiddler, who was described as a pauper in 1643, are less likely to have been involved in a consort, although it is not impossible. There is also a John Vaughan, musician, who with others was presented at the Quarter Sessions for riotous assault on William Worrall on 9 January 1632.[112] Worrall is not specified as a musician in this document, but it seems likely that the musician was the one who was meant. John Vaughan does not appear as a musician in the parish registers, although Roger Vaughan did have a son named John who was buried in 1636.[113] A John Vaughan of Nantwich also appears in 1605, when he was recorded as playing the pipe and tabor at Wistaston, and he may or may not have been the same individual.[114] The two Vaughans are perhaps the most likely to have been connected with William Worrall; we at least have a likely connection, albeit antagonistic, between John Vaughan and Worrall, and we also are fortunate enough to have some evidence of Roger Vaughan's status and instrument. A will and inventory for Roger Vaughan of Nantwich, probated in 1648, is evidently that of the musician. His only musical instrument was a bass viol, valued at £1 10s, mentioned specifically in his will.[115] The will is unfortunately damaged, but it would appear that the bass viol is left, along with his house, to his son Roger.

The bass viol which Roger Vaughan owned is more suited to an independent performer than a town wait, who would have been more likely to own a tenor viol (as did William Madock) which could be suspended from the neck and played while walking.[116] Maybe, since he is repeatedly listed in the parish registers as a musician, he was of sufficient means to be a music teacher to the local gentry. In that case, he is also likely to have been performing at social occasions, either as a soloist or in company with another musician such as Worrall or one of the various individuals in Nantwich who had musical instruments in their inventories.

Worrall was entitled to the designation *musician* in that he was musically literate, as can be seen by the inclusion of instrument books in his inventory. The ability to read music was, as we have seen, one of Whythorne's criteria for professional musicianship, and one that some modern scholars use to determine professionalism. Worrall may also, like Whythorne, have been a music teacher. A number of inventories from the same period in Nantwich list instruments such as a cittern in 1618,[117] bandora and viol da gamba in 1607,[118] and bass viol and bandora in 1638.[119] Richard Heyes, gentleman, had no fewer than four lutes when his will was probated in 1622,[120] and in 1625 Edmund Myles had two as well as a "pair" of virginals.[121] His widow still had them in 1627.[122] Virginals, the most popular gentry instrument, appear in a number of inventories.[123] There are unspecified musical instruments at the inn of Edmund Myles in 1640: "Item In the Parlor, the bedsteadees, beddinge, Table, formes, Cubbordes, Chaires, stooles, Coate Armes, and instrumentes of Musicke, and the rest belonginge to the said Parlor xij li xix s iiij d."[124]

The Nantwich inventories list an unusually high number of stringed instruments. Bandoras, citterns, lutes, and viols of various types do appear in documents from other places, but there are no other instances of orpharions, while bandoras also are rare. It is certainly possible that the presence of a teacher of string instruments contributed to their popularity in Nantwich. Henry Wright's will of 1607 left his viol da gamba to his cousin, Richard Minshull. The name is not unusual, and there are two Richard Minshulls specifically connected with music: Richard Minshull, musician, whose son was baptized in 1606,[125] and Richard Minshull, fiddler, living in Pillory Street, playing on Palm Sunday in 1622,[126] and either receiving or being received as an illegal inmate in 1623.[127] They could be the same individual, but if so, he seems to have fallen on hard times. The will of Richard Minshull, gentleman, probated in 1638, makes no mention of musical instruments, but does not include an inventory.[128]

Individual assessments of the value of the musical instruments in Worrall's inventory are unfortunately lacking, but they collectively make up about one-eighth of his estate. The other goods listed show that he did not live in penury. His house apparently had three rooms: the house proper, which was evidently used for cooking and eating; the "Chamber aboue," which contained beds, trunks, boxes, and some luxury items, and the closet, which contained more beds, clothes, and items such as the musical instruments as well as "One lookeing glass with pictures and other thinges," worth 11s 6d. He also possessed a Bible "with some paper Bookes," worth in all eight shillings, and an hourglass worth the same amount. His wearing apparel was appraised at £3, indicating that he had more than the minimum essentials in the way of clothing. The list of furnishings also shows that he lived comfortably in his degree; he had three beds, and the "Six payer of sheet*es* w*i*th other Napperie" listed for the best bed are worth £2. He also had "5 sowed quishions w*i*th seauen other," worth £1 8*s*, and had three chairs, a bench, and three stools.[129] Yet given the fact that he had at least eight children, although not perhaps all living at once, his furniture was sufficient but not lavish. Worrall's case shows what the divide between *musician* and *minstrel* could be; he is clearly settled, not itinerant, literate both verbally and musically, professional and able to afford some small luxuries.

Music Teachers and Apprentices

Many of the pipers and fiddlers performing on greens and at ale-houses were unlikely to have had any formal musical training or to be able to read music, while professional musicians, such as the Chester waits by the late sixteenth century or William Worrall, were able to read music, as the music books in Worrall's inventory indicate. Min-strels also would not have been involved in teaching music. It has already been suggested that the large number of mixed consort instru-ments in gentry and middle-class wills at Nantwich make it possible that Worrall—and perhaps Vaughan—were teachers as well as performers of music. One member of the gentry at Nantwich certainly had a music teacher, although he was not William Worrall. Mr. Handy, who was paid eight shillings a month by Thomas Wilbraham of Nantwich "to teach me musick,"[130] would seem, like Thomas Whythorne, to have had the status of a gentleman as well as being a professional musician.

For professional musicians such as the Chester waits, teaching music was officially limited to their own apprentices. These might often be their sons, as in 1590–91, when, in the dispute over the musical instruments formerly in the possession of Thomas Williams, wait, it was agreed that the instruments will be the property of the two waits, Christopher Burton and William Madock, or the survivor of them. They will also be the property of two of the apprentices: William Williams, the son of Thomas Williams, and Henry Burton, the son of Christopher Burton, if and when they finish their ap-prenticeship and are found "Apt and fitt for the same *serv*inge w*i*thin the said Citie." Otherwise, the instruments are to revert to the city.[131]

Some of these instruments appear in the inventory of goods of William Madock, although it is not clear if he was in fact the survivor (see also chapter II, part 1, and appendix I).

The apprenticeship of a son could be an expense but also a potential source of income to the family. However, Christopher Burton, whose son Henry was an apprentice in 1590–91, found by 1596–97 that he could not rely on his son. Christopher Burton was at this time no longer one of the waits and found it difficult to maintain himself and his "nomber of smale motherles children." He therefore petitioned to be restored to his place as a wait and also that the Assembly would act with regard to his son, who "is by your worships put over to the said waitmen to vse that trade and to saue for his paines & travell certaine Somes of money which your worships intended to be bestowed towards the relef of his poore brethren & susters / he the same boy so wantonly and extraordenaryly daily wasteth his such gaine and money as neith therwith doeth him self good nor any of his."[132] The petition requests that the money due to his son should be paid directly to Burton himself, and, as the Assembly notes that "Mr Maior will take order for the better gouernment of the Boy,"[133] it seems that his complaint was at least felt to be valid.

Burton's petition reveals another vulnerable point of the professional musician. Only a limited number could be official town waits at one time, and their tenure was at the pleasure of the mayor and assembly. Without that steady source of income and the opportunities for other employment that it gave, making a living might be difficult. As the employment opportunities were restricted, it is not surprising that the sons of musicians were not necessarily apprenticed to learn music. John Williams, son of Thomas Williams, musician, was apprenticed in 1624 to Richard Trafford, tallowchandler.[134] John Williams's father appears to have been alive at the time of his apprenticing. Another son of a musical family, Elias Preston, son of James Preston of Warrington, was apprenticed to Christopher Holme of Chester, painter, but ran away. The apprenticing of the sons of musicians to other crafts may have also been a form of social betterment. City waits were, after all, reliant on city patronage, and there was no guarantee that that patronage would continue from one generation to another. Aptitude was also surely a crucial factor in an apprentice musician, since a musically talented father could not guarantee a musically talented son.

The Chester waits did also take apprentices from outside their own families and even from outside the county. Although the sons of Thomas Williams and Christopher Burton are described as apprentices, teaching music to a member of one's own family was probably less formal than regular apprenticeship. The only formal apprenticeship document relating to the Chester waits is for an apprentice from Lancashire (see chapter II, part 1).[135]

Some of the waits were involved with teaching on a less formal basis, and not necessarily simply music. John Taylor, in 1613, apparently was anxious to learn to dance, and applied to Robert Cally for instruction (see also chapter II, part 1).[136] Robert Cally's brother George was also involved in teaching dancing and had some difficulty with rival teachers from outside Chester to the extent that he sought the protection of the Assembly (see also chapter II, part 1). He stressed that he was a native of Chester and a freeman, and that he should therefore have been given preferential treatment over strangers, namely John Farrar, Thomas Squier, Richard Bell, and Nicholas Webster.[137]

The Musician as Lawbreaker

The musical performer was often a lawbreaker simply by virtue of his occupation, particularly after the Tudor vagabondage laws were introduced. At other times, practicing that occupation could be unlawful, if place or time were considered inappropriate by the authorities. The fact that minstrels were seen as part of the community of "dangerous poor" meant that they were often also suspect in other crimes, as can be seen in the cases of Thomas Yemouth and Edward Clarke mentioned above. Since so much of the evidence that survives is in the form of legal documents, it is hardly surprising that musicians should figure frequently as lawbreakers. Yet evidence from parish registers shows that many performers were never cited for breaking the law. Further, the majority of the lawbreaking done by musicians is of the occupational kind—performing on the sabbath, performing in an illegal alehouse, performing at night, and so on. There were, however, some musical performers who were also lawbreakers in a more serious sense.

Before the establishment of parish registers in the sixteenth century and before the opposition to sabbath entertainment associated with the late sixteenth century puritans, there are two principal ways in which a musical performer could be recorded in a document: as a lawbreaker, or in connection with a money transaction. These documents are correspondingly the ones more likely to survive. The very earliest items show minstrels who are apparently not the dregs of society: William le Synger, minstrel, paying sixty shillings (the reason for the payment is unspecified) in 1342–43,[138] Hugh de Birkenhead, harper, as one of four people standing bail (at £20) for John de Buddeston in 1343,[139] and Hugh de Walay receiving a pardon from the Black Prince for purchase of property without the Prince's consent in 1354.[140]

The early criminals among the musical performers can also have been acting as part of their communities. David le Pyper at Malpas and Roger de Croxton and Robert de Overwhitley at Middlewich took part in riots.[141] Their relative status will be discussed in chapter IV, but they were clearly acting as part of a larger communal group and not as independent lawbreakers. The Malpas riot seems to have occurred because the collectors of a subsidy took six oxen and eight cows as part of the assessed subsidy on the villages of Cuddington, Newton, and Oldcastle, all of which are in Malpas parish and adjacent to Malpas township. The church bells were rung at Malpas to summon the rioters, many of whom had Welsh surnames or are even surnamed "le Walsshmon."[142] The three townships are very near the Welsh border, and the riot could in fact have been connected with objection to English taxation. The Middlewich riot was connected with a land dispute and involved men from both a wider geographical area— including one from Shropshire—and social spectrum, with several gentlemen and squires listed as taking part.

The musician could also appear in criminal cases as the victim, as in the case of Robert le Fysher of Nantwich, who in 1404 was indicted for striking Richard de Bulkeley, piper, on the head with a staff so that he fell to the ground.[143] Bulkeley seems to have survived the assault, but John Savage of Bunbury, a minstrel, was less fortunate in 1421 since William, son of Richard le Cowper of Tarporley, shoemaker, was charged with his death. Details of the manner of death are not given.[144]

Crimes of violence, often combined with theft, are probably the most common of the non-occupational crimes with which musical performers are charged in the earlier records. In 1411, Robert de Whyteley, piper, who is very probably the same as Robert de Overwhitley who was involved in the Middlewich riot, was charged with chasing John le Shermon of Shocklach with a bow and arrows and with robbing him of 1s 11d.[145] John Conason of Chester, piper, was indicted in 1428 for not only stealing 2s 2d from Thomas de Madley but also abducting his servant, Agnes Bayly.[146] It is not clear whether the motive for the abduction was sexual or simply to prevent the servant from raising the alarm. These two crimes seem to be opportunistic, not planned in advance, unless Agnes Bayly was an accomplice. A minstrel who was evidently a more serious criminal was found at Witton in 1406. Thomas Pudgeon, minstrel, who had an alias which does not survive completely because of manuscript damage ("Thomas de <...>ley"), was indicted for an armed assault on the home of Richard de Bulkeley. In the course of the assault, he attacked a servant, Agnes, and carried her off against her will. He also carried off and broke open a chest containing £5 worth of goods, a very considerable sum. He additionally forced the servant Agnes to swear not to tell who had taken the chest, although presumably her testimony was later given.[147] Another minstrel, Thomas Fiddler, attacked the house of Roger Mort at Newton by Frodsham on two days in 1488, allegedly with swords, bows, and arrows. Assaulting Mort's servant John Burches, he broke his forearm with a staff and injured his nose.[148] There is no mention of theft, and there may have been some other motive for the attack; however, it no doubt added to the reputation of the minstrel as violent and dangerous.

The idea of the violent, dangerous piper can perhaps be seen in the early career of Richard Metier. In 1597 he already had a reputation as someone who might be hired to do violence. Roger Stathum testified that his master, William Fallowes of Fallowes, who wanted his neighbor and enemy William Burges "knockt," asked him about Richard Metier as a potential assassin:

> And then the said ffallowes said no I would have him to be conninglie knockt, & further said to this examinate that he beinge acquainted with one Richard Mettyre a pyper, one henry davenport & one william Gibson might procure some of them to knocke him downe of his horse, some eveninge as the said Burges should come from Macclesfeild, for sayth he, he vseth to come late home from thence, & said that if they knockt out his braines he Cared not, & said further also, that if the would so doe, he would geve to him that did it xxtie nobles, or xli, so he weare well knockt & said that if it weare knowen an other Countrey weare as good for them as this.[149]

Metier's reputation for violent behavior was probably also a factor in the paternity suit brought by Katherine Lockett against Thomas

Torkington of Siddington in 1623. According to Lockett, Torkington had promised her marriage, but, having got her with child before marriage, refused to acknowledge it. The chancellor of the diocese had granted Lockett a filiation order, and she was required to appear at Prestbury, seven miles from her home, with the testimony of seven respectable women that the child was Torkington's. Siddington is in the large, detached parish of Prestbury. However, before the filiation could be heard "the said Torkinton by himselfe and one Richard Matwioe a pyper. did solicite the greatest *parte* of the women for the filiac*i*on not to be *present* att that tyme. wheruppon the petic*i*on*er* was forced to *procure* a new filiac*i*on, and before the execuc*i*on therof the childe dyed."[150] Torkington is described by Lockett as "a man of greate estate in wealth," but he nevertheless relied on the help of Richard Metier. Torkington turns up in another case involving Metier, this time in connection with the minister John Fletcher.

The petitions against Metier by Mr. Fletcher reveal the antipathy between them and also the different weapons they used against each other. Mr. Fletcher used both the law and the pulpit; he spoke of preaching against "notorious sinners in his Sermon, as namelie, drunckcardes, whoremungers, and such lyke," which might well have included Metier or might at least affect his business as an alehouse-keeper.[151] Metier countered with openly heckling the sermon and asking :

> when will this preacher . . . speake of Cuckoldes intimatinge there-by as the hearers did conceaue not onely to disgrace and scandalize the doctrine and ministerie of the said Iohn ffletcher, but also to brande him w*i*th the ignominious name of a Cuckolde and didst affirme and saie that the said Iohn ffletcher was a Cuckold and that Margaret ffletcher deceased late wiefe of the said Iohn ffletcher had made the said Iohn a Cuckold and that she had Comitted ^^adulterie^ [adulterie] w*i*th one Thomas Torkington. . . .[152]

Metier's offence against Mr. Fletcher was exacerbated by the fact that the latter was a clergyman, and some of the statements attributed to Metier make it clear that Fletcher's vocation contributed to his enmity. At various times, Metier called Mr. Fletcher "a base paltrie, lowsey, drunken beggarie priest," "a woolfe in sheepes Clothinge," and "a palterie fellowe a paltrie knave, a Consciencelesse fellowe, a puritan."[153] He claimed that Mr. Fletcher had "beene senceles, stark-madd and out of his or thy witt*es* and that he Called himselfe Christ or said he was Christ."[154] Metier also mimicked the curate for the entertainment of the customers in his illegal alehouse, and accused him of keeping a bawdy house. His insults are certainly varied, but the accusation of puritanism is in keeping with his apparent anticlericalism. It is very unfortunate that Metier's responses to the articles do not survive, as it would be very interesting to get some context for his remarks about Mr. Fletcher. It is also very difficult to determine when and how the dispute between them began. Were Metier's slanders invented to annoy the curate, or were they a response to Fletcher's sermons, or to his puritanism? Fletcher, in his petition, referred to events which had been going on for the past two years and made reference to Metier's involvement in earlier offences, which had earned him a period of imprisonment in Chester Castle.[155] Metier's involvement in the Lockett-Torkington case would come within the period to which Mr. Fletcher referred and would bear out his picture of him as a deliberate troublemaker.

Metier was also accused of assaulting and beating Thomas Astle, the constable of Siddington, when he was on official business, and of threatening his own wife with a knife.[156] Much of the trouble seems to have been connected with attempts to suppress Metier's illegal alehouse—attempts which he both resisted and evaded. Mr. Fletcher was very probably involved in these attempts, given both the subject matter of the sermon heckled by Metier and Fletcher's presence at a search of the alehouse in May 1624. Metier was not without a certain ability to use the law for his own ends, as can be seen by his refusal to allow the constables to search his alehouse without a warrant.[157]

Metier's remarks in his defense are mainly attacks on the sexual activities of the wives and daughters of his opponents, as the following extracts show:

> Thomas dayne hath tould this Inform*er* That vppon Barnebe day last past, the s*ai*d Matyer standinge bound (as this Inform*er* thinketh<.>) to the good behauio*ur* vsed theise, or such lyke raylinge speeches against and vnto the s*ai*d Thomas dayne; callinge him a Rouge, and that his wyfe was a whore & a Curtall w*i*th such lyke other speeches and layinge his hand on his sword, said, That the said dayne had but one eye, and that hee would plucke out the other, or to such effect:[158]

> And also hee hath sclaundered dyvers honest mens wyves, And hath saide and affyrmed that Iane Lockett, wieffe of Edwarde

Lockett of Siddington aforesaide hath poysoned a bastard Childe
<...> in the Bellie of her daughter Margrett now wieffe to one
Thomas Bockett, And this Metyer being warned by Edwarde
Lockett then Cunstable of Siddington, to Cease from brewinge and
sellinge of Ale, And hee hath Rayled against the Iusti<.>es that
offered to suppresse him, and spoke opprobrious and most wicked
woordes againt some of the Iustices wyves and daughters then
lyinge at London[161]

Richard Metier was bound to the good behavior at the time that he
was threatening Thomas Dayne, and given the other recognizances
mentioning him, probably also at the time that he railed at the
justices.[160] Mr. Fletcher also obtained a warrant against him as a result
of his petition:

vpon the hearing of the said abuses vnto mr ffletcher a warrant was
graunted for the said Metyer comitted to the Castle of Chester to
remayne there three monthes *wi*thout bayle or maynprise, and after
the three monthes ended then to be bound to his good behauiour,
and for his *pe*rsonall appearance at the next gen*er*all Sessions <...>
&c /[161]

Despite being bound to keep the peace after being committed to
Chester Castle, Metier does not seem to have changed his ways. He
was presented for slander and disturbing the peace at Swettenham by
the jury in 1631,[162] and there is an order for his arrest in 1632.[163] He
was probably also the Richard Metier of Swettenham, husbandman, for
whom a warrant was issued in 1634. Apparently his age and promises of
good behavior had moved the justice to allow him time to find sureties. The
warrant was issued because Metier took advantage of the justice's kindness
to go into hiding, and he continued to annoy his neighbors by various
means.[164] By 1634, he might well have appeared an old man. He had first
appeared in 1597, and, as he was considered capable of physical violence, he
must have been fully grown at the time. Even if he were in his late teens in
1597, he would have been about fifty-five in 1634, an age that would have
been considered "old" at the time but likely exacerbated by a life of violence,
poverty, and intermittent imprisonment.

Richard Metier is an example of how much trouble an unruly
musician could make aside from actually performing music. At no point
was he presented for piping on the sabbath or even for piping in his
alehouse at unseasonable hours. Yet, as noted above, the fact that he

claimed to be a licensed piper was regarded as contributing to his unruly behavior.[165] It may be questioned whether he ever did practice as a piper, or whether he simply obtained the licence because he saw it as a protection from the law. Was he, in fact, a piper who became a lawbreaker, or a lawbreaker who became a piper?

His brother John, also a piper, seems likewise to have had the attitude that the law could safely be broken if one had the protection of a licence or a patron:

> That Iohn metire pyper, brother to Richard metire, commyinge vnto the howse, of the said hvmffray Shawcrosse, did say that he had alreadie killed a man, & by the good helpe of his mayster, had gotten his pardon. yett notwithstandinge, he said that when he did know Thomas Dale he would kill him, for slanderinge of his brother Richard, to be a theefe, which woordes he would not endure. Theise speches weare spoken, about a monthe agone, in the howse aforesaid.[166]

It is not clear to what extent the confidence of the Metiers was justified. Did John Metier (who came from Staffordshire, not Cheshire, and therefore did not have the protection of a minstrel's licence) really kill a man and get a pardon by the help of his master, and if so, what were the circumstances? Was he a liveried minstrel, or did he get protection because his master was in some way approving of the killing, as might have happened to Richard Metier at Chelford in 1597? What protection did the piper's licence actually give to Richard Metier? Despite the licence, or possibly at a time at which he was not licenced, Metier was evidently subject to the punishments decreed in the Statute of Vagabonds. He was "maymed and beatton," which suggests that he was not only whipped, the standard punishment, but also branded as a repeat offender.

The potential for violence from some of the pipers and minstrels was certainly real enough, and those who encountered threats from them took them seriously. In 1612, William Pulford of Littleton complained to the justices of the peace:

> Iohn Browne of Littleton aforesaid in the same Countye Bagpyper maligninge your Oratour hath diuers tymes made reporte vnto his wyfe & others that he would runne your oratour thrugh with a sworde, sayinge, A man is but a blowe, and often tymes endeauored to do ye same when your oratour was Constable of Littleton, but

that he was stayed by neighbours that held him, and after the tyme
of his office of Constableshippe beinge expired the sayd Brown and
his wyfe mett your oratour in the high waye, and there did assault
him and thrust him into a dytch purposinge there to haue murdered
him, in which assault your sayd orator in his owne defence fortuned
to giue the sayd Browne a scarr on ye heade with his dagger &c.[167]

Like John Metier, Browne expressed an indifference to the commission—and, by implicaton, the consequences—of murder. He may, of
course, have been simply threatening with no intention of acting on his
threats. The Littleton case likewise is indicative of the enmity that
existed between the pipers and the constables.

Actual murder involving musicians was rare, although there are two
cases in the sixteenth century. In 1532–33, John Crewe of Chester, a
singingman, had to flee to St. Werburgh's Abbey for sanctuary after
killing Thomas Duke, who was himself a felon, with a knife.[168] A
minstrel was involved in a murder in 1561, but the document is
damaged to such an extent that it is not clear whether he was the
murderer or simply a witness.[169] In both cases, a violent quarrel or
assault resulted in the death of one of the parties; the impression is not
of a premeditated act.

Thomas Dutton, servant to the mason Robert Clare, was in 1621
the victim of a violent robbery by a piper who was also adept at mani-
pulating the law:

your petitcioner beinge at Lathom workinge for the right honourable
the Earle of Derbie and Sendinge his servant ^^Thomas dutton^
vpon the first day of Sept i6i9 beinge [monday] wednesday &
Warington market day to fetch certaine tooles to worke withall one
Thomas Asbie a piper in the eveninge of the same day meetinge the
said Thomas dutton in the Kinges high way did feloniously set vpon
him and tooke his hatt from him and wounded him very greivously
soe that your peticioner was fayne to keepe him eight weeks vpon his
handes payinge ij s vj d a weeke for his diet, & xxiiij s for Curinge
him; And your peticioner vpon the eight of Ianuary last beinge
Monday beinge in Stretton at the howse of one Thomas Millington
the said Asbie and one Iohn Hale a piper Challenginge a Staffe your
peticioner had in his hand to be the staffe of the said Asbie,
alleadginge that the said Thomas dutton had taken yt from him at
the tyme the said Asbie soe wounded him And therevpon did flinge
your petiticioner downe a paire of Staires & broke a ribb in his syde
feloniously tooke from him 4 s 6 d in money

> Soe yt is right Wor*s*hip*fu*lls That *you*r petic*ione*r hath had
> diu*ers* warrants for thapp*re*hendinge of them butt neu*er* cold gett
> them attached and the said Asbie hath lately most vniustly comensed
> an acc*i*on of C*lai*m ag*ainst* your petic*ione*r in Halton Court, &
> Caused him to be taken w*it*h a Capias wherevpon he remayned in
> prison twoe dayes & onely of purpose to keepe *you*r petic*ione*r from
> the Assizes for feare of Indittinge the said Asbie[170]

The claim against Clare in Halton Court (presumably the manor court
for the barony of Halton) would prevent him from appearing at the
assizes, so that the case against Asbie would fail. It argues a superficial
knowledge of the law but also that Asbie was settled enough to be able
to commence an action against Clare. The most dangerous minstrels
seem not to be, as the authorities apparently thought, the vagrants with
no fixed abode but those with a definite dwelling place, a local identity
and reputation, and possibly local patronage.

The puritans were concerned, as indicated in chapter I, with the
effect of alehouse music on the morals of others, and they sometimes
tended also to assume that musicians generally were themselves morally
lax. While not concerning a minstrel but a singingman, sexual mis-
conduct is mentioned in the case of Robert Bower in 1546–47: "The
Jury p*re*sentyth that Marery Redrowe doith kepe badry in hyr howse
that ys to saye betwext Robart bower syngyngman & Jane Chaunterell
late none & the said Robart bower beyng a maryed man etc."[171] There
is also a case of adultery with a piper's wife in 1638,[172] and a case of
bigamy in Rostherne parish in 1590–91.[173] Yet generally speaking the
musicians seem to have been involved in such cases tangentially because
of their music rather than as the principal defendants, as when Old
Towers the piper played for an adulterous couple at an alehouse in
Alvanley.[174] A possible extension of music as an accompaniment for
illicit affairs was the "lewd marriage" which John Tompson, minstrel,
and Allen Wright were charged with making at Nantwich in 1613.[175]
This probably refers to a mock-marriage performed in an alehouse;
Wright, whose occupation is not specified, was evidently the principal
actor, with the minstrel (probably the same John Tompson who is
described as a piper in the parish register) assisting him.

The late sixteenth and early seventeenth centuries saw an increasing
tendency for attempted governmental control over a wide range of activities. The brunt of the responsibility for enforcement fell on the local
authorities, primarily the justices of the peace and the constables. Local
clergy and churchwardens also had a responsibility to report moral

offences at the Visitations or to the Consistory Court. The attitude of the constables or churchwardens towards alehouse music and performing on the sabbath was therefore of great importance since they were responsible for reporting offences. It is hardly surprising to find acrimony between the alehousekeepers and performers on one hand and the constables and local clergy on the other. Some of the problems encountered by constables trying to enforce the justices' orders are discussed in chapter 1. However, it is also not uncommon to find the constables or churchwardens being reported for encouraging, participating in, or even initiating alleged offences such as sabbath or alehouse performances. In 1620, the constables of Lostock presented their fellow constables for sponsoring music on the sabbath in an alehouse:

> The Counstables of Lostock doe pr*es*ent, Thom*as* wyn<...>ton [Adam] and Adam H<...>gkinson of ^lostocke^ being constab<..> for wyningto<.> howse & showld haue seene good orders kept notw*i*thstanding The sayd Thom*as* wynington & Adam hodgkinson did warne A great tumult of people to meet at the sayd wyningtons howse vpon the ixth day of Ianuary last past being the saboath day & there w*i*th a fidler did keepe much disorder all night
> I*te*m wee doe pr*es*ent Thom*as* Allyne the fidler who was not at the church nether morneing nor Evening & would not be taken vp by the sayd constables but gaue them yll word*es*.[176]

Constables could themselves be charged or fined for failing to enforce the laws, as in the case of James Smithe, who was fined for not arresting a piper playing on the sabbath because he was told that the company had permission from Mr. Dutton of Hatton.[177] As well as constables who were actively encouraging sabbath performances or traditional activities such as wakes, there must also have been those who were simply unable to enforce their commands. At Hatton in 1640 both the constables and the justices had difficulty with an alehousekeeper who refused to cooperate: "And a warrant being formerly grantd by the R*igh*t wor*ship*f*u*ll S*i*r George Booth Kn*igh*t & Barro*net* against the said Renshaw to bring him before him to answeare the pr*e*misses hee in contempt refused accordingly to come contrary to the Kings M*aj*esties Lawes & Statut*es* in such Cases pr*o*uided" (see chapter I).[178]

Restraining individual performers could be difficult if they chose not to cooperate. Binding an individual over to keep the peace was probably the most common form of restraint, and a number of recognizances for musicians exist. These could be aimed at specific quarrels between individuals or at specific incidents such as when Thomas Hale of Ince was required to appear at the assizes and "answere his beinge an Aleseller his enterteining of pypers and singgers dansinge and fightinge in his howse in the night tyme vppon the Saboth daye at a wake tyme."[179] An individual could refuse to enter into a recognizance, although at a risk, as when certain offenders at Shotwick were "apprehended & committed to the Castle of Chester for that they refused to enter into Recognizance for their good behaviour & appearance before his Majesties Iustices of Assize, where they continued for foure dayes, before they would be bound, to their good behaviour geveinge fourth threatninge speaches against vs that they would sue vs in the Starrechamber & elswhere."[180]

As the career of Richard Metier shows, some individuals simply chose to ignore their own recognizances while making full use of those which bound others. Imprisonment could and did sometimes follow where recognizances were unsuccessful, but a good many cases seem to have gone no further than binding over, even when this was clearly not working.

Music as a Weapon

One final role of music, usually connected with amateur performers, was that wherein music—or a musical instrument— formed the weapon with which an individual was attacked. This could be a form of social protest, as possibly in the horn-blowing incident at Shotwick, where, as we have seen, the objections to Mr. Burrows as a preacher may have been connected with the fact that he had an illegitimate child.[181] A more common form of musical attack was the making of songs or rhymes about an individual. This might be an expression of disapproval directed at behavior that had otherwise gone unpunished, but it could also be a means of spreading slander. In 1620, the jury at Middlewich presented "Rondle walker and Ione walker and antilie linge of middleweiche in the Countie of Chester laborores for makinge of rimes and tellings of false liyes and [a] breeders of dicention amonge neighbours: and ales biccle of the same towne for the same."[182] Also in 1620, Thomas Hough petitioned against a potentially violent vagabond:

Sheweth vnto your good worships That one Randull Houfeild (who is a Common drunkard & a dissolute lyver hauinge noe certeyne place of aboade) hath bene formerly Committed to the howse of

Correction & afterward*es* to the Castle of Chester for sundry
disorders ^^by him com*m*itted^ against yo*u*r said petitioner. And
beinge now sett at libertie, is so farre from beinge bettered by his
former punishment*es*, that he is growne much more insolent [th] in
his vile Courses, then ever hertofore, threatninge to haue yo*u*r
petitioners bloud & [..] therfore in the night tyme hath sundry
tymes of late [ly] layne about yo*u*r petitioners howse, & in his
ground*es*, and hath made rymes against yo*u*r petitioner & songe
theym amongest his neighbo*u*rs, and hath vowed amongest theym
that he wold haue his lyfe.[183]

The great danger with the songs or rhymes is that they would
become popular, sticking in people's memories and increasing the
damage done by the original slander. Professional musicians could have
had a role in spreading such songs. Stephen, bishop of Winchester,
complained that "Players also & Minstrels railed of me, & others made
ballads & Rhymes of me. but never man had just cause to complain of
any of my sayings, doings, or preachings, or to my knowledge did,
otherwise than before."[184] It is impossible to tell from the surviving
documents which cases were slanderous attacks and which were expressions of communal disapproval. The latter is possibly the case at
Manchester in 1586, when William Stanley sued Elizabeth Mylnes for
defamation. Two children did the actual singing, but they were supported by Mylnes, who sang a song that was recognized by the deponent
as being popularly associated with his master William Stanley. The
rhyme seems to allude to adultery on Stanley's part since it "touched
duckworth wiefe" in connection with him.[185] The song was then taken
up and sung, defiantly and pointedly at the Stanley household, by
Elizabeth Mylnes, who was a neighbor. Whether her action was simply
malicious or whether music was being used as a form of censure is not
capable of proof, but it is clear that music was being used as a weapon
here.

III
MUSIC AND THE GENTRY

Patronage

The role of the gentry in the musical life of Cheshire has three main aspects: as enforcers of the legislation against itinerant musicians, as patrons, and as performers of music. It is principally the two latter aspects that will be discussed in this chapter. However, the involvement of the Dutton family of Dutton and its special responsibility for licensing minstrels in Cheshire—an important right in view of the national legislation aimed at controlling minstrels—also requires attention here.

The Statute of Vagabonds recognized the tradition of minstrels as liveried retainers of the nobility and gentry who were entitled to the protection of their masters. 'Minstrel' itself derives from a term for minor servants of the king.[1] One of the earliest mentions of a specific musician in Cheshire possibly illustrates this type of master-man relationship. In 1354, Edward, the Black Prince, issued a pardon (in both French and Latin)[2] under his privy seal to Hugh de Walay, harper, for Hugh's purchase of a life-interest in land of which the prince was tenant-in-chief. The land, a messuage of two acres with two acres of park and rents of twenty shillings, was in Foulk Stapleford. Hugh de Walay paid a fine of 6*s* 8*d*, and although he does not appear on extant lists of royal minstrels, the whole transaction is reminiscent of royal methods of rewarding retainers.

On the whole, however, the evidence for liveried minstrels in Cheshire is sparse. This is partly because Cheshire is a county of gentry rather than nobility. There are few households of sufficient status in the medieval and early modern periods to have maintained a large retinue, and disappointingly few household accounts have survived from the earlier period. The Legh family of Lyme Hall apparently had household musicians in the time of Sir Piers Legh (1541–90), but by the time of his grandson, Sir Peter Legh (1590–1636), only a piper was recorded. The evidence in this case comes only from an antiquarian source, which refers to an household account book, now missing.[3] The change from a band of musicians to a single piper may reflect a change in family fortunes or in the respective propensity to spend of Sir Piers and Sir Peter. But it probably also reflects both a change in musical taste from formal patronage of liveried musicians to private amateur performance by the gentry themselves—and a decline in the size of gentry households. Had we more household accounts from an early period the picture might be different.

The Minstrel Court

Probably the most important single form of patronage in Cheshire was the Dutton Advowry of Minstrels, or Minstrels' Court, which has already been noticed in chapter I. Importantly, the Duttons were involved in the supervision and control of minstrels in Cheshire throughout the period for which we have evidence. Their control was significant enough, and their claim to it solid enough, for their rights to be explicitly reserved in the Statute of Vagabonds:

> Provided alwayes, That this Acte or any Thing therein conteyned, or any aucthoritye thereby given, shall not in any wyse extend to dysheneryte prejudice or hinder John Dutton of Dutton in the Countye of Chester Esquier, his Heires or Assignes, for towching or concerninge any Libertye Priviledge Preheminence Aucthoritie Jurisdiccion or Inheritaunce which the sayd John Dutton of Dutton nowe lawfully useth or hathe, or lawfully may or ought to use within the Countye Palatyne of Chester and the County of the Cytye of Chester, or eyther of them, by reason of any anncient Chartres of an Kinges of this Land, or by reason of any Prescription of other lawfull Usage or Tytle whatsoever.[4]

This provision was continued in subsequent versions of the Act, although in 1601 a conditional clause was added:

> And towchinge the same Proviso concerning the saide John Dutton, Be it enacted by Auchtoritie of this presente Parliament, That the same Provysion shall contynue and remaine in force to the ende of one yeere nexte ensuynge the firste day of this presente Parliament and no longer; Excepte before the ende of the saide yeare the saide John Dutton or his Heires shall procure the Lorde Chiefe Justice of the Pleas before the Queenes Highnesse to be holden, and the Lorde Chiefe Justice of the Common Pleas, and the Lorde Chiefe Baron of her Majesties Courte of Exchequer, or

two of them, upon hearinge his Allegac*i*ons and Proofes, to make Certificate into her Majesties Courte of Chauncerie that the saide John Dutton or his Heires oughte lawfully, (if no Statute against Rogues or Beggars had byn made) by Charter Tenure or Pre-scripc*i*on, to use have and exercise such Libertie of lycencynge Mynstrels as he claymethe and usethe; And that the said Certificate be inrolled in her Majesties saide Courte of Chancerie within the said yeere: And if he or his Heires shall pr*o*cure such Certificate as aforesaide, then be it enacted by the Aucthoritie of this p*re*sente Parliament, That the same P*ro*vision shall alsoe contynue in force untill the ende of the firste Session of the nexte Parliament.[5]

The Duttons' proofs were satisfactory, as the clause protecting their rights is retained in the form of the statute promulgated in 1603–04 which refers to the section quoted above:

An Acte intituled An Acte for the [punishment] of Rogues Vagabondes and Sturdie Beggers, with this Provison to be annexed thereunto, by authoritie of this p*re*sent Parliament, That the saide laste mentioned Acte, nor any thing therein contained, shall im-peach avoide prejudice or restraine such Libertie and Inheritance as John Dutton of Dutton in the Countie of Chester Esquire, and his Ancestors (whose Heire he is) have lawfullie used and exercised, in allowinge Minstrels in the Countie Palantine and Countie of the Citie of Chester, and for governement of Minstrels there, and keepinge a Court yeerlie for that purpose.[6]

The Duttons had similarly held onto their privileges when earlier at-tempts were made to establish a national system for controlling min-strels: in 1449 when Henry VI authorized a commission of royal minstrels, and in 1469 when Edward IV established a minstrels' guild. The Duttons benefited financially from the licensing system, which required the minstrels to pay four pence each and also to present the Heir of Dutton with four flasks of wine ("Lagenas vini") and "unum Lanciam," which may be translated as either a plate or platter (from *lanx, lancis*) or a small lance (from *lancea, lanceae*, which becomes *lancem* in the accusative).[7] The purpose or significance of either object is not clear.

The licensing date of 24 June coincides with the Midsummer Fair and Midsummer Show at Chester, an event that would attract min-strels from all over the country—a convenient occasion for the licensing even without its traditional association with the rescue of the Earl of Chester. The advowry of minstrels was listed as part of the Dutton property in the fifteenth century. Inquisitions post mortem in 1433 and 1446 list the advowry of minstrels among the assets of the estate. The value of it as a property varied: £5 "repris sex solidos & octo denar'" ("holding back 6s 8d") in 1433; in 1446, only eight pence was held back, and the value was alluded to being as it has been in previous years, but not specifically listed.[8] A reference in 1474 to the inquisition post mortem at the death of Laurence Dutton of Dutton in 1392 gives the value as only twenty shillings.[9] During the minority of Laurence Dutton (1474–1527), who succeeded his father in 1476, commissions to hold the Minstrels' Court were given to various groups of individuals, including the Abbot of St. Werburgh's and the Mayor of Chester.[10] Laurence Dutton of Dutton was the last direct male heir, and after his death there was a protracted dispute between Sir Piers Dutton of Hatton, the next male heir, and the daughters and co-heirs of Thomas Dutton of Dutton, Laurence Dutton's uncle.[11] The dispute was finally resolved by a division of the family lands in 1534, at which time Sir Piers Dutton received the advowry of minstrels as part of his share.[12] A list which is undated (but attributed to c.1534) of lands and tenements of the Duttons of Dutton assigns the granting of the advowry of minstrels to a deed dated 18 Edward III (1344–45).[13] Ormerod's reference to it clearly shows that this was not the original grant: "Robert Monning of Tatenhale grants to Thomas de Dutton and his heirs all the magistracy of minstrels, cùm omnibus pertinentiis, prout in chartâ originali pleniùs continetur. Lib. C. fol. 158, h. I conceive he was but a feofee" ("with all appurtenances, as is more fully contained in the original charter").[14] Sir Peter Leycester, writing in the mid-seventeenth century, assigns the original grant to the reign of Richard I, and the events puzzlingly to "about ye reign of King John."[15] Richard Rastall estimates a date c.1210–14,[16] which makes the Cheshire court both the earliest known organization of minstrels in England and the longest surviving.

Leycester's account describes the ceremony attendant on the licensing of minstrels, at least in his day:

> The Heirs of Dutton Enjoy this power ouer ye Minstralcy even to yis Day. And euery Midsummer Day (being Chester-Fair) Dutton, or his Deputy in a solemn Manner rides thro ye City, attended by all ye Minstrels of Cheshire, playing before him on yer seueral

Instrum*entes*, to St Iohn's Church; where a Court is kept, for y*e*
Renew*ing* of y*er* Licences, under y*e* Hand, & Seal of y*e* Lo*rd*
Dutton, or his Stewa*rd*; w*i*thout w*hi*ch none ought to use y*e*
Ministralcy Eith*er* in y*e* Citie, or County of Chester.[17]

In 1540, the Midsummer licensing of the minstrels coincided
with the marriage of two of the daughters of Sir Piers Dutton. The
brides were brought from Dutton Hall; then on their return the
steward of Dutton met them "at Flookers=brook=bridge . . . attended
by the Pursevant and Standard : bearer of that Family, each properly
habited, and having the several Insignia used at that Midsummer
solemnity, preceded by all the licensed Musicians, with white scarves
across their shoulders, rank'd in pairs, and playing ^^on^ their several
instruments, this procession marched before the Gentlemen and their
Guests, quite thorough the city, to their respective Mansions where
plentifull Entertainment was provided on that occasion."[18]

Although the musicians in the 1540 procession have the appearance of household retainers rather than alehouse minstrels, there
was an ambiguity about the breadth of the original right to license,
which had specifically included prostitutes and shoemakers: "The
anc*ient* Roll of y*e* Barons of Halton s*ai*th, y*at* y*e* Rabble consisted of
plaiers, Fidlers, & Shoomakers: But y*e* Deed mentions ^^only^
Letchers, & Whores: Such loose, & debauchd p*er*sons, drink*ing* w*i*th
y*er* Sweet-hearts in y*e* Fair, as could be gott together: [out] ^which^
Tract of Time and Custome | Custome hath alterd, & reduc'd only to
Minstrels, & com*mon* Fidlers; as necess*ary* Atten=dants on Revellers
in Bawdy-Houses & Taverns."[19]

Richard Rastall argues that a licensing system was already in effect
when Lacy took his rabble army to rescue the Earl of Chester.
Occupations which did not rent booths at the fair—prostitutes and
shoemakers as well as minstrels—would have had to pay a licence fee
for the right to ply their trade. Rastall suggests that these licences may
already have been operating for the entire year since otherwise Lacy
would not have had sufficient authority to compel his army to leave
the profitable fair, march thirty miles, and face the Welsh.[20] This
would help to explain the discrepancy in dates in Leycester's version
of events: a licensing system for minstrels and other itinerant vendors
at the fair was set up in Richard I's reign (1189–99), but the rescue of
the Earl of Chester did not take place until c.1210–14. Leycester's
assumption that minstrels and fiddlers (note the distinction between

the two) are "necessary attendants" in brothels and taverns shows as clearly as Whythorne's fulminations how the status of the minstrel had fallen. It also shows why the term 'musician' might come to be preferred by performers.

The Dutton licensing system was aimed at the lower end of the musical profession, the type of performer who would be found at wakes, fairs, and alehouses. It seems to have worked reasonably well as a system despite some few who abused their privileges. Enforcement was not only left to the Duttons by themselves, however, as shown by a recognizance from 1563–64 that records the Chester mayoral court acting to impose the licensing rules. James Gill was bound for the sum of £10 to appear at the Minstrels' Court and pay his fines:

> The condicion of this Recognizance is suche that if the abouebounden James gill be and personally appere before John dutton Esquier master & conducter of all & singler the Minstyrells within the countie & cytie of chester or his Lefull deputie or deputes vpon the fest of St John Baptiest next comyng after the dat of these presentes at chester within the countie of the Cittie of chester at the court then & their holdon befoore the seid John or his Lefull deput or deputes to Answer to all such fynes as then shalbe Layd against That then etc or elles etc.[21]

The Duttons were evidently also able to attach conditions to the licences. As we have seen above, John Bruen of Bruen Stapleford, a nephew of John Dutton of Dutton[22] who was raised in his household, later prevailed upon his cousin Dutton to forbid minstrels to play on the sabbath.[23] The record shows that the Dutton licensing system was respected as legally binding and enforceable by other members of the gentry and magistracy. The reference to Richard Platt of Tattenhall "abusinge his liberty of pipinge" by playing on the sabbath in 1620 (see chapter I)[24] certainly suggests that he was in possession of a licence which prohibited sabbath playing. Although the phrase may simply denote performing at unlawful times, namely on the sabbath, it is unusual in prosecutions for sabbath infringement.

The puritan gentry must have doubted, perhaps with good reason, the effectiveness of existing laws in suppressing performances on the sabbath and hence generated the concern to have the Dutton licences specifically forbid Sunday performances. There may be an indication here of confusion in the popular mind between the relative authority of the law and the licence. If pipers such as Platt felt that their security lay in the Dutton licence, which gave them rights in spite of the various statutes against vagabonds, then the licence was the place to spell out any restrictions on those rights. There may even have been confusion over who was entitled to grant licences, if the claim for a "tolleracion" from Mr. Dutton of Hatton that fooled the constable in 1617 (see chapter I) traded on the Dutton name. The fact that the licences specifically forbade playing on the sabbath meant that the authorities could simply rescind the minstrel's licence, a quicker sanction than was provided by the law. An unlicensed performer would also become subject to the vagabond laws, which could be enforced against him if necessary, as may have happened to Richard Metier.

All of this was part of the ongoing attempt by the puritans to suppress activities such as music and dancing on the sabbath—an attempt that was to some extent frustrated by James I's *Book of Sports*, initially issued for Lancashire in response to appeals against the puritan suppression of sports in that county and subsequently extended to cover the entire country. The addition to the Dutton licences gives the appearance of a connection with the initial attempt to suppress sabbath entertainment before 1614,[25] against which the *Book of Sports* was to be directed. It may have been subsequently used in an attempt to circumvent the provisions of the *Book of Sports* by making use of the recognized local licensing system.

In addition to their special role in licensing minstrels, the Duttons were also patrons of music in the sense of having musicians as members, even if nominal, of their households. Edmund Cally, one of the Chester dynasty of musicians, described himself in 1575 as "servant to the said John Dutton esquier."[26] Other members of the Cally family were servants of other important local magnates. The brothers Robert and George Cally served, respectively, the Savage family and the Earl of Derby. At least on one occasion Mr. Dutton's servants seem to have objected to performance by other musicians:

> John Barton of the said Cittie of Chester Tallowchanler examined saith That vppon midsommer euen last as this examinate with the reste of his Companie & other Companies of the said Cittie were walkinge together through the streetes hauinge before them iij musitioners with vialls [before them] playinge accordinge to an auncient Custome, there Came ij or iij of mr Duttons men of dutton vnto them and tooke the instrumentes from the musicke whereuppon this examinate nor anie other of his Companie made

noe resistaunce but to p*re*uent anie rumor or contention wente
immediatlie & complayned to mr maior and hee required him this
exa*mina*te to wish mr duttons men to redeliuer the instrumen*tes*
vnto the musicke againe, and this exa*mina*t did then goe vnto them
and signified vnto them what mr maior had Commaunded, and
that one of the iij whose name this exa*mina*te knoweth not, thrust
him w*i*th his hannd uppon the brest and sayd what should wee
talke w*i*th such a skervie boy as this, & did then strike him w*i*th his
hannd vppon the face, and inforced thereby his nose to bleed, and
did strike him w*i*th a rodd vppon the legg*es*, and this exa*mina*te did
then goe towards him and the man then offered to drawe his
sword, and thereuppon other compan<.> Came vnto them, but
this exa*mina*te sayth hee did neither haundle his <.> sword or by
anie meanes ^^did^ breake the same, neither knoweth who did it,
and moore sayth not.[27]

Mr. Dutton's servants were unlikely simply to have been licensed
minstrels objecting to a performance by unlicensed ones. It is possible,
if Edmund Cally were one of them, that there was a dispute between
the Chester musicians and "foreign" musicians over lucrative guild
business. The occasion was evidently the Midsummer Watch, when
the civic authorities and the various guilds marched in procession.
This event would have attracted performers from outside the city, and
the waits would not have been able to provide musicians to march with
every guild. However, other factors may have been involved—for
example, Mr. Dutton's men may have been involved in some quarrel,
either on their own behalf or their master's, which had nothing to do
with music. The term 'servant' covers a range of relationships. Clearly
members of the Chester waits who were also servants to prominent
members of the gentry were not expected to be in regular attendance
on their masters. They may only have had a role within the city of
Chester.

Both the protection of a patron and the protection of a licence
were invoked by minstrels in Cheshire, and we can see these operating
in one family. Richard Metier, who has already been mentioned (see
chapters I and II), evidently had at some point a licence as a minstrel
if the phrase "since this Metyer was p*ro*ferrd to be A pyper" indicates,
as I think, a point at which he received official recognition of his status
as a piper.[28] Metier's identity as an arrogant and contentious person is
definitely associated, at least in the petitioner's mind, with his acquisition of official status. While this may reflect primarily John

Fletcher's negative view of pipers in general, it may also indicate that Metier felt that he had some protection as a result of his licence. It is worth noting that he is never prosecuted for any offence connected with his role as a piper. He does not pipe on the sabbath or at unseasonable times. There are probably more documents dealing with him than with any other Cheshire musician except the Chester waits, but for all the evidence that we have, there is no actual proof of his pipe playing other than the clear though not consistent identification of him as a piper, and this kind of identification may only reflect the status of his licence. Other documents from 1624 refer to him as *yeoman* or *alehousekeeper*, and it may be that he lost his minstrel's licence as a result of Mr. Fletcher's lawsuit, making him liable to the penalties, including whipping and branding, specified in the Statute of Vagabonds.

One should, however, not make too much of the silence of the records about Metier's piping. Music-related activities would not be regarded as very serious crimes, and Metier's other activities would provide more than enough infractions with which he might be charged. Nevertheless, there may have been a certain advantage of having a minstrel's licence to individuals such as Metier since it protected him from the vagabond laws, for one thing, and gave him a recognized role, however marginal, in the community—a role which might serve as a cover for less acceptable activities.

Richard's brother John Metier was resident in Biddulph, Staffordshire, and would therefore be beyond the authority of the Dutton licences. He claimed, however, to have a master who had sufficient influence to protect him, for he said "that he had alreadie killed a man, & by the good helpe of his mayster, had gotten his pardon."[29] It is unfortunate that he does not give the name of his master or any details of the alleged killing since without this information it is impossible to judge the truth of his claim. However, whether John Metier is making an empty boast or not, his story must have been at least plausible enough to be considered a genuine threat. If it were impossible for a piper to have killed a man and to get a pardon through the influence of a patron, there would be no point in trying to make such a threat. Both the patronage system and the licensing system could be abused, and they were. In a positive sense, they offered protection for musicians, who were in a socially, legally, and economically vulnerable occupation. The official criminalization of musicians in the Statute of Vagabonds meant not only that musicians became criminals, but also that, because of the protection afforded by patronage and minstrels' licences, criminals had reason to become musicians.

Sponsorship

Another form of patronage seems to have become more popular in the later sixteenth and early seventeenth centuries. In this arrangement, the musician would not be financially dependent on a single individual. He might travel from one great house to another, as the liveried minstrels did, but would be on more familiar terms with his host. Henry Lawes, a Gentleman of the Chapel Royal, was also a music-teacher to the Earl of Bridgewater's children and therefore available to compose the music for Milton's *Comus* when it was performed at Ludlow Castle on 29 September 1634.[30] But he had visited Lyme Hall in Cheshire, as a guest of Sir Peter Legh, and wrote to him in terms which suggest that he was confident of his welcome. This letter, which is dated from London, 5 February 1635, may indicate that Lawes had visited Lyme Hall the previous summer or autumn when he was in the Northwest for the production at Ludlow Castle. The letter anticipates a return visit:

> Noble S*i*r
> I Am Asham'd my man should be A president of Ciuill respect vnto his Master; but the sev'rall Object<.> And diversity of vnlooked for Occasions (y*a*t Enterpose, And that I daily meet w*i*th) where I Move And haue my beinge, doe soe Often divert me from My best Intentions, that I must Of for<.>e be Liable to much Censure, And in perticular <...> y*ou*r pardon, that I haue not let loose my respects, & <.>mble Thankfullnes to you Longe since for y*e* good welcom & many fauors I receaud from you when I was at Lyme but you haue A Noble way to Oblige all y*a*t make Adress vnto you. I must Ingeniously Confess, I never went more willingly to Schoole, or Euer found better Conversation in A Dog=ken*n*ell then at Lyme whyther I could more willingely retorne (if my fate would guide me) then to Any part of y*e* principallitye I shall be bound for this sum*m*er. but I will not dispaire to vissitt you Once more At Lyme, & greet you w*i*th the Second part of my Lord said to S*i*r Edward &c. or somthinge as ridiculous to make sport w*i*th, though nothinge can be thought on soe Contemptible as S*i*r Edward or his Lor*d*shi*p*; wh*i*ch is the Only thinge y*a*t now remaines of Either of them

S*i*r I dare not trouble you w*i*th much protestation, nor will I
sprinkle you w*i*th Court holye water; yet giue me leaue, hartily to
wish you all y*e* happines A Good man can Expect or desire in this
world that you may Longe Enjoy yo*u*r Health and Abillityes both
of body & mynde, to y*e* good of many y*a*t subsist by | by you, And
to y*e* Generall Ioy of those Numerous ffrends you haue whoe
Really Loue you. as for me that Am scarce worthy of yo*u*r knowledge, I shall In what I can whylst I Am, Euer remaine
          yo*u*r ffaithfull servant
          Henry Lawes

S*i*r if I Apper not too Rude I shall desire you to present my
service to yo*u*r Good Lady for the Rest, I shall Convay my
respects to them by A Second Hand
London, this 5th of ffeb. 1634[31]

The relationship between Lawes and Sir Peter Legh was one of patronage to a certain extent, but not patronage in the same sense as liveried
minstrels were under the patronage of a noble. There may have been
a financial aspect to the relationship, but it is not explicit. The tone of
the letter, despite the conventionally flattering expressions of service
and humility, is assured and relaxed. Both members in this system of
patronage enhance their status: the musician by his association with a
man of wealth and property, and the patron by the implied suggestion
that he is a man not only of wealth but also of breeding, discernment,
and courtly behavior. Modern corporate sponsorship of the arts is
based on similar assumptions.

A further advantage for the musician was that it was not necessary
for him to rely on one patron alone. Francis Pilkington, as noted
above, dedicated works to the Earl of Derby, Sir Thomas Smith of
Hough, and Sir Peter Legh of Lyme.[32] The opening of the final dedication, to Sir Peter Legh, is fulsome but general, and certainly less
familiar than Lawes's letter: "Of him that shall demand of me, why I
presume to send this print of my (now aged) *Muse* to seeke patronage
vnder your worth: my answere shall be this; Aske the little sparks why
they dare flie vpwards to the glorious Sunne, or the small Riverets and
Brookes, why they with a hastie boldnesse strive to be engulphed into
the bosom of the vaste Ocean. . . ."[33] But a far more personal note was
sounded in Pilkington's first dedication, to the Earl of Derby: "I must
confesse my selfe many waies obliged to your Lordships familie, not
onely, for that my Father and Brother receiued many graces of your

Honours noble Father, whom they followed, but that my self had the like of your most honourable Brother, even from the first notice he chanced to take of mee."[34]

Although Pilkington's family is not known, the dedication indicates that his father and brother had been in the service of the Earl of Derby, and that he had received material help in his career from the Stanley family though he was not exclusively bound to them for favors. The dedication of his second work, to Sir Thomas Smith of Hough, speaks of "the many and manifold fauors, which I haue receiued at your hands, and your exquisit skill, both in Theorique and Practique of that excellent Art."[35] Here the patron appears in a dual role as supporter of the musician and as a performer of music himself. The implication of the dedication is that his patronage is not based solely on the desire to appear important, but that, because of his own skill in music and his knowledge of music theory, he is better able to appreciate the qualities of compositions such as Pilkington's. Flattery of the patron doubles as advertisement since the potential buyer of the collection is being alerted to the fact that the songs are prepared for a discriminating patron—and one who is himself a performer. By implication, the songs are suitable for discriminating performers to buy.

Gentry Musicianship

The role of the gentry as performers of music, like their function as patrons and audience, is an important one. The ability to read music and play a musical instrument was one of the hallmarks of a gentleman, provided that it was not indulged in excessively. Peacham's *Compleat Gentleman* reflects an ambiguous attitude towards musical skill: "I might runne into an infinite Sea of the praise and use of so excellent an Art, but I onely shew it you with the finger, because I desire not that any Noble or Gentleman should (save at his private recreation and leasureable houres) proove a Master in the same, or neglect his more weighty imployments: though I avouch it a skill worthy the knowledge and exercise of the greatest Prince."[36] He argues that music is physically beneficial—singing, for example, lengthens one's life and can cure stammering. But music is still only a "trifle." Too much attention to it is condemned: "yea great personages many times are more violently carried, than might well stand with their Honours, and necessity of their affaires: yet were it to these honest and commendable exercises savouring of vertue, it were well: but many neglecting their duties and places, will addict themselues wholly to trifles, and the most ridiculous and childish practices."[37] Peacham's advice "I desire no more in you than to sing your part sure, and at the first sight, withall, to play to same upon your Violl, or the exercise of the Lute, privately to your selfe"[38] is often quoted as the minimum required of a gentleman; however, in its context it also denotes a maximum. Music is an appropriate occupation for leisure time, but the aim is competence rather than expertise. Anything more would allegedly be frivolous wasting of time and beneath the dignity of a gentleman, who should be able to give the appearance of effortlessness in all he does.

The Cheshire records give evidence of this dual attitude towards music on the part of the gentry. Most of it is positive: ownership of musical instruments, payments to music teachers, and so forth. Not even the more puritan members of the gentry were opposed to music as such. John Bruen's biographer relates how, in his youth, when he was sent to the house of his uncle, John Dutton of Dutton, to be educated, he participated in both music and dancing, activities which he later repudiated as "tricks of vanity."[39] The danger for the young man was that music could lead to other things, specifically mixed dancing. That he was not opposed to music itself is shown at his death by the inventory of goods, which included a "Clockbell and bell in the hall" worth £5 1s and a pair of virginals worth twenty shillings.[40]

The attitude that music was properly the occupation of an idle hour is revealed in letters between Elizabeth Winnington of Birches and her sister, Margaret Lowther.[41] On 8 April 1629, Margaret wrote from London to Elizabeth, at Birches. In a postscript her husband, Robert Lowther, says, "Peege is so Idell that shee has tyme to playe. (I mene not the wag) but on hir lute w*hi*ch shee prayes you to send hir by Matacks."[42] Margaret wrote again on 14 April, and once again the lute is mentioned in a postscript: "sister I pray you: sende me my. lute: and: som strings: they are. amongst: the thinges: I left on the bed in the Best chamber. I think. they are in a canuis bage: I pray. you. tell me: whether Richer Iackson: hau paid: my 20 s or not."[43] The lute was sent, as another letter from 1629, unfortunately otherwise undated, mentions that it had been received along with the strings.[44] These letters illustrate in some measure the ambiguous attitude towards music. The lute is only mentioned in the postscript of both the April letters, but is definitely requested in two letters written within a week

of each other. The main sections of the letters are made up of expressions of affection, inquiries after other members of the family, and
covering notes for small gifts sent. That Margaret's inquiry about
whether a debt has been paid or not follows the request for the lute is
indicative that the postscript was not necessarily reserved for un-
important material. Nevertheless, her husband seems to associate
playing the lute with his wife's idleness as if she has nothing better to
do, and so she has time for music. The punning nature of the postscript suggests that playing the lute is preferable to playing the wag.
However, there is no suggestion that is anything more than a playful
term. Robert uses it in a subsequent letter in a double sense of "mischievous child" or "habitual joker."[45] "I haue not got as yet a littell
wage but if God send any if they take at me they wilbe wage
enought."[46] This last letter provides an additional reason for Margaret's leisure time. She has had poor health, and hopes that she may
be pregnant. The lute provides an occupation for her while she is
resting, and a distraction from her poor health.

The fact that Margaret had to send for the lute and that she had
left it in a bag on the bed in the best chamber at first glance seems odd,
but is there is no reason to suppose that this was not a deliberate
choice rather than carelessness. A lute is a delicate instrument and very
sensitive to changes of temperature. A bag provided a certain amount
of protection, and placing a lute in a well-aired bed would be recom-
mended by Thomas Mace, who also warned against tumbling back on
top of the instrument.[47] A bed would provide insulation, and the bed
in the best chamber was probably seldom used for sleeping. A lute
would be at less risk of bumps and knocks than if it were in a cupboard
or a chest, and would also be less susceptible to changes of temperature, which would affect the tuning and could, if extreme, damage the
instrument. Any number of reasons could have influenced Margaret's
leaving the lute behind, including danger to it when bundling it with
the rest of her luggage for the return journey.

A gentleman or gentlewoman might be expected to play more
than one musical instrument. Disbursements on behalf of Mary
Somerford, daughter and heiress of John Somerford, in 1597 included
virginals, costing £4, and a bandora costing £2.[48] In the following year,
"a payer of virgynals" costing £3 13s 4d, a bandora £2, and a lute £3
are listed as being for Mary Somerford, described in the document as
"my doughter in lawe."[49] The bandora at least and probably also the
virginals must have been the same as the ones listed in the previous

year. A cittern (eleven shillings), and lute strings and wire (3*s* 2*d*) bought in 1599 seem also to have been for Mary Somerford.[50] She thus anticipates the image put forward by Thomas Dekker in the *Guls Hornebooke* (1609) of the young gentlewoman who should be able "to read and write, to play upon the virginals, lute and cittern: and to read pricksong at first sight."[51] The bandora is wire-strung and tuned differently than the lute; the cittern and bandora are played with a plectrum, the lute with the fingers.[52] Mary Somerford's versatility would be particularly useful as she would have been able to take any one of half the parts in a broken consort.

A praise-poem on the Stanley family[53] shows that Peacham's reservations about musical expertise were not universal. The poem deals with events during the reign of Henry VII and therefore may reflect an earlier attitude towards musical ability in the gentry. The poet is unequivocal in his praise of Sir Edward Stanley's musical abilities:

> His second sonne Edwarde maried to an heyre
> a thowsand markes a yeare of good landes and fayre
> his plainge [of] of Instrumentes was a good noyse
> his singing as excellent with a sweete voyce
> his countenaunce comely with visage demure
> Not moving nor streining but stedfast and sure
> He would shewe in a single Recorder pipe
> as many partes as anny in a bagge-pipe
> When the King of Castyle was dryuen hyther
> by force and violence of stormye wether
> He broughte with him were thoughte fine musicions
> there was none better in theyre opinions
> kinge of Castile said theyre [w] actes more to able
> they were gentlemen of houses notable
> I have quoth Henry seaventhe a knighte my servante
> one of the greatest Earles sonnes in all my land
> His singinge gallante with a voyce most sweetelye
> his plainge pleasante much better then meetelye
> he playes of all Instrumentes non comes amisse
> Call sir Edward standley lo Sir heere he is
> Come neere good sir Edward Standelaye quod the king
> for the honowre of vs shewe parte of your conninge
> He stoode before the kinges doubtles this was true
> In a fayre gowne of cloth of gould of tissiue

Like no common minstrell to shewe taverne myrth
but like a noble mann both of Land and byrth
he shewed much conning those two kings[54] before
that the others had no Luste to playe any more
He played of all Instrumentes notable well
but of all thinges mused king of Castell
to heare two partes in a single Recorder
that was beyond all their Estimations far
And then king harry made ^^him^ to blowe his horne
they had never hard such one since they were borne
In no Realme any for true and fyne blowinge
since Tristram the prince of huntesmen was liuinge
In two hornes at once would a wonderouse noyse make
In the one Rechate and in the other strake
Blowinge diuers measures was very diffuce
before kings and others he did it of vse
he had more quallities like a gentleman
then in all his time had any other mann
And for his hardines to saye truth and Righte
He was stoute man and a valiante knight
As at the death of King J[a] Jamye did appeere[55]

There is a folktale quality about the contest between Sir Edward
and the King of Castile's musicians, but nevertheless the poem for our
purposes is revealing in the way it treats musicianship. Sir Edward is
specifically declared to be unlike a common minstrel, associated with
"tavern mirth." While he can allegedly play all instruments, he specifically plays the recorder and the horn. His recorder playing is
remarkable for his ability to play more than one part at once and for
the variety of parts he can play. Comparison is specifically made to the
bagpipe, notably a lower-class instrument. The poem gives evidence
not only of his remarkable ability with which the king of Castile is
particularly struck, but also of the relative status of the recorder and
the bagpipe. Sir Edward's musical ambidexterity is further seen in his
ability to blow simultaneously two different signals on two horns. His
opponents are also not common minstrels but, according to the king
of Castile, "gentleman of houses notable" and thus worthy opponents
for Sir Edward. While poetic licence may be involved, the life of
Thomas Whythorne shows that there was nothing inherently im-
probable in the king's claim that his musicians were gentlemen by

birth. In the poem, the king evidently considers that their honorable birth enhances his own status.

Some types of instruments were seen as more appropriate for the gentry to play than others. Matters of fashion and expense come into play here. The lute was singled out by Baldassare Castiglione as more worthy than pricksong because it was a solo instrument, but he also gave his approval to fretted or keyboard instruments and to the music of a consort of viols.[56] These are in fact the instruments principally found in the wills and inventories of the Cheshire gentry. By 1558, the old Latin books had fallen out of favor. An "old boke of prickesonge" was valued at only one penny in the inventory of the goods of Richard Brereton of Lea in that year. In the same inventory, a pair of virginals is valued at 33*s* 4*d*, a lute at four shillings, and even "iij old broken vyall*es*" at four shillings. The price of the music book is the same as that for a "boke of Iest*es*."[57] Music books appear only rarely in wills and inventories, and usually in combination with other books, and of course value would also depend on their condition. In 1618, James Miller, clerk, making a distinction in his will between Latin and ver-nacular songs, left the latter to his daughter: "It*em* I bequeath to James Wilding all my Latine bookes of Diuinity or oth*er* in Latine w*ith* all my songe bookes in Latine except my sett of Balladers w*hich* I giue to my daugh*ter* & th*e* sett of ffrench songes in a Case / & w*hat* oth*er* song bookes James Willdinge shall think*e* ^^most fitt^ for her. . . ."[58] The inventory of his goods values the Latin books, including both the works of divinity and the songbooks, at thirty shillings, and "All the rest of my English bookes Histories Chro=nicles & Diuinity what-soeu*er* w*ith* a sett of Ballad bookes & french songes in a Case" at forty shillings.[59] Unfortunately, this again gives no indication of the specific value of the different music books, but Miller evidently considered the ballads and French songs not only to be more appropriate (and probably more pleasing) to his daughter and but also perhaps not sufficiently serious to interest James Wilding, who received his divinity books and Latin works.

Instrumental music books are included along with instruments in William Worrall's will (see Appendix I), indicating that he was musi-cally literate and putting him above the class of musician castigated by Whythorne as nothing more than minstrels. We do not know what proportion of the £1 18*s* value the music books represent, but as they are grouped with several musical instruments (orpharion, bandora, bass viol, and three treble viols) they cannot have been very valuable.

A lute and luting book were specifically bequeathed by John Coppock, gentleman, in 1587, but again the value of the items is not given.[60] The luting book is probably mentioned because it accompanies the lute, a valuable item, and it may have been a personal collection rather than a printed one.[61] A luting book with a Cheshire connection survives in the Spencer collection at the Royal College of Music. *The Mynshall Lute Book* originally belonged to Richard Mynshall (or Minshull) of Nantwich in the early seventeenth century, and passed from him to his brother-in-law, Ralph Wilbraham.[62]

Musical instruments such as lutes, virginals, and viols were relatively expensive items. As such they figure in inventories and are sometimes specifically mentioned in wills. In 1612, Henry Hardware of Peel left his viol to Thomas Bickerton and his bandora to William Handy.[63] The accounts of Thomas Wilbraham of Nantwich indicate that there was a Mr. Handy teaching music at that time, as he was engaged by Wilbraham in March 1614 when he was paid eight shillings "at the months end."[64] If William Handy and Mr. Handy are the same person, he may well have been a gentleman musician, like Thomas Whythorne, who taught music. In this case, he would have been in Henry Hardware's employ in 1612 or earlier, after which he entered that of Thomas Wilbraham.

But usually musical instruments were left to members of the more immediate family. Thomas Brereton of Barrow left his virginals to his nephew, Edward Savage, in 1587.[65] In 1608, Francis Fitton of Gawsworth left the use of all the furnishings in his dining chamber, specifically including virginals, to his sister to pass to her son on her death.[66] Musical instruments could also become heirlooms, as in the will of Sir Richard Shireburn of Stonyhurst in Lancashire:

> Also it is my will and mind and I give and bequeath vnto the said Richard Shereburn my sonne and Richard Shereburn my grandchild one paire of organes standing in the hall at Stoniehirst. . . . And also all my wyndy instrumentes lyeing in a chist at Lawnd and the chist wherein they are. All which said paire of organnes and other legacyes thereafter and hereinbefore menconed It is my will and mind shalbee and remaine at Stoniehirst for euer as heireloome<.> . . .[67]

Sir Richard also left his daughter, Katherine Pennington, instruments which evidently had some sentimental attachment: "one paire of Virginalls which was her mothers and my litle Lute."[68]

The Cheshire gentry were extensively and intricately interconnected by blood and marriage, and musical instruments hence not surprisingly also moved around in the extended family, as they were lent to a variety of "cousins," a term which loosely covers a range of blood and marriage ties. The lending of instruments could be beneficial to the instrument as well as the borrower. Thomas Wilbraham's Memorandum and Account book includes: "A note of Remembrance made the 5 of Iulye 1614 at my goinge ouer into Fraunce" that "I haue lent vnto my Cosin Ann Whittingham my Base vyall to vse till my retorne."[69] In this instance, the lending of the instrument would hardly have inconvenienced him and presumably would have meant that it was cared for and played during his absence on the Continent.

The Leche family of Carden was at the center of a more complicated web of borrowing and lending of instruments. The account book of John Leche of Carden shows that in 1633 he lent a cittern with case to his cousin, Richard Massey of Coddington. In 1635, he lent a cittern to his cousin, Richard Warde, whose man John Taylor served as courier. This may have been the same cittern that was lent to Richard Massey earlier, although there is no record of its return.[70] The peregrinations of his wife's virginals from 1638 to 1642 show how the borrowing pattern could be extended:

> Mrs Anne Massey
> memorandum that this 2: dye of october i638, my Cossen Mrs: Anne massey of Coddington Borrowed my wifes vergnals to bringe them agayne vppon demande
> The went thence to Chester to my Cossen Harper[71]
> Mr Nuball
> Memorandum that I lent to mr Richard Nuball organest of the Citty of Chester, A payre of vergenals of myne, which were at my Cossen Harpurs of Chester, he had them from thenc in August i641
> I had them agayne & lent them to Cossen wilkenson[72]
> Cossen Wilkenson
> . . .
> memorandum that I lent my Cossen wilkenson A payre of verginals for his daughters vse september i642[73]

The virginals moved from the Leche home at Carden, to Mrs. Massey's, to Mr. Harper's, to Mr. Nuball's, back to Carden, and finally to Mr. Wilkinson. All of the borrowers except Mr. Nuball were relatives of John Leche. Sometimes the virginals moved directly from one borrower to another, as between Mrs. Massey and Mr. Harper, and from there to Mr. Nuball. But they were returned to John Leche before being passed on to his cousin Wilkinson. The virginals were probably available to be lent on this scale because, like the Wilbraham viol, they were not needed at home. The date of Alice Leche's death is not given, but it is likely that she was either dead or unable to play any longer, and there were no daughters of the house to inherit her virginals. Representing what seems to have been a common practice, both Thomas Wilbraham and John Leche were lending instruments that were surplus to their requirements, whether in the short or long term.

We are fortunate to have the memoranda that survive to record the pattern of borrowings. Such notes must have been necessary to keep track of instruments, which might be lost or forgotten if anything happened to the lender. The will of Francis Fitton, dated 31 March 1608, shows how extended borrowing could put the lender at risk of losing his instruments:

Item I will and bequeath to my cosin Edmund ffyton sonne and heire to my late nephew william ffitton the somme of Twenty poundes in money And also I do further bequeath to him a somme of tenn poundes in money which I did lend to him at his going into Spaine with sir Richard Leveson in consideracion of a sett of violles de la gamba of his late fathers and also a sett of Recorders and a great Syterne a Lute and a paire of virginalles which were all his said late fathers and by him left in my keeping which said sett of vialles I did lend to Sir Iohn davers knight deceased and were sithence in the handes of dame Elizabeth davers his late widow and since then also in the handes of Sir Charles davers knight hir sonne attainted by whose fall the said vialles may fortune to be loste but the virginalles and lute are ready for him my said nephew Edmund ffitton and also the said great Sitherne in my owne now lodging in the Strond the red cocke nere the Savoy. And the said somme of Twenty poundes formerly bequeathed to him, my will is shall be deliuered to him my said cosin Edmund ffitton within six monethes next after my decease, if the said Instruments shall not be deliuered to him within that time of the said six monethes or before, safe and sound which I am greatly in doubt will not be donne and so deliuered to him, But if he shall so receiue backe the said Instruments Then the said legacy of twenty poundes to him to cease and to be void.[74]

The situation is a complex one. The instruments, which evidently originally belonged to Francis Fitton's nephew William, were apparently left with Francis Fitton as surety by William's son Edmund in consideration of £10 lent to him at that time. Given the number and range of instruments—a set of viols, a set of recorders, a "great Syterne," a lute, and a pair of virginals—the sum seems small, and the additional £20 left to Edmund is evidently to offset the possible loss of the set of viols. These had been lent to Sir John Danvers, Francis Fitton's brother-in-law,[75] and on his death were used by his wife as well as by their son, Sir Charles Danvers. Unfortunately for the Fitton viols, Sir Charles Danvers was attainted because of his part in the Essex rebellion and was executed 18 March 1601.[76] As a result his large estate in Wiltshire was escheated to the crown. Although James I allowed Henry Danvers to inherit his brother's property in 1603, Fitton was clearly doubtful whether in the initial seizure of the property portable goods such as the viols might not have been sold or removed. As the viols were not his own property, he is seeking in his will to insure that his cousin (actually his great-nephew) is not the loser by it. The virginals, lute, and cittern are, he is quick to assure Edmund, available for him at the Red Cock in the Strand, Francis' lodging. The recorders are not mentioned. They may have been part of the Danvers' loan and therefore lost like the viols. A set of viols consisted of six in all, two each of bass, tenor, and treble.[77] In 1613, a treble viol da gamba for Sir Richard Wilbraham cost 12s 6d, with a further two shillings for the case, and 4s 6d for three dozen strings.[78] This was apparently a gift, as the expense is listed in the account book of Thomas Wilbraham of Nantwich. Sir Richard Wilbraham of Woodhey (c.1578–1643) was Thomas Wilbraham's third cousin, once removed, but he was also the head of the senior branch of the family. The viol was therefore likely to have been intended to impress Sir Richard, whose patronage may have been sought at a time when Thomas was beginning his career at the Inns of Court.[79] Even allowing for a higher price for a matched set in an ornate case, a price of over £10 seems excessive for the Fitton viols. A single bass viol, in the inventory of a professional musician, was valued at £1 10s in 1648.[80] Much does depend on the quality, and beyond these two examples we have very little information about the prices of viols, which could range from four shillings for three old broken viols in 1558, to 6s 8d for a tenor viol belonging to the Chester wait William Madock in 1604, to thirty shillings for a bass viol and a bandora together in 1639, to a bass viol apparently worth £13 4s in 1576–77.[81] This last amount is completely out of line with any of the other sums and either represents an unusually valuable viol or an error on the scribe's part for 13s 4d, a standard sum (one mark), which is more in keeping with the price paid for the Wilbraham viol and even the Vaughan viol. None of the amounts found in other documents combine in any plausible way to make £20, and this sum may include the missing recorders as well as some compensation on Fitton's part for losing the viols that had been entrusted to him.

An important adjunct to music, already discussed in connection with pipers at alehouses and on greens, was dancing. The gentry of course also had their dances and took dancing lessons as well as music lessons. In addition to his payment to Mr. Handy for music lessons, Thomas Wilbraham paid in 1613 paid for "Admittance" to "Mr. Sexton his dauncinge schoole" (15s 6d) and also to "Mr Rowlands dauncinge Schoole" (£1 4s).[82] He further paid £1 3s 4d for admittance to a fencing school in the same month.[83] Since he specifically indicates that he is paying for admittance to the various schools, and that Mr. Handy *began* to teach him music in March, the inference is that he was previously either lacking in—or at least felt himself inadequately equipped with—these skills. In December, at about the same time he was entering the dancing schools, he spent fourteen shillings on "a Bauldrake & a horne," a price comparable to that which he paid for the viol and its case.[84] All this argues a considerable commitment on Wilbraham's part to acquiring social graces. The fact that he was admitted to Lincoln's Inn in May 1613 is important. The Inns of Court provided training for courtiers as much as for lawyers. Wilbraham's attendance at the various dancing and fencing schools and his music lessons cannot have lasted more than about a year, as the memorandum about lending his bass viol (the acquisition of which is not recorded) before going to France in July 1614 shows.

The type of dancing that Thomas Wilbraham was paying to learn was courtly and fashionable, but more traditional country dances were also popular. In a letter to Sir Richard Grosvenor, Sir Richard Wilbraham writes "wee shall wish *you* many times with vs this Crismas to see a horn pipe dansed before oure colefire."[85] Thus if Sir Richard appears more as a country gentleman rather than a courtier, secure in his role as head of the family, his younger cousin Thomas would in contrast have looked to skill at dancing as a means of social advancement. That this was the case at court is shown in a letter from Percy Church to Peter Moreton, who is evidently traveling with Lord Feilding's brother as a tutor or advisor. Church informs Moreton that it is left to Moreton's judgment as to whether the younger Feilding is fit to return, "reflecting both of his wite, discre=tion, language, qualities and behauior, and in them you find him passable and not ridiculous, then to dispose accordingly for *your* returne"—adding that "he desireth you to returne by Turin and so to Paris for some six weekes time where he would haue him diligentlie to ffollow his ex=cersises & especiallie his dawncing it beeing a thing verie much used both by King & Queene in the winter season."[86]

Peter Moreton also considered skill at music a desirable acquisition. Writing to his father, William Moreton, on the eve of his departure for Italy in service of a noblewoman, he expressed his intention to learn Italian and his hopes of studying music as well: "When I heere from you I shall the better know how to fall upon my studyes, I wold gladly acquaint my selfe with som skill in Musike, if my allowance will stretch soe farr."[87] His concern about his allowance reveals a fundamental problem for a young man in his position. The acquisition of social graces such as music and dancing was desirable, but who was to pay for them? The opening part of his letter is taken up with concerns about and requests for money:

> I expected your letter or som direction to my cosen Tucke for his furnishing mee with mooneys for my joyrney: hee wonders much hee had none either from you or his father: yet hee is unwilling to see mee unprovided knowing my occacions: I writt in my last letter by Mr Iohn weld that I shold have use for at least 20: l I have made mee a cloth sute, I did owe at my coming downe, as I then told you, to mrs Clerke & my taylor above 50 s, these somes, and the rest for my inevitable occacions, as I hope my true accounts will informe *you* being deducted out of the 20 l you will *per*ceive what the remainder will bee which I must carry over with mee: If you will send any bill of exchange after mee Mr William Weld will convay it with convenient speede: I thinke one of our companie will stay a fortnight after us.[88]

For a nobleman like Lord Feilding's brother, the opportunity of studying music and dancing is readily provided. For members of the lesser gentry, opportunities had to be taken when they could. Yet though Peter Moreton's anxiety about his allowance comes through clearly in the opening of his letter, he went on to become Charles I's ambassador to Genoa and Tuscany—a sign that he was able to make a successful career as a courtier.[89] Thomas Wilbraham's expenditure on music lessons and dancing schools could, like his purchase of a viol for Sir Richard, have been investments for the future.

A letter from Thomas Maddocks to Charles Mainwaring of Croxton on behalf of the latter's cousin (and probably ward), who had just become a student at Oxford, raises a familiar plea for more money. Oxford life is costing more than is expected, and the student wants a gittern and an archery outfit, interestingly linked together equally:

> Ryght woorshippfull my duety remembred theys may signyfy vnto you that your cosyn ys mery and in good healthe and doethe lyke oxforde very well havynge good hope to obtayne learnynge as no doubte but I trust he wyll sir I haue sent vnto my master and vnto you a note by the perticuler summes of the whole charges and costes that your cosin hathe byne at synce hys commynge fourthe of cheshyre the wyche doe somewhat extende that wyche I receaved of you as the note and byles shall more playnly declare and hys ex=ebytion ys somewhat costly howebeyt as you wolde haue hym to wante nothynge so by godes grace he shall consume nothynge he ys verye desirous to haue a gitterne and bowe and arrowes the wyche I thinke to be necessarye for hym and doe meane to provide for the same verye shortely so that we muste desyre you to be so good as to send vpp some more mony that we may be better able to obtayne thynges necessarye and thus commyttynge you to the tuytion of the seculare powers I cease from oxforde the xviij of [Iulye] Iune
>
> > Yours in all thynges [to] at
> > commaundement your servante
> > Thomas Maddockes[90]

Neither the year nor the name of the student is given in the letter, but other documents in the file indicate that he was John Somerford, who was at Oxford in the early 1560s. Thomas Whythorne mentions learning to play both gittern and cittern as a young man "which ij instruments wer þen stranȝ in England, and þerfor þe mor dezyred and esteemed."[91] Whythorne is referring to a period between 1543 and 1553, slightly earlier than Somerford's time at Oxford. By the 1560s, the gittern would have been more widely known without having yet gone out of fashion.

IV
THE MUSICAL INSTRUMENTS

Over a period of several centuries a variety of instruments were played by performers in Cheshire—a variety that may seem even greater because of the ambiguity of some of the terms used for them. But while shifting terminology may mean that the same name could refer to a different instrument at different times, the form of the instrument also changed over time. The difference between a medieval and a renaissance version of an instrument sometimes was considerable.[1] As most of the evidence comes from the sixteenth and seventeenth centuries, the records largely appear to identify renaissance instruments, but one must also allow for the frequent survival of older instruments well into the renaissance period.

Another problem is encountered because we do not always have specific mentions of an instrument, only its implied use in the terms that identify the performer in the records. There are, for example, many fiddlers but no fiddles as such, although both viols and violins are specifically mentioned. Pipers are mentioned from as early as 1367, but the first specific mention of pipes is in 1597.[2] During the time between, not only did the physical appearance of pipes change but also possibly the range of objects to which the name was given. Terms such as 'minstrel' and 'musician,' already discussed in chapter I, covered a wide range of possible instrumental ability about which the documents are sometimes vague. In some cases, this vagueness is intentional, giving a greater inclusiveness in a legal document where the exact instrument is not known—preventing, for example, a musician from evading a charge by claiming to play a pipe and tabor rather than a pipe. An extreme example is the use of phraseology such as "an instrument of musicke,"[3] though this is not common and occurs only three times in the sample of documents surveyed: once in a recognizance, once in a crown book, and once in a bailiff's presentment.[4] Two of the usages relate to the same case and may indicate an administrative preference for the more inclusive term as much as an uncertainty about the actual instrument played. Vagueness as to musical instrument also occurs, understandably, in accounts, where a musician or minstrel is paid simply for playing. In some cases, the name of the musician is also left

out, and payment simply made "to the music." Terms such as 'piping'
also seem to become almost generic, covering the performance of
music at ales or wakes, as at Tarporley in 1609, when, of four instrumentalists charged with piping on the sabbath, the only one whose
instrument is specified is a harper.[5] As the name of the harper entry is
interlined, it probably represents later information added to an existing
presentation to differentiate one of the performers from the others.
This remains vague in a different way from the specification of the
"instrument of music" in the Frodsham presentation. More problematic still is the case of Thomas Allen, who is described in a number
of documents as a fiddler and is cited for performing on the sabbath.
However, in a diocesan visitation of 1608 he is enjoined not to *pipe* on
the sabbath until after evening prayer.[6] Are there two Thomas Allens,
one a piper and one a fiddler, in the same area and at the same time,
engaged in the same sort of activity? It is certainly possible, but it is
also possible that piping is used here in a general way for performing.

These instances are all exceptions rather than the rule in the
documents, and a more pervasive problem is the simple one that terms
such as 'piping,' while they presume the existence of pipes, give no
information about what type of pipes are intended or how they were
played. In some cases, such as that of Richard Metier, discussed in
chapters I and II, an individual can attract the attention of the authorities and be described as a piper over the course of thirty-five years
without once being recorded as doing anything that clearly involved
pipes. Legal documents are, in the main, useful only as presumptive
evidence of musical instruments. Accounts from the guilds are similarly limited, the more so as the waits were paid collectively, with instruments rarely specified.

Wills and inventories are far more useful as evidence for musical
instruments since they are concerned specifically with the instrument
itself, not with the question of performance. The drawback to evidence
from inventories is that it tends to be associated with the wealthier
portion of the population and therefore misses out the petty musicians
and licensed minstrels who did not have enough goods to be inven-
toried. The majority of named musicians in Cheshire are described as
piper, but if one were to look only at the evidence of inventories, pipes
would appear to be almost non-existent. We are fortunate to have
inventories for three professional musicians, one of whom was a
Chester wait, but given the number of named musicians known to be
in the county during the period, this does not give much of a cross-
section (see chapter II, part 2, and appendix I).

What Were the Instruments?

As the previous discussion will already have implied, the range of instruments played in Cheshire varies from the virginals and lutes of the renaissance gentry, through the ensemble instruments of the waits, to the ubiquitous pipes and fiddles of the alehouses. The tables on the following pages give a general idea of the various instruments, with the date or range of dates of their appearance in the records. A range of dates does not imply continuous appearances within those dates but will give an earliest and latest appearance of the particular instrument. Similarly, a final date in a range does not necessarily mean that this instrument fell out of use by that time. A range in brackets indicates the range of references to the instrumentalist rather than the instrument—e.g., harper rather than harp. This is generally wider than the range of references to instruments as such. Where only bracketed dates are given, it indicates that there are references to performers on an instrument but none to the instrument itself (e.g., fiddler, but no fiddle). The tables are divided according to types of instruments— wind, string, percussion, and so on—but it must be remembered that they were frequently played in combination. Some combinations, such as pipe-and-tabor, were played at the same time by a single performer, amounting in effect to a separate instrument from the plain pipe or drum, but generally do not show up as a separate instrument in the records. Where a date appears in the form "1638–39," that indicates a year, usually an accounting year, which falls in two calendar years.

The String Instruments

String instruments fall into two main groups, plucked and bowed. There are further subdivisions between wire-strung and gut-strung instruments, although these tend to be complementary rather than divisive. The orpharion, for example, could be tuned in the same way as a lute but was wire-strung. Effectively all the lute repertoire could be played on the orpharion.[7] The division between medieval and renaissance forms is less noticeable with the strings, because the majority of examples in this study come from the late sixteenth and early seventeenth centuries. Plucked strings will be treated first in the following discussion.

Harp. The most obvious case of the decline of popularity of an instrument is the harp. That this instrument, frequently seen in iconography, was popular in the fourteenth and fifteenth centuries is seen by the high proportion of harpers to other musicians in those centuries: four out of six named performers in the fourteenth century, and seven out of thirty in the fifteenth.[8] The existence of a harp is indicated in a debt of three pence for harpstrings at Chester in 1436.[9] The design of the harp varied both over time and from region to region, to be sure. The harpers mentioned in the fourteenth century probably played a harp with a range of three octaves, tuned diatonically, or less if one octave had partially chromatic tuning.[10] During the fifteenth century, the range of the harp was extended in the bass registers, and the renaissance harp in Wales had "brays, horsehair strings, bone tuning pins and a mare's skin stretched over the soundbox."[11]

Table I: String Instruments

Alferial (orpharion)	1637
Bandora	1597 — 1638–39
Bass Viol	1594 — 1639
Great Cittern	1608
Cittern	1599 — 1639
Fiddle	{1485 — 1643}
Gittern	c.1562
Harp	1436 {1343–1609}
Irish Harp	1575–76
Kit	1637
Lute	1557 — 1636 {1448 — ?1559–60}
Tenor Viol	1604
Treble Viol	1637
Treble Violin	1637
Viol da gamba	1607 — 1613
Viols	1557— 1659
Violins	1590–91

The harp is especially associated with Celtic countries, and Cheshire, bordering Wales and on the main sea-route to Ireland, is likely to have had influence from both places. Hugh de Walay, the harper who received a reward of land in Cheshire from the Black Prince, may have been Welsh, and it is also possible that harpers from Ireland made their way to Cheshire. Certainly the Irish harp is found at Chester. A Sheriffs' Book memorandum of 1576 appraises an Irish harp and a pair of "tuftmocado gaskyns" (a type of shoe) at 8s 4d.[12] While most medieval and renaissance harps were gut-strung, the Irish harps of this period were strung with brass wire.[13] The Irish harp seems to have regained popularity as a gentry instrument in the seventeenth century, as indicated in Martin Peerson's *Mottects, or Grave Chamber Musique*: "for want of organs, may be performed on virginals, base-lute, bandora or Irish harpe."[14] Possibly this resurgence of interest in the instrument was linked to the development of a chromatic harp towards the end of the sixteenth century, capable of greater range and versatility.[15]

1. Among the angel musicians on the west front of Chester Cathedral is a harp player. The harp, slightly broken at upper left, is probably not an accurate representation of an actual instrument but rather an impressionistic depiction. Line drawing by Marianne Cappelletti, after the photograph by Sally-Beth MacLean (*Chester Art*, pl. 1).

The harp in an earlier form—an example is the Sutton Hoo instrument in the British Museum—had been important in Anglo-Saxon culture, and was associated with the *scop* and the *gleeman*. The conventional distinction is, as the musicologist Gustave Reese indicated, between the *scop* who was "resident in the hall of an atheling (or petty king) and the *gleemen* who traveled about."[16] They thus corresponded to the court minstrel and the itinerant minstrel, and

Reese's suggestion that their role involved poetry and history as much as music still seems viable.[17] Although generally speaking the term 'minstrel' seems to have replaced both 'scop' and 'gleeman' after the coming of the Normans, we do still have one "harper and gleeman" in the Cheshire records. In 1419, Roger de Croxton of Middlewich, described in an indictment as "Rog*er*us de Croxton harp*er* de Medio Wico in eodem Com*itatu* glemon" ("Roger of Croxton harper of Middlewich in the same County gleeman"),[18] was one of a number of people indicted in a case of riot at Ashton in Tarvin parish (Ashton iuxta Mouldsworth in the document). Roger de Croxton's name comes early in the list, immediately after a knight, several gentlemen, a squire, and two yeomen, and well ahead of a minstrel, Robert de Overwhitley, who appears in company with a wright, a yeoman, and a smith. Roger de Croxton was therefore possibly, contrary to the usual distinction, a retainer of one of the gentry families involved in the riot. He was also more probably one of a family of harpers, as in 1394 there is a John de Croxton, harper, taking custody of a minor, Thomas, son of Roger de Croxton (clearly not the same as the Roger de Croxton in the Middlewich riot).[19] In 1416, Roger de Croxton, harper, put in an appearance at the exchequer in Chester and admitted a debt of twenty shillings to the king and William Troutbeck, chamberlain of Chester.[20]

Lute. The lute, bandora, cittern, gittern, and orpharion, as found in the Cheshire records, are principally instruments of the renaissance, although they derive from medieval forms. The lute is described by David Munrow as being "second only to the voice in popularity,"[21] but this must be understood to apply primarily to the gentry and aristocracy. Although waits and musicians such as William Worrall of Nantwich did play lutes by the seventeenth century, there is no evidence that they became popular with musicians or audiences at ales, wakes, and alehouses. Some early professional luters do appear, notably John Haswall, "loter*er*," who was involved in an action for debt in 1488.[22] William Luter, minstrel, who performed for the Smiths' Company in 1557–58 and the Shoemakers' in 1559–60, probably also played the lute.[23] Haswall, at least, would have played the medieval lute.

The renaissance lute was a courtly instrument, delicate both in construction and tone, difficult to keep in tune, and unsuitable to the rigors of outdoor performance or travel. Amongst the gentry, however, it was popular both as a solo instrument and as an accompaniment to singing. It was also played in consort with other instruments, most notably the "broken consort," which consisted of treble viol or violin, flute (which could mean recorder as well as transverse flute), bass viol, lute, cittern, and bandora.[24] The range of dates given for the lute in Table I does represent a continuous appearance of this instrument in wills and inventories between those dates in addition to references in letters and accounts.

The subtlety of tone of the lute was a result of delicacy of construction and the method of playing with the fingertips rather than nails or plectrum which developed in the second half of the fifteenth century—a technique which allowed the performer to play more than one part at a time.[25] The lute characteristically had a pear-shaped back, made up of a series of thin ribs, shaped over a mould and glued together edge to edge. Many different types of hardwood and even ivory were used for making lutes. The neck of the lute was also made of hardwood, with a softwood block to which the ribs and the neck were attached. From the later sixteenth century lute necks were often decorated or veneered with ivory or ebony. The soundboard was made of a flat, straight-grained softwood and had an ornamental soundhole, the "rose," cut into it.[26] The lute was thus a luxury instrument by its very construction and one that had to be handled carefully. The practice of keeping lutes in beds to protect them from changes of temperature has already received notice (see chapter III).

Because the instrument was so sensitive, the stringing had to be light, which meant that strings easily fell out of tune and were subject to breakage. The tension of the strings pulling directly on the soundboard may result in distortion—a tendency which the lute's construction is designed to counter:

> This [distortion] is resisted by a number of transverse bars of the same wood as the soundboard, glued on edge across its underside. These bars, besides supporting the soundboard, have an important effect on the sound quality. By dividing the soundboard into a number of sections, each with a relatively high resonant frequency, they cause it to reinforce the upper harmonics produced by a string rather than its fundamental tone.[27]

Lutes were strung with gut strings in pairs (courses), and hence if one string broke in mid-performance the lute was still playable. Good lute players would select their strings very carefully and paid a premium price for them. In 1599, lists of disbursements for Mary Somerford included 3*s* 2*d* for "lute stryng*es* & wyre," 3*s* 6*d* for "wyre & stryng*es*," and 2*s* 6*d* for "lace & luttes."[28] The total of 9*s* 2*d* is not much less than the eleven shillings paid for a cittern for her in the same year. The wire would have been used for the cittern or the bandora, which she also played.

The number of courses on the lute increased over time. The medieval lutes seem to have had four courses, with a fifth added in the fifteenth century. Tinctoris (c.1481–83) mentions six courses as well as five,[29] and by 1500 six courses (with a range of two octaves) was the form in common use. After 1580 a seventh course became common, with the extra course tuned a fourth below the sixth course. These additions may have been made possible by improvements in string-making.[30] The number of courses continued to increase, with the development of eight-course, ten-course, and eleven-course lutes in the first part of the seventeenth century.

Lutes were, like other instruments, constructed in "families" of sizes and pitches. The "litle Lute" referred to in the will of Richard Shireburn of Stonyhurst, Lancashire, was probably a treble lute rather than the "mean lute" which was the standard.[31] In the sixteenth century, the lute became popular with the growing Tudor middle class, who had leisure and money enough to cultivate an interest in art and music. Books of lute tablature began to appear in the reign of Henry VIII, although none survive from before 1540.[32] The earliest lute mentioned in the Cheshire records is in an inventory of 23 February 1558 which also contains virginals and old, broken viols.[33] The only appearance of a specified luting book is in 1587, when both lute and luting book are bequeathed by John Coppock, gentleman, to John Yeardley.[34]

Cittern and Great Cittern. The cittern was next to the lute in popularity. Descended from the medieval citole, it was a wire-strung instrument, played with a plectrum. The body was usually shallow and pear-shaped in outline, tapering downwards from the neck. The strings were attached at the bottom end and passed over a moveable bridge. The soundboard was usually arched, having been glued to slightly curved internal struts. These acted as counter-supports to the down-ward pressure of the strings at the bridge. From the sixteenth century, the back tended to be slightly convex. There were usually eighteen or nineteen frets, of a hard material such as bone, metal, or ivory, placed in tapered slots and secured with hardwood wedges. These helped to ensure accuracy of intonation. The neck might also be half cut away from behind the fingerboard on the bass side to form a channel along which the thumb of the left hand could slide. Much of the cittern's solo repertory required rapid shifting to high positions, which was made easier by the thumb channel. English citterns usually had a curved pegbox with pegs inserted laterally, unlike the Italian citterns on which the pegs were attached from the front. The number of courses on the cittern varied from country to country. In England, four double courses were the most common, although octave stringing and tripling did occur. Fretting varied widely and could be partially diatonic (as is required by the French and Flemish repertory). In England after the mid-sixteenth century, completely chromatic fretting was standard.[35] From c.1580 to 1621, a new and stronger wire made it possible for the cittern to be tuned six to ten semitones higher.[36] The English cittern at this time was apparently a smaller four-course instrument with tuning derived from the Italian rather than the French manner. In c.1615, Praetorius mentions a small English cittern with Italianate tuning.[37]

Possibly because of its sturdiness compared to the lute, the cittern became popular on a wider social scale. The cittern might be kept in a barber shop for customers who might wish to play on it,[38] and it appears as an instrument played by a saddler at Knutsford in 1639. The decline of the cittern is thus reflected in the Cheshire records from an instrument fashionable with the gentry to one to be played in shops. However, as early as the mid-sixteenth century the *Mulliner Book* contained eight pieces for four-course cittern as well as one for five-course cittern. Adrian Le Roy's cittern tutor of 1565 was translated into English in 1568 (now lost), but the best writing comes with Anthony Holborne's *The Cittharn Schoole* (1597) and Thomas Robinson's *New Citharen Lessons* (1609). James Tyler considers that the "music in these two books represents the highest point in English writing for the instrument."[39] Mary Somerford, for whom a lute and a cittern were purchased in 1599, was thus at the height of the current fashion. Citterns are also found in inventories of goods at Nantwich in 1606 and 1618, although it is never as popular in gentry inventories as either the lute or bandora. The fashionability of the cittern had, however, declined by the 1620s, when the stronger wire was no longer available, and it came to be "associated solely with undemanding popular music."[40] The Leche cittern, which was loaned to family members in 1633,[41] would thus at that time no longer have been a fashionable solo instrument, although it was possibly still used as a continuo instrument in consort playing.

The only other late appearance of a cittern in the Cheshire records definitely takes it out of the gentry sphere. According to the allegations in a sexual assault case at Knutsford in 1639, Thomas Croaker kept the cittern and other instruments in his shop and played on them, and in so doing he attracted an audience of "yonge people."[42] Among those who came to listen to him was Margaret Baxter, a servant girl whom Croaker is alleged to have assaulted. Her story is that she came to hear the music and join the company, and that she was the last to leave the shop. She claims that Croaker shut the shop door and "indeavoured to *pe*rswade her to *pe*rmitt and suffer [Croaker] to have the use of her body, and [Croaker] did alsoe then and there indeavo*ur* offer and contend to have had the vse or rather the abuse of her body."[43] She shrieked, attracting the attention of passers-by, and, after a struggle, escaped through the shop window.

The cittern in this case caused no surprise to the authorities, but was enough of a novelty to attract young folk. Also surviving is Croaker's own side of the story which denies all the above allegations except his playing of the cittern:

> saveinge that this R*es*pondent is a Sadler by trade, and hath a shopp *wi*thin the towne ar*ticu*late, and hath vsed to play somtymes vpon a Citherne and [bel] beleeveth that yonge people have somtymes come into his said shopp to heare him play, And that w*i*thin the tyme ar*ticu*late...[bele] Margaret Baxter ar*ticu*late came into this R*es*pondents shopp, ^^ar*ticu*late^ with a Child in her armes (vt Credit), and then and there gave him some evill word*es* as Lame Gyles ^^or some such word*es*^. . . , And therevpon this R*es*pondent bade her goe forth of the shop, who answered and said that shee would not, and then this R*es*pondent said if shee would not goe foreth through the doore, shee should goe forth some other way, and vpon that this R*es*pondent shutt the said shopp doore and tooke a smale wand in his hand, and said hee would make her goe forth, who forthw*i*th went through the s*ai*d shopp windowe[44]

The facts of the case cannot be finally determined, but it is interesting that the term of abuse—"Lame Giles"—allegedly used by Margaret Baxter suggests that Croaker was physically handicapped. She may have been alluding to a stereotype, since there are sufficient indications of physical handicaps among the musicians in the Cheshire records— blind harpers, club-footed pipers—to suggest a perception that an inability to undertake regular forms of labor gave both the opportunity and the incentive to play a musical instrument. There is room for speculation here, but we should not try to read too much into the statement.

There is one final cittern in the Cheshire records which is of particular interest. The list of instruments in Francis Fitton's will of 1608 unusually includes a "great Syterne." Sizes of this instrument did vary, with string length averaging 42 cm to 49 cm but reaching as much as 62 cm.[45] Normally, as Ephraim Segerman points out, the classification of citterns by size and voice did not come into use until the mid-seventeenth century.[46] The small cittern was evidently in use well before 1615, when Praetorius was aware of it, since the surviving repertoire begins after 1580, and it is possible that the very large type of the instrument co-existed with the smaller in fashionable usage, although the Fitton will appears to be the only evidence—other than that of Praetorius—of more than one size in England.[47] As Fitton had received the cittern along with other instruments as surety for a loan before 1594,[48] it may simply be that the Great Cittern was the older French-style cittern, which was larger than the English cittern of the 1580s and later, and which had become comparatively unusual by 1608 when the will was written.

Gittern. There is only one mention of a gittern in the Cheshire records surveyed, in a letter concerning John Somerford at Oxford (see chapter III). Although undated, the letter comes from the early 1560s. The terminology causes some difficulty, because the medieval gittern is different from the renaissance gittern. The latter is commonly identified as the renaissance guitar to distinguish it from the seventeenth-century gittern, which was a cittern restrung and played like a guitar. The instrument which concerns us here is probably the renaissance guitar, apparently first mentioned in England in a court inventory in 1547.[49] This instrument combined the small size of the medieval gittern with the waisted outline of the vihuela, the shape familiar in the modern guitar. Unlike the medieval gittern, which was lute-shaped, it had a flat back. Unlike the cittern, it was gut-strung (usually with four courses of strings). The gittern (guitar) was linked with the cittern throughout the sixteenth century, and, as noted above, Thomas Whythorne, who was born c.1528, mentions learning to play both of them as a youth though they were unusual at that time.[50] He thus was probably learning to play the gittern when the instrument was still very new to England. Because the instrument was described by him as fashionable, it was all the more likely that the renaissance rather than the medieval form was involved. The "spate of guitar music" published around 1550[51] also favors the renaissance guitar as an instrument likely to be considered desirable for an Oxford student to learn to play in the early 1560s. James Rowbotham's *An Instruction to the Gitterne* (London, c.1569), a translation of an earlier lost French work by Adrian Le Roy (*Briefve et facile instruction pour . . . la guiterne* [Paris, 1551]), is indicative of the reputation of this instrument at this period.[52]

Bandora and Orpharion. The bandora and orpharion are both wire-strung instruments, and differ only in size and tuning. The bandora was invented by John Rose of London in 1562 and is a bass instrument capable of being played solo, as an accompaniment to the voice, or as part of a consort.[53] The orpharion, essentially the wire-strung equivalent of the lute and originally tuned in the same way, developed slightly later than the bandora. After 1621 the stronger wire which made the lute tuning possible was no longer available, and the orpharion would henceforth have had to be tuned at a lower pitch.[54] Both instruments developed an oblique bridge and nut, which had the advantage of shortening the treble strings and stiffening the soundboard.[55] In outline, the instruments were ovoid, but with scalloped edges, and with flat or slightly convex backs, unlike the deeply rounded back of the lute. The strings were of brass, or brass and steel, and the bass strings were made of multiple twisted strands.[56] Both originally had six courses, or pairs, of strings, but by the 1590s the bandora was typically a seven-course instrument, while the orpharion followed the development of the lute and could have as many as nine courses.[57] The development of the oblique bridge seems to date from the 1590s as well.[58]

Both instruments were well established by 1600, and, as Gill notes, twelve of the twenty-nine music books with lute tablature published between 1597 and 1622 "were explicitly for lute and orpharion, and two of the three contemporary lute tutors were for orpharion and bandora as well."[59] Even lute music that was not designated for orpharion as well could be played on either instrument. Francis Pilkington's *Second Set of Madrigals*, dedicated, as we have seen, to the Cheshire gentleman Sir Peter Legh of Lyme, contains "a Pauin made for the Orpharion, by the Right Honourable, *William*, Earle of *Darbie*, and by him consented to be in my Bookes placed."[60]

However, the wire-strung instruments required a different playing technique from the lute. William Barley's *New Book of Tabliture* (London, 1596), a tutor for lute, orpharion, and bandora, warns against the wire strings being "sharplie stroken as the Lute is: for if yee should do so, then the wire stringes would clash or jarre together the one against the other."[61] Despite the different technique, the bandora was considered an easy instrument to play, and as a chromatic instrument, it offered a wider range than the arch-lute with only half the number of strings. It thus was considered a valuable bass instrument.

In the Cheshire records, bandoras are not found as commonly as lutes or virginals, but they do occur in a number of inventories after 1597, when it was recorded, as noted above, that Mary Somerford played this instrument as well as lute, cittern, and virginals. Bandoras are several times the subject of specific bequests, not simply items in inventories. Henry Wright, a Nantwich innkeeper, left his bandora to his brother James in 1607, and Henry Hardware of Peel left his bandora to William Handy in 1612.[62] It is interesting to note that both also left viols to other friends or relatives, which may indicate that the bandoras had been used for consort playing. Henry Wright's inventory mentions a bandora, bass viol, and "other playeinge Instrumentes."[63] Bandoras frequently appear in company with other instruments in inventories: at Chester in 1637 with a kit,[64] at Crewe in 1612 with a lute and case,[65] at Nantwich in 1639 with a bass viol.[66] This is in keeping with its use as a consort instrument.

The orpharion, on the other hand, occurs only once in the Cheshire records, in the inventory of goods of William Worrall, a professional musician at Nantwich in 1637, and even here the identification is to a certain degree conjectural since the spelling "alferiall" used in the document does not apparently occur elsewhere and is not listed as a variant in the *Oxford English Dictionary*. The form "alpharion," however, does occur in a document of 1610.[67] This spelling is unusual and suggests that the instrument was not well-known in the region, but I can find no other possible instrument for which "alferiall" could be a variant spelling. The fact that it is associated with other instruments—a bandora, a bass viol, and three treble viols, and that no lute is mentioned—is also interesting.[68] These instruments may have made up an alternative form of broken consort, which usually consisted of lute, treble viol or violin, bass viol, cittern, bandora, and flute. As the orpharion, as noted above, was capable of playing virtually all lute music, the only missing instruments in this listing are the cittern and flute, but these may have been available for consort playing from other owners than Worrall. It may be noted that two of the four citterns found in the Cheshire records come from Nantwich

inventories slightly earlier than this one. Similarly, the possible involvement of Worrall in a dispute with the piper John Vaughan,
mentioned in chapter II, may provide the name of a potential flute-
player for a broken consort. Although their relationship in 1632
appears to have been hostile, a falling-out between musicians who are
colleagues was by no means unusual, as the evidence for the Chester
waits shows. In any case, even if Worrall was not part of a professional
consort of musicians, he may well have found that the wire-strung
orpharion was more durable than a lute, and it additionally could have
had the appeal of providing a different sound or timbre.

The following section will treat bowed strings, which include
viols, violin and the kit.

Viols. The terms 'viol' and 'violin,' as found in the Cheshire
records, refer primarily to the renaissance instrument. The renaissance
viol is a six-stringed instrument, tuned in fourths with one third in the
middle. It has a long tailpiece, a wide, fretted fingerboard, flat back,
and sloping shoulders. The sides are deep and with round edges. The
sound holes are usually C-shaped, or "flame" shaped, and there are
reinforcing bars inside the body. The pegbox is surmounted by a
curved head.[69] The violin had four strings and was tuned in fifths. It
had a shorter tailpiece, a narrower, unfretted fingerboard, a rounded
back and shoulders with shallow sides, and purfling around the edges
which the viol lacked. Inside there was a reinforcing longitudinal
bassbar, and the sound holes were *f*-shaped. The pegbox was surmounted by a scroll. The violin was a more robust instrument than the
viol, which was preferred by the gentry. The violin, and its medieval
equivalent, the fiddle, were generally associated with taverns. The term
'viol da gamba' is also used for the viol and is strictly speaking more
correct since a distinction was made between viol da gamba, which was
played held between or leaning against the legs, and viol da braccio,
which was held on the arm or shoulder. Reese's statement that "viols
of the *gamba* type were used for chamber music, viols of the *braccio*
variety being considered street instruments" is still generally accepted.

The viol came in a variety of sizes, which were only standardized
after 1600. A consort of viols is first mentioned in England at the
court of Henry VIII in 1540, although the medieval viol was commonly used in England before that time.   A chest of viols, such as is
mentioned in Hinde's *Life of John Bruen*, would have had six viols: two
bass, two tenor, and two treble.   The "set of violles de la gamba"

mentioned in Francis Fitton's will would most likely have been a chest of six viols.[73] All three sizes are found as separate items in the Cheshire records, and there are also viols or viols da gamba of unspecified size. A "base violl" occurs in the inventory of the goods of Sir Peter Legh the Younger of Lyme in 1642. Its exact value is not known since it is grouped with "Cupboards, Tables, Chaires, Cushions, stooles, Laver & Vre, Carpetts, Hangings of Arrase" in the dining room at Lyme Hall, at a value of £35 4s.[74] In 1639, the inventory of Thomas Bickerton of Nantwich lists a bandora and a bass viol at a value of thirty shillings.[75] In 1648, a bass viol in the inventory of a professional musician was valued at £1 10s.[76] Two other occurrences of bass viols in inventories have a probable value of under £1: in 1607, a bandora, bass viol, and other unspecified "playeinge Instrument*es*" were valued at £2 in Nantwich,[77] and the six instruments and music books listed in William Worrall's will came to £1 18s.[78] The value of a used instrument would of course vary according to the original quality of the craftsmanship and the amount of damage the instrument had suffered over the years. The three broken viols in the Brereton inventory were only worth as much as a single lute.[79]

It is interesting to note that all but one of the bass viols in the records come from Nantwich, and these include the viol lent by Thomas Wilbraham to his cousin Ann Whittingham (see chapter III). The numbers here may simply reflect the better survival rate of inventories for Nantwich, but nevertheless the possession of bass viols by two professional musicians there does suggest that consort playing was occurring at this town. William Worrall and Roger Vaughan may have been teachers as well as performers. The bass viol is specifically mentioned as a solo or accompanying instrument in Richard Alison's *Psalmes of David in Meter* (1599), which are "to be sung and plaide upon the Lute, Orpharyon, Citterne or Base Violl, severally or altogether, the singing part to be either Tenor or Treble to the instrument."[80] The bass viol was, of course, also one of the standard instruments in a mixed or "broken" consort.

The tenor viol appears in the Cheshire records only in the inventory of the goods of William Maddock, the Chester wait, where it is valued at six shillings and eight pence.[81] Some of the unspecified viols and viols da gamba may of course be tenor viols, but it is also possible that the lute was preferred as a solo instrument or as an accompaniment to the voice,[82] the tenor viol still occurring in viol consorts. The tenor viol was more suitable for a wait since it could be carried suspended from the neck while walking. The treble viol is also rare in the Cheshire records. One was bought for Sir Richard Wilbraham in 1613, and three are mentioned in the Worrall inventory.[83]

Given the shortage of information about the values of bass viols and the scarcity in the records of mentions of the tenor and treble viols, it is impossible to determine the relative values. Maddock's tenor viol, at 6s 8d in 1604, would at first appear to be worth much less than Vaughan's bass viol at £1 10s, but the difference of over forty years between the two inventories is probably more of a factor than the size or quality of the instruments themselves. Evidence from outside Cheshire shows that viols could be relatively costly instruments: a bass viol bought by the Earl of Cumberland in 1614 cost £2, but there is no indication whether this was a new or a relatively expensive instrument.[84] This price, however, is roughly in keeping with the composite values listed in the Nantwich inventories and the value of the Vaughan bass viol. Woodfill's appendix on Household Records suggests that £4 was a fairly standard price for a *viol da gamba* at the beginning of the seventeenth century. The Earl of Rutland's accounts list viols da gamba bought for £4 in c.1599, 1600, and 1602.[85] Comparisons here too are hard to make since both the Maddock and Vaughan viols were instruments listed in the inventories of professional musicians and most likely to have been valued as used goods. Even when new they were probably designed for use, not prestige—and hence were not the most expensive instruments available.

The treble viol bought for Sir Richard Wilbraham in 1613 cost 12s 6d, with a further 6s 6d for case and strings.[86] As this was a gift, the instrument and case may well have been a relatively expensive. On the other hand, the three treble viols listed in William Worrall's inventory were probably much less valuable even when new and now, suffering from wear and tear, much less so since the combined value of six instruments and an unspecified number of music books was only £1 18s. Yet as Maddock, Vaughan, and Worrall were professional musicians, the variety and relative value of their instruments is of interest. Maddock's inventory, from 1604, contains mainly wind instruments (see Appendix I). The tenor viol is the exception. Worrall's inventory, in 1637, contains no wind instruments at all. This probably reflects the different roles of the two professional musicians and perhaps also the changing tastes of the seventeenth century.

Nantwich was not as large as Chester, and, although it seems to have supported a number of musicians of one sort and another, there nevertheless is no evidence that there was a band of town waits. However, given the number of gentry inventories with instruments that complement those in Worrall's inventory, it seems possible that he was either teaching music or was a professional who was hired to augment the ensembles of the gentry. Not impossibly he might have fulfilled both roles. Vaughan's inventory contains no instruments other than the bass viol, which he also mentions specifically in his will.

Violin and Fiddle. The violin, like the viol, came in different sizes, but during the period covered by the present study it does not figure greatly in the inventories of the Cheshire gentry, perhaps because of its associations with street music.[87] As an instrument it was easier to carry and easier to tune.[88] Indeed, the only specific (rather than implied) mention of violins comes from a Quarter Sessions deposition from Chester in 1594 which mentions both the treble and bass violins. The examinate, Richard Preston, is described as being a musician from Warrington who was playing in St. Werburgh Lane with his "company," very likely a professional group. The Chester waits, at about the same period (1590–91), also had violins among their instruments.[89] Preston's encounter with Mr. Hicock, who borrowed and played his treble violin, has already been quoted (see chapter I).[90]

2–3. Angel musicians playing fiddles on woodcarvings at Nantwich. The instrument at left shows a gouge above the strings which also affects the upper end of the bow. Drawing by Marianne Cappelletti, after photographs by the author.

Mr. Hicock's behavior may well have something to do with the time spent in John Stil's tavern, but it is noteworthy that he was able to play the violin "very excelent well." Preston also shows apparent versatility. It is his treble violin that is borrowed by Mr. Hicock, but he is able to supply an accompaniment, evidently on a bass violin borrowed from one of his companions, as they go up the lane. The fact that Hicock turns violent when invited by Preston to drink with him suggests that the latter had crossed a social divide, though the former's playing of Preston's violin had been acceptable. Preston's claim that he "spake him faier in that he knew not whoe he was" is slightly ambiguous and may imply that he would have been more polite if he had known the identity of Mr. Hicock, clerk. The exact course of events and the reasons for Mr. Hicock's behavior are unclear and were possibly unclear at the time. It is, however, evident that knowledge of violin playing was not confined to street musicians.

Also to be considered in connection with the violin is the fiddle. Although the violin is only mentioned once and the fiddle not at all, *fiddlers* are mentioned frequently from the fifteenth century onwards. The medieval fiddle, which needs to be distinguished from the rebec, was the most important bowed instrument in court society in the medieval period.[91] It suffered a decline in the sixteenth century to become an instrument associated with taverns and alehouses. The renaissance fiddle was a development of the medieval fiddle, and by 1500 had five strings, one of which might be an unstopped drone. It was closer to a violin in size and appearance, and was constructed from separate pieces (neck, fingerboard, top, back, and connecting ribs).[92] Newer instruments played by fifteenth-century fiddlers undoubtedly differed from those played by sixteenth-century fiddlers, although we may assume that the older form of the instrument continued to be played by some musicians after 1500.[93]

4. Organistrum or symphony player with damaged right hand (originally turning crank) on woodcarving at Nantwich. Drawing by Marianne Cappelletti, after photograph by author.

Kit. The kit is described by Mary Remnant in the *New Grove Dictionary of Music and Musicians* as "a small bowed unfretted fiddle, generally with four strings, made in a great variety of shapes and played from the 16th century to the 19th."[94] The only apparent mention of this instrument in the Cheshire records is in the inventory of Thomas Jones of Chester, innholder, in 1637: "Itt [one] 2 Instrvmentes Called a bandore & a Kitte."[95] We need to be cautious since the writer of the inventory does not seem to be very sure of the names of the instruments, and it is possible that the K is written over a C. If this is the case, it may be that the scribe was expecting "cittern," and corrected to "Kitte." Bandora and cittern would be a more usual combination than bandora and kit, but the combination is not an impossible one.

Table II: Wind Instruments

Bagpipes	1597 — 1622 {1597 — 1612}
Cornetts	1590 — 1618–19
Double Curtal	1604
Flute	1613–14
Hoboy	1590–91
Horn	1570 — 1630 {1488–89}
Pipe and Tabor	1605
Pipes	1597 — 1617 {1367 — 1641}
Recorders	c.1502 — 1608
Sackbut	1604
Trumpet	1604–05 — 1609 {1454 — 1623–24}
Whistle	no date
Wind Instrument (unspecified)	1627 & 1625–36

Wind Instruments

The wind instruments, like the strings, can be subdivided according to form of instrument and manner of playing: metal or wood, or even horn, with or without reed, with the air provided either by blowing or by pumping a bag or bellows. It is not, however, always possible to tell to which group a particular instrument actually belongs. The term 'pipe' can refer to a bagpipe, a shawm, or wait-pipe, and a whistle-flute. A flute could be either a transverse flute or a recorder. The same term may describe different instruments at different places and times, and different terms may be used for the same instrument.

Pipes. The pipes are probably the largest and most confusing group in the Cheshire records. Pipers are the most common type of instrumentalist mentioned in the records, but only rarely is any specific information given about their instruments.

Bagpipes. The documents, then, tend to use 'pipes' as a generic term covering a range of instruments, and there does not seem to be a sharp distinction made between terms such as 'piper' and 'bagpiper.' The latter is used less often, but it is clear that some pipers played bagpipes. Robert Laithwood[96] of Runcorn is listed as a piper in 1616 in lists of those presented or indicted for transgressions.[97] A surviving Jury's Presentment and the Crown Books record a charge in 1617 of piping on the sabbath. The Jury's Presentment is a typical one for sabbath piping: "The Iury for our sou<...>igne lord the Kinge present Robert Leathwood of Roncorne [f..] being a piper for playinge on his pipes on the sabboth day ordinarylye in Runcorne [and] contrary to certen Artycles concluded vpon by the Iustice of Chester and in prophanacion of the lords Sabboth."[98]

None of this tells us anything about the type of pipes which Laithwood played, nor would we know more about his pipes than about those of any of the many other pipers who were charged with piping on the sabbath, were it not for his death. Laithwood committed suicide by hanging himself, and such property as he had became the possession of the lord of the manor, in this case Sir Thomas Savage of Rocksavage. The bailiff's accounts for 1622 specify:

> he chargeth himselfe with the receipte of one great paire of droane Bagpipes which he seised vpon att Evensonges howse by the Bridgend in Overton within the parishe of ffrodsham which happened for a deodant vpon Robert Lethwoodes of Runcornes hanging of himselfe in the Marled Earthes feild within the demesnes of Rocksavage and over night before he hanged himselfe had left the same pipes att Evensonges which were estemed to be worthe [blank] as this accomptant estemed them which Pipes mr

> Io Savage sent to him for the same with an intencon to vse them
> the Last *Ch*ristmas att woodhaye [wh] whose request he assented
> vnto with promise to retorne them to this accomptant safe agayne
> or the price ffor w*h*ich this accomptant is to stand still charged
> either to render the pipes or the price [when] att the next accompte
> or when S*i*r Tho Savage or anye from him shall requier the same
> one paire of pipes[99]

Throughout Laithwood has been described as a piper, but the pipes that he evidently played (and which appear to have been his most valuable possession) were bagpipes. It is unfortunate that the estimated value of the pipes is left blank. Evensong, at whose house the pipes were left, was probably himself a fiddler. A Richard Richardson "alias will*ia*mson alias Evensong" was charged with playing on an Instrum*en*t of musicke" on Sunday and collecting "an assembly of people" 1617 at Frodsham, and is mentioned in the crown book for 1617 under the same date as Laithwood is charged with piping on the sabbath.[100] He is likely to be the same person who is described in the information of the High Constable of Eddisbury Hundred as "R<..>hard Ensong fidler" who played on the sabbath in Frodsham, also in 1617.[101] The "mr Io Savage" mentioned is probably Sir Thomas Savage's younger brother, John Savage. "Woodhaye" is Woodhey, home of Sir Richard Wilbraham, who had married Grace Savage, sister of Sir Thomas and John.[102] Evidently John Savage was spending Christmas with his sister's family, and felt that the bagpipes would add to the festivities, although it is unlikely that he played them himself. The bagpipes, described variously as a "pair of bagpipes" and a "pair of great bagpipes," continue to appear, without a monetary value, in the bailiff's accounts until 1625.[103] In 1625 they again are put to use:

> It*em* he praieth to be allowed of one paire of great Bagg Pipes that
> remayned in this accomptant*es* hand*es* seised vpon Laithwait*es*
> hanginge of himself w*h*ich Pipes one Huntsman a piper beinge a
> sutor vnto Cap*ten* W*illia*m Saunders for the havinge of those Pipes
> wiled S*i*r Tho*mas* Savage to bestowe them on Huntesman and for
> that this accomptant charged not to deliu*er* them to anye w*i*thout
> S*i*r Tho*mas* Savage*s* warrant & the Cap*ten* pressing him vpon a
> p*re*tended p*ro*mise fframed a warrant to this accomptant that
> seinge the Cap*ten* alleadged that he had p*ro*mised to geue them to
> the Piper he dared not to disavowe any acte that the Cap*ten* would
> doe And therevpon signed his warr*an*t dated the xxjth of

September i624 as by the same nowe shewen appeareth   one
paire of great Pipes[104]

Huntsman is probably Thomas Foster, alias Huntsman, of Hatton,
which is also in Runcorn parish. He appears as a piper in a recognizance of 1617.[105] Captain Saunders has not been identified, but
evidently had sufficient influence with Sir Thomas that the bailiff felt
able to give him the pipes.

The terms used to describe Laithwood's pipes—"great," "drone,"
"pair"—tell us a little about them, although not as much as could be
wished. "Pair" may indicate that the pipes had more than one drone
pipe, and this would be in keeping with the usage of "drone" and even
with "great" since the instrument "in its commonest forms consists of
a chanter and one or more drones, all supplied with air from the bag,
which is compressed under the player's arm to provide a constant
pressure."[106] Bagpipes can be either mouth-blown or bellows-blown,
the former producing a louder sound, more suited for outdoor playing.
The term 'great' can simply mean a set of pipes with more drones than
the average, but it also suggests the Highland *píob mhór*, literally 'great
pipe,' with three drones (two tenor, one bass), chanter, and blowpipe,
which was known as a martial instrument from the sixteenth century
onwards.[107] References to a similar instrument in Ireland are found
from 1544.[108] Other possible candidates include the Scottish Lowland
pipes and the English Northumbrian half-long pipes, both of which
have three drones in one stock. The Lowland drones are bass, tenor,
and tenor, while the Northumbrian drones are bass, treble, and treble.
These pipes lie across the piper's chest and are played while he is
seated.[109]

It is impossible to determine which, if any, of these pipes Laithwood played. We can only say that he played a bagpipe with probably
more than one drone which was possibly larger than another type of
pipe found in general use, as the bailiff saw fit to comment on its size.
Other evidence about pipers and their pipes indicates, however, that
some at least of the variety of pipes itemized in the preceding
paragraph were being played. At Poynton in 1611, Roger Murgell was
presented at the diocesan visitation "for playeinge on lowde pypes on
the Sabboath daie."[110] These would probably have been mouth-blown
bagpipes rather than a shawm, which, although loud, is not referred to
in the plural, or a bellows-pipe, which has a softer tone. Indeed, when
the records mention a single piper playing on plural pipes, bagpipes are

indicated. However, one very clear mention of bagpipes in the documents occurs in 1597 when Thomas Yemouth described himself as "a mynstrell & dothe vse to playe vpon the bagpipes" (see chapter II, part 2).[111]

The practice of sitting down to play the pipes, which suggests something like the Northumbrian or the Lowland pipes, is found in the metropolitan visitation material for Lancashire. At Wenslow in 1595 several of the parishioners are presented for their participation in a piping in the churchyard. The principal count against three of them is that they "would not helpe to reforme the abuse of pypinge and dauncinge that day but suffred a chaire to be broughte into the churche yard for william harrison the pyper to sitt in that day."[112] It is likely that the provision of a chair was necessary to the performance—that is, that Harrison was playing pipes which had to be played sitting. The piping on this occasion was specifically linked to dancing, and other occasions which feature plural pipes (presumably bagpipes) are also often associated with dancing. In 1616 Humphrey Peacock the elder is cited for performing at the Tarporley Wakes: "in the howse of William Thomasson Alekeeper in ye night season at vnseasonable time contrary to ye law plea on his pipes and a great number of disorder persons did then and there dance and drinck contrary to the statute in that Case provided."[113] Thomas Towers, who was presented in 1610 for "playinge on his pipes in the open street to dawncers vpon sonday the xvth daye of this instant aprill from on of the clock in the afternoone vntill six of the same daye at vpton aforesayd"[114] was probably playing on loud outdoor pipes, as was John Baxter, alias Barne, whose piping at Mobberley in 1597 was, as we have seen, calculated as much to annoy the rector as to entertain the parishioners.[115]

Pipe and Tabor. Piping which is accompanied by dancing in Cheshire was not confined to the bagpipes, for another popular instrument for this purpose was the pipe and tabor, though specific instances of a performer playing these are rare in the county records. John Vaughan of Nantwich played upon a "tabrett & pype" at the neighboring village of Wistaston on the sabbath at service time in 1605,[116] and an undated account of the Chester Midsummer Show specifies a payment of twenty shillings to six morris dancers "& Tabrett & pipe."[117] Further performances with pipe and tabor are implied in the 1608–09 Banns to the Chester plays, in which the Smiths are exhorted to "Gett mynstrelles to that Shewe pype Tabrett and fflute."[118] It is likely, however, that some pipers were in fact pipe-

and-tabor players. The pipe and tabor was a combination particularly suited to providing music for dancing, as can be seen from the Midsummer Show example. Many of the generic references to piping at ales or for dancing may refer to playing the pipe and tabor. There is simply no way of determining which pipe was played in these cases. The pipe in the pipe and tabor combination was a simple three-hole duct flute, held in and played with the left hand. It had a range of about an octave and a half.[119] The tabor in England was generally a shallow side drum with two heads, across one or both of which a gut snare was stretched. It hung from the left wrist or shoulder, and was beaten with a stick held in the right hand.[120] The term 'taborer' could also be used to designate this combination, as found in the diocesan visitation in 1611 at Manchester, where Richard Hampson was presented for having an ale on a Sunday and having "a drum*m*er and a taber that played that daie."[121] The distinction between the drummer and the taborer heightens the probability that the latter played the pipe as well.

5. Angel musician playing shawm. Sculpture on west front of Chester Cathedral. The original is weathered, and the top part of the instrument is broken away (here restored). Drawing by Marianne Cappelletti, after the photograph by Sally-Beth MacLean (*Chester Art*, pl. 1).

Shawm, Hoboy, or Wait Pipe. The third type of pipe that was possibly played by pipers is variously known as the shawm, hoboy, or wait pipe, the latter indicating that this loud (*haut*) instrument was especially associated with waits. However, only the term 'hoboy' actually appears in the Cheshire records, and that only once, in 1590–91, when Alice Williams, the widow of one of the Chester waits, claims a share in the waits' instruments on her husband's behalf. These instruments include "the how boies the Recorders the Cornet*es* and violens."[122] The term 'hoboy' in this period was used interchangeably with 'shawm,' and the instruments referred to here are undoubtedly those known today as shawms rather than the two- or three-key oboe designated by 'hautboy' in the seventeenth century. The shawm is a double-reed instrument with a conical bore. The reed is placed on a staple in a pirouette, against which the player's lips could rest while the reed vibrates freely in the mouth. The shawm came in a family of sizes. Usually only two or three of these sizes were played together: treble, alto-tenor, and bass.[123] Frequently the shawn was played in consort with other instruments, and a painting by Denijs van Alsloot (1616) which shows a band with shawm, cornett, two tenor shawms, sackbut, and curtal may represent actual performance practice.[124] It is thus noteworthy that the inventory of the Chester wait William Maddock in 1604 includes three of the instruments shown in the painting: cornetts, sackbut, and double curtal. The shawms (hoboys) of the 1590–91 Chester Mayors' Book entry supply the rest of the band, with recorders and violins (as well as Maddock's tenor viol) for soft indoor music (*bas*, as opposed to *haut*). There are no other indications in the Cheshire records of pipers who played shawms, but equally no reason why they could not. One would expect that pipers normally were able to play several kinds of pipes, and the waits certainly were able to. Most wind instruments—including cornetts, crumhorns, recorders, bagpipes and shawms—had virtually identical fingering.[125]

Flutes and Recorders. The term 'flute' may designate either a transverse flute or a *flute a bec*, or recorder, whereas 'recorder' refers only to that family of instruments. The flute used in broken consorts was sometimes a recorder, although in England the transverse flute seems to have been preferred. Only one consort book (Matthew Holmes, c.1595), still in manuscript, specifies a recorder.[126] Neither term is common in the Cheshire records. Such mentions of the recorders as do survive are associated with the gentry or the waits. It will be remembered that *The Stanley Poem* tells us that Sir Edward Stanley was noted for his ability to play two recorders simultaneously,[127] and his choice of instrument is in keeping with fifteenth-century paintings of upper-class men and women holding recorders.[128] The Fitton recorders, part of a collection of musical instruments mentioned in Francis Fitton's will, were clearly a matched set, probably in a box. The recorder was a soft (*bas*) instrument, made of wood, suitable for chamber music, to accompany singing or dancing. This instrument appeared among those owned by the Chester waits in 1590–91,[129] and in fact the recorder was one of the regular instruments of professional wind players along with the shawm, cornett, sackbut (all found in the possession of the Chester waits), and sometimes flute or trumpet.[130]

The usage of the term 'flute' in the Cheshire records is also rare, and, in its context, may relate to the military flute rather than the flute used in mixed consorts. The drum and flute were evidently used in combination in the Shrovetide procession of 1613–14 when the players received six pence from the Chester Shoemakers company.[131] This is the only mention of a flute as such in the Cheshire records, although the Banns of 1608–09 refer to a "fflute" which may be something like the three-hole duct flute.[132]

Whistles. Whistles are, like pipes and flutes, a vague category. Jeremy Montagu, writing in the *New Grove Dictionary of Music and Musicians*, describes it as a "short, usually high-pitched flute ('edge aerophone'), either without fingerholes or with no more than one."[133] However, the term as used in the documents could possibly include whistle-flutes as well as simple whistles. In one of the cases the whistle is a toy sent by Margaret Lowther to her sister, Elizabeth Winnington, to be given to Margaret's son, who is evidently still an infant, and being looked after by his aunt. The letter is full of instructions for the child's nurse: "I haue sent: two paire of stocking and a whisell: with a siluer chaine I pray: you: bid her hau^e^ a care of: it that she doe not breake. it."[134] The other mention of a whistle is less precise and involves a professional musician, or at least the son of one. John Cally, son of Peter Cally of the Chester family of waits, appeared before the portmote court in 1588–89 and was ordered not to go about "ludend*um* psallen*es* le whistelinge" (possibly either "sporting playing the whistle" or "playing to the accompaniment of the whistle") after 9 p.m., nor to be outside his lodgings after that hour, under pain of a £40 fine, and a £10 fine if he did not behave in an honest and discreet manner.[135] The whistle in this case is most likely to have been some type of whistle-flute. What is unusual about the item is that the Latin word "psallen*es*" is more properly associated with a stringed instrument or with singing to the accompaniment of a stringed instrument.[136] Could this indicate that Cally was *whistling* while accompanying himself on a stringed instrument, or is playing the whistle sufficiently unusual that a term normally associated with stringed instruments is used here generically for playing any musical instrument?

The whistles used by the shepherds' boys in the Chester play have been discussed by Professor Mills in chapter II, part 1.

Double Curtal and Sackbut. These instruments occur only once each in the Cheshire records, in the 1604 inventory of the goods of the Chester wait William Maddock. The term 'curtal' refers at this period to the dulcian, and a double curtal is the bass form of the instrument. Louder than the bass recorder, more agile than the sackbut, and less cumbersome than the bass shawm, it gradually replaced the latter in the wait bands. The double curtal comprises elements from other instruments: it has the double reed of a shawm, the curved crook of a bass recorder and bass shawm, and the doubled-back bore (within a single block of wood) of the phagotus.[137] It was made of a single shaft of wood (maple or fruit), oval in section, nearly one meter tall, drilled with two bores connected at the bottom to form one continuous conical tube. At the top, a curved brass crook was inserted into the narrow end of the bore, with the other end slightly extended to form a flared bell. The thickness of the walls enabled fingerholes to be drilled obliquely to accommodate the span of the fingers. There were eight fingerholes and two open keys, the latter protected by perforated brass boxes.[138]

By 1604, the double curtal was in fact well established as an instrument regularly played by companies of waits. The combination of bagpipe, curtal, and shawm involved all loud (*haut*) instruments suitable for outdoor use.[139] The sackbut seems to have developed sometime in the late fifteenth century and was essentially a *buisine* type of trumpet, furnished with a telescopic slide.[140] Added to the shawms for loud music, it was, while versatile, not suitable for playing treble parts, which were supplied by shawms for outdoor music and cornetts for indoor music. However, both shawms and cornetts could be used in a mixed band.[141]

Cornetts. Maddock's 1604 inventory also includes two cornetts, and he thus personally lacked only the shawms to make up a full mixed band. Shawms, along with cornetts, are found in the possession of Alice Williams, widow of the wait Thomas Williams, in 1590–91. The cornett, a hybrid form, is an instrument which defies strict classification since it combines the cup-mouthpiece technique of the brass instruments with the finger technique of the woodwinds. The instrument had considerable dynamic range and could be as loud as a trumpet or as soft as a recorder. A great deal of the tonal variety in playing was managed by the embouchure.[142] It came in sets like other instruments, and of the three main sizes—treble, small treble (cornettino), and tenor—the treble was the most important. This also came in three types: straight, curved (the most common), and "mute."[143] Cornetts evidently also were used by themselves on ceremonial occasions, as the Chester Cathedral Treasurers' Accounts list a payment in 1618–19 of 2s 6d to "the Cornetts at the Assises." This item immediately follows, and may be linked to, a payment of £1 14s 6d for "bonefires & triumphes at the Princes returne."[144] The article on this instrument in the *New Grove Dictionary of Music and Musicians* notes that cornetts were sometimes used for virtuoso displays, and it may be that this is what is indicated here.[145]

Trumpets. The medieval trumpet had a limited range of notes and was used mainly for ceremonial music and, as noted above in chapter II, part 1, in stage directions for the Chester Whitsun play, presumably for the Last Judgment pageant where the term that is used is 'tuba.' This instrument was typically straight and over six feet long.[146] The renaissance trumpet was similarly used but developed a characteristic S-shape and the ability to play in the higher register. Trumpeters appear fairly early in the Chester records; for example, Thomas White, trumpeter, is mentioned in a Sheriffs' Roll of 1454.[147] Throughout our period the trumpet was associated with ceremonial occasions such as visits from royalty or nobility or civic events such as the Chester Midsummer Show at which various guilds paid trumpeters as well as other musicians.[148] But trumpets were also military instruments, and this can be seen in combination with the trumpet's role as a perquisite of the nobility in the Congleton accounts for 1623, when six pence was "Bestowed vpon a Trvmpeter of the Earle of Derbeys, who came out of the Lowe Contreys."[149] The Earl of Pembroke's trumpeters apparently visited Lyme Hall, although the date of their visit is not known.[150] Trumpets are found in the inventory of goods of Rowland Dutton of Hatton, but as might be expected are not as common in gentry inventories as lutes or virginals.[151]

This is not to say that trumpets or trumpeters were exclusively found in a courtly context. The Congleton Borough Accounts record expenses in connection with a trumpeter who had, apparently for fraudulent purposes, a badger's licence (see chapter II, part 2).[152] The badger's licence entitled him to beg, and the trumpeter had presumably been making fraudulent use of it. A similarly low-status trumpeter is found at Nether Knutsford in 1609, when Jeffrey Bentley, a local innkeeper, testified of a quarrel between John Crosby, one of the high constables of Bucklow hundred, and William Houlme on 31 August

1609: "At which daye a Tynker came [in] to the sayde howse with pannes vpon his Backe, & a Trumpett in his hande, the said Crossbie bade the saide Tynker sound his trumpett for all hooremaisters, the which hee did; & then the sayd Crossbie bade him sounde againe for all drunkerdes the which hee lykewise did, by Reasoun whereof manie people were drawenn together."[153] The trumpet's role as alarm and summons is essential here. People came at the sound of the trumpet because they associated it with danger, important news, or important visitors. Crosby, however, redefined the terms of the summons, and no doubt informed the people when they arrived that they were the "hooremaisters" and "drunkerdes" he had summoned.

Horn. The horn was primarily a functional rather than a recreational instrument and was used for hunting and for communicating over distance, as presumably implied in the case of the Chester First Shepherd where it is called a *cornu*. It could be part of a gentleman's accouterments, as is the case with the "Bauldrake & a horne" bought by Thomas Wilbraham for fourteen shillings in 1613 at the time when he was commencing dancing and fencing lessons.[154] The horn is also specified as one of the instruments played by Sir Edward Stanley in *The Stanley Poem*.[155] Horn-blowing could also be a form of breach of the peace, as appears to have happened at Shotwick in 1615. The preacher, Mr. Burrows, who had been licensed by the chancellor of the diocese, David Yale, there being at that time no bishop, was forcibly kept out of the pulpit on Christmas Eve with threats, horn-blowing, and "great hallowinge."[156] The horn-blowing and "great hallowinge" did not involve a musical performance as such but, as far as can be determined, were an intentional disruption of the sermon. The reasons for the dispute are not given, but a list of alehousekeepers and infant bastards for the hundred of Wirrall in 1616, in the same bundle of documents, mentions that "There is one Thomas Baggott within this said towne of Capenhurst which doth harbor one Ioane Ianion & a bastard of hirs supposed to bee the Child of one Iohn Burrowes, sometime minister of Shotwicke & there kept & mainteyned since Easter last."[157] This document suggests that the horn-blowing might well have been an expression of moral disapprobation (see also chapter II, part 2).

There is one other doubtful mention of a horn. In 1488–89 the Chester Mayors' Books contain a memorandum that Robert Chalner, fiddler, is to keep the peace towards Richard Hey, horner. Two of his sureties are minstrels (the other two are a hooper and a pardoner), which suggests that Richard Hey may have been a musician as well, though another (less likely) possibility is that he was a person who manufactured goods out of horn.[158]

Table III: Keyboard Instruments	
Desk Virginals	1617
Harpsicalls (harpsichord)	1643
Organs	1518 — 1638 {1504 — 1643}
Regals	1605
Virginals	1557–1643 {single virginal specified in 1643}

The Keyboard Instruments

The Cheshire records report two main groups of keyboard instruments: those which are operated by wind through pipes, including the organ and regals, and those which are plucked by quills. The latter group includes virginals, harpsichords, and spinets, but the term 'virginals' could be used generically for any of these. This seems to have been a particularly English usage since Praetorius considers it worth noting.[159]

Virginals. Virginals could be described as either single, double, or "a pair of," with the latter being perhaps the most common. Single and double probably refer to the range of the instrument, with the double virginal having a full range down to the double notes in the system used at the time, rather than the limited downward compass of the single virginal.[160] The virginal had two bridges, unlike the harpsichord, and a single set of strings, which were oblong, and ran parallel to the keyboards (on the spinet they ran either diagonally or parallel). Dynamic and accentual gradations were not possible, but the player's articulation could produce very subtle effects. Also, variation in the placing of the keyboard produced varying sounds because the strings were plucked in different places.[161]

Virginals were decidedly gentry instruments and were found almost exclusively in the households of the gentry or the aspiring merchant class. The value of the instruments varied, naturally, with both the size (single or double) and quality of the instrument. An early pair of virginals owned by Richard Brereton of Lea in 1558 was worth £1 13s 4d, a considerable sum compared to the four shillings each for the lute and broken viols in the same inventory.[162] An old pair of virginals at Eaton in 1594 was valued at only five shillings, and at Crokeley Bredbury in 1633 another at only two shillings.[163] Inventory valuations of virginals range upwards from these amounts, specifically for "old" instruments and probably indicating some level of decay, to more usual prices of £1 and over, up to £3 for a virginal with a frame at Chester in 1624 and again in 1633.[164] A single virginal listed amongst the goods confiscated from Robert Tatton at Withenshawe in 1643 was valued at £4, suggesting that it was a particularly fine instrument.[165] A new pair of virginals would generally be more expensive than those listed in inventories: virginals bought new for Mary Somerford in 1597 cost £4, and a pair of virginals for her in 1598 cost £3 13s 4d.[166] The virginals, thought according to the popular etymology of the time to have been so named on account of the usual players, were certainly predominantly a lady's instrument. Not only do we see virginals being bought for Mary Somerford but also the instrument lent by John Leche of Carden to various relatives and friends is specifically his wife's. He lent them first to his cousin, Mrs. Anne Massey of Coddington; from there they proceeded to his cousin, Mr. Harper of Chester, and thence to Mr. Nuball, organist of the city of Chester, then, after being returned to Carden, were lent to John Leche's cousin, Mr. Wilkinson, specifically for his daughter's use (see chapter III).[167]

Harpsichord. Like the virginals, the harpsichord's action involves plucking the strings by means of jacks in which quills are inserted. The main difference between the two instruments is in the shape of the soundbox and the placement of the strings.[168] From the evidence of the records, harpsichords would seem to have been very rare in Cheshire, although, as noted above, there may be a difficulty here in that some of the instruments referred to as virginals may have in fact been this instrument. We might speculate that in the case of the virginals bought for Mary Somerford in two consecutive years, one of them—the more expensive "virginals"—might have been in fact a harpsichord or a spinet, although the records allow for no certainty here. The only harpsichord verifiably found in the Cheshire records is a considerably more expensive instrument than the virginals: in the Tatton inventory, a "paire of harpsicalls" was valued at £7.[169]

Organs. Most of the evidence for organs in Cheshire is connected with churches, as might be expected from the size and expense of many of these instruments. Smaller portative organs such as the one in a canopy at Nantwich also existed, but a distinction is not generally made in the records.

At the abbey of St. Werburgh in Chester, later the cathedral of the new diocese of Chester following the Dissolution, considerable building works were done during the late fifteenth and early sixteenth century under the abbots Simon Ripley and John Birchenshaw.[170] It is during the abbacy of the latter that a covenant was drawn up between the Abbey and John Birchley, clerk, of London, who was to act as organist, choirmaster, and music teacher for the Abbey (see chapter II, part 1).[171] The organ at St. Werburgh evidently survived the Dissolution, as John Bircheley continued to hold the post after the Abbey became the Cathedral (see chapter II, part 1). Other foundations were not so lucky. An inventory of saleable goods from the house of Grey Friars (Franciscans) at Chester includes "a pore payer of orgeyns," worth three shillings and four pence.[172] The Grey Friars of Chester do not seem to have been a wealthy house, as the farm of all their lands and tenements only amounted to £2 5*s* 8*d* at the Dissolution, less than either the Black Friars (Dominicans) or White Friars (Carmelites).[173]

Regals. The regals appear only once in the Cheshire records, and then without any valuation, in an inventory of Hugh Calveley of Lea in 1605.[174] This was a small, portable reed instrument, a type first mentioned at Nuremberg in 1460.[175] Like the virginals, it could also be described as "a pair of," as in the 1605 inventory when these two types of instrument are recorded together: "one payer of virginalls & riggalls." But more regals must have been used than have survived in the records. The Chester Smiths' records indicate that regals were being played in connection with their pageant in the Whitsun play since a payment of two pence was made "for Carringe of the Regalls."[176] The regals in this case would undoubtedly have been played by a professional musician, probably someone attached to the cathedral (see also chapter II, part 1).

Table IV: Percussion Instruments

Bells	1492-1625
Clock bell (private household)	1625
Drum	1588–89 — 1639 {1594 — 1641}
Tabor	1596 — 1620 {1611}

The Percussion Instruments

Bells. As expected, bells, like organs, are most frequently found in churches. Their ecclesiastical uses were to mark the canonical hours, to summon people to church, and, by means of the sacring bell, to signal the moment of transubstantiation in the Mass. These are beyond the scope of the present inquiry. But bells were also put to secular use as part of the celebrations for visiting dignitaries as well as for alarms in times of danger and, in announcing the canonical hours, as a means of telling time. In 1615 Congleton paid eighteen pence to the ringers when the Earl of Essex visited.[177] The ringers of Bow Bell were paid a gratuity for ringing by the Innkeepers' Company of Chester.[178] An undated petition from them requests a rise in stipend because the ringers are supported by only a few companies and the costs of maintaining the bell are high:

> wheareas at ye Choysinge of your Offices and at ye makinge of your accowmpts at your meetinge abowtte this time of ye yeare vpon ye accowmpte makinge you did remember the Bowbell; the which I hope at this your meettinge yow will not forgett hopinge by your worshipps meanes you will bee a mydyator vnto your rest of ye companye toe augement your stipend in regard yat theire bee manye of good and able men in ye Companie for I protest but for yow and your companyes with twoe [C..] ^^or three^ companyes moore within the Cittie it showllde cease for ye truth is yat can not bee mayntayned but with greatt Charge, yett wee cowllde, doe well, for ye mayntayninge theireof yf all the Companyes of ye Cittie did contrybuit accordinge too theare abilities, But the one halfe of ye Companies geeue nothinge at all which bee verye riche and of greatt abilitye, and those yat geeues be of ye meannest trads, the which is some halfe a Crowne and some tene grotts yearllie Soe yat my selfe and ye ^^poore^ Ringers; Commit our sellfes vnto

your wor*shi*pp and y*e* Rest of the Companyes gratuitie, hopinge y*at*
some augmentatione will be grauntted in regarde of y*e* forsayde
p*re*mises[179]

The signatories of the petition, and presumably the ringers, are Robert
Gwynne, Richard Done, Mark Butcher, and Arthur Woormsonne. A
further petition, from Robert Gwynne alone and also undated, indicates that he is the chief bellringer and responsible for hiring the
others. He again stresses the cost of maintaining the bell: "Richard
prymett swore a three dayes befor he dyed y*at* he was in xxviij li be-
hynde hande in the Continiwinge toe mayntayne y*e* bowe bell; yett he
had iiij li yearlie from the Church the w*hi*ch I haue not."[180] The
Innkeepers seem to be the only company regularly supporting the Bow
Bell before the Civil War, although other companies do so later.[181] The
Innkeepers' earlier payments (usually ten shillings) are also more
generous than those of other guilds—or than their own post-1642 payments of 2*s* 6*d*.[182]

Bells were regarded with some suspicion after the Reformation although to a lesser degree than organs. This concern principally
centered around the occasions on and purposes for which bells should
be rung, and individuals in communities did not always agree on the
appropriateness of ringing them. At Nantwich in 1625 information
was given to the diocesan visitation against "Ioh*ann*em Browne
Laurentiu*m* Wilkes Thoma*m* Lea Ioh*ann*em Sare Rad*ulph*um Minshall
for ringinge vpon an euen beinge forbidden by y*e* Churchwarden ytt
appearinge to the Iudge y*at* the *sai*d p*ar*ties recreatinge themselves in
ringinge made the Church doores whileste they Continued ringinge
and some of the Church wardens comeinge could not come into the
Church and therevpon p*re*sented them."[183] The ringers were not
punished, and the incident does not seem to have been considered a
serious breach of the law. A similar dispute over bell-ringing occurred
in 1579 at Chester. The mayor and others testify to the Quarter Sessions that on 23 February "at xijth of the clock or ther aboute*s* in
thafter noone [*blank*] dorington p*ar*son of the p*ar*ish Church of St
Peters w*i*th in the citie of chester reported and affirmed in the p*re*sent*es*
and hearing of the p*er*sons whose names are subscribed That the
Quenes Men cam downe to Eaton Colledg*e* to ring the bel*es* ther vpon
A festivall even and Doctor Day then [Deane] ^^privest^ of that same
colledg*e* did bea<.>e them awaye out of the bell fray."[184]

Bells owned by individuals seem to have been rare. Indeed, if one excepts the chapel bell sponsored by the Downes family at Pott Shrigley,[185] there is only one example in private ownership. This comes from the previously mentioned inventory of goods taken on the death of John Bruen of Bruen Stapleford in 1625 and specifies a "Clockbell and bell in the hall" at a value of £5 1s.[186] This is a substantial value—a pair of virginals in the same inventory is only worth £1—and evidently indicates something more than a bell for a clock. Probably a set of chime bells, which were used to teach music as well as played by themselves, are indicated. The bells may also have been valued for the metal weight, which would in some measure account for the high valuation.

Drums and Tabors. As a rhythm instrument, the drum was a useful accompaniment to dancing or processions. John Spencer, who was charged in 1611 with "drumminge on Saboth daies" at Acton,[187] may have been accompanying dancers, as the charge immediately preceding his is against Thomas Hardinge for keeping ales on the sabbath. The Manchester ale mentioned above in connection with the pipe and tabor also had a drummer, and a drummer is listed among those who "one the daye of our faste abussede yat daye moste grosslye in daunsinge and other wantone sportes" at Nantwich in 1605.[188] It is probable that some of the drums used for dancing or entertainment on the sabbath were strictly speaking tabors, although the Manchester case shows that both types could be used for this purpose. The term 'tabor' tended to be displaced by 'drum' in England in the sixteenth century, and came to refer principally to the smaller folk instrument, played with one stick and used in the combination of three-hole pipe and tabor, discussed above.[189] The drum proper was deeper, played with two sticks, and by the sixteenth century had the snare below the head rather than above it as the tabor did.[190]

Drummers accompanied the mayor and aldermen at the Chester Midsummer Show,[191] and individual guilds also sometimes paid a drummer, as in 1620–21, when the Mercers paid twelve pence to "lame Siddall. and the blynde boye that played one Adrome."[192] The latter payment would appear to be partially charitable. Chester had its own town drum, and payments were made for its repair. In 1588–89 "towe snares for the drvme and one Kinge Round of the same drvme" were purchased at a cost of two shillings, and in 1613–14 2s 6d were paid "for headinge and cordinge of the Citties drvm."[193] At Congleton, the drum was used both to summon and to accompany the rushbearing, an occasion when women and children brought fresh rushes to the church.[194] Rushbearing was usually accompanied by music and dancing and was originally associated with the patronal festival of the church, although after the Reformation it was fixed at 25 July for all churches. Congleton also had a drummer performing on other of "the townes occasions,"[195] including such non-celebratory and non-cere-monial activities as "goinge 2 dayes through ye Towne with his drum to gather them yat carryed gravell to ye worke."[196] Both at the rush-bearings and the gravel-bearings the drum served the purpose of gathering people together.

The drum was important too as a military instrument, and town drummers might well be ex-soldiers. This was certainly the case with Roger Lether of Nantwich, who petitioned the justices of the peace in 1639 for a pension. He claimed:

> that where your Peticioner heretofore serued the late Queene Elizabeth of famous memory in her warrs in Ireland and elswere and sithence for many yeeres past hath serued in the Trayned band of this Hundred of Namptwich: but nowe being of the age of lxxxvij yeeres, he is not able for service or to gett his liueing by dayly labour as heretofore, & he is vnwillingly to be burthensome to this Towne if hee could haue any other meanes of liuelyhood and maynteynance, doth therefore humbly beseech your worships
>> That you would be pleased to appoint or allowe vnto your Peticioner a yeerely ^^pencion^ to be paid him quarterly as a mayhmed Souldier duryng his life for his maynteynance and he, as in duty bound, will pray for your worships prosperity long to contynue./ |[197]

Lether was already evidently established in Nantwich in 1602, when his son was baptized.[198] He was charged in 1619 with drumming on the sabbath,[199] and he probably, like the Congleton drummers, played for rushbearings, civic occasions, and gathering people together for important announcements or tasks. He identifies himself, however, primarily with the local militia, and it is likely that other drummers had similar roles to play with the "Trayned band." At Chester in 1614–15, 3s 6d were paid to the "one, who lent the Cittie a drum, in the last trayninge of our souldiers, and also for amendinge of the Citties drum."[200] Mending the drum is a fairly regular expense in the Treasurers' Account Rolls.[201] The ownership of drums by individuals rather than by corporations is not as common but does occur in at least two instances. These drums would have served more for military-ceremonial than recreational purposes. In 1621, Peter Cross of

Wilmslow, identified as "Bachelor," stipulated in his will "that my drumme bee kept in Willmeslowe at the house of Iohn Gibbon, and to bee at the Command of Mr Iohn Newton of Pownall Esquire ffrancis Newton of Pownall ffee yeoman & the said Iohn Gibbon if they haue occassion to vse it. . . ."[202] The drum was valued in his inventory at 3s 4d.[203] The other drum is simply listed in the inventory of goods of Rowland Dutton of Hatton along with "a featherbed a flockbed, a boulster, twoe Coverlettes, a blankett a bedsted an oulde Cheste for provinder," all of which are worth forty shillings collectively.[204]

The drum's roles, as described above, could be the cause of serious conflict. At Timperley in 1630 a petition of the inhabitants showed that "Lawrence Ioneson of Tymperley Alehouse keeper, suffereth evill rule to be kepte in his house, and mens sonnes, and servants, to be feasteing there in ye night [ty..] and at all tymes in ye night to be drinking and Typpling, and to beate a drume at midnight, to ye great disquiet, and terror, of ye Inhabitants recyding neere there aboutes."[205] The neighbors, wakened out of sleep by the sound of a drum, apparently reacted with "terror" because they associated the sound with danger. At Wilmslow in 1629, when the bearward was put in the stocks, several of the townspeople objected, and "Henry Orrell, together alsoe with one William Kellsall and ^^one^ Iohn Robinson went vpp & downe the Towne in an outdaring manner, and caused the drummer to drumme, whilst the said Baxter sate in the same stockes; saying, hee should drumme, in the dispite of any Iustice of the peace whatsoeuer."[206] The drumming is described in another document in the same case: "Iohn Robinson brought Musicke vnto the said Bearewarde, which plaid before him as hee sate in the Stockes."[207] The drumming in this case serves a dual purpose: it is for the entertainment of the bearward (and his supporters), to lessen the punishment of the stocks, and it also serves to attract a crowd, to "drum up support" for the bearward.

Finally, notice may be made of an instrument that appears in Cheshire art but nowhere in the records. This is the set of cymbals that appears on a canopy in the church at Nantwich.

Instrument Makers

Many of the instrumentalists in Cheshire probably repaired and maintained their own instruments, but a few makers also seem to have been present in the county. Instruments for the gentry are likely to have been bought in London or even imported directly from abroad, but importantly there must also have been sufficient local demand to support some local instrument makers. As noted above in chapter II, part 1, in 1592, Thomas Beedle, who describes himself as "Bowier. and maker of Instrumen*tes* of Musick," petitioned the Mayor and Assembly at Chester to be admitted as a freeman of the city. His trade is a double one: "makinge of Instrumen*tes* of Musick and Longe staves, for her Ma*ies*tes seruice," and he is able to pay £1 6*s* 8*d* for the right to practice his trade in Chester.[208] Another petition for the freedom of the city, strictly speaking from outside our period but useful in that it appears to be the only other one, was made in 1670 by John Ward. He described himself as having "made instruments of musicke for diuerse persons of qualitie"[209] and having lived in Chester for several years. He was evidently aiming at the luxury trade. By a vote of twenty-six to fourteen he was assessed £2 for the privilege of freedom, with one alderman urging that he be charged £10.

A much earlier probable maker of musical instruments is Richard Paynter, alias Organmaker, who appears in the Sheriffs' Rolls of 1488 in a dispute with the stewards of the Painters' Guild, evidently for practicing the craft against the wishes of the guild.[210] The difficulty may have been that he was not a regular member of the guild but was decorating his musical instruments. John Lloyd, described in the Malpas parish registers in 1626 as "orgen drawer," may have had a similar occupation.[211] It seems unlikely that there could have been sufficient income in decorating, or even making, organs alone. Virginals and other keyboard instruments were often decorated, and the two men may have had a more general practice.

A final and very intriguing piece of information about an instrument maker is unfortunately available only in a footnote in Rupert H. Morris's *Chester in the Plantagenet and Tudor Reigns* in the context of offenders of the peace at the Mayor's assize: "In Elizabeth's reign the names occur of Wm. Goodeman, virgynall maker, and Thomas Mason, yeoman, al*ias* dictus Thomas Mason, syngynge-man."[212] Morris also mentions an undated inventory of the goods of a William Goodman, al*ias* Goodale, which includes "a pair of virginalls undrest, a lute case," and tools for making musical instruments.[213] Neither Boston's researches in the 1950s nor or the survey of documents for the Cheshire volume of Records of Early English Drama has found the inventory or the reference to the Mayor's Assize.

The documents may have been lost, or Morris's estimate of the date may have been incorrect, and they have been catalogued under a later date. The possibility remains, however, that there was a maker of virginals and lutes resident in Chester in Elizabeth's reign. Like John Ward in the 1670s, he evidently aimed at the luxury trade.

Groups of Instruments

As implied above, many instruments were not designed for solo use, while others could be played either as solo instruments or in groups of like or unlike instruments. The "broken" or mixed consort has already been mentioned in connection with William Worrall's inventory, and another inventory from Nantwich has possibly another set of mixed consort instruments. When Henry Wright, innkeeper, died in 1607, his goods included "one Bandora Base vyoll & other playeinge Instrument*es*" valued at £2.[214] As an innkeeper he may have kept instruments on which his customers might play, but the bandora and bass viol were evidently for his own personal use since he specifically bequeaths them in his will to his brother and cousin respectively.[215] Mary Somerford owned, and presumably could play, lute, bandora, and cittern (half the instruments of a mixed consort) as well as virginals, and it is thus likely that she played in consorts. John Bruen, in his youth, was involved in or at least exposed to consort playing at his uncle John Dutton's, the result being that "by occasion of Musitians and a chest of Viols kept in the house, he was drawn by desire and delight into the Dancing-schoole."[216]

The Chester waits could function as either a wind or string band and were able to perform as a group or separately. They were a formal grouping with instruments that were, at least to some extent, the property of the city. Between the 1590–91 evidence after the death of Thomas Williams and the 1604 inventory of William Maddock, they had a full wind band for loud music (shawms, sackbut, double curtal, and cornetts) and evidently instruments for soft music as well (recorders, violins, and tenor viol, with the cornetts also suitable for this group). As they were musically literate, they probably made use of music written for specific groups such as the mixed consort. It is likely that some of William Worrall's books were for mixed consort as well, given the instruments which he owned. Although his instruments do not form a full mixed consort by themselves, he does have six instruments that could be played in consort. Richard Preston of Warrington refers to his company of musicians, who were also evidently performing on violins in the streets of Chester in 1594 and were staying in the city.[217]

Less formal groupings also occurred, although a group of names that appear in a document such as a Jury Presentment may not necessarily have been played together. Occasions such as wakes attracted performers from surrounding areas, and they need not have performed in groups. Where they appear as a collective group, however, the possibility that they performed as one is stronger, as in the case of "Peter Cooke Iohn Cooke George Ashton & Iohn Hewood minstrells," who were presented for piping in 1618.[218] However, in the Crown Books their names are presented in a list which does not give the same impression. On the other hand, the two fiddlers who in 1588 were singing "of the last Triumphe of england against the spaniard*es*"[219] were evidently performing together. Minstrels, pipers, fiddlers, and harpers did perform together, and iconographic evidence also shows groupings of musical instruments. It is therefore at least a strong possibility that where names of instrumentalists are grouped in the documents they were also grouped in performance. Group sizes tended to be small: two, three, or four musicians together, with two being the most common. Larger numbers could occur, the most extreme case coming from Ribchester in Lancashire. Examinations in a case before the Consistory Court state that the vicar, who ran an illegal alehouse, had "in his howse: wicked p*er*sons vpon the saboth day: & Especially: xi: ffidlers vpon <.>hrid day of Iuly i6i4."[220] Another witness claims to have seen six pipers and fiddlers in the vicar's house on a Sunday, but not to have heard them play, although there is a deposition that the group on 3 July did play as well as drink and gamble.[221]

CONCLUSION

The questions raised in the Introduction concerning the musical life of Cheshire before 1642 can never be fully answered because the evidence will never be complete. Nevertheless, some conclusions can be drawn about the nature of music-making in this county. Music was evidently part of life at all social levels, and even those who might disapprove of it in one sphere or at a particular time would consider it perfectly appropriate in different conditions.

Music could be performed by practically anyone, at any social level. At the top of society, the gentry were active as performers on fashionable instruments such as virginals, lutes, gitterns, and bandoras. They lent and bequeathed musical instruments to one another, and music formed an accompaniment to, and an aspect of, their complex interrelationships. With families such as the Fittons, Leghs, and Winningtons the connections reach beyond the limits of Cheshire, and events of national importance such as the Essex rebellion and the execution of Sir Charles Danvers take on a local significance in the form, as we have seen, of the possible loss of a set of viols.

The gentry were also active in controlling the performance of music by others, whether positively in the form of patronage of artists such as Henry Lawes and Francis Pilkington or negatively in the form of the many prosecutions for piping on the sabbath. The Duttons in particular were involved in the patronage and control of music in their provision of minstrels' licences.

Members of the middle class such as innkeepers in Nantwich also acquired and presumably played musical instruments, which they, like the gentry, left to friends and relations in their wills. Music and dancing were fashionable, and even apprentices sought out instruction in dance from professional musicians. The members of the Chester guilds were regular patrons of local minstrels and groups such as the Chester waits, who provided musical entertainment for guild feasts, for the various pageants of the Chester play, and for the great civic processions such as the Midsummer Show, the Christmas Watch, and the Shrovetide Homages.

Highly visible in the records are the performers at the lower end of the social scale, although often little information is given concerning them. Music formed an accompaniment for dancing, an attraction for ales and alehouses, and an important form of recreation. The question of when and where this recreation was permitted was clearly not universally agreed upon. We know most about those who disobeyed the laws, but the fact that they ran a risk in so doing must suggest that other performances took place which were not illegal and were for that reason not recorded. Nevertheless, as the *Book of Sports* recognized, Sunday was often the only day on which laborers had the leisure for music.

Although not all times and places were considered appropriate for music, the records show that music occurred at virtually all times and all places: by day or by night, in the alehouse, on the green, in private houses, and even disrupting the church services, which of course in the larger churches had their own music and musicians.

The reasons for which different people performed music varied. For someone like Mary Somerford or Margaret Lowther, it was part of a young lady's education. For Peter Moreton, it was a passport to advancement in his career as a courtier. For the young John Bruen it was a temptation to lure him away from the path of righteousness. For the Duttons, the licensing of minstrels was a hereditary responsibility. And for the vast majority of performers, from trained musicians such as George and Robert Cally to Rondull Moreton the tailor, it was a way of making or augmenting a living. For some, the blind or lame harpers, drummers, and pipers, it was a way of surviving when all other ways were closed. For still others, such as Richard Metier, it was an identity which gave them a perceived protection—and which may have in some cases formed a cover for a life of crime.

Generally speaking, there was also a social divide amongst the musical instruments, although this was also subject to fashion. Virginals and lutes remained instruments played by or for the gentry. There are no cases, for instance, of virginals being played in alehouses, unsurprising given the size and delicacy of the instrument. Viols were more adaptable, but the preferred alehouse instruments seem to have been pipes, apparently including a range of instruments, and fiddles, with the term 'fiddler' probably covering the playing of violins by the seventeenth century. Instruments such as the cittern moved from being upper-class to lower-class—a move associated with the change in the type of wire used for the strings of the instrument.

The most important social changes for music in Cheshire were the Reformation and the Renaissance. With the Renaissance came a changing fashion in music with a greater demand for musical literacy. With the Reformation came changes in the liturgy as the Latin services were replaced by the *Book of Common Prayer*, and in the later sixteenth century sabbatarianism arrived with its distrust of music as an potential accompaniment to vice and its advocacy of complete abstention from all secular activity on Sunday, the only day really available for recreation. Music became politicized as a willingness to countenance maypoles and pipings became associated with recusancy. Performers such as Thomas Allen the fiddler were accused of recusancy and active proselytizing. The Church of England itself had difficulty maintaining a middle way between the extremes of the reformers and the traditionalists. Yet even reformers such as John Bruen did not consider music to be completely bad in itself and owned musical instruments. Even a magistrate who patronized musicians and was a performer himself could see the dangers of unlicensed alehouses and unruly pipers such as Richard Metier.

Perhaps most difficult to determine is the extent to which the Dutton licensing system made a difference to Cheshire minstrels. Ostensibly, it gave them exemption from the penalties of the Statute of Vagabonds, yet we see Cheshire minstrels such as Edward Jonson being arrested for offences specifically linked to the statute. No reference is made to whether he was licensed or not, and some complaints, such as those against Richard Platt or Richard Metier, suggest that some licensed performers did abuse their privileges. Minstrels from outside the county are perhaps more likely to be treated as "Rogues by the Statute," but there is no indication that Cheshire was a haven for itinerant minstrels or that vagabond performers were more tolerated there than elsewhere. The Dutton licensing system seems to have worked—or at least to have worked no worse than the Statute of Vagabonds did, the problem in both cases being one of enforcement. The Dutton licences did not give *carte blanche* to the minstrels, but required that they be identified, that they be able to pay an annual sum, and, in the seventeenth century, also that they observe the sabbath and refrain from any seditious activity.

The role of the music-maker shifted with the circumstances and the audience. Making a living as a professional musician was precarious but not impossible, and even a member of the Chester waits such as William Maddock had other sources of income. Minstrels and by extension other musical performers might be below or outside the social scale by both tradition and law, but they were nevertheless not only tolerated but in many cases sought out and encouraged even when to do so might be dangerous. The alehousekeepers who harbored or even hired pipers and fiddlers sometimes did so as a calculated risk. The mayor and assembly of Chester appointed George Cally as an official wait and granted him the status of a freeman of the city despite his previous clashes with them. Music and music-makers had not one role but many, both positive and negative, in the county of Cheshire.

Appendix I
INVENTORIES OF CHESHIRE MUSICIANS

1. Inventory of the goods of William Maddock of Chester, Waitman[1]

An Inventorie taken of the
good*es* & Cattells of Willi*a*m
Maddock one of the waitmen
of the Cittie of Chester decessed
the ffourth daye of September
An*n*o 1604 praysed by Henry
Scarisbrock Thomas Lowe
Tho*mas* Harrison & W: Bedford

ffirst in the hall

A portall dore & wainscott standing at the back of the dore all cont viij*e* yard*es*	x s viij d
more a skrine of wainscote by the said dore cont ij*o* yard*es* D'	iij s iiij d
more aleafe for the Chimney cont v*e* yard*es*	vj s viij d
more xiij*e* yard*es* wainscote atthe back of the table	xvij s iiij d
more one wainscote dore going out of the hall into the gallery & one other wainscott dore going into the backside cont .3. yard*es*	iiij s
one Cubbord w*i*th a testerne	xx s
one table w*i*th a frame & six Ioyned stooles	xx s
ij*o* low Ioyned stooles	xvj d
iij*e* great chaires & ij small cheires	iij s iiij d
aborder of whitework an old Carpett & iij*e* littell shelves	ij s

187

In the littell parlour at	
the back of the hall	
xx yardes & ijo footes winscote	xxvj s viij d
a portall ouer the going ouer the [C]	
seller of Wainscote cont :3.	
yardes D	iiij s viij d
one Ioyned standing bedd with	
a testerne & a truckell bedd	xx s
one littell square table with a	
frame	iij s
one small chest	xviijd
vj footes of glas	ij s
one payer playing tables	xxd
In the kitchine	
one old Cubbort one small squar	
table iiij [srestells] trestells one	
dore out of the entry into the	
kitchine	iiij s
one bord ouer the mantell tree	
& alittell shelf	xij d |
In the buttrye betwene the	
halle and the kitchine	
ijo lattise dores & lockes &	
keyes	ijs viij d
vj shelves & one small stillary	
to sett bere vpon	ij s vj d
iije plaine stooles	iij d
In the bruing howse	
ijo bruing pannes topped with	
lead	xl s
iije cowlers of lead in a frame	xiij s iiij d
one brwing combe ayeyling	
combe ij slainsing sives a	
great turnell & one stonne / trough	xvj s
iiijor crookes ijo littell turnells	
& a gawen crook	ij s
iiijr flaskettes	xij d
iiijr sackes	iiij s
In the streete chamber	
iije payer flaxen sheetes	xxx s
ve payer Reding sheetes	xvj s viij d
iije course sheetes	v s
iije Reding table clothes & one	

flaxen cloth xij s
ij*o* dusson napkins x s
ix pillow berres xij s
vj hand towells xviij d
one prese & one square table xiij s iiij d
iiij*r* flaxen sheet*es* x s
v*e* dubble Ruffe band*es* x s
ij*o* carpett*es* one cloke a
mantell & one cou*er*lett xxvj s viij d
ij*o* steyned clothes for a
square table xxd
one dublett & a payer of
breches x s
one desk & a [payer] close
stoole iij s iiij d
a halbert and a pooleaxe iij s
a suite of Armore vj s viij d
ij*o* chest*es* v s

In the Chamber ou*er* the
p*ar*ler

one standing bedd w*i*th a
testerne one other beddstedd
ij*o* truckell bedd*es* xx s
one counter and one tye chest v s
ij*o* fetherbedd*es* & ij*o* boulsters xl s
v*e* flock bedd*es* & ij*o* pillowes xx s
iij*e* blankett*es* ij*o* caddowes & one
cou*er*lett xxxiij s iiij d |
ij*o* loades of turves vj s viij d
iij*o* little spinnyng whelles v s

In the gallery ou*er* the hall

xvj foot*es* glas v s iiij d
one bird Cage xij d

In the buttry

iiij*r* food of glas xviij d
Nyne drinking glasses iiij d
one bason & ewer vj s viij d
xlviijo² peces pewter [c<..>t
<...> at a <blank> p*er* pound] xliiij s ij d
iiij*r* brasse candelstick*es* iiij s
one hanging candelstick of brasse x d
one ou*er* sea dish iiij d

In the kitchine
vj brasse pott*es* & one fosnett
[c<..>t at p*art*<.>]   liij s iiij d
iij*r* pannes one kettell one
Chafendish one Iron dryping
panne one frying panne one
Skimmer one pestell and
one morter   xx s
                         pewter in the kitchine
ix pewter dishes one
butter plate & ij*o* chamber
poott*es*   vjs viijd
                    Iron ware in the kitchine
one pare Iron golbert*es* one
Iron grate ffyve bar[..]s of
Iron in the Chimney one
spite one payer of tonges
one old fier shouell one
hanging branddred one payer
potte hook*es* one payer Rack*es*
& one chopping knyffe   xljs viij d
                         In the seller
vj barrells   viijs
j iij quarter of a barr   xijd
one firkine   vj d
iij*o* stound*es*   ij s
iij*o* drinking cannes   vj d
iiij*o* dussen trenchers   [vj d] viij d
                    In the p*ar*ler in the Row
one table ij*o*^{3} formes & one
bench   iiij s viij d
one lattice cont iij*o* paines &
one bord   xv d |
                         In the stable
one cradell of Ioyned work
ij*o* old barrells one old hoop
& c*er*taine pec*es* of old tymber   iiij s
ij*o* shootes   xiij s iiij d
iij*o* stoone troughes   iij d
                         Instrument*es*
A Sagbutt   xiij s iiij d

a dubble cvrtall	x s
ij*o* cornett*es*	x s
a tenor viall	vj s viij d
one fishing boate and one	
neat & apece of a nett &	
nett cord*es*	iiij li

Su*mm*a is   xliij li xviij s v d

The praysers names

Henry Skersbroke

the mark[4] of

Thomas Lowe

the mark T H of

Thomas Harison

W: Bedford.

2. Inventory of goods of William Worrall of Nantwich, musician.[5]

A true Inventory taken the 13 of Iune 1637 of all the good*es* of William Wurrall late of Wich Malbanke deceased, praised by vs whose Names are Subscribed

	li – s – d
<.>mpr*imis* In the house one Table one Ioynd presse	0 – 14 – 6
Item three Cheares on forme & three Stooles	0 – 5 – 6
Item One large voyder of peuter and one	
Brasse voydier & other small pewter	2 – 10 – 0
Item Two dreeping pann*es* & one frying pan	0 – 4 – 6
Item One pott 2 kettles 1 posne nett 2 skellett*es*	1 – 5 – 0
Item Butterie Shelues & tickney ware	0 – 4 – 0
Item One Iron Grate 1 fire shoule & tongues	
one pottrack i spitt 1 paier of Bellows	0 – 14 – 0
In the Chamber aboue	
Item One Ioynd Bedsteed one feather bed	
2 Blankett*es* [w*ith* six payer of sheet*es*	
w*ith* other Napperie] w*ith* Boulsters & pillows	
Curtains and Vallance	3 – 0 – 0
Item Six payer of sheet*es* w*ith* other Napperie	2 – 0 – 0
Item One Truckle Bed w*ith* the Beddings belonging to yt	0 – 10 – 0
Item One Trunk 2 Chest*es* & one Boxe	0 – 5 – 0

Item 5 sowed quishions with seauen other	1 – 8 – 0
Item One Byble with some paper Bookes	0 – 8 – 0
Item One houre glasse	0 – 8 – 0

In the Clossett

Item One lookeing glass with pictures and other things	0 – 11 – 6
Item One Chaffe Bedd and fethers	0 – 2 – 6
Item One Chaffe nett	0 – 3 – 0
Item One Bandore One Alferiall one base vyall	
3 treble vyalles with Instrument books	1 – 18 – 0
Item wearing Apparell	3 – 0 – 0

The Sume is   – 19 – 8 – 2

Robarte Bromhall
Exhibitum pro vero &C
Thomas Noden
Edmond Myles
Thomas Shore

3. Will of Roger Vaughan of Nantwich, musician.[6]

In the Name of God Amen; I Roger vaughan of Namptwiche in the Countie
of <...> sence and memory att the Makinge hereof blessed be the Lord,
To<...> aryse betwixte my wiffe and Children after my departure Conser<...>
goodes to settle the same and to dooe as followeth <...> the handes of
Almyghtie God, And my Bodie to the eart<...> mee out of this vale of
Mysery, And as ffor such goodes and Ch<...>in this lyffe, I giue and bequeath
the same viz Imprimis I giue and <...> to an assignement Made, my house
wherein I did latelie liue and <...> And if shee shall Marry or die, Then my
will is that my eldest <...> house duringe his naturall liffe, Alsoe I giue and
beque<...> goodes as are in the said house duringe her liffe if shee <...> be at
her disposinge, soe that shee dispose of <...> or greate age, shee shall <...>
soone Roger vaughan when or before he shall enter vpon t<...> of John Deane
of this towne of Namptwiche, Alsoe I giue & beq<...> paid her in Currant
Englishe money by my sonne Roger vaug<...> The house or groundes of
myne as aforesaid, which he my sonne Roger hath <...> Roger my basse viall;
Item I giue Margrett Brooke my Granchild fforty <...> granchild Tenne
shillings, Item I giue to Humfrey Brooke my Grandch<...> sonneinlawe I
giue Twelfepence in full Satisfaccon of his parte, and <...> sonneinlawe nor
any for hime shall Shue or seeke for an<...> Roger entereth into Possession
of ye aforesaid house or g<...> That my wiffe Maudline vaughan if shee
Contynue wid<...> and <...> my <...> that Iohn deane hath taken in my
groundes in Hendalle, That she ye sai<...> halfe of the ground during her

liffe and widdowehood, and my sonne Ro<...> dep*ar*ture. my will is, That my wiffe Maudline haue the one hal<...> And my sonne Roger the other halfe, The paieinge betwixt <...> my will is, That my ffunerall expencces and <...> which doth belonge vnto my sonne Roger <...> my sonne Roger of neith<...> my will and testament, And doe renownce <...> <.>ther w<...> of effecte, And soe prayeinge to god to blesse yo*w* all <...>

Published sealed and deliuered ffor
the last will and testament of mee
wi*t*hin named Roger vaugahn senio*r* in p*resence* of
Richard Iennings
Thomas Burroughes
Richard Barker senio*r*[7]

4. Inventory of the goods of Roger Vaughan of Nantwich (musician)[8]

A trewe and iust Inventorye, Taken the 24*th* daie of Aprill i648, By them whose names are vnderwritten, of all the good*es* & Chattell that Roger vaughan of Namptwiche died possessed of, whoe dyed the 22*th* daie of aprill last past

A highe ioyntebed, and towe trucklebed	0j *li* – 06 – 08*d*
A ffetherbed, a flockebed, a Chafbed and }	
a strawe bed, 5 old blankitts, a matt }	0ij *li* – i6 – 00*d*
towe ffether boulsters, one boulster stuffed }	
w*i*th flock*es*, 3 pillowes stufd w*i*th fethers }	
Threepere of sheetts, and a old pere, and	
three pillowebeers, nyne Napkins	0ij *li* – 08 – 4*d*
Sixe sett kuckins and 4 old kuckins	00 – 08 – 00
A Basse voyall	0j – j0 – 00
A Ioynt Cheere, a little table	00 – 08 – 00
A Ioynt Chest	00 – 06 – 08
A Bible and towe other book*es*	00 – 00 – 08
A little Boxe with a locke one	00 – 00 – 08
A turnyll to knead in, and a baskett	00 – 02 – 04
all these good*es* are in y*e* loftes aboue	
ffowerteene feaire pew*ter* diches, and 3	
but*ter* diches of pew*ter*, and 8 little sasers of pew*ter*	02 – 03 – 4
a three pinte flagon, and a pinte, towe	
pew*ter* candilsticke and asalte	

One Brassepott, A Bigger brasse kettle and
a lesser, a little Brassine mort*er*, & a skellit   0j – i0 – 00
One Iron grate w*i*th 4 bars, one broche, One
pere of golbort*es*, towe pere of pot rack*es*, a
Iron barr y*at* y*e* hange one, a axe, & a friingpan   00 – i8 – 00
A Ioynt presse   00 – i0 – 00
A longe boord, a short benche, a tressill, towe
ioynt stooles, a throne Cheere, a corded stoolle
Three threeffooted stoolles, a sitting wheelle   0j – 02 – 00
20 fagots 2 little turnels   00 – 03 – 00
ffower knyghts armes in ioynte frames   00 – 08 – 00
his weareinge apparrell   02 – 00 – 00
In Chattell, a house and ground in lease vpon
the racke for one liffe   10 – 00 – 00
                Sume is – xxviiij *li* – iiij *s* – 8*d*

Appendix II
NAMED MUSICIANS

The hundred in which a township is found is given in brackets after the name of the township. The hundreds are abbreviated as follows:

Broxton: BR   Nantwich: NA
Bucklow : BU   Northwich: NO
Eddisbury: ED   Wirral: WI
Macclesfield: MA

Bracketed attributions such as "[piper]" or "[of Nantwich]" indicate that this information is not given in the document, but can be inferred. In the case of "[piper]," it may indicate that an individual of that name is described as a piper in another document. The surname of the Chester dynasty of musicians is variously given as Cally or Kelly, thus indicated below by the use of Cally/Kelly. This does not mean that every member of the family appears under both spellings in the records

The Music-Makers

John Allen, Conduct of the Choir (Chester, 1617)

Thomas Allen of Lostock Gralam, fiddler (Lostock Gralam [NO], 1619, 1620; Nether Peover [NO][1], 1631; Rostherne [BU] 1630)

Thomas Allen, [?piper][2] (Budworth [probably Great Budworth, NO], 1608)

Richard Armes, piper (Wardle [ED], 1640)

Thomas Asbie, piper (Stretton [?BU],[3] 1621)

George Ashton, piper (no place, 1618; Agden [BU], 1630)

William Ashton of Over Knutsford, piper (Over Knutsford [BU], 1618)

Nicholas Ashworth, *alias* Piper, late of Over Tabley (Tabley Superior) (probably a piper by occupation) (Rostherne [BU], 1591)

Thomas Aspshall of Stretton, piper (Stretton [BU], 1617)

John Axon of Nantwich, fiddler (Nantwich [NA], 1643)

Thomas Baker (of Nantwich),[4] harper (Nantwich [NA], 1581, 1592)

Thomas Baker of Wettenhall,[4] minstrel (Wettenhall [NA], 1612)

John Balie, piper (Stockport [MA], 1598)

Banyster the Waitman (Chester, 1626)

Randle Barnes, minor canon of Chester Cathedral (Chester, 1551–68)

Thomas Barnes, master of the choristers at Chester Cathedral (Chester, 1555–56)

Thomas Bateson, organist (Chester, 1604–08)

Henry Baxter, minstrel (Chester, 1490)

John Baxter,[5] piper (no place, 1596)

John Baxter,[5] *alias* Barne, piper (Mobberley [BU], 1597)

John Beamond, piper (Darnhall [ED], 1602; no place,[6] 1602)

Thomas Beedle, instrument maker (Chester, 1592)

James Beggeway, minstrel (no place, 1561)

Richard Bell [musician] (Chester, 1614–15)

Richard Benet, minstrel (Chester, 1483–84)

John Bircheley, clerk, of London, organist and singing teacher (Chester, 1518)

Hugh de Birkenhead, harper (Birkenhead [WI], 1343)

John Blackden of Nether Knutsford, musician (Nether Knutsford [BU], 1612)

Richard Blithe, drummer (Nantwich [NA], 1605)

Henry Boone, piper (no place, 1619; Chelford-cum-Astle [BU], 1619; Marthall [BU], 1619)

Boswicke, harper (Tarporley [ED], 1609)

Richard Boulton of Minshull Vernon, piper (Minshull Vernon [NO], 1609)

Robert Bower, singingman (Chester, 1547)

William Bradbury (also Bredburye),[7] piper (Darnhall [ED]; 1602, no place, 1602)

John Bradley of Bryning, Lancs., apprentice musician (Chester, 1621)

Nicholas Brasey, minstrel (Chester, 1586)

Richard Brimelaw, piper (Utkinton [ED], 1637)

John Browne of Christleton,[8] piper (Christleton, 1605)

John Browne of Littleton,[8] bagpiper (Littleton, 1612)

John Browne of Littleton,[8] musician (Chester, 1614)

William Browne, drummer (Congleton [NO], 1635)

Richard Bruce of Tattenhall,[9] piper (Tattenhall [BR], 1618)

Richard Bruce of Wimbolds Trafford,[9] piper (Wimbolds Trafford [ED], 1617)

Bruce (Bruse),[9] piper (Chester, 1618–19)

Bruchull, minstrel (piper)[10] (Mouldsworth [ED], 1619)

Brughull, piper[10] (no place, 1619)

Richard de Bulkeley, piper (Nantwich [NA], 1404)

Francis Burges, piper (Gawsworth [MA], 1618, 1620)

Christopher Burton of Chester, musician or waitman (Chester, 1580, 1588–89, 1590–91, 1591, 1594–95, 1595–96, 1596–97, 1598–99)

Henry Burton of Chester, apprentice musician/wait, son of Christopher Burton (Chester, 1596–97)

Richard Bury of Northwich, harper, *alias* Richard Bury of Northwich, yeoman (Northwich [NO], 1494, 1495)

Mark Butcher, bell-ringer (Chester, no date)

John Butler, fiddler (Chester, 1485)

Hugh Byrsley, minstrel (Malpas [BR], 1625)

Cally (also known as Kelly) of Chester, musician[11] (Chester, 1589–90, 1601–02, 1602–03, 1604–05, 1605–06, 1607–08, 1609–10, 1610–11, 1611–12, 1624, 1626–27, 1629–30, 1630–31, 1631–32, 1634–35, 1635–36, 1636–37, 1637–38, 1638–39, 1644–45, 1647–48; Congleton, 1620–21)

Edmund Cally/Kelly of Chester, musician (Chester, 1562, 1572–73, 1573–74, 1575)

George Cally/Kelly of Chester, musician (Chester, 1591, 1597–98, 1598–99, 1599–1600, 1601–02, 1602–03, 1603-04, 1605–06, 1607–08, 1608–09, 1609, 1609–10, 1610–11, 1612–13, 1613–14, 1614–15, 1616–17, 1617–18, 1618, 1618–19, 1619, 1619–20, 1620–21, 1621, 1623–24, 1640–41, 1644–45, undated [early 17c.])

John Cally/Kelly (musician), son of Peter Cally, musician (Chester, 1588–89, 1589, 1591)

Peter Cally/Kelly of Chester, musician (Chester, 1567–68, 1572–73, 1574–75, 1575–76, 1589)

Robert Cally/Kelly of Chester, musician (Chester 1598–99, 1599–1600, 1607–08, 1608–09, 1609, 1609–10, 1610–11, 1611–12, 1612–13, 1613, 1613–14, 1614, 1614–15, 1615–16, 1616–17, 1617–18, 1618–19, 1619–20, 1620–21, 1621–22, 1622–23, 1623–24, 1624–25, 1625–26, 1627–28, 1629–30, 1630–31, 1631–32, 1639–40, 1640–41, 1641–42, 1642–43, 1643–44, 1644–45, 1646–47, undated [early 17c.])

Roland Cally/Kelly [possibly a musician] (Chester, 1632–33)

John Challyner of Oswestry, musician (Chester, 1572–73)

Robert Chalner, fiddler (Chester, 1488–89)

Richard Chatterton,[12] minstrel and piper (Chester, 1588–89)

Chatterton,[12] piper (Chester, 1632)

Hugh Chesphord (Congleton [NO], 1602–03)

Chester, drummer (Little Budworth [ED], 1594)

John Cheswood, Jr., piper (Middlewich [NO], 1608)

Christopher, waitman (Chester, 1595–96)

Edward Clarke of the Isle of Ely, musician (Chester, 1607)

Henry Clutton of Malpas, minstrel (piper) (Bickerton [BR], 1618; Malpas [BR], 1625)

John Cona,[13] piper (Chester, 1433)

John Conason of Chester,[13] piper (Chester, 1428)

Henry Concord of Chester, musician (Chester, 1588–89)

John Cook,[14] minstrel (no place, 1618)

John Cook,[14] piper (Rostherne [BU], 1605)

Peter Cook, minstrel (no place, 1618; Over [ED], 1619)

George Cotton, musician (Chester, 1658–59)

Thomas Cowper and his company of Whitchurch, Salop (Shropshire), fiddlers (Chester, 1642)

Randle Crane, minstrel[15] (Chester, 1553–54, 1555–56)

John Crewe of Chester, yeoman, *alias* singingman (Chester, 1532–33)

Thomas Croaker, sadler [cittern-player] (Knutsford [BU], 1639)

Richard Cross,[16] minstrel (Over [ED], 1619; no place, 1619)

Richard Cross of Over,[16] piper (Over [ED], 1603)

John de Croxton, harper (Croxton [NO], 1394)

Roger de Croxton,[17] harper (Croxton [NO], 1416)

Roger de Croxton[17] of Middlewich, harper and gleeman (Middlewich [NO], 1419)

Richard Done, bell-ringer (Chester, undated)

John Dorse, of the Isle of Man, music student (Chester, 1504)

Henry Dowse, piper (Church Lawton [NO], 1595)

Robert Drake, piper (Weaverham [ED], 1608)

Robert Edge, Jr., piper (Barrow [ED], 1625)

Richard Ensong[18] [Evensong?] (of Frodsham), fiddler (Frodsham [ED], 1617, ?1622; no place, 1617)

Mr. Evans, singer in the choir (Chester, 1608–09)

John Everton of Chester, musician (Chester, 1609)

John Farrar [musician] (Chester, 1614–15)

Thomas Fiddler, minstrel (Newton iuxta Kingesley [Newton by Frodsham] [ED], 1488)

Thomas Fidler [?fiddler][19] (Chester, 1575–76)

<...>tium Fiddler of Godley,[20] [?fiddler] (Godley [MA], 1620)

Thomas Fisher, musician (Chester, 1607–08, 1613–14, 1622)

Thomas Foster, *alias* Huntsman,[21] of Hatton, piper (Hatton [BU], 1617; Frodsham [ED], 1625)

Henry Frenway, harper (Chester, 1424)

Fydo, singing man (Chester, 1601–02)

John Garratt, musician (Chester, 1619)

John Genson, precentor of Chester Cathedral (Chester, 1561–67)

James Gill [musician] (Chester, 1563–64)

Zachary Gill (of Nantwich), musician (Nantwich [NA], 1629, 1635, 1637, 1640)

William Goodman, *alias* Goodale, virginal-maker[22] (Chester, ?16c)

Old Griffith? [possibly a musician] (Chester, 1609–10)

Roger Guest, city drummer (Chester, 1612–13, 1613–14, 1614–15, 1616–17, 1617–18, 1618–9, 1619–20, 1622–23, 1625–26, 1626–27, 1632–33, 1638–39, 1641–42)

Mr. Robert Gwynne, bell-ringer (Chester, undated)

Robert Gyster, minstrel (Chester, 1407–09)

John Hale of Stretton, piper (Stretton [BU], 1617)

John Hammeson, harper (Guilden Sutton [BR], 1404)

Mr. Handy, teacher of music (Wilbraham Family [NA], 1614)

John Harrison of Saughton[23] and his boy, fiddlers (Little Neston [WI], 1617)

William Hartleys, piper (Barthomley [NA], 1605)

John Haswall, luterer (Chester, 1488)

William Hearne, singing man (Chester, 1596–97)

John Henshagh, minstrel (Chester, 1493–94)

Richard Henshagh, minstrel (Chester, 1492–93)

Hugh Henshall of Bredbury, minstrel (Wilmslow [MA], 1494)

William Hesketh of Aston[24] [piper] (Tarporley [ED], 1609)

Richard Hey, horner (Chester, 1488–89)

John Heyward, piper (Great Budworth [BU], 1608)

John Heywood of Lostock Gralam, minstrel (no place, 1618)

John Hill, harper (Chester, 1567–68)

Morgan Hopkin,[25] piper (Tarporley [ED], 1609)

Morgan Hopton[25] [piper] (Tarporley [ED], 1609)

Thomas Hough of Chester, musician (Chester, 1591, 1597–98, 1609, 1613–14, 1614, 1615–16, 1616–17, 1617–18, 1618–19, 1619–20)

Robert Hulleboy, piper (Macclesfield Forest [MA], 1366/7)

Richard Hunt of Cheadle, minstrel (Wilmslow [MA], 1494)

John Irish[26] (or Irish John), piper (no place, 1574)

John Jackson of Ince, piper (Ince [ED], 1618, 1633)

John Jackson of Newton,[27] piper (Eccleston [BR], 1634)

Richard Jackson,[28] piper (Chester, 1574)

Roger Jackson, drummer (Congleton [NO], 1630–31, 1631–32)

Jervace, piper (Malpas [BR], 1631, 1641)

Robert Jewett of Dublin, organist (Chester, 1643–46)

William Joett, singingman (Chester, 1546–47)

David Jones of Chester, fiddler, and his fellow[29] (Dodleston [BR], 1620)

Thomas Jones of Chester, Bachelor of Music (Chester, 1625)

Edward Jonson of Handbridge in the County of the City of Chester, musician (Chester, 1572–73)

Kelly; *see* Cally

William Kent, musician (Chester, 1576)

John Kersleye, *alias* Clubfoot, of Malpas, piper (Malpas [BR], 1620)

Thomas Kettle [musician][30] (Chester, 1675–76)

Robert Laithwood[31] of Runcorn, piper (Runcorn [BU], 1616, 1617; Frodsham [ED], 1622, 1623, 1624, 1625)

Richard Laseby of Audlem, piper (Audlem [NA], 1608)

Henry Lawes, musician and composer (Legh Family of Lyme [MA], 1635, undated)

Thomas Lawrenson, musician (Utkinton [ED], 1619; no place, 1619)

Roger Lether (of Nantwich), drummer (Nantwich [NA], 1602, 1619, 1639)

Humphrey Lloyd, singer (Malpas [BR], 1631)

John Lloyd of Malpas, organ drawer (Malpas [BR], 1626)

William Luter, minstrel (Chester, 1552–53, 1557–58, 1559–60, 1560–61, 1562–63)

William Madock/Maddock,[32] waitman/musician (Chester, 1588, 1588–89, 1590–91, 1591, 1604)

William Madock/Maddock, Jr.,[32] waitman (Chester, 1588–89)

John Marshall, harper (Chester, 1448)

William Marshall, minstrel (Chester, 1486, 1488–89, 1490–91)

Thomas Mason, yeoman, *alias* Thomas Mason, singingman (Chester, ?16c)

George Massie [horn-blower][33] (Shotwick [WI], 1615)

Hugh Meaneley, piper (Davenham [NO], 1589)

William Mercer of Chester, waitman (Chester, 1577–78, 1581, 1588, 1588–89)

John Metier of Biddulph, Staffordshire, piper (no place, 1611, 1612)

Richard Metier,[34] piper (Chelford [MA], 1597; no place, 1611, 1612)

Richard Metier[34] of Withington, piper (Withington [MA], ?1609, 1610, 1617, 1623, Lower Withington, 1617, 1618)

Richard Metier[34] of Siddington, piper (Siddington [MA], 1624, 1625)

Richard Metier[34] of Swettenham, piper (Swettenham [NO], 1631, 1632)

Richard Minshull of Nantwich, fiddler/musician (Nantwich [NA], 1606, 1622,[35] 1623)

Rondull Moreton of Harthill, tailor and piper (Bickerton [BR], 1615; Egerton [BR], 1617)

Roger Murgell, piper (Poynton [MA], 1611)

Richard Nuball, organist of Chester (Leche Family of Carden [BR], 1641)

Robert de O<.>uytley[36] of Northwich, minstrel (Middlewich [NO], 1415).

Richard Paynter, organmaker (Chester, 1488)

Christopher Parkynston, singer (Newton Family of Pownall Fee [MA], undated [?c.1502–03])

Peacock of Bunbury,[37] fiddler (Bunbury [ED], 1620)

Peacock,[37] fiddler (Malpas [BR], 1637)

Peacock,[37] piper (Malpas [BR], 1640)

John Peacock of Beeston,[37] piper (Chester, 1612; Beeston [ED], 1615)

Humphrey Peacock,[37] piper (no place, 1609)

Humphrey Peacock, Sr.,[37] piper (Tarporley [ED], 1616)

Robert Pearson, piper (Wybunbury [NA], 1605)

Edward Pemberton, waitman (Chester, 1607–08, 1609)

Thomas Peycock, organmaker (Chester, 1536)

William Phillipps, piper (Wybunbury [NA], 1605)

Pickering[38] [singer] (Chester, 1608–09)

John Piers of Warrington [?piper][39] (Heswall [WI], 1628)

Francis Pilkington, lutenist and composer (Smith Family of Hough [NA], 1614; Chester, 1614–15; Legh Family of Lyme [MA], 1624)

John Pillin of Chester, singingman (Chester, 1575–76, 1576)

Platt,[40] minstrel (Whitegate [ED], with ref. to Middlewich [NO], 1602)

Richard Platt of Tattenhall,[40] piper/minstrel (Bickerton [BR], 1616; Tattenhall [BR], 1619, 1620)

William Plymley, piper (no place, 1630)

Potinger [?of Ireland],[41] scholar and musician (Chester, 1607–08)

Preston, trumpeter (Chester, 1635–36)

James Preston of Warrington, musician (Chester, 1639–40)

John Preston of Warrington, musician (Chester, 1600)

Richard Preston of Warrington, musician[42] (Chester, 1594)

William Pryke, organplayer (Chester, 1504)

Richard Prymett, bell-ringer (Chester, undated)

Thomas Pudgeon *alias* Thomas de <...>ley, minstrel (Witton [NO], 1406)

David le Pyper of Malpas, piper (Malpas [BR], 1417)

James Reynold, fiddler (Chester, 1525–26)

Richard Richardson, *alias* Williamson, *alias* Evensong of Frodsham[43] (Frodsham [ED], 1617; no place, 1617)

James Robinson, musician (Chester, 1658–59)

John Robinson [?drummer][44] (Wilmslow [MA], 1629)

Thomas Roper, minstrel (Chester, 1488–89)

Agnes Rowley of Chester, musician (Chester, 1573–74, 1574)

John Russhall, musician (Chester, 1567–68)

William Ryder, piper (Great Budworth [BU], 1608)

John Salber, harper (Chester, 1467–68)

Arthur Savage, *alias* Buckley, of Wincle, piper (Wincle [MA], 1605)

John Savage of Bunbury, minstrel (Bunbury [ED], 1421)

Francis Seaer, of "the lower wich in Iscoyd" (Flintshire), piper (Malpas [BR], 1617)

John Seton, Jr., of Chester, fiddler (Chester, 1589–90)

Randle Seyvell (of Nantwich), piper (Nantwich, 1597)

Mark Shaw, fiddler (Witton [NO], 1619)

James Shepley, piper (Siddington [MA], 1601)

Shurlock, of Chester,[45] minstrel (Chester, 1575–76, 1577–78)

Henry Shurlock,[45] of Chester, minstrel/piper (Chester, 1588–89, 1593–94, 1594–95, 1595–96, 1598–99, 1599–1600, 1600–01, 1601–02, 1602–03, 1603–04, 1604, 1605–06)

William Siddall [?minstrel][46] (Chester, 1606–07, 1607–08, 1608–09, 1609–10, 1611–12, 1612–13, 1613–14, 1614–15, 1615–16, 1616–17, 1617–18, 1618–19, 1619–20, 1620–21, 1621–22)

Thomas Skinner of Chester, musician (Chester, undated [early 17c])

John Smith, of Clotton Hoofield, piper (Clotton Hoofield [ED], 1611, 1612)

Thomas Smyth, organmaker (Chester, 1534–35)

John Spencer, drummer (Acton [NA],[47] 1611)

Thomas Squier, cornett-player (Chester, 1613–14, 1614–15)

Lawrence Starkey of Stretton, drummer (Stretton [BU or BR],[48] 1617, 1618)

John Stele, piper (Matley [MA], 1592)

Robert Stevenson, organist (Chester, 1570–99)

Thomas Stokes of Stretton (BU or BR),[49] minstrel (Chester, 1567)

Roger Stopporte, drummer (Congleton, 1601–02, 1602–03)

William le Synger, minstrel (no place, 1342–43)

Henry Tailer of Standish, Lancs., musician (Chester, 1588–89)

John Tompson of Nantwich, minstrel[50] (Nantwich [NA], 1613)

John Tompson (of Nantwich), musician[50] (Nantwich [NA], 1589)

John Tompson, piper[50] (Nantwich [NA], 1597, 1624)

Tomson, piper[50] (Nantwich [NA], 1605)

John Tomson of Stockport [musician][51] (Manchester, Lancs., 1601)

Old Towers[52] the piper (Alvanley [ED], 1638)

Thomas Towers of Barrow,[52] piper (Barrow [ED], 1603)

Thomas Towers,[52] yeoman [piper] (Upton [Upton by Chester] [BR], 1610)

Edward Trevis of Nantwich, piper (Nantwich [NA], 1606)

Tyttle [drummer] (Chester, 1591–92, 1593–94)

John Vaughan[53] of Nantwich, piper (Wistaston [NA], 1605)

John Vaughan[53] of Nantwich, musician (Nantwich [NA], 1632)

Roger Vaughan of Nantwich, musician (Nantwich [NA], 1636, 1648)

Richard Vernon of Bunbury,[54] piper (Bunbury [ED], 1620)

Richard Vernon (of Nantwich),[54] piper/musician (Nantwich [NA], 1632, 1635)

Hugh de Walay, harper (Foulk Stapleford [BR], 1354)

Rondle Waker[55] of Budworth, piper ([?Little] Budworth [ED], 1619)

Ralph Waker[55] of Budworth, piper ([?Little] Budworth [ED], 1619)

Rondle Walker[55] of Little Budworth, piper (Tarporley [ED], 1609; Tarvin [ED], 1609, 1611; Little Budworth [ED], 1619)

John Ward, instrument maker (Chester, 1670)

John Waring [drummer] (Chester, 1590–91)

John Waringes of Congleton, minstrel (Congleton [NO], 1575)

George Watt (Watts) of Chester, musician (Chester, 1666, undated [1668–69], 1672)

Nicholas Webster [musician] (Chester, 1614–15)

Thomas Weedall (of Nantwich), musician (Nantwich [NA], 1607)

William Welles, minstrel (Chester, 1492)

Westeid, minstrel (Chester, 1555–56)

Thomas Wewll of Middlewich, piper (Middlewich [NO], 1566)

Robert White of Ely, organist (Chester, 1567–70)

Thomas White, trumpeter (Chester, 1454)

Robert de Whyteley[56] piper (Leftwich [NO], 1411)

Thomas Willard, waitman (Chester, 1609)

Thomas Williams of Chester,[57] waitman (Chester, 1577–78, 1581, 1588, 1588–89, 1589, 1590–91)

Thomas Williams of Chester,[57] waitman (Chester, 1609, 1617–18, 1620, 1623–24, 1624, 1625)

William Williams of Chester, son of Thomas Williams of Chester, apprentice waitman (Chester, 1590–91)

Thomas Williamson,[58] musician (no place, 1620)

Thomas Withenshaw, fiddler (Utkinton [ED], 1619; no place, 1619)

Grace Wood of Warrington [?piper][59] (Heswall [WI], 1628)

Mr. Woodson[60] of Cholmondeley, organist (Malpas [BR], 1643)

Arthur Woormsonne, bell-ringer (Chester, undated)

William Worrall of Nantwich, musician (Nantwich [NA], 1629, 1631, 1632, 1633, 1634, 1635, 1636, 1637)

John le Wrugh, harper (Chester, 1397)

Blind Edward Wyatt [?musician][61] (Chester, 1651–52, 1652–53, 1653–54, 1654–55, 1655–56, 1656–57, 1657–58, 1658–59)

Robert Wythers, piper (also described as "jester or fool") (Norton,[62] 1621)

Thomas Yemouth of "Vn'thorborse"[63] in Derbyshire, minstrel, specifically bagpiper (Chester, 1597)

Richard <...>ase, minstrel (Tattenhall [BR], 1618)

Lancashire Performers (Diocese of Chester)

Henry Arnett of Sefton, piper (Halsall, Lancs., 1630)

James Arnett of Northmeols, piper (Halsall, Lancs., 1630)

William Arnett of Much Crosby, piper (Halsall, Lancs., 1633)

Thomas Barton of Ormskirk, piper (Downholland, Lancs., 1630; Halsall, Lancs., 1633)

James Bickerstaff, minstrel (Halsall, Lancs., 1567)

William Graddell, piper (Kirkham, Lancs., 1629–30)

John Green, piper (Manchester, 1595)

Henry Hallwood,[64] piper (Walton, Lancs., 1590–91)

Thomas Harrison, piper (Much Harwood, Lancs., 1633)

William Harrison, piper (Wenslow, Lancs., 1595)

John Heyhurst, piper (?Salesbury,[65] undated)

John Jackson of Elell, Lancs, piper (Wyredale, Lancs., 1633)

Richard Jackson,[66] piper (Kirkham, Lancs., 1629–30)

Thomas Park, piper (Much Harwood, Lancs., 1633)

John Piper [?piper] (Manchester, 1590)

Thomas Pyper ("the half-faced piper") (Chorlton, Lancs., 1625)

John Starkie of Blackburn, piper (Blackburn, Lancs., 1623)

Alexander Turner of Marsden, piper (Colne, Lancs., 1622)

James Walmesley, drummer (Goosenargh, Lancs., 1633)

NOTES

Abbreviations:

BL	British Library
C&C	Cheshire and Chester Archives
DNB	*Dictionary of National Biography*
GSJ	*Galpin Society Journal*
NG	*The New Grove Dictionary of Music and Musicians,* 2nd ed., ed. Stanley Sadie, 29 vols. (London: Macmillan, 2001).
PRO	Public Record Office
VCH:Chester	*A History of the County of Chester,* vol. 1, ed. B. E. Harris and A. T. Thacker, Victoria History of the Counties of England (Oxford: Oxford University Press, 1987)

Introduction

1. See *Chester,* ed. Lawrence M. Clopper, Records of Early English Drama (Toronto: University of Toronto Press, 1979), vi.

2. F. I. Dunn, *The Ancient Parishes, Townships and Chapelries of Cheshire,* Cheshire Record Office and Cheshire Diocesan Record Office (Chester: Cheshire County Council, 1987), 8.

3. Chester, Frodsham, Macclesfield, Malpas, Middlewich, Nantwich, and Wirral.

4. *VCH: Chester,* 264–65.

5. Ince, part of which was in Chester deanery and part in Wirral deanery. There are a number of townships that fall in two parishes.

6. *Cheshire,* ed. Elizabeth Baldwin and A. D. Mills, Records of Early English Drama, in preparation. Quotations used in the present book have not been checked by an independent reader according to the practice of REED, and, as anyone familiar with the vagaries of early handwriting will know, the final published form of the Cheshire records in the REED volume may differ very slightly from those given here.

7. The cases referred to here, at Little Budworth and Mobberley, are discussed in chapter I.

8. "Acte for the Punishement of Vacabondes, and for Releif of the Poore & Impotent," 14 Elizabeth c. 5 (1572), section 42, in *The Statutes of the Realm,* vol. 4 ([London], 1819).

9. For a more detailed discussion of the geographical formation of Cheshire, see *VCH: Chester*, vol. 1.

10. Ibid., 3.

11. Ibid., 3.

12. Ibid., 4.

13. Congleton Town Hall, Borough Account Book I, fols. 182^v, 185^r.

14. *VCH: Chester*, 33.

15. Ibid., 252.

16. Ibid.

17. Ibid., 265.

18. Ibid., 264.

19. R. C. Richardson, *Puritanism in North-West England: A Regional Study of the Diocese of Chester to 1642* (Manchester: Manchester University Press, 1972), 1.

Chapter I

1. Thomas Whythorne, *The Autobiography*, ed. James M. Osborn (Oxford: Clarendon Press, 1961), 244.

2. Timothy J. McGee, "The Fall of the Noble Minstrel: The Sixteenth-Century Minstrel in a Musical Context," *Medieval and Renaissance Drama in England* 7 (1995): 98.

3. Richard Rastall discusses the difficulty of determining a minstrel's professional status; he points out the necessity for formal apprenticeship for true professionalism, but recognizes that members of other trades were also performing music; see G. Richard Rastall, "Secular Musicians in Later Medieval England," 2 vols. (Ph.D. diss., University of Manchester, 1968), 36.

4. C&C, MB/21, fol. 107^v (Edmund Cally); fol. 65^r (Agnes Rowley). There is no doubt that it is Agnes who is the musician; the recognizance specifies "John Rowley and Agnes his wief (she being a muscon)."

5. C&C, MB/20, fol. 45^v.

6. C&C, P/120/4525/2, 65 (25 December 1589) (musician); P/120/4525/1, fol. 75^v (6 April 1597) (piper); PRO, CHES 24/112/1, single mb, 12 April 1613, CHES 24/112/2, single mb, 27 September 1613, CHES 21/2, fol. 85^r, 22 April 1613 (minstrel); C&C, P 120/4525/2, 271 (7 October 1624) (piper).

7. For instance, William Worrall, described as musician or musicioner from 1629 to 1637, and Zachary Gill, described as musician over the same period. 'Musician' seems to be the preferred term generally in this period, although Richard Vernon is described in the parish registers both as piper in 1632 and as musician in 1634/5.

8. PRO, CHES 24/1/2, single sheet (1342–43).

9. PRO, CHES 2/37, mb 3 (10 June 1354 and 11 May 1354). The

grant is given in both Latin and French.

10. John Southworth, *The English Medieval Minstrel* (Woodbridge: Boydell Press, 1989), 97.

11. *Calendar of the Patent Rolls, Henry VI,* 6 vols. (Norwich and London, 1901–10), 5:262.

12. It has obviously not been possible to examine every document in the Public Record Office, and these numbers are based only on those documents surveyed. As some of the later material is more accessible, there may be some weighting towards evidence from the later period. However, proportionally to the documents examined, there are fewer performers who are designated minstrels in the later period.

13. The term is used most often by the Cordwainers and Shoemakers' Company (C&C, G 8/2, Cordwainers and Shoemakers' Account Book I, 1547–98, *passim*), but also occurs in the Painters, Glaziers, Embroiderers, and Stationers Company, Account Book with Rules and Apprenticeship Enrolment, 1567–1690 (C&C, G 17/1), fol. 38ʳ.

14. Bodleian Library, MS. Rawl. B.282 (William Smith's Description of Cheshire), fols. 54ʳ–54ᵛ. According to the *DNB*, Smith wrote his account in 1585.

15. PRO, CHES 2/105, mb 1 (24 October 1433).

16. Prejudice against performers, particularly those who play instrumental music (*musica instrumentalis*), is very old, for which see Boethius's *De Institutione Musica* 1.2.

17. C&C, QSE 5/46, single sheet (4 October 1594).

18. PRO, CHES 24/113/4, single sheet (1618).

19. McGee, "Fall of the Noble Minstrel," 98.

20. Ibid., 102–03, with reference to Southworth, *English Medieval Minstrel,* 142–43.

21. McGee, "Fall of the Noble Minstrel," 113.

22. Ibid., 116.

23. PRO, CHES 24/1/2, single sheet (William le Synger); C&C, SR/128, mb 1 (1407–09) (Robert Gyster); PRO, CHES 25/16, mb 4d (4 March 1488) (Thomas Fiddler).

24. It is interesting to compare Aristotle's statement: "But professional musicians we speak of as vulgar people, and indeed we think it is not manly to perform music except when drunk or for fun" (*The Politics,* as quoted by Oliver Strunk, *Source Readings in Music History* [London: Faber and Faber, 1952], 17).

25. Richard Rastall, *The Heaven Singing,* Music in Early English Religious Drama 1 (Cambridge: D. S. Brewer, 1996), 300–05.

26. Southworth, *English Medieval Minstrel,* 4. This work focuses mainly on royal minstrels.

27. Rastall, *The Heaven Singing,* 85.

28. Rastall, "Secular Musicians," 242.

29. Ibid., 36, n. 87.

30. Whythorne, *Autobiography*, 232–33.

31. For instance, opera singers who perform in areas of popular music.

32. C&C, QSF/56/35, single sheet (7 September, 1608–09) (Mr. Evans); C&C, CR/385/27, bifolium (7 February, 1625) (Thomas Jones); Manchester, John Rylands University Library, Legh of Lyme Correspondence, Letters to Sir Peter Legh, folder 4, single sheet (5 February 1635) (Henry Lawes); C&C, DLE/87, 29 (from back) (August 1641) (Richard Nuball); C&C, P/21/3607/1/3, 12 (7 January 1643) (Mr. Woodson).

33. C&C, QSF 77/2/97, single sheet (27 July 1642).

34. Whythorne, *Autobiography*, 233–34.

35. For example, C&C, G 2/1, fol. 107^r (six shillings "Giuen the Musicke" on 2 July 1677), or C&C, G 5/1, fol. 82^v (six pence "spent at hireing the musique," 23 June 1678).

36. C&C, G 17/2, fol. 80^r.

37. C&C, G 17/1, fols. 38^r (1568–69), 53^r (1573-4), 84^r (1585–86); C&C, G 8/2, fols. 56^r–56^v (1569–70), 64^r (1573–74), 72^v (1577–78); C&C, G 14/1, fol. 24^r (1581–82).

38. For example, C&C, G 17/1, fol. 84^r (1585–86) (the term 'minstrel' is also used in this account); C&C, G 8/3, fol. 9^v (1600–01).

39. C&C, QJF 39/4/22, single sheet (23 December 1610).

40. C&C, QSF 55/75, single sheet (23 February 1607).

41. The dedications are noted by Joseph C. Bridge, "Francis Pilkington," *Grove's Dictionary of Music and Musicians*, ed. J. A. Fuller Maitland, 5 vols. (Philadelphia: Theodore Presser, 1922), 3:748. The Earls of Derby appear to have been patrons of Pilkington's family. Pilkington's father and brother were in the previous Earl's service, and the Stanley family may have had influence in obtaining Pilkington a post at Chester Cathedral.

42. Congleton, Town Hall, Borough Account Book I, fol. 240^v.

43. Ibid., fols. 170^v, 232^v.

44. Evelyn Caroline Legh, Baroness Newton, *The House of Lyme from its Foundation to the End of the Eighteenth Century* (London: William Heinemann, 1917), 70.

45. David George, *Lancashire*, Records of Early English Drama (Toronto: University of Toronto Press, 1991), 166.

46. See C&C, DBW/P/J/7, fols. 8^v (15 November 1613); 13 December 1613); 11^v (Mr. Handy to teach music; 1 March 1613/4); 12^v (Mr. Handy paid for a month's teaching; June 1614); 14^r (loan of bass viol to Ann Whittingham; 5 July 1614).

47. PRO, STAC 7/2/24, mb 5 (Bill of Complaint of John Egerton).

48. *sayde sayde*: dittography MS.

49. PRO, STAC 7/2/24, mb 1d–2d (Depositions, taken 19 January 1597).

50. PRO, STAC 7/2/24, mb 5 (Bill of Complaint of John Egerton against John Starkey).

51. PRO, STAC 5/E11/3, mb 9 (Interrogatories).

52. PRO, STAC 5/E11/3, mb 8–8d (Deposition of Bennett Hardinge).

53. Philip Stubbes, *The Anatomie of Abuses* (London, 1583), sig. O5ʳ.

54. Richardson, *Puritanism in North-West England*, 18–19.

55. Christopher Haigh, "The Continuity of Catholicism in the English Reformation," in *The English Reformation Revised*, ed. Christoper Haigh (1987; reprint Cambridge: Cambridge University Press, 1988), 184.

56. William Hinde, *A Faithfull Remonstrance of the Holy Life and Happy Death of John Bruen of Bruen-Stapleford, in the County of Chester, Esquire (Brother to that Mirrour of Piety; Mistris Katherin Brettergh) Exhibiting variety of many Memorable and Exemplary passages of his Life, and at his Death, usefull for all sorts and Sexes, but principally intended, as a Path and President of Piety and Charity for the Inhabitants of the Famous County Palatine of Chester* (London, 1641), 10.

57. Ibid., 10–11.

58. Gervase Babington, *On the Ten Commandments* (1588), 318–21, as quoted in the Foreword to Phillip Stubbes, *Anatomy of Abuses in England in Shakspere's Youth*, ed. F. J. Furnivall, New Shakspere Society Publications, series 6, nos. 4, 6, 12 (1877–79; reprint Vaduz: Kraus, 1965), 83. I have not been able to locate Furnivall's exact source.

59. Hinde, *A Faithfull Remonstrance*, 90.

60. William Hinde, *The Very Singular Life of John Bruen, Esquire, of Bruen Stapleford, Cheshire: Exhibitions of a Variety of Memorable and Exemplary Circumstances, Which May Be of Great Utility to All Persons; but Principally Intended as a Precedent of Piety and Charity for the Inhabitants of the County of Chester*, [2nd ed.] (Chester: William Coddington, 1799), 90n.

61. Richardson, *Puritanism in North-West England*, 147.

62. Ibid., 50, with references to John Ley, *Sunday a Sabbath* (1641), R. Cox, *The Literature of the Sabbath Question* (Edinburgh, 1865), and W. B. Whitaker, *Sunday in Tudor and Stuart Times* (London, 1933).

63. Quoted in James Tait, "The Declaration of Sports for Lancashire (1617)," *English Historical Review* 32 (1917): 562; Thomas Morton, the subject of the *Life*, had been bishop of Chester at the time of the issue of the *Declaration for Sports for Lancashire* by James I in 1617.

64. York, Borthwick Institute, V.1629–30/CB, fol. 163ʳ.

65. York, Borthwick Institute, V.1595–6/CB.2, fol. 56ᵛ (15 September 1595).

66. York, Borthwick Institute, V.1595–6/CB.3, fol. 14ʳ (25 September 1595).

67. PRO, CHES 21/3, fol. 12ʳ (15 September 1617).

68. PRO, CHES 24/114/2, single sheet (27 July 1617).

69. PRO, CHES 24/114/3, mb 2 (13 April 1618).

70. Quoted in Joseph Strutt, *The Sports and Pastimes of the People of England from the Earliest Period, Including the Rural and Domestic Recreations, May Games, Mummeries, Pageants, Processions and Pompous Spectacles*, rev. J. Charles Cox (London: Methuen, 1903), xlix. The order is dated 24 May 1618.

71. C&C, EDC 5(1597)/101, two unnumbered sheets (21 April 1597).

72. Ibid.

73. Ibid. The text reads "anno Domini i595 vel anno domini i594."

74. Ibid.

75. Eaton attended Brasenose College, Oxford (B.A. 1577, M.A. 1587) and was one of the four local moderators at Northwich for the Preaching Exercises in the 1580s. In the archdeaconry of Chester twenty-two out of thirty-one moderators were puritans (Richardson, *Puritanism in North-West England*, 63, 66).

76. George Ormerod, *The History of the County Palatine and City of Chester, Compiled from Original Evidences in Public Offices, the Harleian and Cottonian MSS., Parochial Registers, Private Muniments, Unpublished MS. Collections of Successive Cheshire Antiquaries, and a Personal Survey of Every Township in the County: Incorporated with a Republication of King's Vale Royal and Leycester's Cheshire Antiquities*, 2nd ed., rev. and enlarged by Thomas Helsby, 3 vols. (London: G. Routledge and Sons, 1882), 1:411.

77. C&C, EDC 5(1597)/101 (21 April 1597).

78. John Jackson at Ince on Wednesday, 27 November 1633; York, Borthwick Institute, V.1633/CB.2b, fol. 426ʳ.

79. PRO, CHES 24/113/3, unfoliated.

80. "The Kinges' Majesties Declaration Concerning Lawfull Sports," quoted in L. A. Govett, *The King's Book of Sports: A History of the Declarations of King James I. and King Charles I. as to the Use of Lawful Sports on Sundays, with a Reprint of the Declarations and a Description of the Sports then Popular* (London: Elliot Stock, 1890), 37.

81. Ibid.

82. Peter Clark, *The English Alehouse: A Social History 1200–1830* (London: Longman, 1983), 43–44.

83. Ibid., 42 (Table 3.1).

84. Peter Clark, "The Alehouse and the Alternative Society," in *Puritans and Revolutionaries: Essays in Seventeenth-Century History Presented to Christopher Hill*, ed. Donald Pennington and Keith Thomas (Oxford: Clarendon Press, 1978), 48–49.

85. Clarke, *The English Alehouse*, 48.

86. Clark, "The Alehouse and the Alternative Society," 52.

86. Ibid., 48–49.

87. Ibid., 48. It is not always possible to draw an exact line of division between inn, tavern, and alehouse.

88. Chester, C&C, QJF 53/2/152, single sheet (13 July 1624).

89. Clark, *The English Alehouse*, 34.

90. C&C, EDA 2/6, 13.

91. Clark, *The English Alehouse*, 25.

92. C&C, EDV 1/17, fol. 57^r.

93. PRO, CHES 24/114/4, single sheet (20 September 1618).

94. C&C, EDV 1/12b, fol. 71^v.

95. Preston, Hudson's MS Sermons, DP 353, fol. 46; quoted in Richardson, *Puritanism in North-West England*, 52.

96. Clark, "The Alehouse and the Alternative Society," 57 (crime), 59–60 (prostitution and illicit meetings), 58 (disturbance at Malpas).

97. C&C, QJF 10/1/1, single sheet (27 October 1580).

98. C&C, QJF 12/3/36, single mb (24 August 1582).

99. PRO, CHES 24/114/1, unfoliated, (1617).

100. C&C, QJF 60/3/102, single sheet (6 August 1631).

101. PRO, CHES 21/3, fols. 367^v–368^r (1 July 1616).

102. PRO, CHES 24/113/3, unfoliated (1616).

103. Ibid.

104. Ibid.

105. PRO, CHES 24/114/2, single sheet (23–24 August 1617).

106. C&C, QJF 69/3/50, single strip, (22 July 1640).

107. PRO, CHES 21/3, fol. 43^v (24 April 1620).

108. Hinde, *A Faithfull Remonstrance*, 131.

109. Ormerod, *The History of Chester*, 1:651. Thomas Dutton was sheriff of Cheshire in 1611, and was 46 when he died in 1614. John Bruen himself was dead by 1626 (C&C, WS/1625 John Bruen of Stapleford, gentleman, single mb [26 January 1626]).

110. PRO, CHES 24/114/2, bifolium (24 September, 1617). The constable, James Smithe, is constable of either Handley or Hattersley; the document is damaged, and only "Ha<..>ley" remains. Handley seems more likely, given the size of the damaged area.

111. C&C, QJF 31/2/43, single sheet (20 July 1602).

112. Ibid. (referring to events of 2 and 3 July 1602).

113. C&C, QJF 53/2/153, single sheet (12 May 1624). See also Elizabeth Baldwin, "Reformers, Rogues or Recusants? Control of Popular Entertainment and the Flouting of Authority in Cheshire before 1642," *Records of Early English Drama Newsletter* 22, no. 1 (1997): 26–31.

114. C&C, QJF 53/2/153, single sheet (8 July 1624).

115. C&C, QJF 53/2/152, single sheet (13 July 1624).

116. *Chester*, ed. Lawrence M. Clopper, Records of Early English Drama (Toronto: University of Toronto Press, 1979), 43.

117. C&C, QSE 5/46, single sheet (4 October 1594).

118. Ibid.

119. C&C, ML 5/116, single sheet (6 April 1593).

120. For instance, in 1658–59, when the Painters, Glaziers, Embroiderers, and Stationers Company paid 1*s* to the maids at Alderman Holmes' house "for Rubbing the Chamber after their danceing in it" (C&C, G 17/2, fol. 80ʳ).

121. C&C, EDC 5(1571)/8, fol. 3ʳ (1571).

122. C&C, QJF 67/3/33, single sheet (7 August 1638).

123. Clark, "The Alehouse and the Alternative Society," 59.

124. York, Borthwick Institute, V.1578–9, single sheet (12 July 1578).

125. York, Borthwick Institute, V.1578/CB.3, fol. 29ʳ (17 July 1578).

126. PRO, CHES 24/113/4, single sheet (1 August 1616).

127. C&C, QJF 31/2/43, single sheet (20 July 1602) (Darnhall); PRO, CHES 21/2, fol. 51ᵛ (24 April 1609) (Frodsham); PRO, CHES 21/2, fol. 123ᵛ (September 1616) (Tarporley).

128. C&C, EDV 1/29, fol. 4ᵛ (St. John's parish, Chester, 1628).

129. PRO, CHES 24/115/4, single sheet (July–August 1620).

130. Richardson, *Puritanism in North-West England*, 128–29.

131. Southworth, *English Medieval Minstrel*, 4–5.

132. Richard Rastall, "The Minstrel Court in Medieval England," *Proceedings of the Leeds Literary and Philological Society* 18 (1) (1982): 96; Whythorne, *Autobiography*, 244.

Chapter II, Part 1

1. In connection with the topic of the present chapter, see also David Mills, "Music and Musicians in Chester: A Summary Account," *Medieval English Theatre* 17 (1995): 58–75.

2. On the Abbey and Cathedral, see R. V. H. Burne, *The Monks of Chester: The History of St. Werburgh's Abbey* (London: SPCK, 1962), and the same author's *Chester Cathedral from its Founding by Henry VIII to the Accession of Queen Victoria* (London: SPCK, 1958).

3. See William Smith, "A man may stand therein and see into the Markets, or Four principal streets of the city," in *The Vale-Royall of England or the County Palatine of Chester*, ed. Daniel King (London, 1656), 39. A drawing showing the Pentice is reproduced in Clifford Davidson, *Illustrations of the Stage and Acting in England to 1642*, Early Drama, Art, and Music Monograph Series 16 (Kalamazoo: Medieval Institute Publications, 1991), fig. 30.

4. Rupert Morris, *Chester in the Plantagenet and Tudor Reigns* (Chester, n.d.), 150–54.

5. Clopper, *Chester*, 45, 58, 62. For discussion of the Palm Sunday procession, see Davidson, *Illustrations of the Stage*, 15, 17; and the more extended treatment of the context of the rite in Mary C. Erler, "Palm Sunday Prophets and Processions and Eucharistic Controversy," *Renaissance Quarterly*

48 (1995): 58–81. For a translation of the rite from the Sarum Processional and Missal, see William Tydeman, ed., *The Medieval European Stage* (Cambridge: Cambridge University Press, 2001), 61–68.

6. For an account of Chester's Cathedral organists, see Watkins Shaw, *The Succession of Organists of the Chapel Royal and the Cathedrals of England and Wales from c.1538* (Oxford: Clarendon Press, 1991), 60–71.

7. Manchester, John Rylands University Library, Latin MS. 460, fol. 21^r (1518).

8. See *NG* 20:317 (pricksong), 19:825–88 (plainchant and plainsong), and 7:366–74 (discant).

9. C&C, SR/460, mb 1d.

10. Respectively. C&C, SR/360, mb 1d; SR/538, mb 10; SB/7, fol. 67^v.

11. On early English organs, see Stephen Bicknell, *The History of the English Organ* (Cambridge: Cambridge University Press, 1996), 11–90.

12. BL Harley MS. 2095, fol. 146^v.

13. Ibid.

14. Cathedral Statutes 1544, quoted in Burne, *Chester Cathedral*, 10.

15. Bateson was appointed organist at Christ Church Cathedral, Dublin, on 5 April 1609. Barra Boydell comments that "the importance placed by the dean and chapter [of Christ Church] in securing as organist a musician of the calibre of Thomas Bateson is seen in the fact that in no other case between the new foundation and the present day was the wording of the contract appointing an organist at Christ Church deemed worthy of being copied into the chapter acts" ("Music in Reformation and Political Change in Christ Church Cathedral, Dublin," in *Music and Musicians in Renaissance Cities and Towns*, ed. Fiona Kisby [Cambridge: Cambridge University Press, 2001], 138). A further but later link between Dublin and Chester is indicated by the appointment of a Peter Stringer, a member of the choir at Christ Church, as organist in Chester in 1660 (Barra Boydell, *Music at Christ Church before 1800: Documents and Selected Anthems* [Dublin, 1999], 83–84).

16. Shaw, *The Succession of Organists*, 63.

17. Clopper, *Chester*, 436.

18. On the manuscripts and textual history of the plays, see R. M. Lumiansky and David Mills, *The Chester Mystery Cycle: Essays and Documents* (Chapel Hill: University of North Carolina Press, 1983), 1–86 (hereafter *Essays*).

19. David Mills, "James Miller: The Will of a Chester Scribe," *REED Newsletter* 9, no. 1 (1984): 11–12.

20. JoAnna Dutka, *Music in the English Mystery Plays*, Early Drama, Art, and Music Monograph Series 2 (Kalamazoo: Medieval Institute Publications, 1980), 28–29; see also Rastall, *The Heaven Singing*, 152.

21. Rastall, *Heaven Singing*, 154.

22. For the text of the Early and Late Banns to the Plays, see Lumiansky and Mills, *Essays*, 278–310.

23. Quotations from the plays are from *The Chester Mystery Cycle*, ed. R. M. Lumiansky and David Mills, EETS, s.s. 3, 9 (London: Oxford University Press, 1974–86), vol. 1.

24. Translations from the plays are from David Mills, *The Chester Mystery Cycle: A New Edition with Modernised Spelling*, Medieval Texts and Studies 9 (East Lansing, Mich.: Colleagues Press, 1992).

25. Richard Rastall, "Music in the Cycle," in Lumiansky and Mills, *Essays*, 159.

26. Clopper, *Chester*, 53 (1554), 66–67 (1561), 77–78 (1567), 86 (1568).

27. Rastall, "Music in the Cycle," 135.

28. Clopper, *Chester*, 78 (1567).

29. Ibid., 81 (1568), 92 (1572), and 107 (1575).

30. Suzanne R. Westfall, *Patrons and Performance: Early Tudor Household Revels* (Oxford: Clarendon Press, 1990), 62–63.

31. C&C, CHB/3, fol. 103ʳ (23 April, 1612).

32. C&C, TAR 2/37, mb 4; other repairers include Edward Corry in 1588, Thomas Beddell in 1616–17, Peter Ince once more in 1618–19, and James Malbone in 1638–39.

33. Clopper, *Chester*, 325.

34. Ibid., 443.

35. Ibid., 383.

36. Ibid., 407.

37. Ibid., 448.

38. Ibid., 259.

39. Rastall, "Music in the Cycle," 117.

40. Clopper, *Chester*, 43.

41. Ibid., 154–55.

42. Ibid., 166.

43. Ibid., 299.

44. Ibid., 165.

45. Ibid., 368.

46. C&C, MF 87/12 (1668-9); AB/2, fol. 175ᵛ (17 December 1672).

47. Clopper, *Chester*, 164.

48. Ibid., 285.

49. C&C, WS 1604 William Maddock of Chester, Waitman (4 September 1604).

50. Clopper, *Chester*, 169.

51. Ibid., 94.

52. Ibid., 479.

53. Ibid., 443.

54. Ibid., 409.

55. Ibid., 160.

56. Ibid., 119.

57. Ibid., 119.

58. C&C, QSF 67/6, fols. 1–2^v.

59. *Coventry*, ed. R.W. Ingram, Records of Early English Drama (Toronto: University of Toronto Press, 1981), 302.

60. *Shropshire*, ed. J. Alan B. Somerset, Records of Early English Drama, 2 vols. (Toronto: University of Toronto Press, 1994), 1:78.

61. George, *Lancashire*, 170.

62. Clopper, *Chester*, 180.

63. Ibid., 184–85.

64. C&C, QSE 9/2.

65. C&C, QSE 11/71 (31 October 1609).

66. Clopper, *Chester*, 311.

67. C&C, G 2/1, fol. 126^v (29 September, 1624).

68. C&C, QSF 29/122, (12 March 1574).

69. C&C, MB/24, fol. 33^v (21 April 1589).

70. C&C, MB/25, fol. 62^v (4 September 1591).

71. Ibid., fol. 64^v (16 September 1591).

72. C&C, MB/27, fol. 41^r (28 August 1598).

73. Ibid., fol. 25^v (14 January 1599).

74. C&C, QSE 9/8, bifolium unnumbered (31 October 1609).

75. Clopper, *Chester*, 195.

76. Ibid., 265.

77. Ibid., 264.

78. C&C, QSE 9/8, bifolium, unnumbered (31 October 1609).

79. Clopper, *Chester*, 222.

80. Ibid., 280.

81. Ibid., 227.

82. Ibid, 289–90.

83. C&C, MAB/1, fol. 119^r (1621).

84. C&C, QSF 61/84 single sheet (21 April 1613).

85. C&C, MB/20, fol. 45^v (1572–73).

86. Denbigh Record Office, DD/PP/844, single sheet (December, 1583).

87. Ibid.

88. Clopper, *Chester*, 17.

89. Rastall, "The Minstrel Court," 96–105.

90. Clopper, *Chester*, 487. For accounts of the origin of the court, see ibid., 461–66, 487–89.

91. Ibid., 463.

92. Ibid., 464–65.

93. Ibid., 205.

94. C&C, QSE 3/84, fol. 2^r.

95. C&C, QSE 5/82, bifolium (6 May 1597).

96. C&C, SB 5/2, mb 1d (1397); SR/157, mb 1d (1424).

97. C&C, SR/223, mb 1d (1436).
98. C&C, MB/24, fol. 36v (17 May, 1588–99).
99. C&C, QSF 61/84, single sheet (10 December 1612).
100. C&C, MB/7, fol. 61ʳ (1488–89).
101. Clopper, *Chester*, 210.
102. Ibid., 127–28.
103. Clopper, *Chester*, 126.
104. Ibid., 43–44.
105. Ibid., 443.
106. C&C, QSE 9/69 (30 June, 1610).
107. Clopper, *Chester*, 53, 67, 78, 85, 91, 105.
108. Cf. Smiths' acounts for 1553–54 (ibid., 53): "Payd Rand a Crane in yonge Rafe goodmans howse xij d / was ther minstrell."
109. Rastall, "Music in the Cycle," 160–61.
110. Denbigh Record Office, DD/PP/839, 122 (1572).
111. Clopper, *Chester*, 92, 106.
112. Lumiansky and Mills, *Essays*, 118.
113. C&C, QSF 36/58, fol. 1ʳ (3 November, 1585).
114. C&C, G 8/3, fol. 38ᵛ.
115. PRO, CHES 24/126/3, unfoliated.
116. C&C, WS 1579, John Cooper of Chester, alderman, mb 4 (15 July 1579) and WS 1588 William Glaseor of Chester, esquire, fol. 1ʳ (17 January 1588–89).
117. Westfall, *Patrons and Performance*, 214.
118. C&C, EDA 2/2, fol. 115 (3 February 1586).
119. C&C, SBC/22, fol. 301ʳ (13 March 1575–76).
120. C&C, WS 1637 Thomas Jones of Chester, innkeeper, mb 1 (11 August 1637).
121. C&C, QSE 5/46, single sheet (4 October 1594).
122. We must be more cautious about Robert White, who was at Chester only three years, but see P. C. Buck *et al.*, eds. *Robert White*, Tudor Church Music 5 (London: Oxford University Press,1926).

Chapter II, Part 2
1. Peter Burke, *Popular Culture in Early Modern Europe* (New York: Harper and Row, 1978), 97.
2. C&C, QJF 44/2/12, single sheet (18 July 1615).
3. PRO, CHES 24/114/1, unfoliated (27 April 1617).
4. PRO, CHES 21/2, fol. 57ʳ (Tarvin); PRO, CHES 24/110/2, single sheet (Tarporley).
5. A. L. Beier, *Masterless Men: The Vagrancy Problem in England, 1560–1640* (London: Methuen, 1985), 71.
6. Beier, *Masterless Men*, xxii, with reference to G. Dubin and R. H.

Robinson, "The Vagrancy Concept Reconsidered: Problems and Abuses of Status Criminality," *New York University Law Review* 37 (1962): 105, 114–15.

7. C&C, QJF 49/2/47, single sheet (15 June 1620).

8. C&C, EDV 1/14, fol. 64^r (25 October 1605).

9. PRO, CHES 24/110/3, single sheet (15 February 1608/9).

10. C&C, DCH/F/194, 5 (1622).

11. Congleton, Town Hall, Borough Account Book I, fol. 4^r.

12. C&C, QJF 11/4/16, single sheet (24 January 1582).

13. Southworth, *English Medieval Minstrel*, 136.

14. C&C, EDC 5(1625)/67, unnumbered (26 April 1625).

15. C&C, EDD 3913/1/3, 333.

16. C&C, EDD 3913/1/4, 28.

17. C&C, P/120/4525/2, 85 (30 November 1606).

18. C&C, EDV 1/24, fol. 68^v (23 October 1622).

19. PRO, CHES 21/3, fol. 94^r (18 August 1623).

20. C&C, EDD 3913/1/4, 141 (1617–18).

21. C&C, QSF 61/47, single sheet (10 December 1612); C&C, QJF 44/1/96, single sheet (3 April 1615).

22. C&C, QSF 61/47, single sheet (10 December 1612).

23. PRO, CHES 16/1/1, single sheet (14 August 1567). The rent works out at between just over one shilling per week (at six weeks) or just under 15d a week (at five weeks), but most probably it represents a rent of 2d per day for thirty-seven days.

24. C&C, QSE 5/82, single sheet (6 May 1597).

25. Ibid.

26. Ibid.

27. C&C, QSF 55/75, single sheet (23 February 1608).

28. C&C, QJF 58/4/17, single sheet (19 January 1630).

29. Ibid.

30. C&C, EDV 1/12b, fols. 114^v–115^r (7 October 1601).

31. PRO, CHES 24/126/3, unfoliated (22 April 1642).

32. C&C, MB/24, fol. 22^v (22 January 1589).

33. C&C, MB/21, fol. 65^r (29 June 1574).

34. C&C, MB/20, fol. 46^r (20 September 1572).

35. PRO, CHES 2/37, mb 3 (11 May 1354).

36. PRO, CHES 25/11, mb 23d–24 (17 January 1419).

37. C&C, QSE 5/46, single sheet (4 October 1594).

38. Clopper, *Chester*, 290.

39. PRO, CHES 24/110/1, single sheet (15 April 1610). He is described in the Crown Book entry for this incident as "Pyp*er*" (CHES 21/2, fol. 10^v [3 October 1603]).

40. C&C, QJF 67/3/33, bifolium.

41. C&C, P/21/3607/1/2, 23 (21 September 1617).

42. Dunn, *The Ancient Parishes, Townships and Chapelries of Cheshire*, 29.

43. York, Borthwick Institute, V.1590–91/CB.2, fol. 82ʳ.

44. PRO, CHES 24/114/3, single mb (31 August 1610); CHES 24/115/1, single mb (31 August 1610); CHES 24/115/3, single mb, col. 1 (31 August 1610); CHES 24/117/1, single mb (undated, ?1609–10); CHES 24/117/1, single mb, col. 1 (31 March 1617); CHES 21/3, fol. 4ʳ (28 April 1617); C&C, QJB 1/4, fol. 55ʳ (20 January 1612).

45. PRO, CHES 24/115/1, single mb (31 March 1617); CHES 24/114/3, single mb, col. 3 (31 August 1617); CHES 24/115/3, single mb, col. 1 (31 March 1617); CHES 24/115/3, single mb, col. 1 (31 August 1617); CHES 21/3, fol. 11ʳ (15 September 1617); CHES 21/3, fol. 20ᵛ (13 April 1618).

46. C&C, QJF 51/4/163, single sheet (14 January 1623).

47. C&C, QJF 53/2/152, single sheet (13 July 1624).

48. C&C, QJF 60/2/17, single sheet (1 March 1631); C&C, QJB 2/5, fol. 162ʳ (28 June 1631); C&C, QJF 61/2/30, single strip (3 July [but order dated 20 May] 1632).

49. C&C, QJF 27/2/2, single sheet (7 May 1597).

50. C&C, QJF 46/1/54, single sheet (13 May 1617).

51. PRO, CHES 21/3, fol. 11ʳ (13 April 1618).

52. C&C, EDC 5(1624)/7, 3 (3 February 1625).

53. C&C, QJB 1/4, fol. 55ʳ (20 January 1612).

54. C&C, QJF 40/4/15, single sheet. The document is dated 20 October 1611, and the words were alleged to have been spoken "about a month agone," which would put them in late September.

55. C&C, QJB 1/4, fol. 56ʳ (28 April 1612).

56. Congleton, Town Hall, Borough Account Book I, fols. 182ᵛ (14 February), 185ʳ (5 April).

57. Ibid., fol. 240ᵛ (24 June–28 September 1624).

58. C&C, G 17/1, fol. 23ᵛ (1639–40).

59. Clopper, *Chester*, 424.

60. Rastall, "The Minstrel Court," 96.

61. C&C, QJF 53/2/152, single sheet (13 July 1624).

62. PRO, CHES 24/113/3, unfoliated (1616).

63. Clark, "The Alehouse and the Alternative Society," 53.

64. C&C, DDX/69/9, fols. 3ᵛ (26 January 1638) 8ᵛ (22 March 1639) 14ʳ (23 October 1640).

65. *The First Part of the Return from Parnassus* 1.1.370 and note citing *A New Dictionary of the Canting Crew* (London: Smith, Kay, 1899), in *The Three Parnassus Plays (1598–1601)*, ed. J. B. Leishman (London: Ivor Nicholson and Watson, 1949).

66. C&C, QJF 58/4/17, single sheet (19 January 1630).

67. Clopper, *Chester, passim*.

68. C&C, QJB 2/3, fol. 8^v (29 October 1566).

69. C&C, DCH/F/201, 18 (30 September 1625).

70. Whythorne, *Autobiography*, 244.

71. C&C, QJF 67/3/33, single sheet (7 August 1638).

72. C&C, WI 1637 William Worrall of Nantwich, musicioner (13 June 1637); WS 1648 Roger Vaughan of Nantwich, musician (24 April 1648).

73. C&C, WS 1604 William Maddock of Chester, Waitman (4 September 1604).

74. C&C, WS 1648 Roger Vaughan of Nantwich, musician (24 April 1648).

75. C&C, WS 1604 William Maddock of Chester, Waitman (4 September 1604).

76. Clopper, Chester, 60.

77. Ibid., 53.

78. Ibid., 91.

79. PRO, CHES 21/2, fol. 56^v (18 September 1609).

80. C&C, QJF 49/2/47, single sheet (15 June 1620).

81. PRO, CHES 24/114/2, single sheet (27 July 1617).

82. C&C, QSE/3/84, fol. 2^r (30 October 1588).

83. PRO, CHES 24/126/3, unfoliated (22 April 1642).

84. C&C, EDV 1/14, fol. 53^v (24 October 1605).

85. PRO, CHES 24/114/4, fol. 1^r (1618); see also PRO, CHES 21/3, fol. 29^v (21 September 1618).

86. PRO, CHES 24/115/2, single sheet (1619).

87. C&C, QJF 59/4/59, single sheet (3 October 1630).

88. Congleton, Town Hall, Borough Account Book I, fols. 182^v (February 1621); 194^r (14 February 1621); 185^r (5 April 1621).

89. Ibid., fol. 240^v.

90. C&C, P/21/3607/1/2, 45 (8 October 1620).

91. PRO, CHES 25/11, mb 16d–17 (26 February 1417).

92. C&C, P/21/3607/1/2, 23 (21 September 1617); P/21/3607/1/3, 12 (7 January 1642).

93. John Caldwell and Alan Brown, "Leonard Woodson," *NG*, 27:555

94. John Caldwell, "Thomas Woodson," *NG*, 27:555.

95. Ormerod, *The History of Chester*, 2:636.

96. C&C, P/21/3607/1/2, 117 (6 August 1637); P/21/3607/1/3, 3 (28 June 1640).

97. C&C, P/120/4525/2, 242 (13 May 1607).

98. C&C, P/120/4525/1, fols. 11^r (28 October 1581) (marriage); 69^v (10 February 1592) (burial).

99. C&C, P/120/4525/2, 80 (10 July 1602).

100. C&C, QJF 68/2/42, single sheet (9 July 1639).

101. C&C, EDV 1/22, fol. 37^r (7 November 1619).

102. C&C, P/120/4525/2, 280 (27 July 1629) (burial of Anne); 142 (6 January 1635) (baptism of Richard); 148 (19 February 1637) (baptism of Hugh); 308 (9 May 1640) (burial of Margaret and Marie); 308 (15 May 1640) (burial of Zachary Gill).

103. C&C, P/120/4525/2, 130 (28 October 1629) (baptism of John); 134 (20 March 1631) (baptism of Thomas).

104. C&C, P/120/4525/2, 138 (18 February 1633) (baptism of Dudley, Jane and Ellen).

105. C&C, P/120/4525/2, 291 (9 April 1634) (burial of Dudley); 292 (5 January 1635) (burial of William, son of William Worrall).

106. C&C, P/120/4525/2, 146 (13 May 1636) (baptism of William, son of William Worrall); 298 (9 June 1637) (burial of William Worrall, musician).

107. C&C, WI 1637 William Worrall of Nantwich, Musitioner, single sheet (13 June 1637). See Appendix I for the full text.

108. David Munrow, *Instruments of the Middle Ages and Renaissance* (London: Oxford University Press, 1976), 53–54.

109. Ibid., 83.

110. Ephraim Segerman, "A Short History of the Cittern," *GSJ* 52 (1999): 93–94.

111. Ephraim Segerman, private communication (1 September 2001).

112. C&C, QJF 60/4/9, single sheet (24 January 1632).

113. C&C, P/120/4525/2, 297 (15 December 1636).

114. C&C, EDV 1/14, fol. 64^r (25 October 1605).

115. C&C, WS 1648 Roger Vaughan of Nantwich, musician (Inventory, 24 April 1648) (Will, undated, but before 22 April 1648).

116. For a depiction of different sizes of viols, including the bass viol, see Jeremy Montagu, *The World of Medieval and Renaissance Musical Instruments* (Newton Abbot: David and Charles, 1976), pl. 85.

117. C&C, WS 1618 Matthew Hawkes of Nantwich, single sheet (inventory) (6 May 1618).

118. C&C, WS 1607 Henry Wright of Nantwich, Innholder, single sheet (will) (9 August 1607).

119. C&C, WS 1638 Thomas Bickerton of Nantwich, gentleman, fol. 1^v (1639).

120. C&C, WS 1622 Richard Heyes of Nantwich, gentleman, single sheet (4 June 1622).

121. C&C, WS 1625 Edmund Myles of Nantwich, innholder, single sheet (13 August 1625).

122. C&C, WS 1627 Elizabeth Myles of Nantwich, single sheet (20 September 1627).

123. C&C, WS 1604/5 Jasper Rutter of Nantwich, gentleman, 1 (26 February 1605); WS 1627/8 Edward Minshull of Nantwich, esquire, single sheet (11 February 1628); C&C, WS 1633 Richard Arcall of Nantwich, grocer,

single sheet (21 November 1633).

124. C&C, WS 1640 Edmund Myles of Nantwich, innholder, single sheet (13 May 1640).

125. C&C, P/120/4525/2, 85 (30 November 1606).

126. C&C, EDV 1/24, fol. 68ᵛ (23 October 1622).

127. PRO, CHES 21/3, fol. 94ʳ (18 August 1623).

128. C&C, WS 1638 Richard Minshull of Nantwich, gentleman, single sheet.

129. C&C, WI 1637 William Worrall of Nantwich, Musitioner, single sheet (13 June 1637).

130. C&C, DBW/P/J/7, fol. 11ᵛ (1 March 1614).

131. Clopper, *Chester*, 165.

132. Ibid., 184–85.

133. Ibid.

134. C&C, G 2/1, fol. 126ᵛ (29 September 1624). This Thomas Williams is not the same as the Thomas Williams who was dead in 1590–01 but may well have been his son. The Coopers paid "Thomas Williams and his companye for Musicke" at a dinner in 1618 (Clopper, *Chester*, 311).

135. C&C, MAB/1, fol. 119ʳ (2 February 1622).

136. C&C, QSF 61/84, single sheet (21 April 1613).

137. Clopper, *Chester*, 290.

138. PRO, CHES 24/1/2, single sheet (1342–43).

139. PRO, CHES 2/29, mb 2 (24 July 1343)

140. PRO, CHES 2/37, mb 3 (11 May 1354); CHES 2/37, mb 3 (10 June 1354).

141. PRO, CHES 25/11, mb 16d–17 (26 February 1417); mb 23d–24 (17 January 1419). For a discussion of the relative status of the harper and minstrel in the Middlewich riot, see chapter IV.

142. PRO, CHES 25/11, mb 16d (26 February 1417).

143. PRO, CHES 25/9, mb 45 (20 September 1404).

144. PRO, CHES 29/125, mb 12 (5 June 1421).

145. PRO, CHES 25/10, mb 32d (4 May 1411).

146. PRO, CHES 25/12, mb 20 (14 September 1428).

147. PRO, CHES 25/9, mb 70 (14 April 1406).

148. PRO, CHES 25/16, mb 4d (21–23 December, 1488).

149. C&C, QJF 27/2/2, single sheet (7 May 1597). The amount offered *s 4d.*

150. C&C, QJF 51/4/163, single sheet (14 January 1623).

151. C&C, QJF/53/2/152, single sheet (13 July 1624).

152. C&C, EDC 5(1624)/7, fol. 1ᵛ (3 February 1625).

153. Ibid.

154. Ibid.

155. C&C, QJF 53/2/152, single sheet (13 July 1624).

156. Ibid.

157. C&C, QJF 53/2/153, bifolium (12 May 1624).

158. Ibid.

159. C&C, QJF 53/2/152, single sheet (13 July 1624).

160. See C&C, QJF 53/2/82, QJF 53/2/88, and QJF 53/2/92.

161. C&C, QJF 53/2/152, single sheet (13 July 1624).

162. C&C, QJF 60/2/17, single sheet (1 March 1631).

163. C&C, QJF 61/2/30, single strip (3 May 1632).

164. C&C, QJF 63/1/53.

165. See C&C, QJF 53/2/152, single sheet (13 July 1624).

166. C&C, QJF 40/4/15, single sheet (20 October 1611).

167. C&C, QJF 40/4/13, single sheet (21 January 1612).

168. C&C, MB/12, fol. 20ᵛ (29 September).

169. PRO, CHES 24/95/2, single mb (9 June 1561)

170. C&C, QJF 50/1/137, bifolium (24 April 1621).

171. C&C, MB/15, fol. 48ʳ.

172. C&C, EDV 5/5, single sheet (19 January 1638).

173. York, Borthwick Institute, Visitations, V.1590–91/CB.2, fol. 82ʳ.

174. C&C, QJF 67/3/33, bifolium (7 August 1638).

175. PRO, CHES 21/2, fol. 85ʳ (22 April 1613); CHES 24/112/1, single mb, (12 April 1613); CHES 24/112/2, single mb (27 September 1613).

176. PRO, CHES 24/115/3, single sheet (28 April 1620).

177. PRO, CHES 24/114/2, bifolium (24 September 1617).

178. C&C, QJF 69/3/50, single strip (22 July 1640).

179. PRO, CHES 24/113/4, single mb (1 August 1616).

180. PRO, CHES 24/113/3, unfoliated (27 January 1616).

181. See PRO, CHES 24/113/3, single sheet (1616). In one case, unfortunately discovered too late to be included in the main body of this book, a musical instrument was itself used as a weapon. In 1393 Margaret Symphaner, a traveling female harper, used her harp to strike John Plesyngton (C&C, CR 63/2/2339, rot. 1, mb. 2, rot. 2, mb. 2).

182. C&C, QJF 49/2/52, single sheet (18 July 1620).

183. C&C, QJF 49/3/80, bifolium (10 October 1620).

184. Ruthin, Denbigh Record Office, DD/PP/839, 2 (undated).

185. C&C, EDC 5(1586)/77, single sheet (28 April 1586).

Chapter III

1. Southworth, *English Medieval Minstrel*, 3.

2. PRO, CHES 2/37, mb 3, 11 May 1354 (French) and 10 June 1354 (Latin).

3. Newton, *The House of Lyme*, 70–71. The household account book to which reference is made is neither at Lyme Hall nor in the John Rylands University Library with the other Legh papers.

4. *Statutes of the Realm*, 14 Elizabeth c. 5 (1572), section 42.

5. *Statutes of the Realm*, 43 Elizabeth, c. 9 (1601), section 2.

6. *Statutes of the Realm*, 1 Jac. I, c. 25 (1603–04).

7. C&C, DSS/3991/22/1, 12.

8. PRO, CHES 2/105, mb 1 (24 October 1433); CHES 2/119, mb 8d (11 March 1446).

9. PRO, CHES 2/146, mb 12–12d (8 April 1474, but referring to the death of Laurence Dutton of Dutton in 1392).

10. PRO, CHES 2/149, mb 11 (24 June 1477) (Abbot, Mayor and William Thomas); CHES 2/151, mb 5d (23 June 1479) (Abbot, Mayor and Peter Dutton); CHES 2/152, mb 11 (20 June 1480) (John Massy, Peter Dutton of Hatton, Thomas Pole, and John Sotheworth); CHES 2/166, mb 3 (24 June 1496) (Mayor of Chester, William Tatton and Hamon Hassall). See also Clopper, *Chester*, 17–18, 20–21.

11. Ormerod, *The History of Chester*, 1:650.

12. Ibid., 1:650.

13. C&C, DDX/23/1, fol. 2ᵛ.

14. Ormerod, *The History of Chester*, 1:646.

15. Bodleian Library, MS. Sancroft 72, fols. 67–68.

16. Rastall, "The Minstrel Court," 97.

17. Bodleian Library, MS. Sancroft 72, fol. 68.

18. Clopper, *Chester*, 43–44.

19. C&C, DSS/3991/22/1, 12.

20. Rastall, "The Minstrel Court," 98–100.

21. C&C, MB/19, fol. 25ʳ.

22. The relationship is more complicated than it appears: John Bruen's mother was Dorothy, daughter of Thomas Holford of Holford. Her brother, Christopher, was married to Anne Dutton, daughter of Hugh Dutton and sister of John Dutton of Dutton, who succeeded his grandfather, Sir Piers Dutton, Hugh Dutton having died during his father's lifetime. Hugh Dutton's widow, Jane, subsequently married Thomas Holford, John Bruen's maternal grandfather. John Bruen was therefore the nephew of John Dutton's brother-in-law but also the step-grandson of John Dutton's mother (Ormerod, *The History of Chester*, 1:651).

23. Hinde, *A Faithfull Remonstrance*, 131. See also above, chap. 1.

24. PRO, CHES 24/115/3, single sheet (28 April 1620).

25. Tait, "The Declaration of Sports for Lancashire (1617)," 561; L. A. Govett, *The King's Book of Sports*, 1.

26. C&C, QSF 29/122, single sheet (23 March 1575).

27. C&C, QSE 9/69, fol. 1ʳ (30 June 1610).

28. C&C, QJF 53/2/152, single sheet (13 July 1624).

29. C&C, QJF 40/4/15, single sheet (20 October 1611).

30. Ian Spink, "Henry Lawes," *NG*, 14:394. The classic book on Lawes

is Willa McClung Evans, *Henry Lawes: Musician and Friend of Poets* (New York: Modern Language Association, 1941).

31. Manchester, John Rylands University Library, Letters to Sir Peter Legh, folder 4.

32. Sir Thomas Smith of Hough was mayor of Chester in 1596 and sheriff of Cheshire in 1600. He died c.1622–23 (Ormerod, *The History of Chester*, 3:503).

33. Francis Pilkington, *Second Set of Madrigals, and Pastorals of 3, 4, and 5 Parts* (London, 1624), sig. [A2].

34. Francis Pilkington, *First Book of Songs or Ayres of 4 Parts* (London, 1605), sig. [A2].

35. Francis Pilkington, *First Set of Madrigals and Pastorals of 3, 4, 5, and 6 Parts* (London, 1612), sig. [A2].

36. Henry Peacham, *The Compleat Gentleman 1634*, introd. G. S. Gordon (Oxford: Clarendon Press, 1906), 98–99.

37. Ibid., 99–100.

38. Ibid., 100.

39. Hinde, *A Faithfull Remonstrance*, 10.

40. C&C, WS 1625 John Bruen of Stapleford, gentleman, single mb (26 January 1626).

41. Elizabeth and Margaret were both daughters of Sir Thomas Cutler, baronet, of Stainborough, Yorkshire. Elizabeth married Paul Winnington of Birches, Cheshire, and Margaret married Robert Lowther of the City of London (C&C, catalogue).

42. C&C, DSS/1/4/38/11, single sheet (8 April 1629).

43. C&C, DSS/1/4/38/12, single sheet (14 April 1629).

44. C&C, DSS/1/4/38/13, single sheet (1629).

45. See *Oxford English Dictionary*, 'wag' sb. 1. The *OED* does not list the expression "to play the wag" before 1851, when it occurs as a slang expression meaning "to play truant." Lowther's usage seems to mean something closer to "to get up to mischief, to behave like a mischievous child."

46. C&C, DSS/1/4/38/13, single sheet (1629).

47. Thomas Mace, *Musick's Monument* (1676; facsimile reprint Paris: e National de la Recherche Scientifique, 1977), 54–61; reference to this work is made in Thurston Dart, "The Cittern and its English Music," *GSJ* 1 (1948): 47.

48. C&C, DSS/1/7/6/46, fol. 3^r (1597).

49. C&C, DSS/1/7/6/45, fol. 1^r (1598). Note that "daughter in law" could also mean "stepdaughter" at this time. After John Somerford's death, Mary's mother had married Gilbert Domville of Lymme.

50. C&C, DSS/1/7/11/22, fol. 2^r (1599).

51. Thomas Dekker, *Guls Hornebooke* (London, 1609), as quoted by W. Chappell, *Popular Music of the Olden Times* (London, 1855–99), 100.

52. Munrow, *Instruments of the Middle Ages and Renaissance*, 75–78 (lute), 80–82 (cittern), 82–83 (bandora).

53. The poem is attributed by James Orchard Halliwell, who edited it in 1850 (*Palatine Anthology: A Collection of Ancient Poems and Ballads relating the Lancashire and Cheshire* [London, 1850]), to Thomas Stanley (*ob.* 1570), bishop of Sodor and Man (1530–45, 1556–70). However, a more recent argument has been made on stylistic grounds in favor of Richard Sheale, harper, who was a dependent of the Stanley family (see Andrew Taylor, "The Stanley Poem and the Harper Richard Sheale," *Leeds Studies in English*, n.s. 28 [1997]: 99–122).

54. *kings* has been altered from *knights.*

55. Bodleian Library, MS. Rawl. poet.143, 22–23.

56. Baldassare Castiglione, *Il cortegiano*, quoted by Strunk, *Source Readings in Music History*, 284, from the translation of Sir Thomas Hoby (London, 1561).

57. C&C, EDA 2/1, fol. 399ᵛ (23 February 1558).

58. C&C, WS 1618 James Miller of Chester, clerk (will) fol. 1ᵛ (22 July 1617). See also chap. II, pt. 1, above.

59. C&C, WS 1618 James Miller of Chester, clerk (inventory) fol. 1ᵛ (27 July 1618).

60. C&C, EDA 2/2, fol. 115ʳ (3 February 1587).

61. For a discussion of a surviving personal collection of lute pieces, see Gwilym Beechey, "Christopher Lowther's Lute Book," *GSJ* 24 (1971): 51–59. Christopher Lowther was the nephew of the Robert Lowther mentioned in connection with the Winnington correspondence. He was Sheriff of Cumberland in 1640, and was created a baronet in 1642. He died in 1644 ("Lonsdale," *Burke's Peerage and Baronetage*, ed. Peter Townend, 104th ed. [London: Burke's Peerage, 1967], 2:1551–52).

62. See *The Mynshall Lute Book* (Leeds: Boethius Press, 1975); I am grateful to Richard Rastall for calling my attention to this work and for the information concerning it included here.

63. C&C, EDA 2/2, p. 311 (18 March 1612). Henry Hardware of Bromborough and Peel was the son of Henry Hardware, mayor of Chester in 1599. The family was evidently Puritan in sympathy, as the elder Henry Hardware of Chester was actively involved in the suppression of the Chester plays, and his daughter married John Bruen of Bruen Stapleford (Ormerod, *The History of Chester*, 2:320, 322).

64. C&C, DBW/P/J/7, fol. 11ᵛ (1 March 1614).

65. C&C, WS 1587 Thomas Brereton of Barrow, gentleman, fol. 1ᵛ (25 July 1587). Edward Savage (b. 1560) was the fourth, but second surviving, son of Sir John Savage of Rocksavage, Thomas Brereton's half-brother (Ormerod, *The History of Chester*, 1:716).

66. York, Borthwick Institute, Wills/30b, fol. 627^r (31 March 1608). His sister was Margaret, wife of John Englefield, esq., who had been divorced (1546) from her first husband, Francis Warren, son of Sir Edward Warren of Poynton. She died in 1612 (Ormerod, *The History of Chester*, 3:553). Her son was Francis Englefield.

67. York, Borthwick Institute, Wills/40b, fol. 359^r (4 September 1627).

68. York, Borthwick Institute, Wills/40b, fol. 361^v (1627).

69. C&C, DBW/P/J/7, fol. 14^r (5 July 1614).

70. C&C, DLE/86, p. 51 (from back), 11 September 1633; C&C, DLE/87, p. 9 (from back), 18 May 1635. I have been unable to track the exact degree of relation between Leche and his various cousins. None of them appear, from pedigrees in Ormerod's *History of Chester*, to have been first cousins by blood. The Massies of Coddington appear to be connections through William Aldersey, John Leche's father-in-law, and Richard Warde may be the husband of Anne Aldersey, a distant cousin of William Aldersey's (see Ormerod, *The History of Chester*, 2:727 (Massie of Coddington), 2:702 (Leche of Carden), and 2:740 (Aldersey of Aldersey).

71. C&C, DLE/87, 16 (from back) (2 October 1638). The manuscript is paginated both from the front and from the back.

72. C&C, DLE/87, 29 (from back) (August 1641).

73. C&C, DLE/87, 20 (from back) (September 1642).

74. York, Borthwick Institute, Wills/30b, fol. 628^r (31 March 1608).

75. Francis Fitton and John Danvers both married daughters of John Neville, last baron Latimer. John Danvers died 10 December 1594 (*Burke's Peerage and Baronetage*).

76. Sidney Lee, "Sir Charles Danvers," *DNB*, 5:487.

77. Munrow, *Instruments of the Middle Ages and Renaissance*, 86–87.

78. C&C, DBW/P/J/7, fol. 8^v (15 November 1613).

79. Ormerod, *The History of Chester*, 2:137.

80. C&C, WS 1648 Roger Vaughan of Nantwich, musician, single sheet (24 April 1648).

81. C&C, EDA 2/1, fol. 398^v (23 February 1558); C&C, WS 1604 William Maddock of Chester, Waitman, single sheet (4 September 1604); C&C, WS 1638 Thomas Bickerton of Nantwich, gentleman, fol. 1^v (31 January 1639); C&C, SBC/178, fol. 34^r (1576–77).

82. C&C, DBW/P/J/7, fol. 9^v (13 December 1613).

83. Ibid., fol. 10^r (16 December 1613).

84. Ibid., fol. 9^v (December 1613).

85. C&C, CR/63/2/691/6, fol. 1^r (29 December 1634).

86. BL, Add. MS. 33,936, fol. 94^r–94^v (24 June 1634).

87. BL Add. MS. 33,935, fol. 56^r (17 September 1624).

88. Ibid., fol. 56^r (17 September 1624). The Welds may be members of a cadet branch of the Welds of Eaton, and possibly neighbors or even relatives of the Moretons.

89. Ormerod, *The History of Chester*, 3:51.

90. C&C, DSS/1/7/7/2, single sheet (18 June [year not given]).

91. Whythorne, *Autobiography*, 19.

Chapter IV

1. See, for example, Montagu, *The World of Medieval and Renaissance Musical Instruments*, for convenient examples of the differences between earlier and later instruments. The bibliography on historical musical instruments is vast, but for England special notice should also be taken of the following: Bicknell, *The History of the English Organ*; Francis W. Galpin, *Old English Instruments of Music*, 4th ed., rev. Thurston Dart (London: Methuen, 1965); Sibyl Marcuse, *Musical Instruments: A Comprehensive Dictionary* (1964; reprint New York: W. W. Norton, 1975); Mary Remnant, *English Bowed Instruments from Anglo-Saxon to Tudor Times* (Oxford: Clarendon Press, 1986), *Musical Instruments: An Illustrated History from Antiquity to the Present* (London: B. T. Batsford, 1989), and "Musical Instruments in Early English Drama," in *Material Culture and Medieval Drama*, ed. Clifford Davidson, Early Drama, Art, and Music Monograph Series 25 (Kalamazoo: Medieval Institute Publications, 1999), 141–94; and Curt Sachs, *The History of Musical Instruments* (New York: W. W. Norton, 1940). Especially useful are the up-to-date articles and bibliographies in the *NG*.

2. PRO, CHES 25/20, mb 22 (1367); C&C, EDC 5(1597)/101 (21 April 1597).

3. PRO, CHES 21/3, fol. 5ʳ (Monday 23 April 1617).

4. C&C, MB/20, fol. 45ᵛ (24 August–5 September 1572) (recognizance); PRO, CHES 24/114/1, single sheet (27 April 1617) (bailiff's presentment). For crown book, see the preceding note.

5. PRO, CHES 24/110/2, single sheet (20–21 August 1609).

6. C&C, EDV 1/15, fol. 45ʳ (3 October 1608).

7. Munrow, *Instruments of the Middle Ages and Renaissance*, 83.

8. Harpers are overtaken by minstrels in the fifteenth century as the most common designation (twelve individuals), and there is also a greater range of designations. Some minstrels may have been harpers, and some may have been singers. See Richard Rastall, "Some Consort-Groupings of the Late Middle Ages," *Music and Letters* 55 (1974): 179–202, esp. 183. For examples of the harp and other instruments in the visual arts in Chester, see Sally-Beth MacLean, *Chester Art*, Early Drama, Art, and Music Reference Series 3 (1982), 87–88.

9. C&C, SR/223, mb 1 (1436).

10. Joan Rimmer and Robert Evans, "Harp, §V, 1: Europe and the Americas," *NG*, 10:898.

11. Ibid., 10:899.

12. C&C, SBC/22, fol. 301ʳ (13 March 1576).

13. Rimmer and Evans, "Harp, §V, 1: Europe and the Americas," *NG*, 10:898.

14. Martin Peerson, *Mottects, or Grave Chamber Musique* (London, 1630), as quoted in Donald Gill, "The Orpharion and the Bandora," *GSJ* 13 (1960): 14.

15. Gustave Reese, *Music in the Middle Ages* (New York: W. W. Norton, 1940), 326.

16. Ibid., 240–41.

17. Ibid., 241. For the Sutton Hoo instrument, see Rupert Bruce-Mitford's chapter entitled "The Sutton Hoo Lyre, *Beowulf* and the Origins of the Frame Harp," in *Aspects of Anglo-Saxon Archaeology* (New York: Harper and Row, 1974), 188–97.

18. PRO, CHES 25/11, mb 23d–24 (17 January 1419).

19. PRO, CHES 2/66, mb 5d (1394).

20. PRO, CHES 2/89, mb 5 (11 March 1416).

21. Munrow, *Instruments of the Middle Ages and Renaissance*, 75.

22. C&C, SR/358, mb 1d.

23. Clopper, *Chester*, 60; C&C, G 8/2, fol. 36ᵛ (10 November).

24. Warwick Edwards, "Consort," *NG*, 6:329.

25. Ian Harwood, Diana Poulton, and David Van Edwards, "Lute, §4, History," *NG*, 15:336.

26. Ian Harwood, Diana Poulton, and David Van Edwards, "Lute, §3, Structure of the Western Lute," *NG*, 15:331–33.

27. Ibid.,15:334.

28. C&C: DSS/1/7/11/22, fol. 2ʳ–2ᵛ.

29. Johannes Tinctoris, *De inventione et usu musicae* [Naples, c.1481–83], ed. K. Weinman, 2nd ed., rev. W. Fischer (Regensburg, 1961), as cited in Harwood, Poulton, and Van Edwards, "Lute §4, History," *NG* 15:335, 361.

30. Harwood, Poulton, and Van Edwards, "Lute, §4, History," *NG*, 15:336.

31. York, Borthwick Institute: Wills/40b, fol. 361ᵛ (1627). For the "mean lute," see Harwood, Poulton, and Van Edwards, "Lute, §4, History," *NG*, 15:338.

32. Diana Poulton and Tim Crawford, "Lute, §8(v), Repertory: England," *NG*, 15:357. There are earlier Continental sources.

33. C&C: EDA 2/1, fol. 398ᵛ (23 February 1558).

34. C&C, EDA 2/2, fol. 115ʳ (3 February 1587).

35. James Tyler, "Cittern," *NG*, 5:878, 882.

36. Segerman, "A Short History of the Cittern," 94.

37. Michael Praetorius, *Syntagma Musicum* II (1619), as cited in Segerman, "A Short History of the Cittern," 95–96.

38. Munrow, *Instruments of the Middle Ages and Renaissance*, 80.

39. Tyler, "Cittern," *NG*, 5:882.

40. Ibid.

41. C&C, DLE/86, 51 (from back) (11 September 1633); for more detail, see chapter III.

42. C&C, EDC 5(1639)/120, unnumbered (June 1639).

43. Ibid.

44. Ibid.

45. Tyler, "Cittern," *NG*, 5:878.

46. Segerman, "A Short History of the Cittern," 88.

47. Ephraim Segerman, private communication (September 2001).

48. Francis Fitton loaned some of the other instruments to his brother-in-law, Sir John Danvers, who died 10 December 1594. The original deposit of the instruments with Francis Fitton could well have occurred several years earlier.

49. Galpin, *Old English Instruments of Music*, 218.

50. Whythorne, *Autobiography*, 19.

51. Laurence Wright, "Gittern," *NG*, 9:909.

52. James Tyler, "Guitar, §3: The four-course guitar," *NG*, 10:555.

53. Gill, "The Orpharion and Bandora," 14.

54. For a discussion of the Meuler wire used from c.1580–c.1621, see Segerman, "A Short History of the Cittern," 93–96.

55. Gill, "The Orpharion and Bandora," 20.

56. Ibid., 20–21.

57. Ibid., 21.

58. Ibid., 19–20.

59. Ibid., 14.

60. Pilkington, *Second Set of Madrigals, and Pastorals*, no. xxiv.

61. William Barley, *New Book of Tabliture* (London, 1596), as quoted in Gill, "The Orpharion and Bandora," 18.

62. C&C, WS 1607 Henry Wright of Nantwich, innholder, single sheet (will) (9 August 1607); C&C, EDA 2/2, 311 (18 March 1612).

63. C&C, WS 1607 Henry Wright of Nantwich, innholder, mb 3 (inventory) (15 October 1607).

64. C&C, WS 1637 Thomas Jones of Chester, innholder (inventory) (11 August 1637).

65. C&C, WS 1612 John Yardley of Crewe, gentleman, fol. 2^r (inventory) (12 May 1612). The wording suggests that the case was for the lute, but Gill notes that bandoras are often mentioned in inventories with cases (Gill, "The Orpharion and Bandora," 17).

66. C&C, WS 1638 Thomas Bickerton of Nantwich, gentleman, fol. 1^v (31 January 1639). The bass viol in this instance may have been the one left to Thomas Bickerton by Henry Hardware in 1612.

67. *Oxford English Dictionary*, *s.v.* alpharion, orpharion.

68. C&C, WI 1637 William Worrall of Nantwich, Musitioner, single sheet (13 June 1637).

69. Munrow, *Instruments in the Middle Ages and Renaissance*, 85; Remnant, *English Bowed Instruments*, 72–76.

70. Gustave Reese, *Music in the Renaissance* (New York: W. W. Norton, 1959), 547.

71. Walter L. Woodfill, *Musicians in English Society from Elizabeth to Charles I* (Princeton: Princeton University Press, 1953), 297; Reese, *Music in the Middle Ages*, 407.

72. Mace, *Musick's Monument*, 245.

73. York, Borthwick Institute, Wills/30b, fol. 628^r (31 March 1608).

74. C&C, WS 1642 Sir Peter Legh of Lyme the Younger, knight.

75. C&C, WS 1638 Thomas Bickerton of Nantwich, gentleman (31 January 1639).

76. C&C, WS 1648 Roger Vaughan of Nantwich, musician (24 April 1648).

77. C&C, WS 1607 Henry Wright of Nantwich, innholder, mb 3 (inventory) (15 October 1607). This is evidently the same instrument that is referred to in his will as "my vyoll de Gamboe" and is left to his cousin, Richard Minshull.

78. C&C, WI 1637 William Worrall of Nantwich, Musitioner, single sheet (13 June 1637).

79. C&C, EDA 2/1, fol. 398v (23 February 1558).

80. Richard Alison, *Psalmes of David in Meter* (London, 1599), as cited by Reese, *Music in the Renaissance*, 808.

81. C&C, Wills, WS William Maddock of Chester, Waitman, bifolium (4 September 1604).

82. The tenor-alto viol was tuned like a lute, and could play the same repertoire (Reese, *Music in the Renaissance*, 548).

83. C&C, DBW/P/J/7, fol. 8^v (15 November 1613); C&C, WI 1637 William Worrall of Nantwich, Musitioner, single sheet (13 June 1637).

84. Woodfill, *Musicians in English Society*, 258 (Appendix B: Household Records).

85. Ibid., 270. Woodfill lists several viols and other instruments found in inventories, but unfortunately does not give their valuation.

86. C&C, DBW/P/J/7, fol. 8^v (15 November 1613). There were three dozen strings purchased, at a cost of 18d per dozen.

87. See Reese, *Music in the Renaissance*, 547, for the observation that "viols of the *braccio* variety," which included the violin, were considered street instruments.

88. See Munrow, *Instruments of the Middle Ages and Renaissance*, 90–91.

89. Clopper, *Chester*, 164.

90. C&C, QSE 5/46, single sheet (4 October 1594).

91. See Remnant, *English Bowed Instruments*, 61–71.

92. Munrow, Instruments of the Middle Ages and Renaissance, 89-90.

93. For fifteenth-century fiddlers, see C&C, SR/348, mb 1 (1485) and MB/7, fol. 61ʳ (1488–89).

94. Mary Remnant, "Kit," *NG*, 13:635.

95. C&C, WS 1637 Thomas Jones of Chester, innholder, mb 1 (11 August 1637).

96. There are a number of variant spellings—Lethwood, Leathwood, Laithwait, Laithwaite—but all clearly refer to the same individual.

97. PRO, CHES 24/114/3, single mb, col. 3 (31 August 1616); CHES 24/115/1, single mb (31 August 1616); CHES 24/115/3, single mb (31 August 1616).

98. PRO, CHES 24/114/1, single sheet (1617); CHES 21/3, fol. 5ᵛ (28 April 1617).

99. C&C, DCH/F/194, 5.

100. PRO, CHES 24/114/1, single sheet (27 April 1617); CHES 21/3, fol. 5ʳ (28 April 1617).

101. PRO, CHES 24/114/1, single sheet, verso (1617).

102. Ormerod, *The History of Chester*, 1:716.

103. C&C, DCH/F/194, 8, 13 (1622); DCH/F/197, 1, 5, 13 (1623); DCH/F/198, 1, 6, 11, 16 (1624); DCH/F/201, 1, 11 (1625).

104. C&C, DCH/F/201, 18 (30 September 1625).

105. C&C, QJF 46/2/62, single sheet (14 May 1617).

106. William A Cocks, Anthony C. Baines, and Roderick D. Cannon, "Bagpipe," *NG*, 2:471.

107. Ibid., 2:472.

108. Ibid., 2:475.

109. Ibid., 2:473, 476.

110. C&C, EDV 1/17, fol. 92ʳ (15 October 1611).

111. C&C, QSE 5/82, single sheet (15 May 1597).

112. York, Borthwick Institute, V.1595–6/CB.2, fol. 166ᵛ (22 October 1595).

113. PRO, CHES 24/113/4, single sheet (19 August 1616). Peacock's piping is also mentioned in the Crown Books for that year (CHES 21/2, fols. 123ᵛ, 126ʳ, 130ʳ).

114. PRO, CHES 24/110/1, single sheet (15 April 1610).

115. C&C, EDC 5(1597)/101, two unnumbered sheets, folded (21 April 1597).

116. C&C, EDV 1/14, fol. 64r (25 October 1605).

117. Clopper, *Chester*, 481.

118. Ibid., 244.

119. Anthony C. Baines and Hélène La Rue, "Pipe and Tabor," *NG*, 19:768.

120. Ibid., 19:769.

121. C&C, EDV 1/17, fol. 98ᵛ (15 October 1611). Lancashire was part of the diocese of Chester. For the use of 'taborer' to describe pipe-and-tabor player, see Baines and La Rue, "Pipe and tabor," *NG*, 19:769, for reference to William Kemp's *Nine Daies Wonder.*

122. Clopper, *Chester,* 164.

123. Anthony C. Baines and Martin Kirnbauer, "Shawm," *NG*, 23:230.

124. Ibid., 23:233, 235, fig. 9.

125. Jeremy Montagu, "Flute §II, 4(ii): The Western Transverse Flute: 1500 to 1800," *NG*, 9:35.

126. Ibid., 9:36; David Lasocki, "Recorder," *NG*, 21:47. Matthew Holmes's unpublished Consort Book is Cambridge, University Library, MS. Dd.5.21.

127. Bodleian Library, MS. Rawl. poet.143, 22–23.

128. Lasocki, "Recorder," *NG*, 21:45.

129. Clopper, *Chester,* 164.

130. Lasocki, "Recorder," *NG*, 21:44.

131. C&C, G 8/3, fol. 74ᵛ.

132. Clopper, *Chester,* 244.

133. Jeremy Montagu, "Whistle," *NG*, 27:336–37.

134. C&C, DSS/1/4/38/16, single sheet (undated).

135. C&C, MB/24, fol. 33ᵛ (21 April, 1588–89).

136. See C. T. Lewis, *Elementary Latin Dictionary* (Oxford: Oxford University Press, 1891), *s.v.* psallo, -ere; Leo F. Stelten, *Dictionary of Ecclesiastical Latin* (Peabody, Mass.: Hendrikson, 1995), *s.v.* psallo, -ere, psalli.

137. William Waterhouse, "Bassoon," *NG*, 2:877.

138. Ibid., 2:877.

139. See Montagu, *The World of Medieval and Renaissance Musical Instruments,* pls. 45, 73, 75.

140. Remnant, *Musical Instruments,* 151; Reese, *Music in the Middle Ages,* 409.

141. Munrow, *Instruments of the Middle Ages and Renaissance,* 68.

142. Ibid., 69–70.

143. Anthony C. Baines and Bruce Dickey, "Cornett," *NG*, 6:483–84.

144. C&C, EDD 3913/1/4, 167.

145. Baines and Dickey, "Cornett," *NG*, 6:484.

146. Munrow, *Instruments of the Middle Ages,* 19; Remnant, *Musical Instruments,* 147.

147. C&C, SR/304, mb 1.

148. For example, the Innkeepers in 1613–14 (C&C, G 13/42, bifolium). See also Clopper, *Chester, passim,* for the records of the Painters, Glaziers, Embroiders, and Stationers Company, 1624–41. Payments to trumpeters and drummers are a regular feature in the accounts of this guild.

149. Congleton Town Hall, Borough Account Book I, fol. 232^v (29 September–24 December 1623).

150. Newton, *The House of Lyme*, 70–71.

151. C&C, WS 1608 Rowland Dutton of Hatton, esquire, mb 1, col. 1.

152. Congleton, Town Hall, Borough Account Book I, fol. 4^r (25 December 1587–24 March 1588).

153. C&C, QJF 38/3/5, single sheet (18 September 1609).

154. C&C, DBW/P/J/7, fol. 9^v (13 December 1613).

155. Bodleian Library, MS. Rawl. poet.143, 22–23.

156. PRO, CHES 24/113/3, unfoliated (1615).

157. PRO, CHES 24/113/3, unfoliated (1616).

158. C&C, MB/7, fol. 61^r.

159. Michael Praetorius, *Syntagma Musicum*, trans. Harold Blumenfeld (New York: Bärenreiter, 1962), as cited by Munrow, *Instruments of the Middle Ages and Renaissance*, 62; also quoted in translation by Remnant, *Musical Instruments*, 84.

160. Munrow, *Instruments of the Middle Ages and Renaissance*, 60–61; Remnant, *Musical Instruments*, 83.

161. Munrow, *Instruments of the Middle Ages and Renaissance*, 63–65.

162. C&C, EDA 2/1, fol. 398^v (23 February 1558).

163. C&C, WS 1594 Urian Moreton of Yeaton, gentleman, single sheet (16 April 1594); C&C, WS 1633 Ralph Arderne of Crokeley Bredbury, three mbs, unnumbered (30 January 1634).

164. C&C, WS 1624 John Blanchard of Chester, brewer, mb 2 (9 November 1624); C&C, WS 1633 Charles Fitton of Chester, alderman, mb 2 (15 October 1633).

165. Manchester, John Rylands University Library, Tatton MSS. 293, 3 (2 June 1643).

166. C&C, DSS/1/7/6/46, fol. 3^r (1597); C&C, DSS/1/7/6/45, fol. 1^r (1598).

167. C&C, DLE/87, 16 (from back) (2 October 1638); C&C, DLE/87, 29 (from back) (August 1641); C&C, DLE/87, 20 (from back) (September 1642).

168. Galpin, *Old English Instruments of Music*, 89 and, for the virginal's action, 98; Munrow, *Instruments of the Middle Ages and Renaissance*, 63.

169. Manchester, John Rylands University Library, Tatton MSS. 293, 3 (2 June 1643).

170. Ormerod, *The History of Chester*, 1:253–54.

171. Manchester, John Rylands University Library, Latin MS. 460, fol. 21^r (22 June 1518).

172. C&C, DDX 43/54, fol. [1^r] (c.1538).

173. Ormerod, *The History of Chester*, 1:350.

174. C&C, EDA 2/2, fol. 256^v (22 January 1605).

175. Galpin, *Old English Instruments of Music*, 164.

176. Clopper, *Chester*, 78.

177. Congleton, Town Hall, Borough Account Book I, fol. 129ʳ (25 March–24 June 1615).

178. C&C, G 13/42, bifolium (1612–13); G 13/42, bifolium (1613–14); G 13/42, bifolium (1620–21); G 13/42, bifolium (1623–24).

179. C&C, G 13/46, single leaf (undated).

180. Ibid.

181. For example, the Butchers in 1667 (C&C, G 5/1, fol. 41ᵛ), the Barber Surgeons in 1668–69 (C&C, G 2/1, fol. 93ʳ), the Cordwainers and Shoemakers in 1660–61 (C&C, G 8/4, fol. 237ᵛ), the Glovers in 1574–75 (C&C, G 11/1, 207), the Smiths, Cutlers, and Plumbers in 1653–54 (C&C, G 20/1, 60), and the Tanners in 1671 (C&C, G 21/2, fol. 57ʳ).

182. C&C, G 13/43, *passim*.

183. C&C, EDV 1/26, fol. 47ᵛ (4 November 1625).

184. C&C, QSE 3/21, fol. 1ʳ (23 February 1579).

185. C&C, EDA 2/6, 13 (20 June 1492).

186. C&C, WS 1625 John Bruen of Stapleford, gentleman, single mb (26 January 1626).

187. C&C, EDV 1/17, fol. 57ʳ (9 October 1611).

188. C&C, EDV 1/14, single leaf (1605). A piper was also listed.

189. See Anthony King and Mervyn McLean, "Drum, §II, 2: Nontunable Western Drums: Side Drum," *NG*, 7:612.

190. Ibid., 7:612-3.

191. Clopper, *Chester*, 162 (1590–91), 167 (1591–92), 222 (1607–08), 264 (1610–11), 276 (1612–13), 368 (1625–26) and 408 (1632–33).

192. Ibid., 337.

193. C&C, TAR 1/18, mb 5 (1588–89); TAR 2/30, mb 6 (1613–14).

194. Congleton, Town Hall, Borough Account Book I, fols. 67ʳ (24 June–28 September 1602), 307ᵛ (24 June–28 September 1634). In 1602–03 (Borough Account Book I, fol. 72ᵛ) the payment is for "plaing" rather than drumming, and there is a second individual involved as well as Roger Stopport the drummer, which may indicate more music than just drumming. This is supported by the payment of 3s in 1627 to the "pyper or musitioner who played before the Rushbearinge" (Borough Account Book I, fol. 249ᵛ). See also Elizabeth Baldwin, "Rushbearings and Maygames in the Diocese of Chester before 1642," in *English Parish Drama*, ed. Alexandra F. Johnston and Wim Hüsken (Amsterdam: Rodopi, 1996), 31–40.

195. Congleton, Town Hall, Borough Account Book I, fol. 266ʳ (25 March–23 June 1631).

196. Ibid., fol. 272ʳ (29 September–24 December 1631).

197. C&C, QJF 68/2/42, single sheet (9 July 1639).

198. C&C, P/120/4525/2, 80 (10 July 1602).

199. C&C, EDV 1/22, fol. 37ʳ (7 November 1619).

200. C&C, TAR 2/31, mb 5 (1614–15).

201. C&C, TAR 1/18, mb 6 (1588–89); TAR 2/33, mb 2 (1616–17); TAR 2/37, mb 4 (1618–19); TAR 3/44, mb 3 (1626–27); TAR 3/47, fols. 3ᵛ, 4ᵛ (1638–39).

202. C&C, WS 1621 Peter Cross of Wilmslow, bachelor (will), single mb (24 July 1621).

203. C&C, WS 1621 Peter Cross of Wilmslow, bachelor, (inventory), single mb (1 September 1621).

204. C&C, WS 1608 Rowland Dutton of Hatton, esquire, mb 1, col. 2 (28 March 1608).

205. C&C, QJF 58/4/20, single sheet (19 January 1630).

206. C&C, QJF 58/1/37, bifolium (10 April 1629).

207. C&C, QJF 58/1/38, bifolium (10 April 1629).

208. Clopper, *Chester*, 169–70.

209. C&C, AF 40b/20, single leaf (7 January 1670).

210. C&C, SR/360, mb 1d (1488).

211. C&C, P/21/3607/1/2, 90 (1 May 1626).

212. Rupert H. Morris, *Chester in the Plantagenet and Tudor Reigns* (Chester: G. R. Griffin, 1893), 346, as quoted in John Boston, "An Early Virginal-Maker in Chester, and His Tools," *GSJ* 7 (1954): 3.

213. Morris, *Chester in the Plantagenet and Tudor Reigns*, 351, as quoted in Boston, "An Early Virginal-Maker," 3.

214. C&C, WS 1607 Henry Wright, mb 3 (15 October 1607).

215. C&C, WS 1607 Henry Wright, single sheet (9 August 1607).

216. Hinde, *A Faithfull Remonstrance*, 10.

217. C&C, QSE 5/46, single sheet (4 October 1594).

218. PRO, CHES 24/114/4, fol. 1ʳ (1618).

219. C&C, QSE 3/84, fol. 2ʳ (30 October 1588).

220. C&C, EDC 5(1614)/7, single sheet (3 July 1614).

221. C&C, EDC 5(1614)/7, fols. 3, 5 (12 April 1615).

Appendix I

1. C&C, WS 1604 William Maddock of Chester, Waitman, bifolium (4 September 1604); probate granted 7 September 1604.

2. An "x," and possibly "l," seem to be added; "l" runs over "v," and "x" is in a darker ink.

3. Blurred; could be either "ij" or "iij."

4. The mark is possibly a combined TL (not shown here). The names of Henry Skersbroke and W. Bedford are in different hands.

5. C&C, WI 1637 William Worrall of Nantwich, Musitioner, single sheet (13 June 1637). Letters of Administration were granted 29 November 1637 to his widow, Margaret Worrall.

6. C&C, WS 1648 Roger Vaughan of Nantwich, musician (will), single sheet. The will is damaged on the right side of the sheet, with loss of text.

7. The three signatures are all in different hands.

8. C&C, WS 1648 Roger Vaughan of Nantwich, musician (inventory), single sheet (24 April 1648).

Appendix II

1. Lostock Gralam and Nether Peover are both in the large parish of Great Budworth.

2. Possibly the same individual as Thomas Allen of Lostock Gralam, fiddler. Although piping is specified in the document, he is not actually described as a piper, and piping may be used as a generic term here.

3. Probably the Stretton in Great Budworth parish, which is much nearer the Lancashire border. The document mentions Lathom and Warrington, which are in Lancashire but not far from Stretton.

4. Thomas Baker of Nantwich died in 1592, and hence is definitely not the same as Thomas Baker of Wettenhall.

5. Very likely the John Baxter who appears in the 1596 records is the same as John Baxter, *alias* Barne, in 1597.

6. Both documents seem to refer to the same incident, although no location is listed in the second one.

7. William Bradbury and William Bredburye are evidently the same individual, and the two documents cited refer to a single incident since all the other participants are the same.

8. John Browne, musician, and John Browne, bagpiper, seem to be the same individual, and, as Littleton is in Christleton parish and adjacent to Christleton, John Browne of Christleton, piper, is probably also the same person.

9. Because Tattenhall and Wimbolds Trafford are a considerable distance apart, two separate performers named Richard Bruce are probaby designated in the records, as it would be unlikely for a piper to be described as "of Wimbolds Trafford" and "of Tattenhall" in consecutive years. However, the "Bruse the piper" who appears at Chester in 1618–19 is correspondingly more likely to be the same individual as one of the two Richard Bruces, given the closeness of the date and the attraction of a city like Chester for performers from the rest of the county. Richard Bruce of Tattenhall is perhaps more likely, as Tattenhall is closer to Chester.

10. Bruchull and Brughull are possibly the same individual, but the evidence is not sufficient to be conclusive.

11. Entries referring to the Callys as a group are also included here.

12. The time-lapse between the two appearances of Chatterton is sufficiently large to make it doubtful that the same individual was involved in both instances.

13. Given the closeness of the two dates, the similarity of the names, and the association of both with Chester, John Cona and John Conason may be the same individual.

14. Though John Cook, minstrel, and John Cook, piper, could have been the same individual, the name is not an unusual one, and the evidence is not conclusive.

15. In the Chester Smiths' accounts for 1553–54, Randle Crane is described as "ther minstrell."

16. Given the links of Richard Cross, minstrel, with Over, he likely was the same as Richard Cross of Over, piper.

17. Probably the same individual.

18. See also Richard Richardson, *alias* Williamson, *alias* Evensong, below.

19. The payment to Thomas Fidler immediately follows payments to Peter Cally and "shurlocke the menstrell," both of whom received the same amount; hence Thomas Fidler was probably paid for performing.

20. The document is damaged, and the entire name cannot be read, nor is it certain whether "ffidler" is a surname or an occupation.

21. Most probably Thomas Foster, *alias* Huntsman, of Hatton, who is put under recognizance in 1617, is the same as "Huntsman a piper" who received the pipes of Laithwood of Frodsham in 1625.

22. Morris (*Chester in the Plantagenet and Tudor Reigns*, 346, 351) makes reference to a William Goodman, virginal-maker, and quotes his will. However, neither Professor Mills nor I could find the original will in the Cheshire and Chester Archives.

23. Saughton is given in both documents in this case, but there is no Cheshire township of that name. Probably it is a variant of Sutton, represented by three townships in Cheshire as well as Great Sutton, Little Sutton, and Guilden Sutton. One of the documents further specifies "Saughton vpon the hill or there aboutes." As the other place names in the incident are all on the Wirral, one of the Wirral Suttons is more likely—that is, Great Sutton or Little Sutton.

24. Since William Hesketh was charged with piping at Tarporley, it is likely that Aston represents a township not too far away. The most likely places are Aston iuxta Mondrem (Nantwich Hundred) and Ashton in Tarvin parish (Eddisbury Hundred). Tarporley is also in Eddisbury Hundred.

25. Morgan Hopkin and Morgan Hopton are clearly the same. The fact that he is specifically mentioned as "a stranger" makes the variant spellings of his name more likely.

26. The text reads "Iohannem hibernicum," which would appear to indicate the piper's national origin.

27. Of the nine townships named Newton in Cheshire, the most probable are Newton by Chester and Newton by Tattenhall, both of which are in Broxton Hundred.

28. The name Richard Jackson, piper, occurs twice in the Cheshire records, but the lapse of more than fifty years between the two entries strongly suggests that different individuals are signified, especially since one of them was recorded in Lancashire rather than Cheshire.

29. Possibly John Yockin of Chester.

30. He is described in the document as "Tho Kettle the musick."

31. The name is spelled in a variety of ways: Laithwood, Lethwood, Laithwait, Leithwood, Leathwood. Most of the documents refer to a pair of bagpipes taken as a deodand after he hanged himself. Only the 1616 and 1617 entries relate to actual performance.

32. William Madock and William Madock, Jr., are evidently the same individual. William Madock, Sr., was surety for his son in 1588–89.

33. George Massie need not have been a musician. The horn-blowing incident seems to have been intentionally disruptive and possibly a form of social comment.

34. I have separated the references to Richard Metier, who apparently was one individual who lived in more than one location. All the townships associated with him are near one another, and his pattern of behavior is consistent. John Metier of Biddulph was his brother.

35. In 1622, Richard Minshull was described as being "of Pillory Streete"; in the 1606 parish register entry he is described as a musician, a fiddler in the later Visitation and Crown Book entries.

36. Likely to be the same as Robert de Whyteley, who appears at Leftwich, near Northwich, in 1411. "O<.>uytley" must designate Over Whitley, a variant of Higher Whitley, which is to the north of Northwich.

37. A number of musicians named Peacock apparently lived in the Malpas-Bunbury area. The two parishes are adjacent, and possibly the parish register entries for Malpas, which are quite late, are indicative of a gradual move from one parish to another. Beeston, the home of John Peacock, is in Bunbury parish, and it may be that Peacock the fiddler who is described as "of Bunbury parish" in 1620 is linked somehow to John Peacock. Humphrey Peacock may also have been linked to the parish of Malpas, as the child of Peacock the piper baptized in 1640 was named Humphrey. Humphrey Peacock, piper, and Humphrey Peacock, Sr., piper, are very probably the same individual. The gap between his description as "Sr." in 1616 and the baptism of a piper's child named Humphrey in 1640 is long enough to make it likely that there was an intervening generation. Peacock of Bunbury, fiddler, in 1620, and Peacock the fiddler, who had a child baptized in Malpas parish in 1637, may or may not have been the same.

38. Identified in one document as "Richard barlow man pickeringe" (Clopper, *Chester*, 228), and therefore more likely to have been an amateur than a professional musician.

39. John Piers of Warrington is charged with drinking, dancing, and

piping on a fast day but is not specifically identified as a piper. See also Grace Wood (n. 59, below).

40. Although possibly only one individual was concerned here, the locations are sufficiently distant—and the time between incidents sufficiently long—to make two individuals more probable.

41. Potinger is specified in the document as having come "bare out of Ireland," but it is not clear that he was Irish.

42. Described in the record as "musicioner," but the scribe had begun to write "piper" and then canceled it.

43. Two documents are extant relating to a fiddler in Frodsham in 1617. The name in one case is Richard Richardson, *alias* Williamson, *alias* Evensong, and in the other Richard Ensong. The two are almost certainly identical, and may be the same individual as the Evensong at whose house Robert Laithwood left his pipes when he committed suicide.

44. The document states that John Robinson "brought Musicke" to the bearward while the latter was in the stocks. Drumming is specifically mentioned in another document in the same case, but it is not clear whether John Robinson was himself the drummer or only the one who fetched the drummer.

45. Shurlock the minstrel and Henry Shurlock, piper, are probably the same person.

46. Variously described as "Lame Siddall," "old Siddall," and "poore siddall beinge a lame man," he is not designated as a minstrel, but payments to him occur nearby to payments for music. He is described as "Siddall the Cobler" in 1617–18, but a payment in 1620–21 to "lame Siddall. and the blynde boye that played one Adrome" may indicate that he was connected with musical performance.

47. As John Spencer was tried for drumming at Acton in a diocesan visitation of Nantwich Deanery, the Acton lying in Nantwich Hundred and Deanery must be the location.

48. There are two Strettons in Cheshire, one in Bucklow Hundred and one in Broxton Hundred, but the document gives no indication of which of these is intended in the document. However, the connection of Laurence Starkey with John Hale of Stretton makes the Stretton in Bucklow Hundred seem the more likely as a complaint about him mentions several placenames in that vicinity.

49. Although there no indication is given concerning which of the two Strettons in Cheshire is Thomas Stokes's home, the Stretton in Broxton Hundred is closer to Chester and may be the more likely.

50. Despite the different spellings and designations, four names evidently all refer to a single individual who died in 1624. As he is "of Nantwich" consistently from 1597 to 1624, he seems unlikely to have been the same person as John Tomson of Stockport.

51. Tomson's instrument is not specified, only that he played on the sabbath.

52. Alvanley, Barrow, and Upton-by-Chester are located sufficiently close together to allow one individual to have been intended in all three cases. Thomas Towers, who was actively piping in 1603, could well become "Old Towers" by 1638. Although he is described as "yoman" in the Upton incident, the offence is piping, and a Crown Book entry for the same incident refers to him as a piper.

53. References are probably to the same person. Wistaston is adjacent to Nantwich parish. The document specifies that Vaughan played the pipe and tabor at Wistaston.

54. Richard Vernon of Bunbury is described as being of Bunbury parish rather than of the township. The parish is a large one, and there is only one parish between it and Nantwich. The entries for Richard Vernon in the Nantwich parish register suggest that he was resident in the parish. While these two references are not impossibly to the same individual, more likely they were in fact two separate musicians.

55. All three variants of Rondle Waker or Walker would appear to refer to the same individual. The Budworth to which reference is made is likely to have been Little Budworth in all cases. Great Budworth and Little Budworth are not adjacent, and are in different hundreds.

56. See n. 36, above.

57. Two waits named Thomas Williams are definitely involved since the 1590–91 document refers to the earlier as deceased. The second Thomas Williams may well have been the son of the first. Another son, William Williams, was an apprentice wait in 1590–91.

58. Very probably Thomas Williams, the Chester wait. Another Crown Book entry for the same year refers to him as "Thomam Williams[son] de Civitat<..> Cestr' musitian," and the error may have been uncorrected in the Crown Book.

59. Grace Wood is charged, along with John Piers, with drinking, dancing, and piping on a fast day. She is not specifically described as a piper, and it is likely that she was involved as a dancer rather than a musical performer (see n. 36, above). However, as the document does not make it clear which one is the piper, if either, I have included both individuals.

60. Possibly Leonard Woodson or Thomas Woodson. See chapter III, above, for discussion.

61. Although he is not described as a musical performer of any sort, payments to "blind Edward wyatt" regularly follow payments for music. He may have been an object of charity, but he may also have been performing at the guild feasts.

62. Norton is described as being in the diocese of Coventry and Lichfield, but at this time Chester was a separate diocese. Was the reference therefore to

a place in one of the counties bordering on Cheshire?

63. "Vn'thorborse" is described in the document as being five miles from Derby, but no exact match for the name has been found.

64. Probably the same as Henry Halewood, Liverpool wait. See George, *Lancashire*, 39–40, 45, 47.

65. The document reads "Sausburie," which does not correspond to any Cheshire township. The information, coming from a diocesan visitation, may refer to Salesbury in Lancashire, a town which was within the diocese of Chester.

66. See n. 28, above.

BIBLIOGRAPHY

Abbreviations

C&C	Cheshire and Chester Archives
GSJ	*Galpin Society Journal*
PRO	Public Record Office
REED	Records of Early English Drama

Primary Sources

Documents:

Chester
Assembly Books
C&C, AB/2
Civic Records
Assembly Files
Petition of John Ward: C&C, AF 40b/20.
Mayors' Books
C&C, MB/7; C&C, MB/12; C&C, MB/15; C&C, MB/19; C&C,
MB/20; C&C, MB/21; C&C, MB/24; C&C, MB/25; C&C, MB/27.
Mayors' Files
C&C, MF 87/12
Mayors' Letters
C&C, ML 5/116
Sheriffs' Books
C&C, SB/7, C&C, SB/5/2.
Sheriffs' Court Books
C&C, SBC/22; C&C, SBC/178.
Sheriffs' Rolls
C&C, SR/128; C&C, SR/157; C&C, SR/223;C&C, SR/304; C&C,
SR/348; C&C, SR/358; C&C, SR/360; C&C, SR/460.
Corporation Lease Book
C&C, CHB/3.
City Treasurers' Accounts
C&C, TAR 1/18; C&C, TAR 2/30; C&C, TAR 2/31; C&C, TAR

2/33; C&C, TAR 2/37; C&C, TAR 3/44; C&C, TAR 3/47.
Apprenticeship Indenture Register
C&C, MAB/1.

Ecclesiastical Records
Bishop's Registers
EDA 2/1; EDA 2/2; EDA 2/6.
Chester Cathedral Treasurers' Accounts
C&C, EDD 3913/1/3; C&C, EDD 3913/1/4.
Consistory Court
C&C, EDC 5 (1571)/8; C&C, EDC 5 (1586)/77; C&C, EDC 5
(1597)/101; C&C, EDC 5 (1614)/7; C&C, EDC 5 (1624)/7; C&C,
EDC 5 (1625)/67; C&C, EDC 5 (1639)/120.
Chester Diocesan Visitation Proceedings
C&C, EDV 1/12b; C&C, EDV 1/14; C&C, EDV 1/15; C&C, EDV
1/17; C&C, EDV 1/22; C&C, EDV 1/24; C&C, EDV 1/26; C&C,
EDV 1/29; C&C, EDV 5/5.

Parish Registers
St. Oswald's, Malpas
C&C, P/21/3607/1/2; C&C, P/21/3607/1/3.
St. Mary's, Nantwich
C&C, P/120/4525/1; C&C, P/120/4525/2.

Wills and Inventories
C&C, WS 1633 Richard Arcall of Nantwich, grocer.
C&C, WS 1633 Ralph Arderne of Crokeley Bredbury.
C&C, WS 1638 Thomas Bickerton of Nantwich, gentleman.
C&C, WS 1624 John Blanchard of Chester, brewer.
C&C, WS 1587 Thomas Brereton of Barrow, gentleman.
C&C, WS 1625 John Bruen of Stapleford, gentleman.
C&C, WS 1579 John Cooper of Chester, alderman.
C&C, WS 1621 Peter Cross of Wilmslow, bachelor.
C&C, WS 1608 Rowland Dutton of Hatton, esquire.
C&C, WS 1633 Charles Fitton of Chester, alderman.
C&C, WS 1588 William Glaseor of Chester, esquire
C&C, WS 1618 Matthew Hawkes of Nantwich.
C&C, WS 1622 Richard Heyes of Nantwich, gentleman.
C&C, WS 1637 Thomas Jones of Chester, innholder.
C&C, WS 1642 Sir Peter Legh of Lyme the younger, knight.

C&C, WS 1604 William Maddock of Chester, Waitman.
C&C, WS 1618 James Miller of Chester, clerk.
C&C, WS 1627/8 Edward Minshull of Nantwich, esquire.
C&C, WS 1638 Richard Minshull of Nantwich, gentleman.
C&C, WS 1594 Urian Moreton of Yeaton, gentleman.
C&C, WS 1625 Edmund Myles of Nantwich, innholder.
C&C, WS 1640 Edmund Myles of Nantwich, innholder
C&C, WS 1627 Elizabeth Myles of Nantwich, widow.
C&C, WS 1604/5 Jasper Rutter of Nantwich, gentleman.
C&C, WS 1648 Roger Vaughan of Nantwich, musician.
C&C, WI 1637 William Worrall of Nantwich, musicioner.
C&C, WS 1607 Henry Wright of Nantwich, Innholder.
C&C, WS 1612 John Yardley of Crewe, gentleman.

Indenture of Goods of Grey Friars of Chester
C&C, DDX 43/54.

Guild Records
Barber Surgeons' Company Book 1606–98
C&C, G 2/1.
Butchers' Account and Fines Book
C&C, G 5/1.
Cordwainers and Shoemakers' Account Book I, 1547–98
C&C, G 8/2.
Cordwainers and Shoemakers' Accounts Book II 1598–1615
C&C, G 8/3.
Cordwainers and Shoemakers' Accounts Book III 1615–61
C&C, G 8/4.
Wet and Dry Glovers' Minute Book 1629-1968
C&C, G 11/1.
Innkeepers', Cooks' and Victuallers' Financial Papers
C&C, G 13/42; C&C, G 13/43.
Petitions to the Innholders
C&C, G 13/46.
Joiners', Carvers', and Turners' Company Book 1576–1756
C&C, G 14/1.
Painters, Glaziers, Embroiderers and Stationers' Account Book
with Rules and Apprenticeship Enrolment, 1567–1690
C&C, G 17/1.

Painters, Glaziers, Embroiderers, and Stationers' Account Book II
1620–1806
C&C, G 17/2.
Smiths, Cutlers, and Plumbers' Order and Account Book 1637–
1902
C&C, G 20/1.
Tanners' Account and Minute Book 1646–97
C&C, G 21/2.

Family Records
Bradshaw Family of Marple
Henry Bradshaw's Account Book
C&C, DDX 69/9.
Leche Family of Carden
Account book of John Leche of Carden, sergeant-at-law
C&C: DLE/86.
Debts and Financial Transactions of John Leche of Carden, sergeant-at-law
C&C, DLE/87.
Dutton Family of Dutton
Advowry of Minstrels, Quo Warranto Plea
C&C, DSS/3991/22/1.
List of Lands and Tenements belonging to Duttons of Dutton
C&C, DDX 23/1.
Savage Family of Rocksavage
Accounts of Richard Wilkinson, bailiff to Sir Thomas Savage for
Frodsham manor
C&C, DCH/F/194; C&C, DCH/F/197; C&C, DCH/F/198; C&C,
DCH/F/201.
Somerford Family of Somerford
Disbursements for Mary Somerford
C&C, DSS/1/7/6/45; C&C, DSS/1/7/6/46; C&C, DSS/1/7/11/22.
Letter from Thomas Maddock to Mr. Charles Mainwaring
C&C, DSS/1/7/7/2.
Trafford Family of Bridge Trafford
Indenture between William Trafford and Thomas and Anne
Johnes
C&C, CR/385/27.
Wilbraham Family of Nantwich
Wilbraham Account Book
C&C, DBW/P/J/7.

Letter from Sir Richard Wilbraham to Sir Richard Grosvenor
C&C, CR/63/2/691/6.
Winnington Family of Birches
Letters from Margaret and Robert Lowther to Elizabeth Winning-
ton
C&C, DSS/1/4/38/11; C&C, DSS/1/4/38/13.
Letter from Margaret Lowther to Elizabeth Winnington
C&C, DSS/1/4/38/12.
Letter from Margaret Lowther and Gervase Cutler to Elizabeth
Winnington
C&C, DSS/1/4/38/16.

Judicial Records
Quarter Sessions
Quarter Sessions Recognizances
C&C, QJB 1/4.
Quarter Sessions Indictments
C&C, QJB 2/3; C&C, QJB 2/5.
Quarter Sessions Files
Affidavit
C&C, QSE 3/21.
Depositions
C&C, QSF 29/122.
Examinations of Witnesses
C&C, QJF 11/4/16; C&C, QJF 27/2/2; C&C, QJF 38/3/5; C&C,
QJF 58/1/37; C&C, QJF 58/1/38; C&C, QJF 59/4/59; C&C, QJF
67/3/33; C&C, QSE 3/84; C&C, QSE 5/46; C&C, QSE 5/82; C&C,
QSE 9/2; C&C, QSE 9/8; C&C, QSE 9/69; C&C, QSE 11/71;
C&C, QSF 55/75; C&C, QSF 61/47; C&C, QSF 61/84; C&C, QSF
67/6.
Indictments
C&C, QJF 60/2/17; C&C, QJF 60/4/9.
Informations
C&C, QJF 39/4/22; C&C, QJF 40/4/15; C&C, QJF 44/1/96; C&C,
QJF 53/2/153; C&C, QJF 58/4/20; C&C, QSF 77/2/97.
Orders
C&C, QJF 60/3/102.
Petitions
C&C, QJF 40/4/13; C&C, QJF 49/3/80; C&C, QJF 50/1/137;
C&C, QJF 51/4/163; C&C, QJF 53/2/152; C&C, QJF 58/4/17;

C&C, QJF 68/2/42; C&C, QSF 36/58.
Presentments
C&C, QJF 31/2/43; C&C, QJF 44/2/12; C&C, QJF 46/1/54; C&C, QJF 49/2/47; C&C, QJF 49/2/52; C&C, QSF 56/35.
Recognizances
C&C, QJF 10/1/1; C&C, QJF 12/3/36; C&C, QJF 46/2/62; C&C, QJF 53/2/82; C&C, QJF 53/2/88; C&C, QJF 53/2/92; C&C, QJF 69/3/50.
Warrant for Arrest
C&C, QJF 61/2/30; C&C, QJF 63/1/53.

Congleton Town Hall
Borough Account Book I.

London
British Library
Letter from Peter Moreton to his father, William Moreton of Moreton
Additional MS. 33,935.
Letter from Percy Church to Peter Moreton
Additional MS. 33,936.
Indenture
Harley MS. 2095, fol 146^v.

Public Record Office (PRO)
Enrolments
PRO, CHES 2/29; PRO, CHES 2/37; PRO, CHES 2/66; PRO, CHES 2/89; PRO, CHES 2/105; PRO, CHES 2/109; PRO, CHES 2/146; PRO, CHES 2/149; PRO, CHES 2/151; PRO, CHES 2/152; PRO, CHES 2/166.
Pleadings
PRO, CHES 16/1/1.
Crown Books
PRO, CHES 21/2; PRO, CHES 21/3.
Files of the County Court and Court of Great Sessions
PRO, CHES 24/1/2; PRO, CHES 24/95/2; PRO, CHES 24/110/1; PRO, CHES 24/110/2; PRO, CHES 24/110/3; PRO, CHES 24/112/1; PRO, CHES 24/112/2; PRO, CHES 24/113/3; PRO, CHES 24/113/4; PRO, CHES 24/114/1; PRO, CHES 24/114/2; PRO, CHES 24/114/3; PRO, CHES 24/114/4; PRO, CHES

24/115/1; PRO, CHES 24/115/2; PRO, CHES 24/115/3 PRO, CHES 24/115/4; PRO, CHES 24/117/1; PRO, CHES 24/126/3.
Indictment Rolls
PRO, CHES 25/9; PRO, CHES 25/10; PRO, CHES 25/11; PRO, CHES 25/12; PRO, CHES 25/16; PRO, CHES 25/20.
Plea Rolls
PRO, CHES 29/125.
Star Chamber Cases
PRO, STAC 5/E11/3; PRO, STAC 7/2/24.

Manchester
John Rylands University Library
Letter from Henry Lawes to Sir Peter Legh, Lord of Lyme (1590–1636)
Legh of Lyme Correspondence, Letters to Sir Peter Legh, folder 4.
Contract between the Monastery of St. Werburgh and John Bircheley, clerk, of London
Latin MS. 460.
Inventory of goods taken from Robert Tatton at Withenshawe by parliamentary forces
Tatton MSS. 293.

Oxford
Bodleian Library
William Smith's *Description of Cheshire*
Bodl. Rawl. B.282.
The Stanley Poem
Bodl. Rawl. poet.143.
The Magistracy of Minstrels
Bodl. MS. Sancroft 72.

Ruthin
Denbighshire Record Office
Plas Power MSS.
Answer of Steven, Bishop of Winchester, to the six articles
DD/PP/839.
Letter from Christopher Goodman to the Archbishop of York
DD/PP/839
Copy of Letter from Christopher Goodman to the Earl of Derby
DD/PP/844

York
Borthwick Institute
Metropolitan Visitation Proceedings
Answers to the Articles of the Archbishop of York re: Chester
Cathedral
V.1578–9.
Archbishop Sandys' Visitation Book
V.1578/CB.3.
"Detecta" for Archbishop Piers' Visitation
V.1590–1/CB.2.
Archbishop Hutton's Visitation Books
V.1595–96/CB.2.
V.1595–96/CB.3.
Archbishop Harsnett's Visitation Book
V.1629–30/CB.
Archbishop Neile's Visitation Book
V.1633/CB.2b.
Will of Francis Fitton of Gawsworth
Wills/30b.
Will of Sir Richard Shireburn of Stonyhurst
Wills/40b.

Books:

Boydell, Barra. *Music at Christ Church before 1800: Documents and Selected Anthems*. Dublin, 1999.

Buck, P. C., *et al.*, eds. *Robert White*, Tudor Church Music 5. London: Oxford University Press, 1926.

Calendar of the Patent Rolls, Henry VI, 6 vols. Norwich and London, 1901–10.

Clopper, Lawrence M., ed. *Chester*, REED. Toronto: University of Toronto Press, 1979.

George, David, ed. *Lancashire*, REED. Toronto: University of Toronto Press, 1991.

Hinde, William. *A Faithfull Remonstrance of the Holy Life and Happy Death of John Bruen of Bruen-Stapleford, in the County of Chester, Esquire (Brother to that Mirrour of Piety; Mistris Katherin Brettergh) Exhibiting variety of many Memorable and Exemplary passages of his Life, and at his Death, usefull for all sorts and Sexes, but principally intended, as a Path and President of Piety and*

Charity for the Inhabitants of the Famous County Palatine of Chester, By the late reverend Divine William Hinde, sometimes fellow of Queenes Colledge in Oxon., and Preacher of Gods Word at Bunb. in Cheshire, Published since his Death. London, 1641.

_____. *The Very Singular Life of John Bruen, Esquire, of Bruen Stapleford, Cheshire: Exhibitions of a Variety of memorable and exemplary Circumstances, which may be of great Utility to all Persons; but Principally intended as a Precedent of Piety and Charity for the Inhabitants of the County of Chester,* revised ed. Chester: William Coddington, 1799.

Ingram, R. W., ed. *Coventry,* REED. Toronto: University of Toronto Press, 1981.

Lumiansky, R. M., and David Mills, eds. *The Chester Mystery Cycle,* EETS, s.s. 3, 9. London: Oxford University Press, 1974–86.

Pilkington, Francis. *First Book of Songs or Ayres.* London, 1605.

_____. *First Set of Madrigals and Pastorals.* London, 1612.

_____. *Second Set of Madrigals, and Pastorals.* London, 1624.

Somerset, J. Alan B. *Shropshire,* 2 vols., REED. Toronto: University of Toronto Press, 1994.

Statutes of the Realm, Printed by Command of His Majesty King George III in pursuance of an address of the House of Commons of Great Britain, The. Vol. 4. 1819.

Secondary Sources

Abbott, Djilda, and Ephraim Segerman. "Strings in the 16th and 17th Centuries," *GSJ* 27 (1974): 48–73.

Armstrong-Davies, M. H. "A Note on the History of the Northumbrian Small Pipes," *GSJ* 22 (1969): 78–80.

Aydelotte, Frank. *Elizabethan Rogues and Vagabonds,* Oxford Historical and Literary Studies 1. Oxford: Clarendon Press, 1913.

Baines, Anthony. *Bagpipes,* Pitt Rivers Museum Occasional Papers on Technology 9. Oxford: Oxford University Press, 1960.

Baldwin, Elizabeth. "Reformers, Rogues or Recusants? Control of Popular Entertainment and the Flouting of Authority in Cheshire before 1642," *Records of Early English Drama Newsletter* 22, no. 1 (1997): 26–31.

_____. "Rushbearings and Maygames in the Diocese of Chester before 1642." In *English Parish Drama,* ed. Alexandra F. Johnston and Wim Hüsken, 31–40. Amsterdam: Rodopi, 1996.

Beechey, Gwilym. "Christopher Lowther's Lute Book," *GSJ* 24 (1971): 51–59.

Beier, A. L. *Masterless Men: The Vagrancy Problem in England, 1560–1640*. London and New York: Methuen, 1985.

_____. "Vagrants and the Social Order in Elizabethan England," *Past and Present* 64 (1974): 3–29.

Bicknell, Stephen. *The History of the English Organ*. Cambridge: Cambridge University Press, 1996.

Boston, John. "An Early Virginal-Maker in Chester, and His Tools," *GSJ* 7 (1954): 3–6.

Boydell, Barra. "Music in Reformation and Political Change in Christ Church Cathedral, Dublin." In *Music and Musicians in Renaissance Cities and Towns*, ed. Fiona Kisby, 131–42. Cambridge: Cambridge University Press, 2001.

Bray, Roger, ed. *Music in Britain: The Sixteenth Century*, The Blackwell History of Music in Britain 2. Oxford: Blackwell, 1995.

Bruce-Mitford, Rupert. *Aspects of Anglo-Saxon Archaeology*. New York: Harper and Row, 1974.

Bullock-Davies, Constance. *Menestrellorum Multitudo: Minstrels at a Royal Feast*. Cardiff: University of Wales Press, 1978.

Burke, Peter. *Popular Culture in Early Modern Europe*. New York: Harper and Row, 1978.

Burke's Peerage and Baronetage, ed. Peter Townend, 104th ed. London: Burke's Peerage Limited, 1967.

Burne, R. V. H. *Chester Cathedral from Its Founding by Henry VII to the Accession of Queen Victoria*. London: SPCK, 1958.

_____. *The Monks of Chester: The History of St. Werburgh's Abbey*. London: SPCK, 1962.

Cannon, R. D. "Bagpipes in English Works of Art," *GSJ* 42 (1989): 10–31.

Carpenter, Nan Cooke. "Music in the Chester Plays," *Papers in English Language and Literature* 1 (1965): 195–216.

_____. "Music in the English Mystery Plays." In *Music in English Renaissance Drama*, ed. John H. Long, 1–31. Lexington: University of Kentucky Press, 1968.

Chappell, W. *Popular Music of the Olden Times*. 2 vols. (London, 1855–59.

Clark, Peter. "The Alehouse and the Alternative Society." In *Puritans and Revolutionaries: Essays in Seventeenth-Century History presented to Christopher Hill*, ed. Donald Pennington and Keith Thomas, 47–72. Oxford: Clarendon Press, 1978.

_____. *The English Alehouse: A Social History 1200–1830.* London: Longman, 1983.

Collinson, Patrick. *The Birthpangs of Protestant England: Religious and Cultural Change in the Sixteenth and Seventeenth Centuries.* Basingstoke and London: Macmillan, 1988.

_____. *The Religion of Protestants: The Church in English Society 1559–1625.* Oxford: Clarendon Press, 1982.

Dart, Thurston. "The Cittern and its English Music," *GSJ* 1 (1948): 46–63.

_____. "Music and Musical Instruments in Cotgrave's *Dictionarie* (1611)," *GSJ* 21 (1968): 70–80.

Davidson, Clifford. *Illustrations of the Stage and Acting in England to 1580.* Early Drama, Art, and Music Monograph Series 16. Kalamazoo: Medieval Institute Publications, 1991.

Dictionary of National Biography, ed. Leslie Stephen and Sidney Lee. 22 vols. London: Smith, Elder, 1908.

Dunn, F. I. *The Ancient Parishes, Townships and Chapelries of Cheshire,* Cheshire Record Office and Cheshire Diocesan Record Office. Chester: Cheshire County Council, 1987.

Dutka, JoAnna. "Music and the English Mystery Plays," *Comparative Drama* 7 (1973): 135–49.

_____. *Music in the English Mystery Plays,* Early Drama, Art, and Music, Reference Series 2. Kalamazoo: Medieval Institute Publications, 1980.

_____. "Mysteries, Minstrels, and Music," *Comparative Drama* 8 (1974): 112–24.

Erler, Mary C. "Palm Sunday Prophets and Processions and Eucharistic Controversy," *Renaissance Quarterly* 48 (1995): 58–81.

Evans, Willa McClung. *Henry Lawes: Musician and Friend of Poets.* New York: Modern Language Association, 1941.

Frere, A. H. "Shawms and Waits," *Music and Letters* 4 (1923): 170–77.

Galpin, Francis W. *Old English Instruments of Music,* 4th ed. London: Methuen, 1965.

Gill, Donald. "The Elizabethan Lute," *GSJ* 12 (1959): 60–62.

_____. "James Talbot's Manuscript V: Plucked Strings," *GSJ* 15 (1962): 60–69.

_____. "The Orpharion and the Bandora," *GSJ* 13 (1960): 14–31.

Gosson, Stephen. *The Schoole of Abuse [August?] 1579, and A Short*

Apologie of the Schoole of Abuse [November?] 1579, ed. Edward Arber. Westminster: A. Constable, 1895.

Govett, L. A. *The King's Book of Sports: A History of the Declarations of King James I. and King Charles I. as to the use of Lawful Sports on Sundays, with a Reprint of the Declarations and a Description of the Sports Then Popular.* London: Elliot Stock, 1890.

Grove's Dictionary of Music and Musicians, 4th ed., ed. J. A. Fuller Maitland. 5 vols. Philadelphia: Theodore Presser, 1922.

Haigh, Christopher, ed. *The English Reformation Revised.* 1987; reprint Cambridge: Cambridge University Press, 1988.

Halliwell, James Orchard. *Palatine Anthology: A Collection of Ancient Poems and Ballads Relating the Lancashire and Cheshire.* London, 1850.

Heartz, Daniel. "An Elizabethan Tutor for the Guitar," *GSJ* 16 (1963): 3–21.

History of the County of Chester, A, vol. 1, ed. B. E. Harris and A. T. Thacker, Victoria History of the Counties of England. Oxford: Oxford University Press, 1987.

Higham, N. J. *The Origins of Cheshire.* Manchester: Manchester University Press, 1993.

Hill, Christopher. *The World Turned Upside Down: Radical Ideas During the English Revolution.* 1972; reprint Harmondsworth: Penguin Books, 1991.

Jusserand, J. J. *English Wayfaring Life in the Middle Ages*, trans. Lucy Toulmin Smith. London: T. Fisher Unwin, 1889.

Legh, Evelyn Caroline, Baroness Newton. *The House of Lyme from its Foundation to the End of the Eighteenth Century.* London: William Heinemann, 1917.

Le Huray, Peter. *Music and the Reformation in England, 1549–1660.* London: Herbert Jenkins, 1967.

Leishman, J. B., ed. *The Three Parnassus Plays (1598–1601).* London: Ivor Nicholson and Watson, 1949.

Lewis, C. T. *Elementary Latin Dictionary.* Oxford: Oxford University Press, 1891.

Lowe, Michael. "The Historical Development of the Lute in the 17th Century," *GSJ* 29 (1976), 11–25.

Lumiansky, R. M., and David Mills. *The Chester Mystery Cycle: Essays and Documents.* Chapel Hill: University of North Carolina Press, 1983.

Mace, Thomas. *Musick's Monument.* 1676; facsimile reprint Paris:

Éditions du Centre National de la Recherche Scientifique, 1977.

Marcuse, Sybil. *Musical Instruments: A Comprehensive Dictionary.* 1964; reprint New York: W. W. Norton, 1975.

McGee, Timothy J. "The Fall of the Noble Minstrel: The Sixteenth-Century Minstrel in a Musical Context," *Medieval and Renaissance Drama in England* 7 (1995): 98–120.

MacLean, Sally-Beth. *Chester Art: A Subject List of Extant and Lost Art Including Items Relevant to Early Drama,* Early Drama Art and Music, Reference Series 3. Kalamazoo: Medieval Institute Publications, 1982.

Mills, David. *The Chester Mystery Cycle: A New Edition with Modernised Spelling.* East Lansing, Mich.: Colleagues Press, 1992.

_____. "James Miller: The Will of a Chester Scribe," *REED Newsletter* 9, no. 1 (1984): 11–12.

_____. "Music and Musicians in Chester," *Medieval English Theatre* 17 (1995): 58–75.

_____. *Recycling the Cycle: The City of Chester and Its Whitsun Plays,* Studies in Early English Drama, 4. Toronto: University of Toronto Press, 1998.

Montagu, Jeremy. "Was the Tabor Pipe Always as We Know It?" *GSJ* 50 (1997): 16–30.

_____. *The World of Medieval and Renaissance Musical Instruments.* Newton Abbot: David and Charles, 1976.

Morris, Rupert H. *Chester in the Plantagenet and Tudor Reigns.* Chester, 1894.

Mountney, Hugh. "The Regal," *GSJ* 22 (1969): 3–22.

Munrow, David. *Instruments of the Middle Ages and Renaissance.* London: Oxford University Press, 1976.

New Grove Dictionary of Music and Musicians, The, 2nd ed., ed. Stanley Sadie. 29 vols. London: Macmillan, 2001.

Ormerod, George. *The History of the County Palatine and City of Chester, Compiled from original evidences in public offices, the Harleian and Cottonian MSS., Parochial Registers, Private Muniments, Unpublished MS. Collections of Successive Cheshire Antiquaries, and a Personal Survey of Every Township in the County: Incorporated with a Republication of King's Vale Royal and Leycester's Cheshire Antiquities,* 2nd ed., rev. and enlarged by Thomas Helsby, 3 vols. London: G. Routledge and Sons, 1882.

Peacham, Henry. *Peacham's Compleat Gentleman 1634,* introd. G. S. Gordon. Oxford: Clarendon Press, 1906.

Pound, John. *Poverty and Vagrancy in Tudor England*. Harlow: Longman, 1971.

Puttenham, George. *The Arte of English Poesie*, ed. Gladys Doidge Willcock and Alice Walker. 1936; reprint Cambridge: Cambridge University Press, 1970.

Rastall, Richard. "Alle hefne makyth melody." In Paula Neuss, ed., *Aspects of Early English Drama*, 1–12. Cambridge: D. S. Brewer, 1983.

_____. *The Heaven Singing: Music in Early English Religious Drama*, 2 vols. (Cambridge: D. S. Brewer, 1996–2001).

_____. "The Minstrel Court in Medieval England," *Proceedings of the Leeds Literary and Philological Society* 18, no. 1 (1982): 96–105.

_____. "Music in the Cycle." In R. M. Lumiansky and David Mills, *The Chester Mystery Cycle: Essays and Documents*, 111–64. Chapel Hill: University of North Carolina Press, 1983.

_____. "Secular Musicians in Later Medieval England," 2 vols. Ph.D. diss., University of Manchester, 1968.

_____. "Some English Consort-Groupings of the Late Middle Ages," *Music and Letters* 55 (1974): 179–202.

_____. "'Some Myrth to his Majestee': Music in the Chester Cycle." In David Mills, ed., *Staging the Chester Cycle*, Leeds Texts and Monographs, n.s. 9, 77–99. Leeds: The University of Leeds School of English, 1985.

Raynor, Henry. *A Social History of Music from the Middle Ages to the Renaissance*. 1972; reprint New York: Taplinger, 1978.

Reay, Barry, ed. *Popular Culture in Seventeenth-Century England*. 1985; reprint London: Routledge, 1988.

Reese, Gustave. *Music in the Middle Ages*. New York: W. W. Norton, 1940.

_____. *Music in the Renaissance*. New York: W. W. Norton, 1959.

Remnant, Mary. *English Bowed Instruments from Anglo-Saxon to Tudor Times*. Oxford: Clarendon Press, 1986.

_____. "The Gittern in English Medieval Art," *GSJ* 18 (1965): 104–09.

_____. *Musical Instruments: An Illustrated History from Antiquity to the Present*. London: B. T. Batsford, 1989.

_____. "Musical Instruments in Early English Drama." In Clifford Davidson, ed., *Material Culture and Medieval Drama*, 141–

94. Kalamazoo: Medieval Institute Publications, 1999.

Richardson, R. C. *Puritanism in North-West England: A Regional Study of the Diocese of Chester to 1642*. Manchester: Manchester University Press, 1972.

Roberts, Peter. "Elizabethan players and minstrels and the legislation of 1572." In Anthony Fletcher and Peter Roberts, eds., *Religion, Culture and Society in Early Modern Britain: Essays in Honour of Patrick Collinson*, 29–55. Cambridge: Cambridge University Press, 1994.

Sachs, Curt. *The History of Musical Instruments*. New York: W. W. Norton, 1940.

Salgādo, Gāmini. *The Elizabethan Underworld*. 1977; reprint Gloucester: Alan Sutton, 1984.

Segerman, Ephraim. "A Short History of the Cittern," *GSJ* 52 (1999): 77–107.

Shaw, Watkins. *The Succession of Organists of the Chapel Royal and the Cathedrals of England and Wales from c.1538*. Oxford: Clarendon Press, 1991.

Slack, Paul. *Poverty and Policy in Tudor and Stuart England*. London: Longman, 1988.

_____. "Vagrants and Vagrancy in England, 1598–1664," *Economic History Review*, 2nd series, 27 (1974): 360–79.

Smith, William. "A man may stand therein and see into the Markets, or Four principal streets of the city." In *The Vale-Royall of England or the County Palatine of Chester*, ed. David King. London, 1656.

Southworth, John. *The English Medieval Minstrel*. Woodbridge: Boydell Press, 1989.

Stelten, Leo F. *Dictionary of Ecclesiastical Latin*. Peabody, Mass.: Hendrikson, 1995.

Stokes, James. "Musicians and Performance in Lincolnshire," *Early Drama, Art, and Music Review* 24 (Spring 2002): 121–51.

Strunk, Oliver. *Source Readings in Music History: From Classical Antiquity to the Romantic Era*. London: Faber and Faber, 1952.

Strutt, Joseph. *The Sports and Pastimes of the People of England from the Earliest Period, Including the Rural and Domestic Recreations, May Games, Mummeries, Pageants, Processions and Pompous Spectacles, Illustrated by Reproductions from Ancient Paintings in Which Are Represented Most of the Popular Diversions*, rev. J. Charles Cox. London: Methuen, 1903.

Stubbes, Philip. *The Anatomie of Abuses*. London, 1583.

_____. *Phillip Stubbes's Anatomy of the Abuses in England in Shakspere's Youth, A.D. 1583*, ed. F. J. Furnivall, New Shakspere Society Publications, ser. 6, Shakspere's England, nos. 4, 6, 12. 1877–79; reprint Vaduz: Kraus, 1965.

Tait, James. "The Declaration of Sports for Lancashire (1617)," *The English Historical Review* 32 (1917): 561–68.

Taylor, Andrew. "*The Stanley Poem* and the Harper Richard Sheale," *Leeds Studies in English*, n.s. 28 (1997): 99–122.

Tydeman, William, ed. *The Medieval European Stage, 500–1550*. Cambridge: Cambridge University Press, 2001.

Westfall, Suzanne R. *Patrons and Performance: Early Tudor Household Revels*. Oxford: Clarendon Press, 1990.

Woodfill, Walter L. *Musicians in English Society from Elizabeth to Charles I*. Princeton: Princeton University Press, 1953.

Whythorne, Thomas. *The Autobiography*, ed. James M. Osborn. Oxford: Clarendon Press, 1961.

Wright, Laurence. "Medieval Cittern and Citole: A Case of Mistaken Identity," *GSJ* 30 (1977): 8–42.

INDEX

Acton *41, 177, 207, 245*
Actors (*see also* Players) *20, 59, 70*
Affray *26, 45*
Agden *98, 195*
Alderley Edge *11*
Aldersey, Anne *232*
Aldersey, William, mayor of Chester *232*
Alehouses *1–2, 9–10, 18, 20, 22, 24–25, 27, 38–53, 81–83, 88–90, 93–96, 105, 107, 110–12, 115–17, 123–24, 127, 140, 145, 148, 160, 165, 171, 179, 182, 184–86, 217*
Ales *10, 25, 35, 38–49, 53, 144, 148, 166, 177, 184*
Alferiall *see* Orpharion
Alison, Richard, *Psalmes of David in Meter 157, 236*
Allen, John, conduct of the choir at Chester Cathedral *58, 195*
Allen, Katherine, wife of Thomas Allen, fiddler *33*
Allen, Thomas, of Lostock Gralam, fiddler *33, 116, 144, 185, 195, 242*
Allen, Thomas, possibly a piper *144, 195, 242*
Allostock *90*
Alsloot, Denijs van, painting by *167*
Alvanley *50, 88, 95, 115, 207, 246*
Apprentices *21, 50, 63, 70, 92, 98, 105–07, 183, 197–98, 209, 246*
Arcall, Richard, of Nantwich, grocer *226*
Archery *35, 38, 142*
Arch-lute *155*
Arderne, Ralph, of Crokeley

Bredbury *239*
Armes, Richard, piper *195*
Arnett, Henry of Sefton, Lancs., piper *209*
Arnett, James, of Northmeols, Lancs., piper *210*
Arnett, William, of Much Crosby, Lancs., piper *210*
Arrowsmith, William *52*
Asbie, Thomas, piper *114–15, 195*
Ash, Alice *50, 95*
Ashton in Tarvin parish *148, 243*
Ashton iuxta Mouldsworth *148, 243*
Ashton, George, piper *98, 182, 195*
Ashton, Thomas *33*
Ashton, William, of Over Knutsford, piper *35, 195*
Ashworth, Nicholas, alias Piper, of Over Tabley (Tabley Superior) *88, 195*
Aspshall, Thomas, of Stretton, piper *196*
Astbury *41, 89*
Astle (*also* Ascell), Thomas, constable of Siddington *47–48, 111*
Aston *97, 202, 243*
Aston iuxta Mondrum *243*
Audience *24, 53, 75, 79–80, 93–95, 130, 148, 152, 185*
Audlem *203*
Axon, John, of Nantwich, fiddler *103, 196*

Babington, Bishop *31, 215*
Baggott, Thomas *171*
Bagpiper *162, 197, 209, 242*
Bagpipes *72, 82, 84, 95, 133–34, 161–67, 169, 244*

Baker, Thomas, of Nantwich, harper *101, 196, 242*

Baker, Thomas, of Wettenhall, minstrel *196, 242*

Balie, John, piper *196*

Ballads *20, 29, 77, 98, 118, 135*

Bandora *78, 102, 104, 132–33, 135–36, 140, 146–50, 154–55, 157, 161, 181, 183, 192, 230, 235*

Banquets *22, 24, 65*

Banyster the waitman *196*

Barker, Elizabeth *50*

Barker, Richard, Sr. *193*

Barley, William, *New Book of Tabliture 154, 235*

Barlow, Francis *98*

Barlow, Richard *77*

Barnard, John, *First Book of Selected Church Musick 100*

Barnes, Randle, minor canon of Chester Cathedral *60–61, 196*

Barnes, Thomas, master of the choristers at Chester cathedral *56, 60*

Barrow *87–88, 136, 200, 207, 246*

Barrowe, William, constable of Ness *34*

Barthomley *201*

Barton, John, tallowchandler *125–26*

Barton, Thomas, of Ormskirk, Lancs., piper *210*

Barwick, John, dean of St. Paul's *32*

Baskervyle, Mr. *89*

Bastwick, Dr. *77*

Bateson, Thomas, organist *58, 78, 196*

Bawdry *29, 50–51, 111, 115, 123*

Baxter, bearward *179*

Baxter, Henry, minstrel *196*

Baxter, John, piper *196, 242*

Baxter, John, alias Barne, piper *36–37, 165, 196, 242*

Baxter, Margaret *152*

Bayly, Agnes, servant to Thomas de

Madley *109*

Beamond, John, piper *196*

Bearbaiting *24–25, 32, 35, 42–43, 45, 47, 71, 81*

Bearwards *15, 32, 42, 44, 47, 70–71, 80–81, 93, 99, 179, 245*

Beddell, Thomas *220*

Bedford, W. *187, 191, 241*

Beedle, Thomas, instrument maker *64, 180, 196*

Beeston *84, 204*

Beggeway, James, minstrel *196*

Bellows-pipe *164*

Bell, Richard (musician) *69–70, 107, 196*

Bellman (town crier) of Chester *62*

Bell-ringers *175–76, 198, 200–01, 205, 209*

Bells *131, 175–77*; bow bell *175–76*; chime bells *177*; clock bell *131, 175, 177*

Benet, Richard, minstrel *196*

Bentley, Galfridus, of Knutsford *90; see also* Bentley, Jeffrey, of Nether Knutsford

Bentley, Jeffrey, of Nether Knutsford, innkeeper *170–71; see also* Bentley, Galfridus, of Knutsford

Bentley, John, of Knutsford *90*

Betteley, Margaret *52*

Biccle, Alice *117*

Bickerstaff, James, minstrel *210*

Bickerton *79, 199, 204–05*

Bickerton, Thomas *136*

Bickerton, Thomas, of Nantwich, gentleman *157, 226, 232, 235–36*

Biddulph, Staffs. *90–91, 127, 204*

Bigamy *88, 115*

Bircheley, John, clerk, of London, organist and singing teacher *56–58, 174, 196*

Birchenshaw, John, Abbot of St. Werburgh's Abbey *56, 174*

Birkenhead *196*

Birkenhead, Hugh de, harper *108, 196*

Blackburn, Lancs. *210*

Blackden, John, of Nether Knutsford, musician *196*

Blanchard, John, of Chester, brewer *239*

Blind boy playing drum *177, 245*

Blithe, Richard, drummer *197*

Blundeville, Ranulph or Randle (Ranulph III), Earl of Chester (1181–1232) *18, 71*

Blymson, John *65*

Bockett, Margaret, née Lockett, wife of Thomas Bockett *112*

Bockett, Thomas *112*

Bockos, Peter *73*

Boden, John, of Rowton *45*

Boethius, *De Institutione Musica 213*

Book of Sports (also *Declaration for Sports*) *35, 37–39, 46, 125, 184*

Boone, Henry, piper *82, 197*

Booth, Sir George, knight and baronet *116*

Boswicke, harper *97, 197*

Boulton, Richard, of Minshull Vernon, piper *197*

Bower, Robert, singingman *115, 197*

Bowling *35*

Brachgirdle, John *37*

Brachgirdle, Thomas *36*

Bradbury, William (*also* Bredburye) *197, 242*

Bradford, Thomas *73*

Bradley, John, of Bryning, Lancs., apprentice musician *70, 107, 197*

Bradshaw, Henry, of Marple *93–94*

Bradshaw, John, of Allostock *90*

Brasey, Nicholas, minstrel *197*

Brawling *40–41, 68*

Bredbury *201*

Bredburye, William *see* Bradbury, William

Brereton, Sir John *26, 99*

Brereton, Richard, of Lea *135, 157, 173*

Brereton, Thomas, of Barrow *136, 231*

Bressie, Thomas, high constable of Broxton Hundred *42*

Brettar, Flintshire *66*

Bridgend in Overton, Frodsham parish *82, 162*

Bridge Street, Chester *55, 65*

Bridgewater, Earl of *128*

Brimelaw, Richard, piper *197*

Bromhall, Robert *192*

Brooke, Humphrey *192*

Brooke, Margaret *192*

Brooke, Thomas *52*

Brothels *41, 50, 111, 123–24*

Browne, John, of Christleton, piper *197, 242*

Browne, John, of Littleton, bagpiper *113–14, 197, 242*

Browne, John, of Littleton, musician *197*

Browne, John, of Nantwich *176*

Browne, William, drummer *197*

Broxton Hundred *12, 42, 243, 245*; high constable of *42*

Bruce, Richard, of Tattenhall, piper *197, 242*

Bruce, Richard, of Wimbolds Trafford, piper *197, 242*

Bruce (Bruse), piper *197, 242*

Bruchull, minstrel *197, 242*

Bruen, Dorothy, daughter of Thomas Holford of Holford *229*

Bruen, John, of Bruen Stapleford *7, 30–32, 46, 124, 131, 156, 177, 181, 184–85, 217, 229–31, 240*

Brughull, piper *197, 242*

Bryning, Lancs. *70, 107, 197*

Buckley, Mr. Robert, of Congleton *99*

Bucklow Hundred *12, 245*; high constable of *170*

Buddeston, John de *108*
Buisine *62, 169*
Bulkeley, Richard de *109*
Bulkeley, Richard de, piper *108, 197*
Bullbaiting *35, 71*
Bunbury *30, 51–53, 108, 204, 206, 208, 244, 246*
Burches, John *109*
Burges, Francis, piper *197*
Burges, William *109*
Burroughes, Thomas *193*
Burrows, John, Mr., preacher at Shotwick *38, 117, 171*
Burton, Christopher, of Chester, waitman *65–68, 105–07, 198*
Burton, Henry, of Chester, apprentice musician/wait, son of Christopher Burton, waitman *66, 105–06, 198*
Bury, Richard, of Northwich, harper, alias Richard Bury of Northwich, yeoman *198*
Butcher, Mark, bell-ringer *176, 198*
Butler, John, fiddler *72, 198*
Byrsley, Hugh, of Malpas, minstrel *83, 198*

Cally/Kelly *7, 67–70, 73, 92, 100, 198, 242;* travels to Congleton *11, 91–92, 99*
Cally, Edmund, musician *15, 67, 125–26, 198, 212*
Cally, George, musician and wait *26–27, 66–70, 87, 107, 125, 184, 186, 198*
Cally, John, son of Peter, musician *67, 77, 168, 198*
Cally, Peter, musician *67, 168, 198, 243*
Cally, Robert, musician and wait *26–27, 67–68, 70, 107, 125, 184, 198*
Cally, Roland, possibly a musician *198*
Calveley, Hugh, of Lea *174*

Capenhurst *171*
Carden *137–38, 173*
Carter, William *28*
Castiglione, Baldassare *135, 231*
Castile, King of *133–34*
Challyner, John, of Oswestry, musician *87, 199*
Chalner, Robert, fiddler *72–73, 171, 199*
Chamberlain, Sir Thomas *46*
Chanter, Mr., probably John Genson *60–61*
Chanter, Roger *73*
Chapel Royal *100, 128*
Charles I *141–42*
Chatterton, piper *199, 242*
Chatterton, Richard, minstrel and piper *73, 199, 242*
Chauntrell, Jane, former nun *115*
Chelford cum Astle *82, 89, 109, 113, 197, 204*
Cheshire, county of *1–4, 8–12, 17–18, 30, 32, 35, 38–40, 71, 83, 86, 91, 93, 95, 99, 101, 113, 119–20, 126–28, 131, 135, 137, 143–45, 147–48, 150, 152–62, 165, 167–69, 173–74, 179–80, 183–86, 244–47;* administrative boundaries of *2–3, 10, 12, 211;* economy of *8–9;* geography of *2–3, 10–12, 212;* recusancy in *9, 11;* sheriff of *217, 230*
Chesphord, Hugh *199*
Chester, bishop of *215*
Chester Castle *89, 111–12, 117–18*
Chester, churches at *55*
    Cathedral (formerly St. Werburgh's Abbey) *1, 23, 26, 55–61, 74, 83–84, 114, 129, 170, 174, 195–96, 201, 214, 218–19;* Palm Sunday celebrations at *56, 218–19*
    St. Bridget's *23*
    St. John's *55, 56, 72, 78, 123, 218*
    St. Mary's *56*

St. Michael's *59*

St. Peter's *55–56, 65, 176*

St. Werburgh's Abbey *1, 3, 5, 55, 114, 122, 174, 218, 229*

Chester, city of *6–12, 23, 48–50, 54–78, 81, 83–87, 91–94, 96–97, 100, 105–08, 114–15, 121–27, 137, 140, 144, 146–48, 155–59, 161, 166–71, 173–78, 180–83, 186–87, 195–209, 230, 242–43, 245–46;* Christmas Watch at *56, 183;* constable of *18, 71;* Entry of Lord Deputy to *65;* mayor of *55–56, 63, 66, 106, 122, 177, 180, 186, 229–31;* Midsummer Fair at *25, 71, 121–23;* Midsummer Show at *25, 56, 64, 71–72, 74, 121, 165–66, 170, 177, 183;* Midsummer Watch at *25, 125–26;* St. George's Day Races at *56, 62, 64–65;* Shrovetide ceremonies at *25, 56, 64, 66, 168, 183;* Whitsun plays at *56, 58–61, 74–75, 77, 165, 170–71, 174, 183, 231*

Chester, deanery of *211*

Chester, diocese of *12, 211, 216, 238, 246–47*

Chester, drummer *29, 199*

Chester, Earl of *18–19, 54–55, 71, 122–23*

Chester, Thomas *85, 94*

Cheswood, John, Jr., piper *199*

Cholmondeley *23, 100, 209*

Cholmondeley, family of *100*

Chorlton, Lancs. *210*

Christleton *197, 242*

Christopher, waitman *199*

Church, attendance at *32–33, 38, 116, 175;* disruption in *89, 184;* music of the *55–61, 174–75, 184;* performance in or near *25, 36–38, 52, 72, 171, 176–77, 184*

Church Lawton *33, 200*

Church, Percy *141*

Churchyard *25, 37, 165*

Citole *150*

Cittern *2, 102, 104, 133, 137, 142, 146, 148–53, 155, 157, 161, 181, 184, 230;* great cittern *138–39, 146, 150, 153*

Clare, Robert, stonemason *114–15*

Clarke, Edward, of the Isle of Ely, musician *26, 85, 107, 199*

Clerke, Mrs. *141*

Clotton Hoofield *207*

Clowghe, William, yeoman *84*

Clutton, Henry, of Malpas, minstrel *19, 83, 199*

Coddington *137, 173*

Coddington, Richard *52*

Coller, Mr., parson of Swettenham *89*

Collier, of Alvanley *95*

Colne, Lancs. *210*

Cona, John, piper *199, 243*

Conason, John, of Chester, piper *108, 199, 243*

Concord, Henry, of Chester, musician *86, 199*

Congleton *11, 26–27, 82, 91–92, 99, 170, 175, 177–78, 197–99, 202, 207–08*

Congleton Edge *11*

Conpares, Ralph *73*

Consorts *68, 73, 96–99, 102–03, 105, 133, 135, 148–49, 151, 154–57, 167–68, 181–82*

Cook, John, minstrel *199, 243*

Cook, John, piper *98, 182, 199, 243*

Cook, Peter, minstrel *98, 182, 199*

Cooper, John, of Chester *78, 222*

Coppock, John, of Chester, gentleman *78, 136, 150*

Cornetts *64, 161, 166–70, 181, 191*

Cornish, William *76*

Corry, Edward *220*

Cotton, George, musician *199*

Coventry, Warks. *65, 92*

Coventry and Lichfield, diocese of *3, 12, 246*

Cowper, Thomas, and his company, of Whitchurch, Shrops., fiddlers *77–78, 86, 98, 199*

Cowper, William, son of Richard le Cowper, of Tarporley, shoemaker *108*

Craddock, Elizabeth *73*

Crane, Randle, minstrel *97, 199, 222, 243*

Crewe *155*

Crewe, John, of Chester, yeoman, alias singingman *114, 199*

Crime *31, 41, 44, 50, 72, 81, 83–85, 88–89, 92–93, 107–17, 127, 152, 184, 217*

Croaker, Thomas, of Knutsford, sadler (cittern player) *151–52, 199*

Crokeley Bredbury *173*

Crosby, John, high constable of Bucklow Hundred *170–71*

Cross, Peter, of Wilmslow, bachelor *178–79, 241*

Cross, Richard, minstrel *200, 243*

Cross, Richard, of Over, piper *98, 200*

Croxton *142, 148, 200*

Croxton, John de, harper *148, 200*

Croxton, Roger de, harper *148, 200*

Croxton, Roger de, of Middlewich, harper and gleeman *108, 148, 200, 227*

Croxton, Thomas, son of Roger de Croxton *148*

Crumhorns *167*

Cuddington 108

Cumberland 3, 8

Cumberland, Earl of *158*

Curtal *167, 169;* Double *64, 161, 167, 169, 181, 191*

Cutler, Sir Thomas, of Stainborough, Yorks. *230*

Cymbals *179*

Dale, Thomas *90–91, 113*

Dancing *7, 20, 22, 24–25, 27–35, 38, 40–42, 45–46, 50–53, 56, 69–70, 73, 77, 79–80, 87–88, 93, 95, 98, 107, 117, 125, 131, 140–41, 165–67, 171, 177–78, 181, 183–84, 218, 244, 246;* hornpipe at Christmas *140*

Dancing school *140, 181*

Danvers, Sir Charles *138–39, 183, 232*

Danvers, Dame Elizabeth, widow of Sir John Danvers *138–39*

Danvers, Henry *139*

Danvers, Sir John *138–39, 232, 235*

Darley *28*

Darnhall *51, 196–97, 218*

Davenham *203*

Davenport, Henry *109*

Day, Dr., provost of Eaton college *176*

Dayne, Thomas *48, 111–12*

Deane, John, of Nantwich *192*

Declaration for Sports; see *Book of Sports*

Dee, river at Chester *10–11, 54–55*

Dee Bridge *55*

Dekker, Thomas, *Guls Hornebooke 133, 230*

Derby, Derbs. *72, 85, 247*

Derby, Earl of, Chamberlain of Chester *26–27, 67, 70–72, 114, 125, 129–30, 170, 214;* trumpeter of *170*

Derby, Earl of, William *154*

Derbyshire *11, 85*

Descant *57–58*

Disorder *32, 34, 37, 40–41, 43, 45, 49, 51–53, 68, 70, 77–79, 89–90, 99–100, 108, 116–18, 165, 171*

Dod, Richard, of Harthill, aleseller,

and constable of Harthill *42, 43*

Dodleston *81, 97, 202*

Domville, Gilbert, of Lymme *230*

Done, Richard, bell-ringer *176, 200*

Dorington, parson of St. Peter's, Chester *176*

Dorse, John, of the Isle of Man, music student *57–58, 200*

Downes, Geoffrey *40, 177*

Downes, Robert *40*

Downholland *210*

Dowse, Henry, piper *33–34, 200*

Drake, Robert, piper *200*

Drum *28–29, 62, 145, 166, 168, 175, 177–79, 245*

Drummers *19, 29, 62, 72, 101, 166, 177–79, 184, 197, 199, 201–03, 206–08, 210, 238, 240, 245*

Drumming *28–29, 41, 62, 99, 101, 177–79, 240, 245*

Drunkenness *29, 38, 44–45, 48–49, 81, 110, 117, 171, 213*

Dublin *10, 58;* Christ Church Cathedral at *219*

Duckworth's wife *118*

Due, Richard *50*

Duke, Thomas *114*

Dulcian *169*

Dutton Hall *123*

Dutton, of Dutton, family of *55, 183;* herald of *62;* licensing of minstrels *9–10, 17–19, 46, 56, 70–72, 91, 119, 121–28, 183–85;* Minstrels' Court *10, 56, 62, 71–73, 78, 83, 85–86, 119–28, 221;* patronage of minstrels as liveried servants *125–26;* servants in affray with other musicians *74, 125–26*

Dutton, Anne, wife of Christopher Holford *229*

Dutton, Hugh *229*

Dutton, Jane, widow of Hugh Dutton, subsequently married Thomas Holford *229*

Dutton, John, of Dutton *67, 120–21, 124–25, 131, 181, 229*

Dutton, Laurence, of Dutton *122, 229*

Dutton, Peter *229*

Dutton, Sir Piers *73, 123, 229*

Dutton, Ralf *19, 71*

Dutton, Thomas, of Dutton (14th century) *122*

Dutton, Thomas, of Dutton (17th century) *46, 124, 217*

Dutton, of Hatton, Mr. *46, 116, 125*

Dutton, of Hatton, Peter *229*

Dutton, of Hatton, Sir Piers *122*

Dutton, of Hatton, Rowland *170, 179, 239, 241*

Dutton, Thomas, servant to Robert Clare, stonemason *114*

Eaton *173*

Eaton [?Eton] College *176*

Eaton, Robert, rector of Mobberley *36–37, 165, 216*

Eccleston *202*

Eddisbury Hundred *12, 243;* high constable of *163*

Edge, Robert, Jr., piper *200*

Edward, Prince of Wales (the Black Prince) *17, 87, 108, 119, 147*

Edward IV *121*

Egerton *79–80, 204*

Egerton, John, of Oulton *27–29, 214–15*

Elell, Lancs. *210*

Elizabeth I *29, 101, 178, 180–81*

Elizabethan Poor Laws *3*

Ellam, Thomas *60*

Ellesmere *10*

Englefield, Francis *232*

Englefield, John, esquire *232*

Englefield, Margaret *232*

Ensong (?Evensong), Richard, of Frodsham, fiddler *163, 200, 245*

Essex, Earl of *139, 175, 183*
Eton College *100*
Evans, of Flintshire *34*
Evans, Mr., singer in the choir at
    Chester Cathedral *23, 200,
    214*
Evensong, *see* Richardson, Richard,
    alias Williamson, alias Even-
    song
Everton, John, of Chester, musician
    200

*Faithfull Remonstrance, A (Life of
    John Bruen)* 7, 30–32, 46, 215
Fallowes, William, of Fallowes *109*
Fargery, Derbyshire *85*
Farrar, John (musician) *69–70, 107,
    200*
Feilding, Lord, brother of *141*
Fencers *42*
Fencing school *140, 171*
Fiddle *98, 143, 145–46, 156, 159–
    61, 184*
Fiddler, <...>tium, of Godley (?fidd-
    ler) *200*
Fiddlers *17, 19, 24, 32–34, 45, 53,
    71–73, 77–78, 81–83, 86,
    93–94, 97–98, 100–01, 103–
    05, 123, 143–45, 160, 163,
    171, 182, 184, 186, 195–96,
    198–202, 204–06, 209, 237,
    242, 244–45*
Fiddling *34–35, 40, 42, 45, 83, 97–
    98, 163*
Fidler, Thomas, minstrel *17, 20,
    109, 200, 213, 243*
Fighting *51, 89, 117*
*First Part of the Return from Par-
    nassus* 94, 224
Fisher, Thomas, musician *69, 200*
Fisher, Thomas, of Rowton *45*
Fitton, Charles, of Chester, alder-
    man *239*
Fitton, Edmund *138–39*

Fitton family, of Gawsworth *183*
Fitton, Francis, of Gawsworth *136,
    138–40, 153, 157, 167, 232,
    235*
Fitton, William *138–39*
Fletcher, John, curate of Siddington
    *47–48, 89–90, 110–11, 126–
    27*
Fletcher, Margaret, wife of John
    Fletcher *110*
Fletcher, Mr., of Chester, draper *63*
Flintshire *3, 10, 66, 88, 99*
Flookers Brook Bridge *123*
Flute *74, 102, 149, 155–56, 161–
    62, 165–68*
Foden, William, of Lower Withing-
    ton *90*
Foster, Thomas, alias Huntsman,
    piper *95, 163–64, 200, 243*
Foulk Stapleford *87, 119, 208*
Foxall *48–49, 87*
France *54, 140*
Frenway, Henry, harper *73, 200*
Friars, orders of *174*
Frodsham *47, 51, 82, 144, 162–63,
    200, 203, 206, 218, 243, 245*
Frodsham, deanery of *211*
Fydo, singingman *201*
Fysher, Robert le, of Nantwich *108*

Gambling *32, 47, 50–51, 182*
Games, unlawful *35, 42*
Gamesters *32*
Gamul, William, mayor of Chester
    66–67
Garratt, John, musician *201*
Gawsworth *12, 136, 197*
Gee, Henry, mayor of Chester *63*
Genoa *142*
Genson, John, precentor of Chester
    Cathedral *60–61, 201*
Gentry *1–2, 6–9, 20, 25–27, 30,
    56, 67, 70, 78, 92, 94–95, 99,
    104–05, 119–20, 124, 126,
    128–42, 145, 147–48, 151–*

52, 156, 159, 167, 170, 172, 180, 183–84

Gest, *see* Guest, Roger

Gibbon, John *179*

Gibson, William *109*

Gill, Anne *226*

Gill, Hugh *226*

Gill, James (musician) *124, 201*

Gill, Margaret *101, 226*

Gill, Marie *101, 226*

Gill, Richard *226*

Gill, Zachary, of Nantwich, musician *101–03, 201, 212, 226*

Gittern *142, 146, 148, 153–54, 183*

Glaseor, William, of Chester *78, 222*

Gleeman 147–48, 200

Gloria, sung in Whitsun plays *59, 61, 76*

Godley *200*

Good Gossipes Songe, sung in Whitsun plays *77*

Goodman, Christopher, puritan cleric *70–71, 76*

Goodman, young Rafe *222*

Goodman, alias Goodale, William, virginal-maker *180, 201, 243*

Goosenargh, Lancs. *210*

Graddell, William, piper *210*

Grappenhall *37*

Great Boughton *40*

Great Budworth *195, 202, 206, 242, 246*

Green, John, piper *210*

Greene, Mr., of Congleton *92*

Greens *25, 53, 80, 95, 105, 140, 184*

Griffith, Old (possibly a musician) *201*

Grosvenor, Sir Richard *140*

Guest, Roger (Gest), drummer of city of Chester *62, 201*

Guilden Sutton *201, 243*

Guilds *1, 6, 13, 18, 20, 22, 25, 27, 50, 55, 60, 62, 73, 93–94,* 125–26, *144, 170, 176–77, 183, 246*

Barber Surgeons *240*

Beerbrewers *68*

Butchers *240*

Coopers *66, 73, 227*

Drapers *75*

Glovers *240*

Haberdashers, of London *52*

Innkeepers *175–76, 238*

Joiners *25, 72*

Mercers/Merchants *75, 177*

Painters (Painters, Glaziers, Embroiderers and Stationers) *25, 59, 61–62, 75–77, 92, 180, 213, 218, 238*

Shoemakers (Cordwainers and Shoemakers) *25, 65, 67–68, 71, 73, 123, 148, 168, 213, 240*

Smiths *60–61, 65, 74–75, 97, 148, 165, 174, 240, 243*

Tallowchandlers *125*

Tanners *240*

Walkers *62*

Waterleaders and Drawers in Dee *59*

Wrights *59*

Guitar, renaissance *153*

Gwynne, Robert, Mr., bell-ringer *176, 201*

Gyster, Robert, minstrel *20, 201, 213*

Hale, John, of Stretton, piper *114, 201, 245*

Hale, Thomas, of Ince *51, 117*

Halewood, Henry, Liverpool wait *247*

Hallwood, Henry, piper *210, 247*

Halsall, Lancs. *209–10*

Halton *115*

Halton, Barons of *123*

Hamestan, ancient district of *12*

Hammeson, John, harper *201*

Hampson, Richard *166*

Handbridge, suburb of Chester *15, 70, 202*

Handley *217*

Handy, Mr., teacher of music *105, 136, 140, 201, 214*

Handy, William *136, 155*

Hardinge, Bennet *28, 215*

Hardinge, Thomas *41, 177*

Hardware, Henry, mayor of Chester *231*

Hardware, Henry, of Peel and Bromborough *136, 155, 231, 235*

Harp *145–48, 228, 233;* harpstrings *73;* Irish harp *78, 146–47;* Sutton Hoo harp *147, 234*

Harper, cousin to John Leche of Carden *137, 173*

Harper, John, hooper *73*

Harpers *17, 19, 72–73, 97, 101, 108, 119, 144–48, 152, 182, 184, 196–98, 200–03, 206, 208–09, 227, 228, 231, 233*

Harping *17, 41*

Harpsichord *172–74*

Harrison, John, of "Saughton" (Great or Little Sutton) fiddler, and his boy *34–35, 97, 201*

Harrison, Thomas *187, 191*

Harrison, Thomas, piper *210*

Harrison, William, piper *165, 210*

Harthill *42–43, 79–80, 204*

Hartleys, William, piper *201*

Hassall, Hamon *229*

Haswall, John, luter *148, 201*

Hattersley *217*

Hatton *45, 116, 179, 200, 243*

Hawkes, Matthew, of Nantwich *226*

Hawking *51*

Hearne, William, singing man *201*

Helen, William *77*

Hendalle (?Henhull) *192*

Henrietta Maria, wife of Charles I *141*

Henry VI *121*

Henry VII *54, 133*

Henry VIII *156*

Henshagh, John, minstrel *201*

Henshagh, Richard, minstrel *201*

Henshall, Hugh, of Bredbury, minstrel *201*

Heralds *62*

Hesketh, William, of Aston (piper) *97, 202, 243*

Heswall *205, 209*

Hey, Richard, horner *73, 171, 202*

Heyes, Richard, of Nantwich, gentleman *104, 226*

Heyhurst, John, piper *210*

Heyward, John, piper *202*

Heywood, John, of Lostock Gralam, minstrel *98, 182, 202*

Hicock, William, Mr., clerk *49, 78, 159–60*

Higher Whitley (Over Whitley) *87, 244*

Hill, John, harper *202*

Hinde, William, vicar of Bunbury *7, 30, 32, 46, 156, 215*

Hoboys *64, 161, 166–67*

Hoby, Sir Thomas *231*

Hodgkinson, Adam, constable of Lostock Gralam *116*

Holborne, Anthony, *The Cittharen Schoole 151*

Holford, Christopher *229*

Holford, Thomas, grandfather of John Bruen *229*

Holland, Richard, of Little Neston, miller *34*

Holme, Christopher, of Chester, painter *106*

Holmes, Alderman, of Chester *25, 218*

Holmes, Matthew *167, 238*

Holywell, pilgrimage to *34, 97*

Hopkin, Morgan, piper *202, 243*

Hopkins, John *59*

Hopton, Morgan, piper *97, 202, 243*

Horn *38, 76, 117, 134, 140, 161,*
    171–72, 244
Horner *17, 73, 202*
Hornpipe, danced at Christmas *140*
Horsebaiting *47*
Houfield, Randle *117–18*
Hough, Ann *67*
Hough, Thomas *117–18*
Hough, Thomas, of Chester, wait-
    man *67, 202*
Houlme, William *170–71*
Hudson, Christopher, of Preston
    41, 217
Hughes, Anne, wife of Richard *51*
Hughes, Henry, sub-sub-sexton of
    St. Bridget's, Chester *23*
Hugh Lupus, 2nd Earl of Chester *55*
Hulleboy, Robert, piper *202*
Hunt, Richard, of Cheadle, minstrel
    202
Hunting *51*
Huntsman, piper *see* Foster,
    Thomas, *alias* Huntsman
Huntsman, Raph *82*

Ince *51, 117, 202, 211, 216*
Ince, Peter *62, 220*
Ince, Rondull *61*
Inns *29, 39–40, 49, 72, 104, 217*
Inns of Court *139–40*
Instrument makers *61, 64, 179–81,*
    196, 204–05, 207–08, 243
Interludes *35, 62, 71*
Ireland *10, 54, 101, 147, 164, 178;*
    musicians from *83, 245*
Irish, John, piper *202, 243*
Irish Sea *10–11, 54*
Iscoyd *88, 206*
Italy *141*

Jackson, John, of Elell, Lancs., piper
    210
Jackson, John, of Ince, piper *202,*
    216
Jackson, John, of Newton, piper
    202

Jackson, Richard *131*
Jackson, Richard, piper *73, 202,*
    244
Jackson, Richard, of Lancashire,
    piper *210, 244*
Jackson, Roger, drummer *202*
James I *35, 38, 46, 125, 139, 215*
Janion, Joan *171*
Jenion's wife *85*
Jennings, Richard *193*
Jervace, piper *202*
Jewett, Robert, of Dublin, organist
    58, 202
Joett, William, singing man *202*
John, king of England *122*
Johnson, David, pardoner *73*
Jones, David, of Chester, fiddler,
    and his fellow *81, 97, 202*
Jones, Thomas, of Chester, bachelor
    of music *23, 202, 214, 222*
Jones, Thomas, of Chester, inn-
    keeper *78, 161, 237*
Joneson, Laurence, alehousekeeper
    179
Jonson, Edward, of Handbridge,
    suburb of Chester, musician
    15, 70, 185, 202
Jonson, Mr., alleged father of Alice
    Ash *95*
Jonson, Thomas *61*
Jugglers *15, 42, 44*

Kellsall, William *179*
Kelly, *see* Cally
Kemp, Thomas, of Chester, smith
    65
Kemp, William, *Nine Daies Wonder*
    237
Kendericke, of Chester, alderman
    72
Kent, William, musician *203*
Kersleye, John, alias Clubfoot, of
    Malpas, piper *99, 203*
Kettle, Thomas (musician) *203, 244*

Kinderton, baron of *97*
Kirkham, Lancs. *210*
Kit *78, 146, 155–56, 161*
Knutsford *90, 151–52, 199;* Nether
 Knutsford *170–71, 196;* Over
 Knutsford *35, 195*

Lacy, Roger, surnamed Hell, con-
 stable of Chester *18–19, 71,*
 123
Laithwood, Robert, of Runcorn,
 piper *95, 162–64, 203, 237,*
 243–45
Lancashire *3, 8, 10, 12, 27, 35, 65,*
 67, 70, 87, 92, 107, 125, 136,
 150, 165, 182, 238, 242, 244,
 247
Lancaster *54*
Laseby, Richard, of Audlem, piper
 203
Lathom, Lancs., seat of the Earl of
 Derby *67, 114, 242*
Lawes, Henry, musician and com-
 poser *23, 26, 128–29, 183,*
 203, 214, 229–30
Lawrenson, Thomas, musician *203*
Layton, Mary, wife of William
 Layton *33*
Lea, Thomas *176*
Leaping and vaulting, as sabbath
 activities *35, 38*
Leche family, of Carden *137–38,*
 151, 173, 204, 232
Leche, Alice, wife of John Leche of
 Carden *137–38, 173*
Leche, John, of Carden *137–38,*
 173, 232
Leevesley, Alice *67*
Leftwich *206, 244*
Legh, Mr., of Baguley *26*
Legh family, of Lyme *23, 26, 119,*
 128, 183, 203, 205
Legh, Sir Peter, of Lyme (Lord of
 Lyme 1590–1636) *26, 119,*
 128–29, 154; piper of *26, 119*

Legh, Sir Peter, of Lyme the
 Younger *157, 236*
Legh, Sir Piers, of Lyme (Lord of
 Lyme 1541–90), musicians of
 27, 92, 119
Le Roy, Adrian *151, 154*
Lether, Roger, of Nantwich, drum-
 mer *101, 178, 203*
Leveson, Sir Richard *138*
Leycester, Sir Peter, antiquarian
 72–73, 122–23
Lichfield, Bishop of *55*
Lichfield, diocese of *12*
Lincoln's Inn *140*
Linge, Antilie, of Middlewich *117*
Little Budworth *27–29, 80, 199,*
 208, 211, 246
Little Neston *34, 201*
Littleton *85, 113–14, 197, 242*
Liverpool, Lancs. *247*
Lloyd, Humphrey, singer *100, 203*
Lloyd, John, of Malpas, organ
 drawer *100, 180, 203*
Locker, Thomas *65*
Lockett, Edward, of Siddington,
 constable *111–12*
Lockett, Jane, wife of Edward
 Lockett of Siddington *111*
Lockett, Katherine *109–11*
London *10, 52, 56, 112, 128–29,*
 131, 154, 174, 180, 230
Lostock Gralam *33, 98, 116, 195,*
 202, 242
Lowe, Thomas *187, 191*
Lowther, Christopher *231*
Lowther, Margaret, of London *131–*
 32, 168, 184, 230
Lowther, Robert, of London *131–*
 32, 230–31
Ludlow Castle *128*
Ludlow, Shrops. *65, 92*
Lute *78, 102, 104, 131–33, 135–*
 36, 138–39, 145–51, 153–57,
 170, 173, 180–81, 183–84,
 231, 235–36; bass lute *147;*
 mean lute *150, 234;* treble lute
 150

Lutenist *26, 129, 205*
Luter *17, 148, 201, 203*
Luter, William, minstrel *97, 148, 203*
Luting books *78, 136, 150, 154, 231*
Lyme Hall *23, 27, 128, 157, 170, 228*

Macclesfield *109*
Macclesfield, deanery of *211*
Macclesfield Forest *202*
Macclesfield Hundred *12*
Mace, Thomas, *Musick's Monument 132, 230*
Macebearer, of Chester *61–62*
Madley, Thomas de *108*
Maddocks, Thomas *142*
Madock/Maddock, William, of Chester, waitman *64, 67–68, 96, 103, 105–06, 140, 157–58, 167, 169, 181, 185, 187–91, 203, 220, 225, 232, 236, 241, 244*
Madock/Maddock, William, Jr., of Chester, waitman *67–68, 203, 244*
Mainwaring, Charles, of Croxton *142*
Mainwaring, Henry *26, 99*
Mainwaring, Sir Randle *26, 99*
Malbone, James *220*
Malpas *3, 30, 41, 82–83, 88, 99–100, 108, 180, 198–99, 202–06, 209, 217, 244*
Malpas, deanery of *211*
Man, Isle of *57–58*
Man, Jane, wife of William Man, M.A. *50*
Manchester, Lancs. *54, 86, 118, 166, 177, 207, 210*
Manning, Thomas *52*
Manslaughter *44, 50*
Manx women dancing *77*
Marple *93*
Marsden, Lancs. *210*

Marshall, John, harper *203*
Marshall, William, minstrel *73, 203*
Marthall *82, 197*
Maskers *22, 24*
Mason, Thomas, yeoman, alias singingman *180, 203*
Massey, Anne, of Coddington *137, 173, 232*
Massey, Richard, of Coddington *137, 232*
Massie, George *38, 203, 244*
Massy, John *229*
Matacks *131*
Matley *207*
Maygames *28, 35, 38, 51–52*
Maypoles *27, 33, 35, 38, 51–52, 185*
Meaneley, Hugh, piper *203*
Mercer, William, of Chester, waitman *204*
Mersey, river *10–11*
Metier, John, of Biddulph, Staffs., piper *90–91, 113–14, 127, 204, 244*
Metier, Richard, piper *8, 40, 47–48, 83, 88–91, 93, 109–13, 117, 125–27, 144, 184–85, 204, 244*
Middleton, Ralph *82*
Middlewich *11, 95, 108, 117, 148, 199–200, 204–05, 208, 227*
Middlewich, deanery of *211*
Midland Gap *11*
Midlands *10–11*
Migrancy *81, 87–88*
Miller, James, vicar of St. Michael's, Chester, and precentor of Chester cathedral *59, 76–77, 135, 231*
Millington, Thomas *114*
Milton's *Comus 26, 128*
Minshall, Ralph *176*
Minshull, Edward, of Nantwich, esquire *226*
Minshull, Margery *84*
Minshull, Richard *104*
Minshull, Richard, of Nantwich,

fiddler *83–84, 103–04, 204,*
244
Minshull, Richard, of Nantwich,
gentleman *104, 136, 227, 236*
Minshull, Richard, of Nantwich,
musician *83, 103–04, 204,*
244
Minshull Vernon *197*
Minstrels *1–9, 14–27, 29, 31, 36,*
42–44, 53, 56, 62, 65, 70–75,
79–87, 92–93, 95, 97, 99,
105, 107–09, 113–15, 118–
29, 134–35, 143–44, 147–48,
165, 172, 182–85, 196–210,
213–14, 222, 227, 233, 242–
43, 245; as lawbreakers *107–*
17; economic situation of *2,*
8–9, 53, 85, 92–97, 106, 127;
licences of *42, 46, 78, 82, 93,*
113
Mobberley *36–38, 165, 196, 211*
Monning, Robert, of Tattenhall *122*
Moores, William, vintner *73, 84*
Moreton family, of Moreton *232*
Moreton, Peter *141–42, 184*
Moreton, Rondull, of Harthill,
tailor (piper) *79–80, 93, 184,*
204
Moreton, Urian, of Yeaton *239*
Moreton, William, of Moreton *142*
Morris dances *29, 35, 38, 165*
Mort, Roger *109*
Mouldsworth *197*
Mow Cop *11*
Much Harwood, Lancs. *210*
Mulliner Book 151
Mummers *22, 24*
Murgell, Roger, piper *164, 204*
Music books *59, 78, 96, 102–03,*
105, 135–36, 151, 154, 157–
58, 181, 192, 231
Music teachers *22, 24, 56–57, 69,*
103–07, 128, 131, 136, 140,
157, 159, 174, 196, 201
Musical instruments *8, 17, 64, 70,*
74, 78, 96, 102–05, 117–18,

123, 125–26, 130–39, 142–
82, 183–85, 235–36, 245;
gentry ownership of *27,*
130–42, 170, 180; groups of
96, 181–82; keyboard instruments *172–74, 180;* makers of
64, 179–81; percussion instruments *145, 175–79;* string
instruments *145–61, 168,*
181; wind instruments *136,*
145, 158, 161–172, 181
Musical taste, change in *19–20,*
120, 158, 184–85
Musicians *1–2, 8, 14–27, 29–31,*
33, 36, 38, 43, 48–49, 51, 53,
55–56, 58, 62–70, 72, 74–75,
78, 83–88, 91–103, 105–06,
118–20, 123–30, 133–36,
139, 143–44, 146, 148, 152,
155–60, 168, 170, 172, 174,
181–85, 195–209, 212, 219,
240, 242, 244–46; as lawbreakers *107–17;* inventories
of *95–96, 144, 158, 187–94*
Myles, Edmund, of Nantwich,
innkeeper *104, 226*
Myles, Edmund, of Nantwich, innkeeper (presumably son of
Edmund Myles, *see above*)
104, 192, 227
Myles, Elizabeth, of Nantwich,
widow of Edmund Myles (*see
above*) *104, 226*
Mylnes, Elizabeth *118*
Mynshall Lute Book 231

Nantwich *11, 15–16, 23, 81, 83–*
84, 96, 101–05, 108, 115,
136, 139, 148, 151, 155,
157– 58, 165, 174, 176–79,
181, 183, 191–93, 196–97,
201, 203–04, 206–09, 242,
245–46
Nantwich, deanery of *211*
Nantwich Hundred *12, 243*
Ness, constable of *34*

Nether Alderley *12*
Nether Peover *42, 51, 195, 242*
Neville, John, baron Latimer *232*
Newton *202, 243*
Newton by Chester *243*
Newton by Frodsham (Newton iuxta Kingesley) *109, 200*
Newton by Malpas *108*
Newton by Tattenhall *243*
Newton family, of Pownall Fee *204*
Newton, Francis, of Pownall Fee *179*
Newton, John, of Pownall Fee *179*
Noden, Thomas *192*
Nomenclature *7–9, 14–20*
Northgate jail, Chester *66*
Northgate Street, Chester *65*
Northmeols, Lancs. *210*
Northwich *87, 198, 204, 216, 244*
Northwich Hundred *12*
Norton *209, 246–47*
Nuball, Richard, Mr., of Chester, organist *23, 137, 173, 204, 214*
Nunc dimittis, sung in Smiths' play *61*
Nuremberg *174*

Oldcastle *108*
Organ drawer *100, 203*
Organistrum *160*
Organists *22–23, 57–58, 61, 100, 137, 173–74, 196, 202, 204– 05, 207–09, 219*
Organmaker *17, 61, 64, 204–05, 207*
Organs *56, 58, 136, 147, 172, 174– 76, 180, 219*
Ormskirk, Lancs. *210*
Orpharion (alferiall) *102, 104, 135, 145–46, 148, 154–57, 192*
Orrell, Henry *179*
Oswestry, Wales *87, 199*
Over *98, 199, 200, 243*
Overton *82, 162*
Over Whitley *see* Higher Whitley

Overwhitley, Robert de, of North- wich, minstrel *87, 108, 148, 204, 227, 244*
Oxford *142, 153–54, 216*

Paris *141*
Parish *3, 6–7, 9, 12, 15–16, 23, 30– 31, 33–34, 36–37, 42, 52, 80– 84, 88–91, 98–101, 108, 110, 115, 148, 162, 164–65, 176, 180, 211, 218, 242–44, 246*
Park, Thomas, piper *210*
Parkynston, Christopher, singer *204*
Patronage *7, 9, 23, 53, 56, 67–71, 73, 87, 91, 95, 97, 106, 113, 115, 119–20, 125–30, 139, 183, 185, 214*
Paynter, Richard, alias Organmaker *57, 180, 204*
Peacham, Henry, *The Compleat Gentleman* *130–31, 133, 230*
Peacock, fiddler *52, 100, 204, 244*
Peacock, piper *100, 204*
Peacock, Humphrey, piper *100, 165, 204, 237, 244*
Peacock, Humphrey, Sr., piper *100, 165, 204, 244*
Peacock, Jane, of Beeston *84*
Peacock, John, piper (*see also* Pea- cock, John, of Beeston, piper) *73, 84, 204*
Peacock, John, of Beeston, piper (*see also* Peacock, John, piper) *84, 204, 244*
Pearson, Robert, piper *205*
Peckforton *84*
Peel *136, 155*
Peerson, Martin, *Mottects, or Grave Chamber Musique* *147*
Pemburton, Edward, waitman *68– 69, 205*
Pembroke, Earl of *27, 170*
Penkett, Thomas *50, 95*

Pennines *10–11*

Pennington, Katherine, daughter of
  Sir Richard Shireburn of
  Stonyhurst, Lancs. *136, 150*

Pentice, The *55, 218;* Sheriffs'
  Procession to *69*

Perk, William *57–58*

Peycock, Thomas, organmaker *57,
  205*

Phagotus *169*

Pickering, Richard Barlow's man
  77, 205, 244

Pickering, Thomas, constable of
  Hatton *45, 116*

Phillipps, William, piper *205*

Piers, John, of Warrington (possibly
  a piper) *205, 244–46*

Pilgrimages *34, 40*

Pilkington, Francis, lutenist and
  composer *26, 58, 78, 129–30,
  154, 183, 205, 214, 230*

Pillin, John, of Chester, singingman
  205

Pillory Street, Nantwich *244*

Pipe and tabor *81, 103, 143, 145,
  161, 165–66, 177, 238, 246*

Piper, in livery of Legh family of
  Lyme *26, 119*

Piper, John, possibly a piper *210*

Piper, of Sir Thomas Smith *27*

Pipers *4, 6, 9, 15–17, 19, 22, 24,
  26–27, 32–33, 35–38, 40,
  42–43, 46–47, 50–53, 73–74,
  80–82, 84–85, 88, 90, 92–95,
  98–101, 105, 108–17, 124,
  126–27, 140, 143–44, 152,
  156, 162–67, 182, 184–86,
  195–97, 199–210, 212, 223,
  240, 242–46*

Pipes *2, 24, 36–37, 74, 76–77, 87,
  95, 127, 133, 143–45, 161–
  68, 184, 243–45*

Piping *4–5, 7, 10, 25, 31, 42, 45–
  47, 49, 79–80, 82, 84, 86–87,
  94, 97–98, 100, 112, 124,
  126, 144, 162–63, 165–66,*

  182–83, 185, 237, 242–46

Plague, fears of *32, 42–43, 56*

Plainsong *56–58*

Plante, Edward, constable of
  Siddington *48*

Platt, minstrel *205*

Platt, Richard, of Tattenhall, piper/
  minstrel *45–46, 124, 185, 205*

Players *19–20, 22, 24, 32, 42, 62,
  71, 79, 81, 93, 99, 118, 123*

Playing *20, 25, 27, 33–34, 36–38,
  46, 51, 81, 83–84, 87–88,
  91–94, 96, 98, 101–04, 115–
  16, 122–25, 130–35, 137–38,
  142–46, 148–57, 159–71,
  174, 177–78, 181–82, 230,
  236, 240, 245–46*

Plays (*see also* Whitsun Plays) *11,
  24, 56, 58–62, 71, 74–77,
  91–92, 99, 165, 168, 174,
  183, 219–20, 231*

Plesyngton, John *228*

Plymley, James, son of William
  Plymley *85, 94*

Plymley, William, piper *85, 94–95,
  205*

Pole, Thomas *229*

Poole, Mr. *60*

Potinger (?of Ireland), scholar and
  musician *83, 205, 245*

Pott Shrigley *40, 177*

Pownall Fee *179*

Poynton *164, 204*

Praetorius, Michael *151, 153, 172*

Prestbury *3, 12, 88–91, 110*

Preston, trumpeter *92, 205*

Preston family of Warrington,
  musicians *92, 97*

Preston, Elias, son of James *106*

Preston, James, of Warrington,
  musician *92, 106, 205*

Preston, John, of Warrington,
  musician *92, 205*

Preston, Richard, of Warrington,
  musician *19, 48–49, 78, 87,
  92, 159–60, 181–82, 205*

Pricksong *22, 56–58, 133, 135*
Professionalism *1, 9, 15–17, 20–24, 49, 66, 68, 73–74, 78, 85–86, 95, 104–06, 118, 124, 139, 144, 148, 155–59, 168, 174, 244*
Pryke, William, organplayer *57, 205*
Prymett, Richard, bell-ringer *176, 205*
Prynne, Mr. *77*
Puddington *34*
Pudgeon, Thomas, *alias* Thomas de <...>ley, minstrel *109, 205*
Pulford, William, of Littleton *113*
Puritanism *2, 5–6, 8, 18, 27, 29– 33, 35–39, 50, 70, 86, 99, 107, 110–11, 115, 124–25, 131, 216, 231*
Pyper, David le, of Malpas, piper *99, 108, 205*
Pyper, Thomas, "the half-faced piper" *210*

Quarrelling *41, 44, 47, 67, 89, 96, 114, 117, 126, 170*
Queen's Men *176*

Raby *34*
Rebec *98, 160*
Recognizance *15, 18, 86, 90, 112, 116–17, 124, 143, 164, 212, 243*
Recorders *64, 102, 133–34, 138– 39, 149, 161–62, 166–69, 181;* bass recorder *169*
Recusancy *9, 29–36, 40, 51, 185*
Redrowe, Margery *115*
Regals *61, 75, 172, 174*
Renshaw, Thomas, of Hatton *45, 116*
Revelers *22, 24, 123*
Reveling *51*
Reynold, James, fiddler *72, 205*
Rhuddlan Castle, Wales *18, 71*
Rhymes *29, 117–18*
Ribchester, Lancs. *182*

Richard I *122–23*
Richardson, Richard, alias William- son, alias Evensong, of Frods- ham *47, 82, 162–63, 206, 243, 245*
Richmond, deanery of *3*
Ripley, Simon, abbot of St. Wer- burgh's *174*
Robinson, James, musician *25, 206*
Robinson, John, possibly a drummer *179, 206, 245*
Robinson, Thomas, *New Citharen Lessons 151*
Rocksavage, seat of the Savage family *67, 162*
Rogers, David, antiquarian *58*
Roper, Thomas, minstrel *73, 206*
Rose, John, of London *154*
Rostherne *33, 88, 98, 115, 195, 199*
Rowbotham, James, *An Instruction to the Gitterne 154*
Rowland, John, of Peckforton *84*
Rowland, Mr. *140*
Rowley, Agnes, of Chester, musi- cian *15, 86, 206, 212*
Rowley, John, of Chester, tinker *15, 86*
Rowton *44–45*
Runcorn *67, 162, 203*
Rushbearings *25, 53, 99, 177–78, 240*
Rushen Abbey, Isle of Man *57–58*
Russhall, John, musician *206*
Rutland, Earl of *158*
Rutter, Jasper, of Nantwich, gentle- man *226*
Ryder, William, piper *206*

Sabbatarianism *5, 29–32, 38, 72, 107, 124–25, 185*
Sabbath infringements *4–5, 7, 20, 25, 27, 32–39, 41–42, 45–46, 51, 72, 79–83, 86, 92, 95, 97– 98, 101, 103–04, 107, 112, 116–17, 124–25, 127,*

144, 162–66, 177–78, 182–85, 245

Sabbath sports *32–39, 125*

Sackbut *64, 161, 167–69, 181, 190*

St. Werburgh's Abbey *see* Chester, churches at

St. Werburgh Lane, Chester *48, 159*

Salber, John, harper *206*

Salesbury, Lancs. *210, 247*

Salte, Elizabeth, alias Bouncing Bess *28*

Sare, John *176*

Saunders, William, Captain *95, 163–64*

Savage, of Clifton and Rocksavage, family of *55, 67, 95, 125*

Savage, Arthur, *alias* Buckley, of Wincle, piper *206*

Savage, Edward *136, 231*

Savage, Grace, wife of Sir Richard Wilbraham *163*

Savage, John *163*

Savage, John, of Bunbury, minstrel *108, 206*

Savage, Sir John, of Rocksavage *26, 67–68, 125, 231*

Savage, Sir Thomas *95, 162–64*

Save me, O God, sung in Water-leaders' play *59*

Scarisbrock (*also* Skersbroke), Henry *187, 191, 241*

Scop 147

Scotland *54, 164*

Seaer, Francis, of Lower Wich in Iscoyd (Flintshire), piper *88, 100, 206*

Sedition, fears of *32, 34–35, 38, 42, 185*

Sefton, Lancs. *209*

Seton, John, Jr., of Chester, fiddler *72, 206*

Sexton, Mr. *140*

Seyvell, Randle (of Nantwich), piper *206*

Shaw, Mark, fiddler *206*

Shawcrosse, Humphrey *113*

Shawm *162, 164, 166–69, 181;* bass shawm *169*

Sheale, Richard, harper *231*

Shepley, James, piper *206*

Shermon, John le, of Shocklach *108*

Shireburn, Sir Richard, of Stony-hurst, Lancs. *136, 150*

Shireburn, Richard, son of Sir Richard Shireburn, of Stony-hurst, Lancs. *136*

Shireburn, Richard, grandson of Sir Richard Shireburn, of Stony-hurst, Lancs. *136*

Shocklach *108*

Shore, Thomas *192*

Shotwick *34, 38, 117, 171, 203*

Shrewsbury *92*

Shurlock, Henry, minstrel/piper *73, 206, 243, 245*

Shuttleworth, Sir Richard, of Smithills, Lancs. *27, 65, 92*

Siddall, William (Lame Siddall), possibly a minstrel *177, 206, 245*

Siddington *47, 89, 91, 110–12, 204, 206*

Singers *17, 21–23, 26, 51, 56–61, 74, 77–78, 83–84, 100, 114–15, 117, 197, 199–205, 214*

Singing *17, 21, 29, 56–61, 74–78, 118, 130–31, 133, 148, 157, 167–68, 182*

Skersbroke, Henry *see* Scarisbrock, Henry

Skinner, Thomas, of Chester, musician *206*

Slander *89, 117–18*

Smith family, of Hough *205*

Smith, John, of Clotton Hoofield, piper *207*

Smith, Sir Thomas, of Hough *26, 129–30, 205, 230;* piper of *27*

Smith, William, *Description of Cheshire 213, 218*

Smithe, James, constable *46, 116*

Smithills, Lancs., home of Shuttleworth family *27, 65, 92*

Smyth, Thomas, organmaker *57, 207*

Somerford, John, of Somerford *132, 142, 153, 230*

Somerford, Mary, of Somerford *132–33, 149–51, 155, 173, 181, 184, 230*

Songs *29, 59–61, 75–78, 86, 98, 117–18, 130, 135*

Sotheworth, John *229*

Spain *54, 138*

Spanish Armada, defeat of, subject for song *72, 77, 98, 182*

Spencer, John, drummer *41, 177, 207, 245*

Spinet *172–73*

Squier, Thomas, cornett-player *69–70, 107, 207*

Staffordshire *10, 90, 113, 127*

Stainborough, Yorks. *230*

Standish, Lancs. *86, 207*

Stanley, family of (Earls of Derby) *130, 133*

Stanley, Sir Edward *133–34, 167, 174*

Stanley, Thomas (*ob.* 1570), bishop of Sodor and Man *231*

Stanley, William *118*

Stanley Poem, The 133–34, 167, 174

Stanne, Margaret *42*

Starkey, John, of Darley *27–29, 215*

Starkey, Laurence, of Stretton, drummer *207, 245*

Starkie, John, of Blackburn, Lancs., piper *210*

Stathum, Roger *109*

Statute of Vagabonds *2, 9–10, 15–16, 18–19, 23, 25, 70, 79, 81–83, 85–87, 90–91, 94, 107, 113, 119–21, 127, 185, 211*

Stele, John, piper *207*

Stevenson, Robert, organist *58, 207*

Stil, John *49, 159*

Stockport *86, 93, 196, 207, 245*

Stocks *25, 179, 245*

Stokes, Thomas, of Stretton, minstrel *84, 207, 245*

Stonyhurst, Lancs. *136, 150*

Stopporte, Roger, drummer *207, 240*

Strand, Red Cock in, near the Savoy *138–39*

Stretton *84, 114, 195–96, 201, 207, 242, 245*

Stringer, Peter, organist *219*

Stubbes, Phillip, *The Anatomie of Abuses 29, 31, 215*

Stubbs, Isabella *33;* Ellen, servant of *33*

Stubbs, Richard *52*

Sutton *82;* Great or Little Sutton *34, 97, 201, 243*

Swaggering *51*

Swettenham *89, 91, 112, 204*

Swordbearer *61*

Symme, Elizabeth *52*

Symme, Thomas *52*

Symphaner, Margaret *228*

Symphony *160*

Synger, William le, minstrel *17, 20, 108, 207, 213*

Tabley Superior (Over Tabley) *88, 195*

Tabor (*see also* pipe and tabor) *28, 74, 143, 145, 161, 165–66, 175, 177, 238*

Taborer *166, 177, 238*

Tailer, Henry, of Standish, Lancs., musician *86, 207*

Tarporley *51, 80–81, 97, 100, 144, 165, 197, 202, 204, 208, 218, 222, 243*

Tarvin *31–32, 80–81, 208, 222*

Tattenhall *46, 124, 197, 205, 209, 242*

Tatton, Robert, of Withenshawe *173–74*

Tatton, William 229

Taverns 22, 24, 29, 39–40, 49, 77, 95–97, 123–24, 134, 156, 159–60, 217

Taxal 12

Taylor, John, apprentice 70, 107, 183

Taylor, John, servant to Richard Warde 137

Thomas, William 229

Thomasson, William, alekeeper 165

Timperley 179

Tinctoris, J., De inventione et usu musicae 150

Tinker with trumpet 171

Tompson, John, of Nantwich, minstrel 15–16, 115, 207

Tompson, John, of Nantwich, musician 15–16, 103, 207

Tompson, John, of Nantwich, piper 15–16, 103, 115, 207

Tomson, John, of Stockport, musician 86, 207, 245

Torkington, Thomas, of Siddington 109–11

Towers, "Old Towers", piper 88, 95, 115, 207, 246

Towers, Thomas, of Barrow, piper 87, 207, 246

Towers, Thomas, yeoman (piper) 87, 165, 207, 246

Trafford, Richard, tallowchandler 106

Trevis, Edward, of Nantwich, piper 207

Troly loly loly loo, song sung in Painters' play 76

Troutbeck, William, chamberlain of Chester 148

Trowle, character in Shepherds' play 61, 75–77

Trumpet 62, 161, 168–71

Trumpeters 15, 17, 62, 72, 82, 92, 170, 205, 208, 238; of Earl of Derby 27, 170; of Earl of Pembroke 27, 170

Tucke, cousin of Peter Moreton 141

Tumblers 15, 22, 24, 42, 71, 73

Turin 141

Turner, Alexander, of Marsden, Lancs., piper 210

Tuscany 142

Tyttle (drummer) 207

Upton by Chester 87–88, 165, 207, 246

Utkinton 197, 203, 209

Vagrancy 3, 43–44, 72, 81–91, 94, 115

Vaughan, John, of Nantwich, piper/ musician 81, 103, 156, 165, 208, 246

Vaughan, Maudline, wife of Roger Vaughan, musician 192–93

Vaughan, Roger, of Nantwich, musician 96, 103, 105, 157–59, 192–94, 208, 225–26, 232, 236, 242

Vaughan, Roger, of Nantwich, son of Roger Vaughan 192–93

Vernon, Richard, of Bunbury, piper 52, 208, 246

Vernon, Richard, of Nantwich, piper/musician 208, 212, 246

Vihuela 153

Violins 64, 143, 146, 155–56, 159–60, 167, 181–82, 184, 236; bass violin 49, 159–60; treble violin 49, 78, 102, 149, 155, 159–60

Viols 125–26, 131, 135–36, 139–40, 143, 146, 150, 155–59, 173, 183–84, 226, 236; bass viol 102–04, 135, 137–40, 146, 149, 155–59, 181, 192–93, 226, 235; chest of viols 131, 156, 157, 181; set of viols 138–39, 183; tenor viol 64, 103, 140, 146, 156–58, 167, 181, 191, 236; treble viols 102, 135, 139, 146, 149, 155–56, 158, 192

Viol da braccio *156, 236*
Viol da gamba *104, 138–39, 146, 156, 158, 236*
Virginals *78, 104, 131–33, 135–39, 145, 147, 150, 155, 170, 172–74, 177, 180–81, 183–84, 239*
"Vn'thorborse," Derbyshire *85, 209, 247*

Wait pipe *162, 166–67*
Waits *15–16, 19, 24–48, 87, 92, 95, 103, 144–45, 148, 157, 159, 166–67, 169;* of Chester *6–9, 11, 23, 25–27, 55, 63–70, 73–75, 87, 91–92, 96–97, 105–07, 126–27, 139, 144–45, 156–57, 159, 166–69, 181, 183, 185–87, 196, 198–99, 203–05, 209, 246;* of Liverpool *247;* of Shrewsbury *92*
Waker, Ralph/Rondle, of Budworth, piper (*see also* Rondle Walker) *208, 246*
Wakes *7, 10, 25, 27–28, 30–32, 34, 42–45, 50–51, 53, 79–81, 97, 116–17, 124, 144, 148, 165, 181*
Walay, Hugh de, harper *17, 87, 108, 119, 147, 208*
Wales *3, 10–11, 17, 34–35, 54, 87–88, 100, 146–47*
Walker, Joan, of Middlewich *117*
Walker, Randle, of Middlewich, laborer *117*
Walker, Rondle, of Little Budworth, piper *80–81, 208, 246*
Walmesley, James, drummer *210*
Walton, Lancs. *210*
Ward, John, instrument maker *180–81, 208*
Warde, Hugh, of Astbury *41*
Warde, Richard *137, 232*
Wardle *195*

Waring, John, drummer *208*
Waringes, John, of Congleton, minstrel *99, 208*
Warren, Francis, son of Sir Edward Warren of Poynton *232*
Warrington *54, 87, 92, 97, 106, 114, 159, 181–82, 205, 242*
Watt/Watts, George, of Chester, musician *208*
Weaver, river *101*
Weaverham *200*
Webster, Nicholas, musician *69–70, 107, 208*
Weedall, Thomas, musician *101, 208*
Weld family, of Eaton *232*
Weld, John *141*
Weld, William *141*
Welles, William, minstrel *208*
Wenslow, Lancs. *165, 210*
West, William, of Canterbury *100*
Westeid, minstrel *208*
Westmorland *3, 8*
Wettenhall *196, 242*
Wewll, Thomas, of Middlewich, piper *95, 208*
Whistle *76–77, 161, 168–69*
Whistle-flute *162, 168*
Whistling *67, 77, 168*
Whitchurch, Shrops. *54, 77–78, 86, 199*
White, Robert, of Ely, organist *58, 60–61, 78, 208, 222*
White, Thomas, trumpeter *170, 208*
Whitegate *205*
Whitsun ales *35, 38*
Whitsun Plays *56, 58–61, 74–77, 165, 183, 219–20, 231;* banns, post-Reformation *59, 74, 165, 168, 219;* Drapers, play 2 ("Creation and Fall of Man: Cain and Abel") *75;* Merchants, play 8 ("The Magi") *75;* Painters, play 7 ("The Shepherds") *59, 61, 75–77, 168, 171;* Smiths, play 11

("The Purification: Christ
Before the Doctors") *60–61,
74, 165, 174;* Walkers, play
24 ("The Judgment") *62, 170;*
Waterleaders and Drawers in
Dee, play 3 ("The Flood") *59,
77;* Wrights, play 6 ("The
Nativity") *59–60*
Whittingham, Ann *137, 157, 214*
Whyteley, Robert de, piper *108,
209, 244*
Whythorne, Thomas *14–16, 20,
22–26, 53, 95, 102, 104–05,
124, 134–36, 142, 153*
Wilbraham family, of Nantwich
201
Wilbraham, Ralph *136*
Wilbraham, Sir Richard, of Wood-
hey *46, 139–40, 142, 158,
163*
Wilbraham, Thomas *27, 105, 136–
42, 157, 171*
Wilding, James *59, 135*
Wilkes, Laurence *176*
Wilkinson, cousin of John Leche of
Carden *137–38, 173*
Wilkinson, David *52*
Willard, Thomas, waitman *209*
Williams, Alice, widow of Thomas
64, 66, 105, 166, 169
Williams, John, son of Thomas
Williams Jr. *66, 106*
Williams, Thomas, of Chester,
waitman *64, 66, 105, 169,
181, 209, 227, 246*
Williams, Thomas, Jr., of Chester,
waitman *66, 106–07, 209,
227, 246*
Williams, William, of Chester, son
of Thomas Williams (*see
above*), apprentice waitman
105, 209, 246
Williamson, Richard *47*
Williamson, Thomas, musician
209, 246
Wilmslow *26, 179, 201–02, 206*

Wimbolds Trafford *197, 242*
Winchester, Stephen, bishop of *118*
Wincle *206*
Winnington family, of Birches *183,
231*
Winnington, Elizabeth, of Birches
131–32, 168, 230
Winnington, Paul, of Birches *230*
Winnington, Thomas, constable of
Lostock Gralam *116*
Wirral *11, 34, 70, 97, 243*
Wirral, deanery of *211*
Wirral Hundred *12, 171*
Wistaston *81, 103, 165, 208, 246*
Withenshaw, Thomas, fiddler *209*
Withenshawe *173–74*
Withington *88–91, 204;* Lower
Withington *88–89, 204;* Old
Withington *88–89*
Witton *108, 205, 206*
Wood, Grace *209, 245–46*
Woodhey, seat of Sir Richard
Wilbraham *163*
Woodson, Leonard, organist *100,
225, 246*
Woodson, Mr., of Cholmondeley,
organist *23, 100, 209, 214*
Woodson, Thomas, organist and
composer *100, 225, 246*
Woormsonne, Arthur, bell-ringer
176, 209
Worrall, Dudley *102, 226*
Worrall, Ellen *102, 226*
Worrall, Jane *102, 226*
Worrall, John *102, 226*
Worrall, Margaret, widow of
William Worrall *241*
Worrall, Thomas *102, 226*
Worrall, William, of Nantwich,
musician *96, 102–05, 135,
148, 155–59, 181, 191–92,
209, 212, 225–27, 236, 241*
Worrall, William, Jr. *102*
Wrenbury *50*

Wright, Alan *115*
Wright, Henry, of Nantwich, inn-
  holder *104, 155, 181, 226,*
  235–36, 241
Wright, James *155*
Wright, Richard *49–50*
Wrugh, John le, harper *73, 209*
Wyatt, Blind Edward, possibly a
  musician *209, 246*
Wybunbury *205*
Wyredale, Lancs. *210*
Wythers, Robert, piper/jester/fool
  209

Yale, David, chancellor of diocese of

Chester *37, 171*
Yardley, John, of Crewe, gentleman
  235
Yeardley, John *150*
Yemouth, Thomas, of Derbyshire,
  minstrel, specifically bagpiper
  72, 84–85, 87, 107, 165, 209
Yerton, Jehan *85*
Yewood, Laurence *28*
Yockin, John, of Chester, possibly a
  fiddler *244*
York, archbishop of *36–37, 51, 76,*
  88
Yorkshire *3, 11–12*